All Bound Up Together

The John Hope Franklin

Series in African American

History and Culture

Waldo E. Martin Jr. and

Patricia Sullivan, editors

All Bound Up Together

The
Woman Question
in African American
Public Culture,
1830–1900

MARTHA S. JONES

The University of North Carolina Press
Chapel Hill

© 2007 The University of North Carolina Press
All rights reserved
Manufactured in the United States of America

Designed by Jacquline Johnson
Set in Baskerville MT
by Keystone Typesetting, Inc.

The paper in this book meets the guidelines for
permanence and durability of the Committee on
Production Guidelines for Book Longevity of the
Council on Library Resources.

Library of Congress Cataloging-in-Publication
Data
Jones, Martha S.
    All bound up together : the woman question in
African American public culture, 1830–1900 /
Martha S. Jones.
    p. cm. — (The John Hope Franklin series in
African American history and culture)
    Includes bibliographical references and index.
ISBN 978-0-8078-3152-6 (cloth: alk. paper)
ISBN 978-0-8078-5845-5 (pbk.: alk. paper)
    1. African American women political activists
—History—19th century. 2. African American
women—History—19th century. 3. African
American women—Social conditions—19th
century. 4. United States—Race relations—
History—19th century. 5. Sex role—United
States—History—19th century. 6. Women's
rights—United States—History—19th century.
7. Feminism—United States—History—19th
century. 8. African Americans—Politics and
government—19th century. 9. Community
life—United States—History—19th century.
10. African Americans—Social conditions—
19th century. I. Title.
E185.86.J663 2007
305.48′896073009034—dc22
2007010367

cloth   11 10 09 08 07   5 4 3 2 1
paper   11 10 09 08 07   5 4 3 2 1

Parts of Chapters 5 and 6 appeared earlier, in
a somewhat different form, in " 'Make Us a
Power': African-American Methodists Debate
the Rights of Women, 1870–1900," in *Women
and Religion in the African Diaspora*, ed. R. Marie
Griffith and Barbara D. Savage (Baltimore:
Johns Hopkins University Press, 2006), and
are reprinted here with permission.

for Musie

Contents

Illustrations

Introduction

When African American poet and essayist Frances E. W. Harper took the podium during the inaugural meeting of the American Equal Rights Association, she spoke with both trepidation and conviction. Aiming to set forth a creed that might guide the fledgling women's rights organization, Harper declared: "We are all bound up together in one great bundle of humanity." The year was 1866, and the nation was in the midst of what Harper termed a "grand and glorious revolution." In the wake of the Civil War, all Americans—especially those of African descent were engaged in a highly charged debate over freedom, citizenship, and the nation itself. Harper argued that any endeavor to transform the standing of American women required consideration of society's "weakest and feeblest" members alongside those individuals with their hands "across the helm." In making her case, Harper drew upon her vantage point as a "colored woman" who, she explained, had felt every man's hand against her, and hers against every man. Using the term "man" as a universal, Harper underscored how race and gender intersected in her experience of oppression.[1]

Harper, a relative newcomer to public speaking, had recently endured a series of personal degradations. After the death of her husband, she explained, a neighbor attempted to seize the few possessions left to Harper and her four children. In this circumstance, Harper understood herself to be bound up with the fate of the many American women who were deprived of meaningful property rights. Harper then told the audience of the difficulties she encountered when searching for a new home. She felt unwelcome in the many cities that limited her access to streetcars and discriminated against her in the housing market—this had been the case even in Philadelphia, the "city of brotherly love," and in Boston, where she finally settled. Thus, Harper cast herself as bound up with the burdens of blackness and the myriad injustices that flowed from race, as well as sex. But, if being an African American woman in the mid-nineteenth century might have engendered self-doubt, in Harper it fostered confidence and conviction. She was among the unprivileged class of Americans, yet Harper held herself out as the embodiment of the country's crossroads. The most vexing challenges of freedom, citizenship, and the nation's identity were all bound up together in her.

The life of Frances Ellen Watkins Harper vividly illustrates the multifaceted lives of mid-nineteenth-century African American female activists. Born to free parents in the slave state of Maryland and orphaned at three, Harper was raised by her uncle, William Watkins, a teacher and Methodist minister.[2] Her early life was spent working as a domestic and then a teacher. Harper began her public life as a writer in the antebellum decades. She went on to defy convention by penning poetry, prose, and polemic in the black press. As a teacher, she accrued important insights into the educational challenges of the Reconstruction era. In 1866, she took the podium at the first postwar women's rights meeting. Over the course of her life, Harper was celebrated as an antislavery and civil rights advocate, a religious worker, journalist, women's suffragist, fraternal order affiliate, poet, essayist, and commanding public speaker. She well knew the many convergences that characterized nineteenth-century America, and she urged her audience members—who were variously black and white, male and female, northern and southern, young and no longer young—to see them too. Her ideas reflected antebellum political culture, in which civil rights and women's rights had been intertwined. But she also spoke to the challenges facing a new generation of men and women who were navigating the meanings of freedom and citizenship in a world where earlier alliances appeared fragile. "We are all bound up together," Harper urged, and with this she placed African American women at the center of the century's greatest challenges.

All Bound Up Together explains how African American activist women, who occupied what was termed by many a marginal position in public life during the 1830s, became visible and authoritative community leaders by the 1890s. Across these seven decades, black female activists transformed their public standing through a process that was always bound up with the shifting fortunes of all black Americans. Three generations of women, often with male allies, engaged in a sustained and multifaceted debate about women in public life. Black women's prospects for public engagement were bound up with the revolutions and reforms that transformed American society over the century: slavery and abolitionism, women's rights, war, emancipation, institution building, the Fourteenth Amendment, and Jim Crow. Among African

Frances Ellen Watkins Harper. Frontispiece, Iola Leroy; Or, Shadows Uplifted *(1892).*
Courtesy of the Library Company of Philadelphia.

American activists, the nineteenth-century women's movement—the collective processes by which women asserted rights and claimed a central place in public life—occurred not within a distinct female sphere but in those spaces that men and women shared: churches, political organizations, mutual aid societies, and schools.[3]

In nineteenth-century America, the "woman question" took a variety of forms, from a woman's right to control her body to her right to the vote. This book takes up one crucial aspect of the debate: the extent to which African American women would exercise autonomy and authority within their community's public culture.[4] Black activist thought on the question changed over the course of the century. In some cases convergences fostered the enhancement of women's public standing; at other times disagreements thwarted women's claims and threatened the well-being of the institutions of which they were a part. Always, the woman question generated challenges over power. In churches, it concerned the propriety of female preachers, the governance of missionary societies, and the ordination of women to the ministry. In political organizations, it was manifest in disagreements over the election of female delegates and officers and the inclusion of women's rights on the platforms of "race" organizations. In fraternal orders, the woman question arose over access to the secrets of Masonry and the creation of female auxiliaries such as the Order of the Eastern Star. In literary societies, the question was provoked when women took the podium and engaged their male counterparts in debate. In lyceums, as in the press, the woman question was often squarely put: Who and what could women be? Public speakers, preachers, delegates, officers, voters, teachers, principals, fund-raisers, mothers, ministers? The parameters of the debate cut across institutional boundaries. Biblical precepts were employed to support the seating of women in political conventions, and political theory was used to argue against the elevation of women to the ministry. Finally, the debate emerged across a broad geographic terrain. Black Americans, initially in the free states and territories and later throughout the United States, were knit together by the threads of a public culture through which ideas and practices related to women in public life circulated.

This book adopts a frame termed "public culture" to highlight the interrelatedness of various sites of African American life, sketching out the contours of a world in which activists engaged a broad array of intellectual currents.[5] Activists gave such ideas lived meaning as they moved through varied social spaces. In its formative period, black public culture encompassed the many communal associations founded between the Revolution and the Civil War: churches, political organizations, secret societies, literary clubs, and antislavery societies. In these spaces, black Americans came together to address their mutual needs, creating schools and lyceums, burial societies and cemeteries, widows' pensions and funds for the destitute. These were bounded spaces whose parameters were defined to a significant degree by racism.[6] With notable but limited exceptions, black Americans were marginalized within, if not wholly excluded from, institutions operated by white Americans, and they often sought out the authority and autonomy that independent institutions made possible. Most lived and died, worshipped and mourned, read and debated, strategized and sought assistance in African American institutions.[7]

However, institutions and the material sustenance they provided are not all that the term "public culture" is intended to convey. Public culture also encompassed a realm of ideas, a community of interpretation, and a collective understanding of the issues of the day.[8] Through exchanges at conferences and conventions, the written word, and lively debates, African American activists built an intellectual community. They deliberated and developed tactics and strategies to sustain communal well-being and enhance their standing in the broader society.[9] This aspect of public culture did not suffer from the same bounded quality that institutions did. In the realm of ideas, African American activists were as cosmopolitan as any.[10] They were as likely to take up world cultures or national politics as the Sunday sermon or the upcoming ladies' bazaar. They read widely and attended public forums when welcome and, in doing so, forged connections to the broader culture, its issues and trends, its challenges and triumphs.

This book's adoption of a public culture perspective does not elide differences and divisions among African Americans. Indeed, it is in part public culture's broad-stroke point of view that brings into relief differences among and between black activists. Most pointedly for the purpose of this study, differences manifested themselves through the various ways in which black activists answered the woman question. We might then ask, however, how such differences mapped onto other fissures that divided black Americans. Here, lines drawn by nineteenth-century politics are often salient. Prior to emancipation, black activists in the free states and territories constructed a public culture that largely elided the lives and the ideas of black southerners, most of whom remained enslaved. Enslaved people did develop their own public culture, as historian Steven Hahn argues, but it generally lacked the elaborate institutional frameworks that activists in the antebellum North had built.[11] Thus, the woman question debate, as this book takes it up, was largely among black people in the free states and territories prior to the Civil War. The political geography of African American public culture underwent a sea change in the postwar period. Formerly free people and formerly enslaved people confronted one another as the public lives of all black Americans were transformed through the challenges of emancipation and citizenship. Public culture served as a place of convergence, and in politics, religion, and associational life generally, the woman question continued to give shape to communal institutions. In some sense, the center of public culture shifted to the South, pulled there by the millions of freed people who might be incorporated into what had been before the war northern, regional institutions. But there remained a North-South, or perhaps a formerly free–formerly enslaved divide in another sense. Northern activists, their experiences and their ideas, exerted a disproportionate influence, particularly in those spaces where the woman question was most squarely confronted, black churches. When negotiating the woman question, some denominations deftly elided this potential fissure, others saw it dramatically split apart female activists, and in yet others, regional differences lent the woman question a unique character.

The framework of public culture illuminates a great deal about the nineteenth-century African American past, bringing into relief the women's movement that emerged therein while also demonstrating the ways in which black activists engaged with various publics, only some of which they constructed and controlled. In this sense, I use public culture in the manner that Thomas Bender promotes.[12] This book begins with those sites of African American life in which power was constructed and then shows how those sites were intertwined, at times, with realms of power dominated by white Americans. The result does not approach the sort of synthesis that Bender calls for, but it does suggest an approach to the telling of African American history that knits it into the fabric of some of U.S. history's other narratives while also preserving its particularity. The rubric of public culture also brings African American history into dialogue with numerous already existing interpretive approaches to the period. The problem of separate, or private versus public, spheres that has long engaged women's historians is present. This book embraces the notion of the public as both an ideological construction and a social fact and then reexamines it as a space in which gendered power was contested rather than merely reified or lived. Jürgen Habermas's theory of the historical emergence of the public sphere and its progeny, particularly the conceptualization of women and minorities as counterpublics, also has relevance. *All Bound Up Together* contributes to ongoing discussions about the dynamics of democracy and citizenship and captures the ways in which African Americans generally and African American women in particular positioned themselves in relation to the nation-state throughout the nineteenth century. Public culture is an expansive rubric that encompasses the deliberations of African Americans within their own institutions and their engagements with overlapping publics.[13]

This public culture approach reveals how debates about black women's standing in public life occurred in three phases. Chapters 1 and 2 begin in the early 1830s, a period in which singular women such as Boston reformer and public thinker Maria Stewart and itinerant preachers Jarena Lee and Julia A. J. Foote forced discussion of the woman question. These path breakers defied convention, speaking publicly without the sanction of male leaders. At the same time, they used the podium and the pulpit to call attention to the contradictions embedded in a public culture that sought to undo discrimination based on race while letting stand differences rationalized through gender. By the 1840s, the implications of this tension were dramatically manifest when the leadership of the American Anti-Slavery Society split over the standing of women within that organization. Black Americans were foremost among those who grappled with the principles of universal rights and the practical task of organizing a movement to achieve them. Could the political culture of African Americans be broadened to encompass antislavery, civil rights, and the rights of women? The women's rights conventions of the late 1840s infused the question with new urgency as female activists adapted the rhetoric of abolitionism to their cause and incorporated male and female antislavery reformers into their ranks. Briefly in 1848, black American political conventions embraced the rights of women.

Chapters 3 and 4 open with the passage of the Fugitive Slave Act of 1850 and the crisis that accompanied this grave piece of legislation. Black public culture became singularly focused on matters of race and freedom, with most male activists persuaded that women's rights had no relevance for them. Only the turmoil of the Civil War era created new openings for women, propelling them onto the public stage. For enslaved women, emancipation opened the door to public culture. Although these women were not entirely free from ideas about gendered difference, their lives and labors were not imbued with a Victorian ideology of separate spheres. The exigencies of war permitted all black women to enter public culture in unprecedented ways. Through public speaking, fund-raising, soldiers' aid, and teaching, women staked out new turf. Their efforts bore fruit in the Reconstruction years and had enduring consequences. Many black institutions were remade by, in part, extending new authority to women. Formal sites of female authority, such as the Methodist office of the stewardess and the Masons' auxiliary Order of the Eastern Star, created public roles for women that were no longer subject to the capriciousness of male leaders.

Chapters 5 and 6 assess how the collapse of Reconstruction transformed the debate on the woman question, leading to a contentious rethinking of the relation of gender to power among African American activists. Black men lost their authority in the political realm, and as they turned inward, especially toward their church communities, a reconsideration of women's religious authority occurred. Forcibly evicted from southern politics, black men placed increased value on their authority in churches, and women's religious aspirations were checked. But women did not abandon public culture. Instead, they founded autonomous women's clubs as vehicles for their continued exercise of public authority and standing. By the century's end, ideas about women's place in public life had been transformed. Women were influential and independent forces in causes ranging from temperance to the campaign against lynching and from missionary work to party politics.

Writing Black Women into Public Culture

This book seeks out black women in public, looking for them in those sites often associated with male authority and domination. One rationale for this approach is set out in *Women in Public: Between Banners and Ballots, 1825–1880*, where historian Mary Ryan returns to a dichotomy that had, for an earlier generation, distinguished between the male public sphere and the female private sphere. Ryan observes that feminist scholarship had all but extinguished the view that this dualism contained any explanatory power relative to the lived experiences of women and men. Still, Ryan suggests we might retain the "concept of the public but shun its gender correlate . . . and go defiantly in search of women in public" where we may find them as subjects, a linguistic construction, and a set of social relationships.[14] Ryan's formulation raises an important question for historians of nineteenth-century African American life. Has the field thrown off entirely the male-public versus female-private dichotomy? Do the frequent characterizations of black institutions as "male-dominated" or "patriarchal" signal a continued deference to this outmoded scheme? This book is an exploration that, as Ryan urges, "defiantly" seeks out African American women in unexpected public places. Once there, what might we find? Ryan, for one, suggests the answer is women as "subjects" and gender as "a linguistic construction and a set of social relationships." Perhaps we will also find women themselves.

Long before Mary Ryan issued her call, African American women's historians sought out, found, and memorialized the nineteenth century's African American public women. This book is most deeply indebted to those who knew how and where to look. For over a century, editors, chroniclers, and historians have found black women active in churches, antislavery societies, literary circles, mutual aid organizations, schools, war relief agencies, and politics.[15] Today, a rich and important body of scholarship explores the lives of black women in the vexed period known as both the "woman's era" and the "nadir" of American race relations. Some historians, notably Evelyn Brooks Higginbotham, examine this shift in churches. Others, such as Deborah Gray White, focus on the emergence of independent women's clubs.[16] Still others, such as Glenda Gilmore, examine the interplay between the sacred and secular realms of women's activism.[17] These and other scholars suggest that the late-nineteenth-century emergence of black women into public culture is best understood as an extended process that spanned generations and nurtured the ambitions of young women through families and communities.[18] This book expands upon these insights about black women in the late nineteenth century by demonstrating the half-century-long debates that facilitated their public capacities.

In *All Bound Up Together*, readers from the field of African American history will discover the extent to which the woman question shaped nearly every dimension of black public culture from the 1830s forward. Nearly all African American activists were required to consider the nature of female influence and women's rights and grappled with the consequences of those ideas for the institutions of which they were a part. Here I use the term "activist" much in the same sense as scholars James and Lois Horton have, to capture a collective of individuals, some of whom were highly visible but many more of whom were working people for whom public activism was but a small facet of their lives. For many, activism, be it in politics, the church, or any one of a number of associations, was not a vocation but a part of a life's fabric that included work, family, and community building. Throughout this book, many such individuals come to the surface of the historical record for just a moment, mentioned in a newspaper report, conference minutes, or a letter. As individuals they often quickly recede from view, but as a cumulative presence they are highly suggestive of the extent to which the woman question permeated African American life.[19] Rather than patriarchal or male-dominated, black public culture was an openly and often heatedly contested space in which activists self-consciously wrestled with the meanings of manhood and womanhood and the implications of those ideas for the structures and practices of institutions. Thus, this book offers new insights about familiar terrain, including free black communities of the North and the struggle against slavery; the Civil War and emancipation; the promises of Reconstruction; and the disappointments and degradations of Jim Crow.

For readers from the field of American women's history, which has taken the position of white women as its paradigm, this book offers striking new insights into the history of women's rights and the origins of feminism. Throughout the nineteenth century, there was a distinct movement for women's rights among black Americans, but this movement defined its objectives relative to the parameters of African American society rather than American society writ large. Black women did not privilege matters of race over those of gender. Rather, they were active at the intersection of these two salient social categories and fashioned their tactics and their aims to suit this circumstance. In a significant revision of earlier accounts and analyses, this work demonstrates that the differences long associated with the terms of the Fourteenth and Fifteenth Amendments were already present during the 1850s. African American activists, in the face of the increasing degradations that followed the Fugitive Slave Act, generally purged women's rights and women themselves from the realm of black politics. Looking forward from the moment of the Reconstruction-era constitutional amendments, women's historians will discover that among African Americans, agitation for women's rights increased. The evidence for this renewed commitment to women's rights issues is found not in politics but in churches, where black women seized upon three decades of women's rights discourse and transformed their roles in what was a most important institution. Thus, this book revises prevailing views of a well-studied past, including the emergence of Victorian domesticity; the Seneca Falls convention and development of the women's rights movement; the work of the Civil War; the campaign for women's suffrage; and the club movement of the woman's era.[20]

African American women, their ideas, their activism, and the contours of their lives, are at the core of this story. This book adopts a perspective that Elsa Barkley Brown has termed "pivoting the center."[21] Centered on black women, this book does not leave them to stand alone. The character of African American public culture, both its gender-integrated aspects and its frequent alliances with white activists and institutions, means that to pivot is to confront multiple voices: female as well as male and black as well as white.

Readers may be particularly struck by the prominence of male "allies" in this story, men who spoke, and often acted, in support of women's claims for rights and public authority.[22] Their presence complicates previous understandings of African American feminism and echoes the question posed by literary critic Michael Awkward: Can men be feminists, or merely feminism's supporters or sympathizers?[23] The men in this story are as complex as the women with whom they were allied. Some "women's rights men" were converted to the rights of women by moral suasion, many before the Civil War. Their words and deeds flowed from a transformation that had already taken place in their hearts and minds. Others did so less out of personal conviction than from a sense that to call for women's rights would mark them and, perhaps more significantly, their institutions as advanced and civilized. From this perspective, to recognize the rights of women was one means by which black institutions distinguished themselves as forward-thinking, if not as superior to white-run institutions. Few, if any, did so out of baldly strategic or cynical thinking. Why not? The price to be paid by any African American who openly advocated the rights of women was high, as evidenced by minstrelsy's persistent fascination with this confluence of interests. Mindful of the cruel parodies to which they would likely be subjected, those African Americans who spoke of women's rights opened the door to a form of public ridicule that few would invite lightly. Men's voices joined those of women to produce what Brown terms a historical "gumbo ya ya," many voices speaking simultaneously, debating the woman question in African American public culture.[24]

Among the earliest inspirations for this study was a photograph buried in a 1908 church conference "souvenir volume." Digging through early black church records, I came upon a collage of portraits and, noticing women in the group, scanned the caption. Image number nine was labeled "Rev. Mary J. Small, widow of Bishop and Evangelist." No, it did not say "Mrs. Rev.," the honorific typically bestowed upon ministers' wives. (Image twelve's caption, for example, read "Mrs. Rev. F. U. A. Brooks.") There she was, in the volume's biographical sketches: Rev. Mary J. Small had been ordained a deacon and then elder in the African Methodist Episcopal Zion (AME Zion) Church (in 1895 and 1898, respectively); she was the "first and only woman receiving Holy Orders in a Methodist Church," the sketch's author boasted.[25] In Small was woman as subject: her ordination was the focus of a heated debate among religious activists. Constructions of gender and power were posited and contested through the ideas about the nature of manhood and womanhood that circulated through the debate. And gender functioned as a set of social relations as men and women arrayed themselves around Small in varying and complex ways. Not the least of all, I had found woman as lived experience. Mary Small had donned the robe, occupied the pulpit, and preached the gospel, all with as much authority as her "male-dominated" institution could confer.

Locating an African American Public Culture

Thomas Holt took up the question of how to locate an African American public in his afterword written for a 1995 edited volume titled *The Black Public Sphere*, a text that remains the most thoughtful examination of the subject to date.[26] In his essay, "Mapping the Black Public Sphere," Holt asserts that prior to the Civil War and emancipation, African Americans did not constitute a public of which historians might speak in Habermasian terms. Given the parameters of the volume's essays, most of which center on twentieth-century black life and politics (a notable exception is Elsa Barkley Brown's "Race, Identity, and Political Activism: The Shifting Contours of the African American Public Sphere"), Holt's conclusion holds. But it is more difficult to discern how Holt's analysis might have been altered had the volume included essays from historians Leon Litwack, Leonard Curry, George Walker, Philip Foner, James and Lois Horton, Julie Winch, or Leslie Harris, all of whom have vividly captured the complex social, intellectual, and political world constructed by African Americans living in the free states and territories prior to the Civil War and emancipation.

This book is allied with these and other histories of African Americans in the antebellum period, arguing that the African American public culture that emerged by the early 1830s is critical to understanding subsequent debates over women and their rights in African American life through the end of the nineteenth century. The woman question took shape during, indeed was an important feature of, what was emerging as an ambitious collective of African American ideas and institutions. While constrained in practice, the ambition of most black public activists was to incorporate people of African descent throughout the United States into their institutions and deliberations. African American public culture was a place of material sustenance and ideological contestation. The lives of African Americans in the free states and territories were transformed by the economic, social, and cultural changes brought about by the market revolution. Yet slavery and racism continued to shape their experiences in distinctive ways.[27] Gradual-emancipation acts had brought about the end of slavery as an institution, even though a small number of individuals remained enslaved. For black northerners, the 1830s most clearly marked the first full decade in the transition from slavery to freedom.[28]

During this period, African Americans joined westward migrations. No longer was free black life confined to cities on the eastern seaboard, such as New York, Philadelphia, and Boston. For example, Ohio's black population increased fivefold between 1810 and 1830, when the 9,574 black residents of Ohio outnumbered their counterparts in any one of the New England states.[29] Black migrants were not welcomed by whites in these western regions, however. Beyond the seaboard states, they confronted exclusionary "black laws" in most free states and territories that conditioned the entry of black Americans on the posting of a bond, or which absolutely prohibited their in-migration. Those African Americans who successfully established residency found their citizenship rights severely curtailed. For example, the Ohio constitution of 1802 denied black people the right to vote, hold office, and testify against whites in court.[30] Even in the face of such restrictions, African Americans sought out the opportunities that these places might offer. By the 1830s, black settlements had taken hold in Chillicothe, Milton Township, Cincinnati, and Cleveland, Ohio; Pittsburgh; Buffalo; St. Louis; and Detroit.

At the same time, African Americans participated actively in the process of urbanization. The pulls of family ties, jobs, sociability, and security all brought free black people from outlying rural communities to cities. Places with long-standing free black communities experienced dramatic growth between 1820 and 1830: 54 percent in Philadelphia, 72 percent in New York City, and 272 percent in Baltimore.[31] In newer, western cities, population changes reflected the combined impact of westward migration and urbanization. In Buffalo, Pittsburgh, and Cincinnati, the free black populations multiplied over a hundredfold.[32]

Class divisions deepened as capitalist economic relations spread throughout the North, and by 1837, class conflict had become overt, and occasionally even violent. The urban labor market was reshaped by capitalist relations of production even before industrialization. Artisans were threatened by the loss of their independence and the debasement of skilled trades; many responded by organizing trade unions. The new manufacturing industries demanded an ample supply of cheap labor, and the ranks of factory workers were filled largely by single women who had migrated from rural areas and by European immigrant families. The social separation between artisans and factory hands was only gradually overcome by the organization of labor reform groups. African Americans, whether new migrants or longtime residents, confronted an additional tension: the race-based stratification of the urban labor market.

In some instances the restrictions black workers faced were imposed by laws that denied them apprenticeships, licenses, and permits for specific trades. But in most cases, custom, enforced by employers and defended by white workingmen, limited employment opportunities for black city-dwellers. When African American men managed to be hired in skilled trades, they were the targets of work stoppages by white workers. These forces conspired to push black workers into jobs that were low-paying, transient, menial, and back-breaking.[33] Black women were relegated to the most laborious and least lucrative female occupations; most were domestics and laundresses.[34] There were always black artisans and entrepreneurs in these cities, but their numbers were few and their status vulnerable. As historian James Horton has pointed out, the "line between the relatively affluent and the very poor in black society was never fixed."[35] Even the Fortens of Philadelphia, often held out as the epitome of an antebellum black elite, saw their fortune largely dissipated after the death of their patriarch, James Forten.[36] Very few black families sustained even a modest "competency" to ensure over the course of generations what among white Americans might have been termed a middle-class position.

These same cities were the site of Jacksonian-era political struggles that brought about simultaneous though seemingly contradictory changes. Propertyless white men received the vote, while black men were formally excluded from the full privileges of citizenship. African American men were denied the franchise by the founding documents of the western territories. In those seaboard states where free black men had enjoyed the vote under post-Revolutionary constitutions, they lost this increasingly salient marker of political competency. Between 1822 and 1842, New Jersey, Pennsylvania, Connecticut, and Rhode Island all revised their laws to exclude African American men from voting. New York did not go quite so far. Yet by 1821 that state had imposed a property qualification on black but not white men.[37] Their exclusion from the polls did not prevent black men and women from taking part in the mass politics that emerged during the Jacksonian era, however. Through communitywide gatherings, African Americans created their own political culture. While only a select few men attended such meetings with a delegate's formal credentials, many more men, women, and children filled meeting halls and public assembly grounds. The right to "vote" was fully exercised within these gatherings, as activists took up the issues of the day. Black Americans took to the streets and, through parades, marches, and other public demonstrations, asserted their citizenship amid the shifting political parameters of the Jacksonian era.[38] For black activists, even as they were excluded from the electoral arena, mass politics conducted in city streets and squares contained subversive, even transformative, possibilities.

Black communities were increasingly bound together in a public culture of institutions and ideas. Urban-dwellers concentrated in predominantly black enclaves founded churches, schools, literary societies, fraternal orders, mutual aid societies, and political conventions. Although African American associational life had its beginnings in more localized endeavors during the late eighteenth century, by the early 1830s regional conferences, associations, and conventions brought these institutions together.[39] These networks extended to incorporate new African American communities as far west as San Francisco. While they were prevented from fully incorporating those free black institutions that managed to sustain themselves in the slave South, they reached out to religious and political organizations in such border cities as Baltimore and Washington more often than to their counterparts in Charleston and New Orleans. Ambitions were constrained by competing notions of how the public might be constituted in a nation that increasingly saw itself as divided between North and South, slave and free.

The problems that impeded unification are vividly illustrated through the story of the free black Methodists of Charleston, South Carolina. As had been true in many northern cities in the post-Revolutionary era, tensions emerged between white and black congregants over control of the governance and finances of a local congregation. In the wake of a dispute over operation of the African American burial ground, the black members of the congregation seceded from the mixed church and founded the Charleston African Methodist Episcopal (AME) Church, a move they undertook after consulting with Richard Allen, the denomination's Philadelphia-based bishop. This vision of a truly national black Methodist organization, which would include congregations in both free and slave states, was soon thwarted, however. Although Charleston's AME Church purchased a lot, built a hall, and met regularly over four years, by 1822 threats and intimidation disrupted the congregation. Its leader, Morris Brown, was run out of town. The AME Church's nineteenth-century historian, Daniel Payne, explained that the congregation's demise was attributable to white fears generated by rumors about a conspiracy led by Denmark Vesey to incite a slave insurrection.[40] The fate of Charleston's AME Church reflected the constraints imposed upon what many activists envisioned as an African American public culture of truly nationwide proportion; in the pre–Civil War period public culture was generally limited to the free states and territories.

By 1831, an African American convention movement generated an overlapping network of state and local political bodies that brought black activists together through the Civil War era and beyond. During the 1830s, too, African American religious denominations—Methodist, Baptist, Presbyterian, Congregationalist, and Episcopalian—coalesced into networks of governing bodies with regional, if not nationwide, jurisdiction. Through a complex matrix of conferences, associations, and synods, black Christians collaborated to advance their spiritual, as well as material, well-being, supporting ministers, congregations, benevolent organizations, mutual aid societies, and literary associations. Among fraternal orders and secret societies, the Prince Hall Masons, which originated in late-eighteenth-century Boston, brought together free black activists across the country. By 1830, the order had affiliates in Massachusetts, Rhode Island, Pennsylvania, and New York, and by 1850, lodges in New Jersey, Indiana, Ohio, Delaware, and Maryland had joined the organization. Through Grand Lodge gatherings, local chapters were linked to lodges nationwide.[41] Despite the more general violent anti-Masonic agitation of the 1820s and 1830s, African American activists moved easily between churches, fraternal orders, and political organizations.[42] Black temperance activism also originated in the post-Revolutionary era, and by the early 1830s organized temperance societies existed in cities from New Haven, Hartford, and Middletown in Connecticut, to Boston, New York City, Brooklyn, Troy, and Baltimore. The subject ranked high on the agenda of black political conventions, and the Coloured American Conventional Temperance Society eventually had twenty-three branches in eighteen cities.[43]

Finally, free black activists embraced print culture, using newspapers and pamphlets to facilitate institutional life and sustain long-distance communication. African American editors published the *Weekly Advocate* and the *Colored American*, both of which offered coverage of far-flung gatherings. These papers were complemented by the antislavery press, particularly William Lloyd Garrison's *Liberator*, which also provided extensive coverage of African American public culture. Churches and political conventions saw to it that their proceedings were recorded and published in the press and in pamphlet form, bringing those who had not traveled to a particular gathering into the debates that had taken place there.

Although most of these institutions had as their express objective the spiritual and material well-being of their members and of African Americans generally, they also served as centers for deliberation and the development of ideas. In the 1830s, an African American intellectual culture that transcended local concerns emerged to address the most pressing questions confronting black communities.[44] Activists could be heard debating the nature of citizenship, the value of integration, the worth of manual training, the relationship of religion to politics, the objectives of education, the consequences of urbanization, and the evils of slavery. These discussions were never neatly demarcated or narrowly defined. Church conferences and political conventions were as concerned as temperance gatherings about excessive alcohol use; ministers were as concerned as political leaders about the role of the church in antislavery politics.[45] As activists moved between the many sites of public culture—from Sunday sermon to Tuesday evening literary society meeting, from temperance convention to antislavery society fair—they carried the ideas generated in each of those venues with them.

African American public culture was constructed through the forces that were reshaping American society during the early nineteenth century. At the same time, African Americans confronted notions about racial inferiority that had been developing since the earliest encounters between Africans and Europeans. Beliefs about African womanhood, particularly women's physical strength, capacity for manual labor, physicality, overt sexuality, and child-bearing and child-rearing capacities, were critical building blocks in the construction of the racial ideology that undergirded the transatlantic slave trade and a southern plantation system dependent on slave labor.[46] Historian Deborah Gray White explains that two principal images of black women emerged in the context of enslavement. The first and most prevalent was "Jezebel," a woman "governed almost entirely by her libido," impious, unchaste, and indifferent to the needs of the men and children in her midst. The second was "Mammy," a "premiere house servant" and "surrogate mistress and mother" who was devoid of sexuality and singularly devoted to the white family she served.[47] Notions of racial difference were no less central to the imposition and reconstruction of a racial hierarchy in the North, particularly as gradual emancipation augmented the number of free persons of African descent. In this context, too, ideas about black women constituted an essential component of a brand of racism that rationalized the economic, social, and political subordination of African Americans. The circulation of these caricatures through popular culture helps to explain why some black women embraced a politics of respectability for the moral dignity it offered as they endeavored to distance themselves legally, economically, socially, and above all ideologically from the degradations of servitude. But white racism was malleable and hence inescapable. Even as they were no longer slaves, African American women found themselves subject to ideas about racialized difference.

As they entered public culture in the late 1820s, black women encountered new images that sought to delimit the parameters of their freedom. Freedom came to be associated with the manners, dress, leisure, and associational life of white bourgeois culture, but whites doubted whether black women had the capacity to inhabit such roles.[48] Even though only a few African Americans aspired to participate in bourgeois culture, white commentators defined it as off-limits to all black urban-dwellers. Blackness marked them as outside the boundaries of middle-class circles, and caricatures depicting black women's fatally flawed attempts to appear to be "ladies" were used to fix such lines of demarcation. Whatever their ambitions, free black women could never achieve the pious, refined, demure, and modest brand of womanhood reserved for their white counterparts.

This racist view became pervasive as it circulated through images as well as words. Pictures—vivid, engaging, and accessible even to the preliterate—controlled the climate in which free black women entered public culture. One such set of images, titled "Life in Philadelphia," originally appeared in the late 1820s as a series of fourteen lithographs, eleven of which featured African Americans in a variety of settings. Local booksellers advertised these cartoons as sold as a set.[49] The artist, Edward W. Clay, frequently portrayed black women as engaged in middle-class undertakings: shopping for luxury goods, strolling through a park, hosting tea parties, attending dances, and bantering with the opposite sex. Yet Clay's women always appear to miss the mark. By uttering malapropisms, wearing clothing of exaggerated proportions, and adopting ungraceful postures, Clay's caricatures consistently conveyed the view that free black women, despite great efforts, could never be more than amusingly inadequate imitations of white ladies. The implications were far-reaching. Black women might enter public culture, but in doing so they would be required to battle a well-developed array of stereotypes that compromised their standing.[50]

New ideas and images of black women circulated during the 1830s in antislavery circles as well. Iconography became a powerful tool with which to elicit sympathy for the abolitionist cause. The image of the enslaved supplicant—kneeling, bare-breasted, in chains, and often accompanied by the plea, "Am I not a woman and a sister?"—was offered up as an alternative not only to the images of Jezebel and Mammy but also to that of the bourgeois aspirant, appearing ubiquitously in abolitionist newspapers, pamphlets, stationery, and broadsides. As historian Jean Yellin explains, a major variant of this image depicted the female slave alongside her white female liberator, a juxtaposition that underscored the black woman's relative powerlessness. This narrative of slavery's demise offered no role for the free black women of the North.[51]

It was within this public culture that the woman question debate began for

"I aspire too much." Edward W. Clay, "Life in Philadelphia."
Courtesy of the William L. Clements Library.

African Americans. Whether understood as sites of power, scenes of contestation, one side of the ideological public-private coin, a community of interpretation, or the place from which black Americans challenged the state, the print culture, institutions, and deliberations of African Americans in the antebellum era's free states and territories had constructed a public culture

"Morgan's deduction." Edward W. Clay, "Life in Philadelphia."
Courtesy of the William L. Clements Library.

"Am I not a Woman and a Sister?" Antislavery token (1838).
Courtesy of the William L. Clements Library.

that was an essential component of their struggles for civil rights and against slavery. Gender—ideas about manhood and womanhood—was at the core of this public culture from its first moments and would continue to shape its contours and possibilities for decades to come. Certainly, as Thomas Holt suggests, the Civil War and emancipation would have profound consequences for public culture; but for former slaves, freedom did not present them with a blank cultural slate, ideologically or institutionally, and confrontations within spaces and deliberations born in the antebellum decades would be among freedom's critical challenges.

All Bound Up Together examines the woman question debate among African Americans as a series of contests that were bound up, to borrow Frances Ellen Watkins Harper's phrase, with economic and legal transformations; challenges of geographic migrations; institution building, including churches, political organizations, and print culture; and resistance to a range of denigrating images. These were formidable endeavors, and in everyday life women were indispensable partners as black people took them up. For decades to come commentators and historians would laud the women who were present at these scenes, opening their homes, preparing meals, filling pews, and raising funds as public culture came into being. It did not take long, however, before a most-pointed woman question came to be asked: What sort of authority and autonomy could women exercise in this emerging public culture? The following chapter begins with those women who were first to insist upon an answer, those singular women of the 1830s who deemed themselves called by God and by their communities' needs, defied expectations, and took the public stage.

I

Female Influence Is Powerful
Respectability, Responsibility, and Setting the Terms of the Woman Question Debate

Maria Stewart need not have posed the woman question; she was its embodiment. In September 1832, Stewart spoke at Boston's Franklin Hall on the prejudice to which African Americans were subjected. She shattered long-standing proscriptions against women speaking on politics. Stewart is often cited by historians as one of the first American women to address a "promiscuous" audience comprised of both men and women. It is of no small significance that Stewart was black. Yet what drew her to the podium were as much concerns about womanhood as about blackness. She queried her audience: "Who shall go forward, and take off the reproach that is cast upon the people of color? Shall it be a woman?"[1] With this, Stewart provoked a new debate, asking forthrightly what many African American activists only quietly pondered. What was the nature of female influence on public life? Was it defined by duties or rights, by restraint or innovation? Did it respect a public-private divide, and what was its relationship to movements to abolish slavery and earn civil rights? For Stewart, the future of black Americans was all bound up with the woman question.

While based in Boston, Stewart was never a merely local figure. Her ideas assumed national proportions with relevance for black communities throughout the free states and territories. Her primary audience was Boston's free black community, numbering just under 1,900 people in 1830.[2] They existed largely on the city's economic edges yet supported a flourishing public culture that included a primary school, five churches, and various mutual aid societies, fraternal orders, and lyceums. Through this associational life, black Bostonians challenged their economic marginalization, their segregation in schools and places of public accommodation, and the institution of slavery.[3] Print culture was essential to community building and contestation. By tracts and newspapers Stewart lobbed her earliest volleys. Her *Religion and the Pure*

Principles of Morality, published in 1831, was a collaboration born out of radical abolitionism's early cross-racial alliances. Among Stewart's allies was William Lloyd Garrison. She likely knew him through their mutual association with David Walker, author of the incendiary tract *Walker's Appeal . . . To the Coloured Citizens of the World.* Garrison published Stewart's writings and advertised them in the *Liberator*, the antislavery weekly and paper of record for free African Americans in the early 1830s. Stewart garnered some favorable notice, with "a highly respectable clergyman" deeming her "practical" and "truly eloquent" while also praising her "sterling wit."[4] By 1832, Stewart was delivering public lectures.[5] Local audiences, comprised of black and white people of both sexes, were eager to hear her speak, and Stewart filled popular venues.[6] Her topics included the evils of intemperance, the need for education, the degradations of proposals to colonize black Americans in Africa, and the capacity of moral suasion to abolish slavery. Garrison continued to support Stewart's ambitions. Notices of her speaking engagements, along with excerpts from her pamphlets and speeches, were printed for the readers of the *Liberator* and thereby reached the newspaper's broad-based readership.

A skilled rhetorician, Stewart crafted her message such that her provocations were muted by reassurances. Seemingly aware that some might question her right to speak in public, Stewart attempted to deflect overt criticism. It was God who had called upon her to ameliorate the community's ills, Stewart explained. She celebrated female domesticity, urging women to influence husbands, children, and circles of "acquaintance."[7] Piety, "delicacy of manners," "gentleness and dignity," contempt for the vulgar and vile, prudence, and economy were qualities to which she advised women to aspire.[8] When espoused by an African American woman, these strictures, which also circulated in white middle-class circles, took on distinct meaning.[9] Respectability marked the difference between slavery and freedom far more than it did that between private and public for women like Stewart. When she recommended that her sisters embrace domesticity, she was not urging their retreat to a separate female realm. Stewart well knew that most of the women whom she addressed moved daily between their homes, the streets, and their places of work. Not only would piety, manners, dignity, and the roles of mother and wife help protect African American women as they traversed crowded streets and entered places of work; they were ideals intended to distance them from the degradations that enslavement had imposed upon their lives.[10]

Tributes to domesticity were only her starting place. Stewart was not satisfied to fulfill duties to God and the home alone. She donned the cloak of wife and mother, neither of which she herself was, and set out to conquer public culture. Stewart lamented how rigid adherence to domesticity constrained black women's public lives. To take pen to paper or stand at the podium were, for Stewart, reflections of a new notion of womanhood.[11] She scoffed at the idea that African American women should be confined to domestic labor, burying "their minds and talents beneath a load of iron pots and kettles."[12] Here, Stewart echoed the sarcasm expressed by Matilda, a black female correspondent to *Freedom's Journal*, who chided her readers that a woman's influence over her family could not be properly exercised if her "mathematical knowledge should be limited to fathoming the dish-kettle."[13] Struggles against prejudice and slavery should also be their sphere of influence, and Stewart positioned women as key activists in African American public culture, united in "heart" and in action.[14] In her analysis, black women's "female influence" extended beyond the parameters of white, middle-class domesticity and incorporated an ambitious range of women's extra-domestic endeavors. Stewart drew upon the Bible, history, political theory, and the example of white women's benevolent work to construct a view in which female influence might be harnessed against what she described as "the strong current of prejudice" that led to economic misfortune among African Americans.[15] Urging her "sisters" to raise funds, erect buildings, operate retail establishments, and "sue" for their "rights and privileges," Stewart tailored the notion of female influence to African American life and circumstances. She called upon the "daughters of Africa" to distinguish themselves and direct their expanding influence toward achieving the "rights and privileges of equal citizens."[16]

Only with the benefit of hindsight can Stewart be said to have been a visionary. No aspect of her ideas was commonplace or foreordained in the 1830s. For most black activists, they were, instead, unsettling. Sensing disdain from within Boston's black community, in 1833 Stewart resolved to leave the city, and her "Farewell Address" reflected this. Nearly twenty years later, William C. Nell recalled that the opposition Stewart encountered "even from her Boston circle of friends . . . would have dampened the ardor of most women."[17] Scholars have sought to explain this turn of events with little more to rely upon than Stewart's own reflections. Some suggest that there were black men in her audiences who would not tolerate a woman's public critique of their leadership.[18] Others have surmised that some black women in Stewart's audiences, unwilling to "abandon the façade of feminine propriety," shunned her.[19] Whatever her listeners' objections, there is no doubt that Stewart was a provocative figure in her time.

What was the nature of Stewart's provocation? Her radical views were not without precedent. David Walker had openly advocated slavery's violent overthrow, ministers often criticized men's moral conduct. Female preachers had long spoken before promiscuous gatherings. Stewart raised issues already well-known to free African Americans in the early nineteenth century, including politics, leadership, faith, morals, institutional well-being, slavery, family, labor, and the future of a community with a fragile grip on freedom. Unique perhaps was the subversive power of her questions about black womanhood. In her analyses, no realm of African American life was immune from a wholesale reconsideration of the relationship between gender and power. Both by her physical presence at the podium and her forceful pronouncements, Stewart provoked a highly charged and enduring debate about black women in public life. She asked the woman question at a moment when most African American activists lacked the language for such a conversation and many wondered if there was anything to talk about at all.

It would be a mistake to leave Stewart's story to stand alone, as that of a singular, extraordinary woman. Her career as a public speaker was but one episode among many in the earliest years of an emerging African American public culture. This chapter situates the challenges encountered by this woman of exceptional talents as characteristic of a broader debate over the proper uses of female influence. This debate emerged within print culture— as reflected in the pages of *Freedom's Journal*, the nation's first black newspaper. It was also central to the character of abolitionism's political culture— generating divisions among antislavery activists. Female influence, with its emphasis on women's supremacy in the domestic sphere, was the rubric that most black activists used to frame the relationship of women to public culture. However, its parameters expanded as African Americans sought to address the material challenges their communities faced. Maria Stewart may have stepped too far beyond the parameters of female influence for many black Bostonians, but the questions she posed lingered. "Who shall go forward, and take off the reproach that is cast upon the people of color? Shall it be a woman?"

For most black activists in this period the answer was a qualified yes. Most agreed that women's domestic and moral influence were powerful tools in the battle to "take off reproach." In many circles of public life, women's efforts at self-improvement through entities such as literary societies were lauded. Their support for male leaders, particularly through religious and political fund-raising, met with widespread approval. Female influence clearly allowed for black women to take up activities beyond the home, but the character of those endeavors was a matter of debate. Political exigencies, the irrepressible drive of singular women, and quiet experiments in power shared across gender lines all tested the limits of female influence.

Few activists escaped the woman question debate. In the realm of education, polite exchanges about limiting the proper methods of educating young women gave way to an endorsement of their broadest education. In religious circles, female preachers sought official sanction for their efforts and in doing so, set off a debate about the character of religious leadership. In politics, apprehension surrounded the claim that female influence might encompass women's leadership on antislavery and other political matters. Still, experiments in female political activism got under way, with striving organizations inviting women to contribute their signatures to petitions and to sit as delegates in deliberative bodies. With increasing frequency, African American activists were called upon to consider the public standing of women as they built institutions and developed campaigns against slavery and for civil rights.

Had black activists taken lessons from Maria Stewart's inauspicious exit from Boston? Perhaps. Their quiet and often tentative engagements with the woman question suggest an awareness of its ability to provoke rancor and division. By the end of the 1830s, black antislavery organizers openly disagreed about the place of women within the American Anti-Slavery Society's leadership, as did their white counterparts. Many continued to believe, as Stewart's audience had, that public women were out of bounds. But these activists were confronted by an emerging opposition, one that claimed more expansive roles for women in religious and political circles. Still, black women had reason to remain cautious. They did not stand in precisely the same shoes as their white counterparts. They were the special targets of public disdain as expressed through popular culture. And they were charged with singular responsibility for the well-being of their communities. Even with the support of allies, male and female, black women in public more often than not faced the sort of rebuff that had led Maria Stewart to leave Boston.

The Matter of Female Influence

In the 1830s, ideas about the influence of African American women were refracted through thoughts about the collective aims of all black activists. Female influence was the primary rubric through which African American activists considered women's standing in early antebellum public culture. While in her person Maria Stewart may have confounded free black activists, her ideas aptly captured the conflicts and contradictions that soon characterized a broader debate. Female influence had emerged in the post-Revolutionary era to capture a new set of assumptions about how middle-class, white, Republican wives might exert moral force over men's public virtue.[20] In exchanges between antebellum African Americans, female influence was recrafted to reflect the particular challenges facing black public culture. Some invoked female influence as a prescriptive, attempting to police women's extradomestic endeavors. For others, female influence was a malleable and capacious rubric. Cloaked in it, black women might foray into public culture, particularly politics. African American activists pushed and pulled at the parameters of female influence. Sometimes it was stretched beyond recognition.[21]

For black women only a short generation from enslavement, to claim supremacy in the home was an expansive gesture. The home was explained as the most powerful realm of female influence. Woman's well-executed direction of her home, husband, and children reflected collective respectability and illustrated the distance from slavery that free black people had traveled. Prescriptive commentators urged black women, through their roles as wives, mothers, daughters, and sisters, to fulfill a distinct duty. Some used flattery to articulate the view that women's ambitions should be confined to the home, that "elevated sphere" in which she might exercise all the "powers with which . . . her Divine Benefactor" had endowed her.[22] Charles B. Ray, a Congregationalist minister and antislavery leader in New York City, asserted that the "destiny" of woman and her duties in life were "not only dissimilar, but entirely distinct" from those of men.[23] The aim of family relations was to mold the religious, moral, and literary or intellectual dimensions of individuals and, thus, society. How women were to exercise domestic influence was equally critical to African American claims to respectability. The art of persuasive "conversation," "reason," and "gentleness," rather than "thunder with her tongue," women were told, would ensure their greatest influence on their families.[24] Other commentators put forth a view of women as socially inferior to men, even when morally and mentally equal, adding that to challenge this was futile because men did not intend to give up their power.[25] Even as such commentators appeared to distinguish between the public world of men and the private sphere of women, few black writers argued for the imposition of a narrow domesticity upon black women.

The domination of men in exchanges on the woman question was not mere hypocrisy in the 1830s; it was the target of the debate. Women first broke through, not by challenging their male peers, but by accommodating

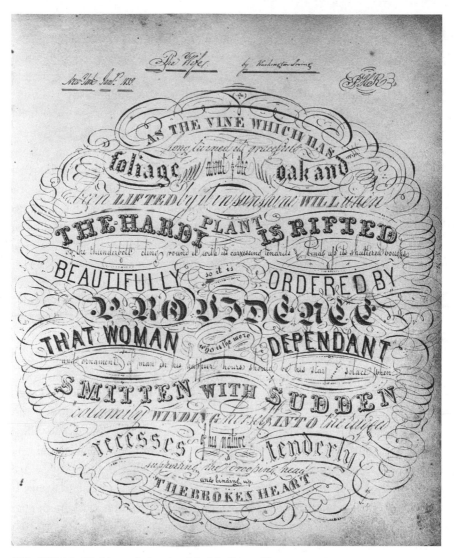

"The Wife," by Washington Irving. Amy Matilda Cassey Album.
Calligraphy by Patrick H. Reason. Courtesy of the Library Company of Philadelphia.

and agreeing with them. Their vehicle? The pages of black and antislavery newspapers. As Maria Stewart's example suggests, speaking before mixed assemblies largely remained a dangerous, but not impossible, outlet for black women activists. It was print culture, however, that presented the best avenue for women's entry into the debate. The African American and antislavery press were venues in which black women tested their own capacities to shape opinion and set the terms of the debates that framed their lives.[26] Some women drew a sharp line between the proper provinces of men and women. "Beatrice," probably a member of Philadelphia's black Female Literary Association, argued that women were not destined to possess the "physical strength" or "moral courage or ambition" of man.[27] It was these female writers who underscored the distinct challenges that debates over female influence held for black women. Matilda, for example, writing on the subject of women's education for *Freedom's Journal*, referred to the "great difficulties" that stood in the way of what she termed "our advancement," a phrase intended to convey the sense that the purpose of black women's education was the amelioration of the prejudices that confronted all African Americans. She further emphasized the peculiar standing of black women, lamenting, "We possess not the advantages with those of our sex whose skins are not colored like our own." Clearly, black women possessed neither the material resources nor the presumption of respectability enjoyed by white women. Hence, the risks and the burdens of reconstructing the nature of female influence were formidable.[28] Some of these views echoed the proscriptive views espoused by male commentators. Yet by writing in the press, black women added layers of complexity to the meanings of female influence.

But whatever the content of women's writings, the very appearance of female-authored commentary took women activists out of their homes and into public culture. A most poignant example was that of Ellen, who wrote for the readers of the *Colored American* in 1837. The appropriate sphere of female influence was the "domestic fireside," she urged. Women would shape their communities by their virtuous and moral examples. Yet, even as she made her case, Ellen appeared compelled to acknowledge that her very act of writing to a newspaper was a departure from her own recommendations. It was "risky" for a young woman to write in the press, she explained, suggesting that when women entered public debate they invited criticism that might undercut their respectability. Nevertheless, Ellen felt compelled to correct what she viewed as the lack of attention given to the "improvement of women." Yet, by doing so in print, she breached her self-defined boundaries.[29] Drawn into public culture by both women's needs and those of African Americans more broadly, Ellen undercut the logic of the very ideas she espoused. And she was not alone. As one editor remarked, gone were the "gloomy days" when women "had not rights" and were unappreciated for their talents; now, he continued, a woman could rightly expect to assert herself and attain those rights and privileges "to which her talents and her worth entitle her."[30] All who sought to define the parameters of female influence found the ground underneath them shifting.

Educating Women for Influence

The exercise of influence was the privilege of well-educated women. By the late 1820s, education was understood to be a constitutive element of female influence and a precursor to any role that a woman might play.[31] The earliest discussions about female education were framed within broader concerns about female influence. Literary societies were celebrated universally as spaces of improvement for women of all ages. Regarding the formal training of young women, commentators differed. Some advocated that they be educated in homes or single-sex seminaries, reflecting the belief that women would bring their learning to bear primarily on their homes and families. This view was countered by those who envisioned women's education as a means toward extending female influence into public culture's antislavery activism. Rather than remaining at odds, however, these views arrived at a point of convergence in the case of Prudence Crandall's Canterbury, Connecticut, school. When that short-lived academy for young African American women came under attack by local whites and its directress faced a jail term for violating the state's black laws, the prevailing perspectives on female education merged. Young black women should attend female academies, activists agreed, whether as an extension of their special charge as future wives and mothers or as an assertion of their civil rights—or both. At the center of the fray were Crandall's young female students. For the first time, they entered public culture, publishing heartfelt letters in the antislavery press pleading that the public rise up to support their school.

For many female activists, single-sex literary societies were a principal training ground. Their female-only character led most commentators to laud such societies as an extension of the domestic realm. Still, such venues often equipped women with skills essential to leadership in public life. Women's literary societies were regular features of public culture's landscape by the 1830s, serving as venues for the moral and intellectual improvement of women who had not the opportunity for formal schooling. Literary historian Elizabeth McHenry explains that antebellum literary societies grew out of the black mutual aid organizations of the post-Revolutionary era. By the 1830s, women's literary societies may have outnumbered those for men, though they typically had smaller memberships that held meetings in members' homes rather than in public halls.[32] Commentators universally encouraged female literary societies as efforts to improve the power of women's minds and hence their influence through methods that included acquiring basic literacy, composing original essays, and delivering orations and dialogues.[33] Society members were expected, in turn, to assist and instruct others and, by their example, to undermine prejudice grounded in stereotypically racist visions. One speaker before a Buffalo, New York, society characterized such women's organizations as among the hallmarks of freedom; "your parents and forefathers had not the opportunities to engage" in such pursuits, he reminded his audience.[34] And while most commentators imagined the education that literary societies made possible would enhance women's domestic capacities, society members went further and established more explicit ties to public culture by sponsoring public exhibitions and fund-raising fairs.[35]

Consideration of formal schooling for women and girls provoked more pronounced disagreements. Some commentators advocated a distinct approach to black women's education that reinforced the boundaries between gendered spheres of influence. Preparing women to be respectable wives and mothers as well as ladies was held up as education's foremost purpose. Abolitionist and minister Charles Ray, for example, argued that, prior to receiving training outside their homes, young women should spend their early years being educated by their mothers, learning to govern a household and raise children.[36] Beyond the training within the domestic realm, others argued, a style of education similar to that already available to white women in academies and seminaries should be extended to African Americans. Lewis Woodson, a Pittsburgh-based minister, temperance lecturer, antislavery activist, and education reformer, urged that black women be educated like those of the other "classes of society." Woodson's vision was the flip side of the coin minted by Ray. Women required training in the "elegant and ornamental" branches, including needlework, painting, drawing, and music in order to wholly fulfill their obligations to family, the home and society.[37] Without any hint of irony, Woodson characterized his vision for women's education as a progressive one when contrasted with that of those who continued to oppose female education, thus leaving them "savage" rather than "citizen" and "better qualified for the wigwam than the parlor."[38] These were multifaceted objectives that aimed to distinguish between male and female realms of influence while simultaneously elevating black women to the status of ladies and thus distancing them from the image of the ignorant and ill-mannered slave.

On one side were those who espoused a separate spheres ideology in the realm of education. Commentators such as Lewis Woodson claimed for their wives and daughters an education that would buttress their claims to a brand of respectable womanhood that was on a par with women of other "classes," most obviously, white middle-class women. Among commentators were women who concurred with Woodson. "Beatrice," a "young lady of color," wrote to the *Liberator* that "woman has a high destiny to fill," but qualified this by explaining that while man had "physical strength," "moral courage," and "ambition," woman had "the wide field of the domestic circle to interest her."[39] While neither needlework nor exemplary homemaking would excuse most black women from the demands of employment outside the home, perhaps such skills would mark them as women who were not enslaved, but free. Few, however, objected to taking women's education a step further and encouraging the development of their intellectual capacities, be it in a female seminary, a coeducational academy, or a literary society. Even those who believed women's province to be limited to the home saw their intellectual development as key to fulfilling the roles of wife and mother.

For other activists, education should put women and men on equal intellectual footing. Philadelphia's James Forten Jr. promoted education as a means of making women the intellectual peers of men and thereby suited to join the ranks of antislavery activists. As a member of Philadelphia's black-led American Moral Reform Society (AMRS) and as a correspondent to the *Liberator*, Forten was a highly respected member of the antislavery community.[40] In a speech to an annual AMRS gathering, he strongly endorsed black women's intellectual aspirations and encouraged the formation of female literary societies. He leveled harshly worded accusations at those who opposed such endeavors, charging that only hypocrisy, false pride, and vanity would lead black men—the very men who complained of being persecuted—to, in turn, persecute women.[41] Many joined Forten in supporting black women's educational aspirations. One member of Philadelphia's Female Literary Association termed education along with religion "powerful weapons" against prejudice and slavery. "Every effort you make in this way . . . helps to unbind the fetters of the slave," she urged her "friends" on the occasion of the association's first anniversary.[42] No narrowly drawn sphere could contain a perspective that encouraged bringing female influence to bear in the interest of enterprises "for the improvement of our people." In this view, female influence might be properly harnessed to improve not only the home but also public culture and those institutions through which most African Americans made their way.

Rarely did sharp distinctions hold. Some commentators developed an approach that appeared to bridge the two perspectives on female education, as was the case with a speaker before the black Female Literary Association of Philadelphia. The speaker, likely a man, began by describing the "influence that females possess": training young minds and instilling governing principles and thus shaping the actions of citizens, patriots, philanthropists, lawgivers, presidents, and kings. In this, he concurred with Woodson and Ray. But "superficial learning"—likely a reference to Woodson's curriculum of needlework, painting, drawing, and music—fell short of preparing women for this mission, rendering them "incapable of filling the stations allotted them" and discharging their duties. Declaring that only "a liberal, classical education" would equip women to exert their proper influence, the speaker decried the "corruption and error" that characterized much of women's education, and endorsed the quest for intellectual advancement embodied by the literary society. James Forten, had he been present, likely would have signed on to this latter sentiment. Most significantly, the speaker pointed out that much discussion, if not outright debate, surrounded the matter of female education. It was, he explained, a "fashionable theme" about which a "great deal has been said and written." Yet still open was the question of what sort of learning women had the "capacity" to receive.[43]

Only a genuine crisis forced black activists to reconcile their competing points of view. For a time, debates about the nature of female education appeared to unfold only in the abstract, with little grounding in the day-to-day challenges that confronted African American communities. Cloaked in domesticity, literary societies were the primary avenue for young women's education. Whether their style was "superficial" or "classical," such societies were generally shielded from criticism.[44] White women's academies and seminaries were not sites of lived contestation because they did not admit African American students. Until, that is, controversy erupted over the admittance of young black women to Prudence Crandall's Canterbury Female Seminary. The debate over female education took on a pointed relevance that led to the forging of a common ground.

Crandall defied the color line in her small-town Connecticut school in 1833. The Quaker teacher became the target of communitywide ridicule when she invited a young African American woman, Sarah Harris, to join the student body. Abandoned by her white clientele, Crandall in consultation with antislavery activists, including William Lloyd Garrison, remade her school into an academy for young black women. African American leaders endorsed Crandall's effort early on when she made personal appeals in Providence and New York. They also lent their reputations to Crandall's enterprise. When she advertised for pupils in the *Liberator*, activists, including journalists, ministers, and antislavery leaders, offered their endorsement.[45] As new students arrived in Canterbury, the orderly complaints of the town's white residents gave way to a vile campaign that saw a boycott by local merchants, the school's drinking well contaminated, its building set on fire, and the scholars harassed. A jury convicted Crandall of violating a recently enacted black law that prohibited the teaching of African American students from outside of the state. After she spent a brief time in jail, her conviction was overthrown. Still, relentless harassment led Crandall and her students, who numbered somewhere between fifteen and twenty, to abandon the school permanently.[16]

Activists mourned the defeat of Crandall's school for girls as but one in a series of educational defeats. In the Canterbury case was an unfortunate reminder of another recent defeat in the realm of education. In 1831, a long-standing proposal to establish a manual labor school for young African American men in New Haven had been voted down, victim of the fear generated by the Nat Turner rebellion.[47] With Crandall's school stamped out of existence, activists were left to wonder what shape the future of black education might take. They had followed closely the saga of Crandall's school and, from the outset, had rallied to support her female academy. The same year that Crandall's school was burnt and Crandall arrested, black activist leaders in Boston condemned the formation of a new "Young Men's Colonization Society" because societies like it encouraged the "scandalous proceedings of the inhabitants of Canterbury." The implication was that colonizationist ideas had, in part, fueled the opposition to Crandall's seminary.[48] The school's plight was on the agenda of the Third Annual Convention for the Improvement of the Free People of Colour, convened in Philadelphia.[49] In Boston, throngs of African Americans "poured their benedictions upon [Crandall's] head, in strong and fervent language, evidencing their 'gratitude and respect' for the school mistress."[50] She was the subject of a resolution expressing "patronage and affection" of "the people of color" during the Fourth Annual Convention for the Improvement of Free People of Colour held in New York.[51] In Philadelphia, Crandall was introduced to some fifty African American families in a meeting arranged by antislavery activist Lucretia Mott, who judged that black people stood ready to patronize Crandall should she decide to open a new school.[52]

The strife surrounding Crandall and her students reframed the woman question debate in education. Those who had previously debated young women's education in female influence terms set aside their differences. All commentators endorsed the model of female education offered at the Canterbury school, which was a separate female seminary that combined "classical" and "superficial" subjects: "Reading, Writing, Arithmetic, English

Grammar, Geography, History, Natural and Moral Philosophy, Chemistry, Astronomy, Drawing and Painting, Music on the Piano, together with the French language."[53] Their point of convergence was not curricular, however. It was the politics of black women's education and its implications for black people generally that muted differences.

The rights of African Americans generally and women's right to education were joined. The implications of the Crandall case for women and public culture went beyond debates about what women should learn and under what conditions. Black abolitionists, speaking on both sides of the Atlantic, included public recountings of the Crandall case as an example of the wrongs to which African Americans were subjected in a nation that countenanced prejudice and slavery. Writing from London with biting sarcasm, black Baptist minister Nathaniel Paul thanked those who had opposed Crandall, explaining that their "patriotic" and "heroic" acts gave his British audience a keen sense of the "condition of free people of color" in the United States.[54] For Paul, the Crandall case became a powerful element of his antislavery appeals. For black activists more generally, the story endured as a touchstone long after the Connecticut school had closed, with Crandall venerated as a model defender of racial justice.[55] The Reverend Theodore Wright, a second-generation black abolitionist, Presbyterian minister, and New York City vigilance committee organizer, had been one of Crandall's early supporters. He surely had her example in mind when he addressed an audience of New York City antislavery activists: "When we hear your talk of female seminaries and of sending your daughters to them, we weep to think our daughters are deprived of such advantages. Not a single high school or female seminary in the land is open to our daughters."[56] Wright knew that antislavery ideals were not always accompanied by racial egalitarianism. Still, over time the Crandall case became a means by which men like Wright challenged the racism of their white allies. Their tacit support of racially discriminatory admissions policies exposed the hypocrisy of white activists who pleaded the cause of the enslaved while refusing to abandon the prejudice in their own midst.[57]

Print culture once again served as an opening by which women entered public culture. Crandall's young students penned commentaries and delivered addresses on their circumstance, and their words made their way into the antislavery press. In this process young women's ideas about the strife that surrounded them, ones that originated in a small enclave of female scholars, were transformed into admonitions for an entire community. These young women provided firsthand accounts of the "trial and struggles" to which prejudice subjected them in Canterbury. They counseled Christian "forgiveness," condemned the "great evil" of slavery, stood fast against colonization, and championed their teacher.[58] In this crucible, the public lives of at least two of Crandall's students were forged. Julia Williams continued her education at Noyes Academy (another institution beset by white violence) and the Oneida Institute, along the way meeting her future husband, Henry Highland Garnet.[59] Williams's public endeavors later included fund-raising in support of the antislavery press in Syracuse, New York, in the 1840s, and soldier's relief in Washington, D.C., during the Civil War.[60] Sarah Harris, the first of Crandall's African American students, married and settled in nearby Kingston, Rhode Island. Harris's years of antislavery work won her a tribute in Hallie Quinn Brown's 1926 volume, *Homespun Heroines*. Harris exemplified, in Brown's pantheon of black women activists, "a group of unhonored heroes" who aided fugitive slaves in the prewar years.[61] In a sense, Crandall's school brought young women into public culture. Yet, for women already engaged in activism, Crandall's was a cautionary tale. For challenging her community's racial order, Prudence Crandall was in a sense stripped of her standing as a white woman. Her lifelong adherence to respectability, piousness, and dutifulness had not shielded Crandall from the retribution that her transgressions engendered. For black women activists, whose claims to respectability were fragile, Crandall's story likely informed their sense of the material and the psychic risks associated with their own aspirations as teachers and beyond.

Women's Religious Influence

The Crandall case moved the woman question across the sacred-secular divide. African American religious activists were among those following events as they unfolded in Canterbury. Indeed, Crandall's supporters included leading ministers who early on endorsed her school and later decried its persecution. Among female church activists of the 1830s, Crandall's reputation for piousness and her steadfast commitment to Christian principles may have elicited special sympathy. Those who practiced their faiths in interracial settings, such as women who like Crandall were Quakers, recognized the strife associated with crossing the color line. Lives spent in the separate churches of African American public culture partially shielded some black women from such confrontations. In black Methodist and Baptist churches, women found their benevolent and mutual aid work welcomed and encouraged much in the way that female literary societies were received.

However, as a small but forceful number of female preachers challenged their marginalization within black Christian sects, the woman question embedded in Crandall's story took on newfound relevance for the gender politics of religious culture. Eventually, church activists, like educational leaders, would be forced to confront questions about the standing of the women who had long filled church pews.

The power of female influence in the religious realm was reflected in the case of African American Quaker Sarah Mapps Douglass. Douglass was the potent embodiment of a brand of female influence that had the capacity to disrupt long-standing religious beliefs and practices. Douglass was an already well established figure within African American public culture when, in the late 1830s, she brought to light the racially discriminatory practices of the Society of Friends, or Quakers.[62] Douglass was the daughter of Philadelphia-based antislavery activists and distinguished herself as a member of the Female Literary Society of Philadelphia and the Philadelphia Female Anti-Slavery Society (PFASS). Under the pen name Zillah, Douglass regularly tutored readers of the *Liberator* on subjects ranging from child rearing and friendship to slavery, colonization, and the civil rights of Pennsylvania's free black community.[63] By 1837, she was a seasoned teacher of over fifteen years, operating a school that offered, in the words of one commentator, "good and solid female education . . . together with many of the more ornamental sciences."[64] In that same year, Douglass, prompted by her friend and anti-slavery lecturer Sarah Grimké, joined ranks with antislavery Quakers to expose the second-class status of African Americans within Philadelphia's Arch Street meetinghouse. For many years, Douglass, her mother, and numerous friends had been required to sit apart from whites on "the Negro Pew." While her mother had never joined the congregation for fear that she would be refused, others of Douglass's friends had left the sect, unable to endure the "scorn" and "contempt" with which they were treated.

Douglass's earliest criticisms were contained within her private letters to antislavery friends. Her testimony surfaced only indirectly. British abolitionist and Quaker Elizabeth Pease relied upon Douglass's private writings for her tract *Society of Friends: Their Views of the Anti-Slavery Question, and Treatment of the People of Colour*.[65] By 1839, when the veracity of her white allies was drawn into question, Douglass revealed herself as the source of their allegations. She then repeated, for the readers of *The Friend*, a Quaker weekly, the decades-long indignities to which her family and friends had been subjected in New York City and Philadelphia.[66] When Douglass stepped forward publicly, her literary demeanor changed dramatically. At one time, Douglass had voiced her criticisms of the Quakers through self-described "weakness" and trembling "flesh." Not only did she replace her earlier pen name with her own, but she also set aside her reticence and self-conscious rhetorical posture. By 1840 she forthrightly declared to the editor of *The Friend*: "I am persuaded the Lord has a controversy with Friends on this account. Let them see to it."[67] Strife within her religious community drew Douglass into public culture. This evolution grew, in part, out of her collaborations with white women activists, but her sharpening skills would be most directly felt within African American public culture as Douglass matured into a teacher, lecturer, organizer, and commentator.

Battles in the religious realm enhanced women's public visibility. Such confrontations were still rare in the 1830s, however. Many more women adopted an approach to female influence that affirmed the stature of churches and the supremacy of male leaders. Women's religious societies dotted the landscape of public culture, and, while not formally provided for by church law, they generally received hearty endorsement for their labors. Black Methodist denominations, still in the early years of their independence, acknowledged the work of female societies, such as the Daughters of Conference. These female religious activists joined together to raise funds for the clergys' salaries and missionary expenses. Working within local congregations, they mended ministers' suits, prepared their meals, and housed visiting itinerants.[68] Also within local churches, women extended their influence into mutual aid and benevolent efforts. The Female Branch of Zion of the African Methodist Episcopal Zion (AME Zion) Church was only one of many such societies that acted upon an ambitious agenda that included providing death benefits to widows, caring for orphaned children, and generally aiding the "sick and distressed." Oftentimes such church-based societies were linked by way of a growing network of female leaders to self-improvement organizations, including mutual aid societies, literary societies, and reform associations.

Many activist women moved easily between their families and their associational lives. Such was the case in Boston, where, as historian Anne Boylan explains, roles as wives, mothers, workers, and community activists were complimentary for the members of the Afric-American Female Intelligence Society. Established for the "diffusion of knowledge" and the "suppression of vice," the society was led by Elizabeth Riley, who later brought her leadership experience to the work of the Baptist Church–based Colored Female Union, a benevolent society devoted to aiding widows and orphans.[69] Similarly, Henrietta Regulus, secretary of New York City's African Dorcas Association, later led the Colored Ladies' Literary Society. But Regulus's example is a reminder that often early women's associations did not act independently but maintained close, dependent ties to male-led churches and other religious organizations. Both the African Dorcas Association and the Colored Ladies' Literary Society came into being under the auspices of the New York Vigilance Committee, a men's organization devoted to the defense of fugitive slaves. Sometimes organizational structures reflected the ongoing reach of male leaders. The African Dorcas Association, for example, operated under an advisory committee comprised of ministers from the city's black churches.[70] Their access to the African American and antislavery press gave women's associations enhanced public visibility, at the same time as it subjected them to the rhetorical discipline of male editors. Such was the case for the Daughters of Israel, who were criticized by the editor of *Freedom's Journal* for violating "principles of morality and economy" by staging an evening procession in which they were adorned in "white dress and cap and ribbon."[71] Still, such criticisms were rare and most often churchwomen were lauded and encouraged for deploying their influence in support of ministers, church organizations, and the broader community through benevolent and mutual aid work.

Churchwomen turned print culture toward subversive ends, unwilling to leave their words in the hands of male editors. Much in the way Maria Stewart had made her mark by publishing her tract *Religion and the Pure Principles of Morality*, Methodist preacher Jarena Lee ignited a debate about the standing of women within the religious realm by publishing her spiritual autobiography, *The Life and Religious Experience of Jarena Lee, A Coloured Lady*, in 1836. Since the 1760s, black women who took the pulpit had provoked concerns about religious and sexual "disorder." Generally, these women did not criticize their subordination in churches or the broader society.[72] By the 1830s, however, African American preaching women were less likely to accept their wholesale exclusion from the privileges and benefits associated with formal standing in the church. Lee was not alone, either as a female preacher or as one questioning her role within religious institutions. She made her mark, however, by setting out her challenge in the pages of her self-published memoir.

Lee faced off against the African Methodist Episcopal (AME) Church's most senior authority, Bishop Richard Allen. Her claim of a divine call to preach did not deflect conflict. Early in her life as an evangelical itinerant, Lee confided to Allen that "the Lord" had directed that she "must preach the gospel." Allen received this revelation with doubt. According to Lee, Allen explained that, while she might be permitted to preach occasionally with the permission of her local minister, church law "did not call for women preachers." Lee persisted, convinced that she was uniquely qualified by way of her effectiveness in the field. By her own account, she confronted Allen by delivering an impromptu exhortation that so inspired the bishop that he relented, declaring Lee's calling equal to that of "any of the preachers present." Allen gave his tacit approval to Lee's prayer meetings, yet he never advocated that she be granted formal standing within the church.

Local congregants did not share the unease of the denomination's national leadership. Lee provoked ministers as she called into question the reasoning of those who would deny women the right to preach. Her question—"Why should it be thought impossible, heterodox, or improper, for a woman to preach?"—required an institutional response. Lee found her answer in the wonder of the divine and in the unequivocal authority of the Bible: "For as unseemly as it may appear now-a-days for a woman to preach, it should be remembered that nothing is impossible with God . . . did not Mary, a woman, preach the Gospel?" Lee also based her claim on the evidence of her success: "I have frequently found families who told me that they had not for several years been to a meeting, and yet, while listening to hear what God would say by his poor coloured female instrument, have believed with trembling—tears rolling down their cheeks, the signs of contrition and repentance towards God."[73] Lee's success suggested that women's talents had the capacity to transform the lives of individual believers. Did they also have the power to alter the institutions with which they were affiliated? The framing of Lee's tract suggested yes, as it circulated with her from churches to revivals and camp meetings. Lee reframed the struggles of individual female preachers in woman question terms.

Print culture itself emerged as a religious battleground. In the mid-1840s, Lee approached the AME Church's General Conference Book Concern requesting support for a reprinting of her text. In his church history of the period, Bishop Daniel Payne remembered that the state of the book concern was especially dire in those years. Financial constraints prevented the church from supporting a number of indisputably worthy books, including a "history and life" of the denomination's founding bishop, Richard Allen. For Lee's request, the committee had a special word, however. Her manuscript was ridiculed for having been "written in such a manner that it is impossible to decipher much of the meaning contained in it." Resolving to "apply to Sister Lee to favor us with an explanation of such portions of the manuscript as are not understood by us," the committee curtly dismissed Lee's request and the controversial claims contained therein.[74] Despite the church's refusal of support, Lee secured the resources to commission what was to be a third printing of the autobiography, which was issued in 1849.

Julia A. J. Foote, an itinerant AME Zion Church preacher, shared Lee's aspirations to religious leadership. While there is no evidence that she read Lee's autobiography, had Boston's Julia A. J. Foote done so, she would have found much that affirmed her aspirations to religious leadership. In the late 1830s, Foote was a member of Boston's AME Zion Church, a congregation established after "unjust" treatment caused seventeen African American congregants to withdraw from the May Street Methodist Episcopal Church and affiliate with the black Methodist sect.[75] With this, Boston's black Methodists joined a growing denomination with fourteen congregations in Massachusetts, Rhode Island, New York City, and upstate New York.[76] Foote had migrated to Boston from upstate New York, and, after experiencing a religious conversion at the age of fifteen, she set out to preach the gospel.[77] Called by God, Foote approached Jehiel Beman, her local minister, for permission to preach from the pulpit. Beman, an antislavery and temperance activist, flatly refused. When Foote persisted, convening prayer meetings in the homes of local congregants, he excommunicated her.

Foote experienced her own ambivalences about the woman question, as reflected in her 1879 spiritual memoir, *A Brand Plucked from the Fire*.[78] Recounting a confrontation with Beman, Foote confessed that at one time she too had been "opposed to the preaching of women." Only the relentless intensity of her calling had enabled her to overcome such misgivings. Beman challenged her from the outset, convening numerous committees and tribunals to establish that Foote was acting in violation of *The Doctrines and Discipline*, the church law. According to Foote, Beman objected to her conduct on a number of grounds. He accused her of promoting the doctrine of sanctification or holiness. This stage of salvation, in which an individual is "free from the power of sin by virtue of the indwelling of the Holy Spirit," was not formally recognized by black Methodist sects. He also alleged that she preached the gospel without an exhorter's or preacher's license. Both of these charges might have been leveled at a man or a woman. But, in Foote's view, all of Beman's objections were grounded in her being a woman. "Even ministers of Christ did not feel that women had any rights which they were bound to respect," she concluded.[79]

Foote was joined by a growing cadre of black Methodist preaching women. At the outset of her dispute with Beman, Foote had acted alone. But as it moved through the AME Church's conference structure, her claim took on churchwide significance. Authority in the denomination was hierarchically arranged through a series of local, regional, and national ministerial bodies. It was by way of this structure that Foote could initiate and then appeal the

Bethel African Methodist Episcopal Church, Philadelphia (1829). Note male and female congregants use separate entrances, which mirror sex-segregated seating in the sanctuary. Courtesy of the Library Company of Philadelphia.

determination of her local minister. Foote penned a letter of protest and then carried it to Philadelphia, where a regional conference also rebuffed her. Her letter was "slightly noticed, and then thrown under the table." Thus, while the church's governance structure provided Foote with an avenue for redress, nothing required ministerial leaders to give her a full hearing, much less to find in her favor. Just as she had not been dissuaded by Beman's condemnation, Foote was not wholly thwarted by the conference's silent rebuke. Instead, she took the opportunity to join forces with other preaching women.

A women's prayer meeting, held just after the close of the AME Church annual conference, added a new layer of public visibility to contests over churchwomen's power. With Foote in Philadelphia were black Methodist women whom Foote described as, like her, "sisters who believed they were called to public labors in their Master's vineyard." This coming together appears to have emboldened the women and fostered their collective sense as preaching women. They shared stories of encountering "more opposition from ministers than from any one else," which discouraged them from "their duty." Denied a hearing at the conference, Foote and her sisters hired their own hall, where they held what she later described as the city's first religious gathering "under the sole charge of women." For eleven nights the women presided over prayer meetings. Some attendees sneered, others said "hard things," but also present were those who came "to receive good" and were converted.[80] Though beyond the walls of the church conference, the women's meeting was no less a confrontation over authority in the religious realm. Foote went beyond the relatively private settings of local parishioners' homes to a public hall where she and like-minded women acted with religious authority. Their challenge to the institutional strictures that sought to constrain preaching women was underscored when some of the conference ministers attended the meeting. These men mocked the women, disingenuously asking if they intended to form their own conference (or denomination). But no amount of ridicule could effectively undermine the questions implicitly posed by the women's meeting. Like Jarena Lee's spiritual memoir and Foote's petition, the women's prayer meeting questioned the exclusion of women from religious authority, further fueling the debate about female influence in the religious realm.[81]

Throughout the 1830s, religious communities were a rich terrain for rethinking black women's public authority. In the examples of Douglass, Lee, and Foote is evidence of how their deep commitments to communities of faith transformed women's consciousness and led them to adopt new postures. Not merely stand-alone commentators or critics, female religious activists began to turn their long-standing associations to transformative ends. The contests generated by these early activists are also a reminder of how deeply entrenched black religious institutions were in strict gender conventions. On the national or the denominational level, decision-making and leadership were a carefully guarded, male province. Julia Foote's case suggests, however, that on the local level such lines were not so starkly drawn. Congregants welcomed Foote's assumption of spiritual leadership in Boston, and at least some sought out her women's circle in Philadelphia. Only as her work was subjected to the scrutiny of highly placed male church leaders was it ridiculed and subjected to sanction.

The Politics of Female Influence

Political culture was being similarly challenged by the woman question during the 1830s. Black women shaped public opinion about education. They built religious institutions and were agents of self-help, benevolence, and spiritual leadership. Singular women often forced the woman question onto the public agenda, testing limits by way of the podium, the pen, and the pulpit. The unease that greeted these innovations also surfaced in politics. Most frequently, women's political aspirations met with a condemnatory silence. The records of the first "colored" conventions do not make even passing mention of female attendees, even as providers of meals or entertainment, roles women most assuredly filled during men's extended deliberations. But by 1836, women emerged at the center of black-led conventions, in some cases seated as delegates and signing petitions. In interracial antislavery politics, black activists confronted the woman question as national and international conventions split over the inclusion of women within their deliberative and leadership echelons. By the decade's end, the possibilities for black women's political activism had broadened vastly, but how they would step into such possibilities, if at all, remained unclear.

White women's antislavery activism, particularly in its most radical forms, was one touchstone for black activists. They strained to incorporate such developments into their overall thinking on the woman question. One example was the case of Angelina and Sarah Grimké. These daughters of a South Carolina planter had forsaken slave society and moved north, where they endured ridicule and threats of bodily harm for their abolitionist activism. Generally, their work generated positive reviews by black activists, and the sisters counted among their closest allies black women including Sarah Mapps Douglass. However, the publication of Sarah Grimké's essay "What Are the Duties of Woman at the Present Time?" in 1838 threatened the unquestioned acceptance the sisters enjoyed. Initially published in New York's Female Moral Reform Society's *Advocate of Moral Reform*, the essay insisted that men and women were equal before God and urged women to think for themselves and "lose . . . the consciousness of sex." As "duties belong to situation, not to sex," Grimké explained, women were required to embrace moral reform and abolition societies as emancipated selves, giving money, writing, speaking, and spreading periodicals. Thus, Grimké pushed female influence to its outer limits, terming women bearers of "essential rights" rather than "peculiar privileges."[82]

Their radical and unflagging commitment to the antislavery cause made assailing the Grimké sisters for their breach of gender conventions an awkward undertaking for African American commentators. For Samuel Cornish, editor of the *Colored American*, Grimké's claim for women's rights opened the door to a subtle rebuke. He never published Grimké's own words. Instead, Cornish reprinted the writings of her opponents that appeared in the *Advocate of Moral Reform*. Without comment, Cornish presented his readers with the concern that Grimké's ideas threatened to "weaken" women's influence. His vehicle was the voice of a female writer. Cornish eschewed "rights" in favor of "duties" and asserted that the Bible made clear woman's "social inferiority" to man, such that in marriage a woman "voluntarily vests her civil rights" in her husband, while in the social world, men were supreme.[83] Cornish walked a fine line. His aim was to leave antislavery unassailed while critiquing those women who were the face of its public ambitions. There was an irony in Cornish's approach. As noted, Cornish borrowed from a debate among the white women affiliated with the Female Moral Reform Society. As a reader of the *Advocate* Cornish knew that the essay he relied upon to make his point was not typical of that organization's perspective. Quite to the contrary: the Female Moral Reform Society and its weekly organ were known to be among the era's most pointed critics of the inequalities of marriage, as well as champions of women's capacities beyond the domestic realm.[84]

Mindful of women's increasing impact on antislavery activism, some commentators attempted to locate a common ground between domesticity and women's political activism. One such approach was to cloak women's antislavery work in the rhetoric of domesticity, arguing that opposition to slavery was a religious and moral duty, as well as a political one. In the view of Philadelphia activist James Forten, antislavery was not only a cause founded in "sympathy and Christianity"; it was also an extension of women's "legal privileges." Forten made this point when addressing the PFASS, an interracial women's group. He endorsed women's "managing the reigns of improvement" and dismissed those who stood in their way as "less than respectable men." Philadelphia's women should look not to such naysayers but to Britain's female abolitionists. "There shone the influence of woman!" he declared. And he specifically endorsed women's circulation of antislavery petitions.[85] Forten turned respectability on its head.

It was, however, murkiness and ambivalence that characterized views about black women's political activism by the early 1840s. Events surrounding an 1841 New York State convention to "extend the franchise" illustrated this state of affairs. Prior to the convention, William Johnson, a New York City–based vigilance committee activist, urged prospective delegates: "If you wish to make your visit more agreeable, bring your wives with you, and let them inhale some of the healthful atmosphere of the city of Troy."[86] Johnson's remark elicited a sharp response from Charles Ray, who asserted that for delegates to bring their wives would be "a great mistake." Whatever comfort they might enjoy, or bring to their husbands, Ray insisted, women should not attend the Troy meeting because "a man can do more work abroad without his wife than with her." His conclusion—"we hope, therefore, [that] the wives will not go with the view of doing business"—was seemingly directed not toward Johnson, who had recommended women come to Troy for leisure. Ray addressed an unstated but palpable concern that women might seek to take part in the convention's deliberations.[87] In the months following the Troy convention, activists continued to clash over whether women should sign the petitions circulated by the convention's delegates. Few denied that women might take part in petitioning, but they disagreed about what such activity by women meant. "A Friend" framed his view in terms of women's *rights*, arguing that because they suffered many of the same disadvantages endured by men, women had the *right* to sign political petitions. Charles Ray, on the other hand, while noting his general agreement, twice repeated a qualification: women should sign petitions only "if they wish to."[88] While Ray left the door open to women's political activism, his comment suggests that some women might still eschew politics. By 1840, a discourse about women's rights had begun to compete with the more established female influence. Terming women's public endeavors rights rather than duties reflected a significant shift—one that threatened to splinter gatherings such as the Troy convention.

A quiet consensus led to a different result as women assumed positions of political leadership in the Philadelphia-based American Moral Reform Society. In 1936, the AMRS emerged as heir to the earliest meetings of the national black convention movement. Founded in 1835 during the Fifth Annual Convention for the Improvement of the Free People of Colour, the AMRS set an ambitious agenda: to eliminate vice, greed, corruption, slavery, and war through education, temperance, economics, and universal liberty.[89] Although the organization drew members from throughout the free states and territories, it was dominated by a cadre of activists from Philadelphia.[90] The group self-consciously distinguished itself from preceding African American political bodies, eschewing distinctions of color by welcoming whites as members. The AMRS also broke with prior conventions by gradually incorporating women into its leadership ranks. In 1837, when Pittsburgh's black activists established a local branch of the AMRS, its constitution provided for a leadership structure that included a "standing committee" of twelve females, along with twelve male officers and managers.[91] By 1839, the national AMRS extended formal equality to women in its proceedings. The possibilities for black women's political influence were being redefined.

Women never were mere helpmeets in the AMRS, figuring prominently in annual meetings from the outset. At its first convention in 1836, two women—one "a Lady, distinguished for her unceasing advocacy of the rights of the oppressed," and the other a "Lady of kindred principles [and] philanthropic practices"—addressed the gathering.[92] The following year, the minutes lauded the establishment of allied female societies. Women spoke for themselves: "a Lady, eminent for her untiring zeal in the cause of human rights," shared the platform with male leaders. James Forten Jr. gave meaning to the presence of women. Chiding those who, out of "unmanly and selfish" motives, opposed "woman rising equal to them, in the sphere of intellectual strength," Forten urged the AMRS to "cooperate" with women's organizations. To do otherwise would be to indulge in a profound contradiction, "to cry aloud against persecution, and in the meantime play the part of persecutors." This was not an unqualified call for the public authority of women; Forten made clear that his female counterparts must act within the bounds of a respectability that would "reflect honour upon any community."[93] The following year's call for an annual meeting instructed any female society intending to send delegates to send their "male supervisor," if they had one, a request that suggests that recognizing women's authority as moral reform workers did not always lead to their autonomy.[94]

Women's full equality was not far off, however. By 1839, the AMRS initiated a scheme to extend the organization's constituency. Their work had long been hampered by tensions between its Philadelphia-based leaders and activists elsewhere and by criticisms of its expansive and idealistic goals.[95] Still, the rationale for amending its constitution to admit members "without regard to sex" was forthright.[96] Quoting nearly verbatim from Sarah Grimké's "Letters on the Equality of the Sexes," the delegates resolved: "What is morally right for a man to do, is morally right for women."[97] In the AMRS, moral equality was neither an abstract principle nor an endorsement of women's behind-the-scenes efforts. It guaranteed women access to the organization's leadership ranks as conference delegates.[98]

The integration of women into the AMRS has been explained through the ties of kinship and friendship that united the leadership. Delegates Grace Douglass (mother of Sarah Mapps Douglass), Mary Ann Whipper, Amelia Lewis, and Eliza Ann Bias were in the company of their activist husbands, while Mary Bustill was in the company of her sister and brother-in-law, Grace and Robert Douglass.[99] But the seventeen female AMRS delegates also entered the conference hall carrying experience in public leadership. Grace Douglass and Mary Bustill were seasoned antislavery activists. Douglass, the owner of a millinery store, was a founder and officer of the interracial Philadelphia Female Anti-Slavery Society, while Bustill was among the founders of the city's female vigilance committee.[100] These were veteran activists who had spearheaded speakers' series, petition drives, and fund-raising in a period during which abolitionists frequently met violence on Philadelphia's streets. In May 1838, for example, Pennsylvania Hall, an abolitionist meetinghouse that the members of the PFASS had helped to finance, was burned to the ground by a riotous mob.[101]

The cross-generation development of women's political leadership was reflected in the AMRS. Among the younger female delegates, Eliza Ann Bias, Mary Ann Whipper, Elizabeth Proctor, and Hannah Purnell had collaborated with Douglass and Bustill under the auspices of the PFASS and the local female vigilance committee.[102] The presence of Esther Moore, a white Philadelphia Quaker and PFASS activist, underscored the comprehensive nature of the political coalition imagined by the AMRS leadership. This movement not only embraced a brand of female influence that acknowledged women in leadership but also endorsed women's *rights*. Many of the women who joined the AMRS had long been allied with some of the earliest calls for American women's political equality. In Pennsylvania, whether inspired by Lucretia Mott's service on the executive committee of the Pennsylvania Anti-Slavery Society or Angelina Grimké's call for women to expand their sphere of influence, women had already begun to take an active part in antislavery politics alongside men.[103]

This was not a shift toward women's rights comparable to the dramatic emergences of that discourse that were characteristic of the late-1840s. Instead, what was most striking about the incorporation of women into the AMRS is that this innovation remained largely unremarked upon. In Philadelphia, this was not a radical overturning of a gendered social order but instead came out of local political alliances. Female influence was a malleable concept that might permit black women to move beyond the domestic realm while remaining shrouded in a cloak of respectability. Moreover, it allowed them to exercise leadership on political issues without undermining the effectiveness of the movements in which they participated. This move to empower women in black politics might also be read as a commentary on the 1838 disfranchisement of black men in the state of Pennsylvania. Acting upon a principle of broad political inclusion, the AMRS's increasingly democratic practices contrasted starkly with the exclusivity of politics as practiced by the state legislature.

The silence on the national front is more difficult to interpret. By the late 1830s, leaders of the AMRS were locked in a heated debate with the many activists who decried the organization for its welcoming of white members and its overly ambitious agenda that sought moral reform of nearly all facets of African American society.[104] Even amidst such contentious wranglings, as leaders aggressively vied for the loyalty of black activists generally, not one of the AMRS's detractors used the society's women's rights stance to undermine its standing. Can this silence be read as a tacit endorsement of the AMRS's policy? It is difficult to say. But it is clear that, nationally, black activists closely followed AMRS proceedings and likely made a deliberate choice to let the organization's move toward women's equality stand uncriticized.

The role of women in petition campaigns was more openly controversial. The mid-1830s marked the height of white women's antislavery petition campaigns in the United States. Even the careful crafting of such petitions, cloaked in a rhetoric of humility, did not insulate such women from opposition and derision.[105] The African American press followed these developments closely. For example, the editor of the *Colored American* reprinted John Quincy Adams's speech endorsing women's right to petition Congress on political subjects and praised him as a "gallant and eloquent advocate" for the "ladies."[106] Chronicling African American petitioning efforts throughout the North, such as the 1840 Massachusetts campaign to repeal laws banning interracial marriage, black newspapers encouraged women's participation.[107] In New York, petitioning had been one of the tactics adopted by African Americans in as early as 1821 during the debates surrounding franchise restrictions enacted in the state's new constitution. Similar tactics were adopted in 1837 when New York City's black activists organized to secure legal protections for fugitives and regain the vote for black men. Such petitions, while only occasionally stimulating legislative debate, became a commonly called upon weapon in the arsenal of political activists. While political rights, including the right to sit on juries and vote, were spoken of as men's aspirations, women were not wholly excluded from the processes deemed essential to achieving such ends.[108] Thus, when David Ruggles, a leader of New York City's Committee of Vigilance, announced a meeting to honor the third anniversary of emancipation in the British West Indies, he encouraged "all persons . . . male and female" to add their signatures to protests against slavery in the United States, the District of Columbia, and the state of New York, and in opposition to the admission of Texas to the Union.[109]

Ruggles articulated a place for women in politics. When it came to antislavery and civil rights activism, African Americans generally did not promote the construction of a separate female political culture, advocating instead that women combine their influence with that of their male counterparts to challenge slavery and prejudice. Yet, despite the endorsement of men like Forten and Ruggles, some continued to question whether women should be permitted to sign petitions. An 1837 report on African American petitions to the New York State legislature demonstrated how women's signatures added weight to political appeals, the strengths of which were reinforced by depictions of their length. Measured in linear feet, a petition for the repeal of all extant laws authorizing slavery was twenty-five feet long, with 271 female and 605 male signers. A petition in support of jury trials for those alleged to be fugitive slaves measured twenty-three feet, endorsed by 272 females and 489 males. Petitioning campaigns did draw gendered distinctions, however. A final petition that called for the right to vote for all male citizens of the state was the shortest of the spring 1837 petitions, only twenty feet in length. Its 620 signatories were all men.[110] Women had not, it appears, been invited to endorse this final objective.

The ambivalence that surrounded women's local political work was amplified many times over in debates over women's leadership within national antislavery society ranks. In 1839 and 1840, antislavery activists pointedly debated the woman question. In some cases black activists were at the center of these controversies, while many thousands of others watched this conflict unfold. Their sight was fixed upon the disagreements over white women's access to political leadership. And the lesson was one about how deeply divisive the woman question could be.

The 1840 schism between American abolitionists grew out of two questions: what was the clergy's culpability for sustaining slavery and what should be the standing of women within antislavery societies? During the 1840 meeting of the American Anti-Slavery Society (AASS), leaders withdrew in opposition to William Lloyd Garrison's support for women's rights and his opposition to political action. Establishing the new American and Foreign Anti-Slavery Society (AFASS), these politically oriented men were convinced that advocating women's rights would hinder the cause of the slave by alienating the clergy and that part of the all-male electorate that might be persuaded to vote against slavery.[111]

African American activists were fully part of this debate, and they, too, were divided.[112] When the tally was taken at an 1839 meeting of the AASS, eight of the ten black delegates voted against the appointment of female officeholders, a position that put them at odds with Garrison and his followers. Charles Ray was one of the few African Americans who stood with Garrison; along with David Ruggles and Henry Highland Garnet, Ray endorsed the view that women's votes should be counted. In 1840, eight African Americans were among those delegates who permanently left the ranks of the AASS to join the newly formed AFASS. Among them was Jehiel Beman, who just a few years earlier had put Julia Foote out of the AME Zion Church.[113]

Even before the decisive May 1840 meeting of the AASS, African American abolitionists rallied community members to take one side or the other on the woman question. In Boston, "a large body of colored citizens, male and female," voiced their opposition to "the new organization [the AFASS]." They declared themselves to be "friendly to the course pursued by William Lloyd Garrison" and urged all "colored inhabitants of Boston, without distinction of sex," to attend a public meeting. The rallying cry used strikingly martial imagery: "Fail not—everyone to his post."[114] Thomas Van Rensellaer reached out further, publishing a notice in the *Colored American* calling upon "every male and female Anti-Slavery Society among our people" to send their "most talented men and women" to the meeting. Their charge, as Van Rensellaer saw it, was to "watch the movements, and save the Society from Destruction."[115]

As activists chose sides they were required to confront their views on the woman question. The alternatives were clear. The Garrisonian AASS argued that women and men should take equal roles in the organization's proceedings, while the AFASS believed that the formal admittance of women, and the issues that might accompany them, would detract from its pursuit of the antislavery cause. African Americans weighed in on this state of affairs. Junius Morel, a journalist and abolitionist activist from Harrisburg, Pennsylvania, conveyed to Charles Ray his esteem for the AASS and those who had remained associated with it.[116] He lauded the "regenerated and regenerating spirit of Universal Liberty" that continued to guide it; Garrisonian antislavery activists were "infusing a higher and holier principle of justice and humanity throughout the world."[117] Solomon Peneton and AME minister Jeremiah Sanderson led a "large and respectable" meeting of "the colored people of New Bedford" at which the split was the topic of an "animated discussion." They condemned the AFASS for dividing the movement and depriving women of their right to speak merely "on account of their sex." For these Massachusetts reformers, this "foul spirit of prejudice" against women had an ominous significance for the standing of African Americans within antislavery societies. They wondered if the next step of the AFASS would be to exclude them "on account of colour."[118]

The black activists who joined the new AFASS did so based upon their views about women in politics, at least in part. "A Colored Man" wrote in Garrison's *Liberator* that "some of the very colored people who have become new organized" had become so because they viewed the AASS as "too leveling in principles; it places us all on a common platform, without regard to age, sex, color or condition."[119] Samuel Cornish and Theodore Wright penned a rebuttal claiming that the dispute was grounded in "a great diversity of views as to the manner of conducting the anti-slavery cause." They insisted that "the Woman question, as it is called, was not the cause—it was only the occasion" of the split. No one had aimed to "disfranchise" women "on account of their sex"; they had only sought to "decide who were members."[120] This explanation was strained and contradicted by widespread press coverage that squarely attributed the split among abolitionists to arguments over whether the AASS was a "woman's rights society."[121]

Those black activists who remained allied with the AASS recommitted themselves to women's political elevation as they watched the woman question embroil the World's Anti-Slavery Convention in 1840.[122] The British and Foreign Anti-Slavery Society had organized the conference to bring leaders from both sides of the Atlantic together in London and encourage their increased cooperation. Yet, when female delegates from the AASS presented themselves, they were refused. Their male allies gave up their seats and observed the proceedings from the gallery alongside the women. This incident forced both British and American reformers to define themselves in relation to the emerging concern for women's rights, and African Americans again confronted the consequences of the woman question for the antislavery cause. Their collective gaze fixed upon Charles Remond, the convention's sole African American delegate. They watched as Remond and a small group of AASS delegates, declined their places in this esteemed, international gathering.

Bold as his actions in London had been, Remond was unsure about how his African American constituency would view his commitment to the rights of women in antislavery politics. He thus explained to the readers of the *Colored American* that circumstances "forbid" him from taking his seat. He had declined his place at the convention out of indebtedness to those women who raised the funds to make his journey to London possible.[123] Given this support, Remond reasoned, he could not take part in any convention that excluded female delegates. Still, Remond felt vulnerable to the tensions that his advocacy of women's rights might generate, and he endeavored to reaffirm his leadership status. He reassured his supporters that women's rights did not rival the relative superiority of the antislavery cause: "Thanks be to Providence, I have yet to learn, that the emancipation of the American slave . . . is not of more importance than the rejection of females from the platform."[124] With these remarks, Remond erected a hierarchy of political interests. Priority would be given to antislavery and civil rights relative to women's rights.

Remond was lauded by many. For example, a crowd of 2,500 gathered in Boston's Marlboro Chapel in August 1840 to welcome the returning AASS delegates and to praise their performance at the World's Convention. William Nell, the African American historian, antislavery activist, and education reformer, reported that the assembly formally endorsed the "course of Messrs. Garrison, Rogers, Remond, and Adams, at the World's Convention, (falsely so called,) in refusing to lower a noble principle to accommodate a barbarous custom." A special resolution read: "We, the colored citizens of Boston, feel ourselves ably represented at antislavery meetings in England in the person of Charles Lenox Remond."[125] Among the interests so ably represented by Remond was that which claimed political rights for women.

Still, Remond's insecurities persisted, suggesting his sense that a quiet opposition to his actions remained. Perhaps there were still mutterings that threatened Remond's standing because he continued to clarify his position. He was emphatic on one point. His allegiance to women's rights would not compromise his effectiveness as an antislavery agitator. Antislavery was paramount, Remond insisted: "Happy as I should have been to see the ladies seated as delegates, I have not lost a night's sleep in consequence of their rejection; and I hope I am not far behind friend Garrison as a woman's rights man; at least, I don't mean to be. I would yield to them the same rights I claim for myself—and no man can do more."[126] Remond's effort to impose order inevitably drew attention to a complication that the intersection of race and gender created within African American understandings of nineteenth-century public culture. How would the rights of African American women be defined? Remond's view was that women should enjoy all the rights he claimed for himself. Thus, he advocated that women should be seated alongside him as delegates to antislavery conventions. Yet Remond's rights, as contrasted with those of his white counterparts, were significantly constrained. Would a movement for African American women's rights define its aims relative to the rights already claimed by men? And, if so, were those rights relative to the rights enjoyed by white men, or those sought by African American men?

Hester Lane and Intersectionality of Race and Gender

Gender, race, and politics remained a fraught terrain, however, even in Garrisonian circles. When an African American woman, Hester Lane, was nominated to the executive committee of the American Anti-Slavery

Society in 1840, unease about how black women fit into emerging discourses about women and politics was exposed. The scene had changed since Maria Stewart's rancorous foray into antebellum black politics. Ideas about African American womanhood were firmly woven into the fabric of black public culture. It had been a decade of women's firsts.

By 1840, a more pointed question surfaced in antislavery politics: Was an emerging women's rights discourse sufficient to encompass the challenges confronted by female African American activists, or would the intersection of gender and race require a unique framing? Early ideas about respectability and the stakes for all African Americans in having women conform to such expectations suggest that a discrete analysis would be necessary. This need for an intersectional analysis was further illustrated during a lesser-known incident involving an attempt to elevate an African American woman, Hester Lane, to the leadership of the American Anti-Slavery Society.[127] The precise obstacles Lane confronted suggested that it was still difficult for activists to fully articulate the challenges that confronted black women in antebellum public culture.

Black and white women did not stand in the same shoes. Historians have long attended to the 1840 nomination of Abby Kelley to the AASS business committee in an effort to understand the intersections of gender and politics in that moment. Kelley eventually won her seat among the society's male-dominated leadership cadre. It is the case of Hester Lane, however, that best illuminates the place of black women in this scene. Unlike Kelley, Lane's effort to join the society's executive board failed.

Born a slave in Maryland, Lane was a mature woman of approximately sixty. A resident of New York City, she was reputed to be an effective antislavery activist. British writer Edward Abdy, who met her in 1833, noted that Lane had "obtained a comfortable competency for herself" by operating her own shop. Lane told Abdy that she had spent much of her adult life earning the funds with which to purchase the freedom of other enslaved people.[128] Lane supported mutual aid efforts as a member of the African Dorcas Association's board of managers, worked with David Ruggles and New York City's Vigilance Committee to raise funds for Garrison's *Liberator*, and organized fairs in support of churches, including Philadelphia's Second African Presbyterian.[129] In May 1840, Lane's long-standing commitment to antislavery activism brought her to the annual meeting of the AASS.

The control of the Garrisonians was absolute once the "new organizationists" defected on the second day of that tumultuous meeting. The way was opened for women's leadership. The slate proposed by the committee on nominations included one African American man, New York City restaurateur, newspaper editor, and Vigilance Committee activist Thomas Van Rensellaer, who was approved.[130] A number of vacant slots remained. David Lee Child, a lawyer who was best known as the husband of author Lydia Maria Child, proposed that, having prevailed on the principle that all persons enjoyed equal rights "in the Antislavery ranks, without distinctions of sex or color," the society should show that "its practice was consistent with its theory." The group then nominated three white women, Lucretia Mott, Lydia Maria Child, and Maria Chapman, all of whom were confirmed by the assembled delegates. The society made manifest its commitment to making no distinctions of "sex or color." Or had it?

It was Charles Ray who put Lane's name forward. The two were likely well acquainted. Ray's first wife, Henrietta, had served with Lane as a manager of the African Dorcas Association, and both Ray and Lane had been active in Vigilance Committee work during the mid-1830s. When Ray reported on the Society's proceedings in the pages of the *Colored American*, he noted that Lane's nomination was "lost" and she was not elevated to the executive committee. In an editorial note, Ray hinted at his view of Lane's case: "Hester Lane is well known in this city as a woman of good character and sense, and has been a slave, but [t]he 'principle' could not carry her color—eh!" Ray was quick to indict antislavery activists, black and white. Equality of the races might apply to African American men, such as Van Rensellaer. Equality of the sexes might apply to white women, such as Mott, Child, and Chapman. But Hester Lane, as the potent embodiment of both blackness and womanhood, was beyond the reach of such principles. Despite her personal experience as a slave and her standing as a "woman of good character and sense," Lane was denied the public authority that membership on the executive committee would have conferred.[131]

Word of Lane's defeat spread, and the African American men who were involved in the controversy offered less than convincing explanations. Ray amended his early reportage. Lane had not been denied an executive committee seat by a vote of the AASS delegates; rather, her nomination had been "withdrawn by us, rather reluctantly, by persuasion."[132] Thomas Van Rensellaer, the sole black member of the executive committee, explained that the AASS had rejected Lane's nomination not because of her race but because of her position on the "woman question." Van Rensellaer reported that he questioned Lane about her point of view on the issue and found her "opposed to us [the AASS], and strongly in favor of the new organizationists [the AFASS]." If anyone were to blame, he added, it was Ray, who should have known that he was putting forth the name of someone opposed to "us."[133] The historical record does not allow for a full accounting of what led to the failure of Hester Lane's nomination. If Lane disagreed with the Garrisonians on the woman question and thus opposed the elevation of women to formal leadership positions, as Van Rensellaer alleged, why did she permit Ray to nominate her? Why, in a gathering of seasoned activists well-versed in arguments about the rights of women in antislavery societies was the debate over Lane's nomination confined to an exchange between two black male abolitionists?

Lane's case demonstrates how the woman question had the power to divide antislavery activists, not simply between Garrisonian and political abolitionists, but even among such longtime allies as Ray and Van Rensellaer. It also signaled that, through such debates, ideas about the place of women in public culture were being transformed. Just three years before nominating Lane to the AASS executive committee, Charles Ray had asserted that daughters were "destined to be wives and mothers," never hinting that they should also be prepared to meet the challenges of political life. Hester Lane, who had begun her public life in the late 1820s as a manager of the African Dorcas Association, which historian Anne Boylan has described as a mutual aid society that was "called into existence" and overseen by a committee of men, was by 1840 at the center of a debate about the capacity of black women to exercise leadership at the highest level of the antislavery movement. Thomas Van Rensellaer was a reminder of those who had caused Maria Stewart to abandon her public life in Boston. If Stewart was present during the 1840 AASS meeting (which, as a then resident of New York City, she may have been), she would have been troubled by the terms of a debate in which the principle of the equality of the sexes was apparently applied differently to black and white women. But she would also have been encouraged. African American women aspired to public authority and dared to challenge the judgment of the male leaders in their midst. Her questions about women's public standing had come to the fore during the 1830s, and in this debate men and women exchanged ideas and beliefs rather than vitriol and ridicule.

2

Right Is of No Sex
Reframing the Debate through
the Rights of Women

Of the many resolutions adopted during the September 1848 National Convention of Colored Freedmen, none was more novel than that which called for women's "equal" participation in the proceedings.[1] During three days of deliberations in Cleveland, Ohio, delegates considered a dizzying array of issues, including the upcoming presidential election, armed opposition to slavery, the defense of fugitives, temperance, patronage of the black press, and the dignity of labor. Late in the final day, Frederick Douglass and Martin Delany petitioned for women to be "speaking and voting as men did."[2] When met with defeat in committee, an undeterred Delany brought the issue before the full assembly. An animated exchange ensued as men on both sides of the resolution spoke out.

Douglass then called upon a woman, Rebecca Sanford, to make the case for "the rights of woman." Sanford, a white woman and Quaker from Ann Arbor, Michigan, began by endorsing the convention's objectives: "God speed you in your efforts . . . stop not; shirk not; look not back, till you have justly secured an unqualified citizenship of the United States."[3] She continued, advocating for the rights to which she believed women aspired: "True, we ask for the Elective Franchise; for right of property in the marriage covenant, whether earned or bequeathed. True, we pray to co-operate in making the laws we obey." In a closing attempt to garner sympathy for her position, Sanford set forth a complex claim: "There are duties around us, and we weep at our inability." This formulation mobilized domesticity's tearful womanhood in service of the rights-bearing and duty-bound female activist.

Sanford's speech appears to have had the desired effect. In its wake, the only remaining objection was hardly that. Ohio representatives Charles Langston and William Howard Day argued that the Douglass-Delany proposal was redundant. The convention had already passed a resolution making "all colored persons present, delegates to this Convention." As "they considered women persons," the two reasoned, they saw no need for further measures— women were already full members of the convention. With this, the delegates endorsed a final resolution that read, "We fully believe in the equality of the sexes, therefore, Resolved, That we hereby invite females hereafter to take part in our deliberations."[4] The minutes report that this outcome was met with an outburst. "Three cheers for woman's rights" rang from the convention floor.[5]

Such a seemingly out of place episode in antebellum African American history has long given historians pause.[6] This chapter's discussion lifts the debate over women at the Cleveland convention out of the realm of the novel and resituates it as a reflection of the many streams of influence that were shaping African American public culture during the 1840s. Female influence was giving way to women's rights in black activist circles, a shift that opened a door to a rethinking of the gendered character of fraternal orders, churches, and political organizations. Key in this moment was a new understanding about the underpinnings of inequality. Prejudice grounded in sex was no less arbitrary than that grounded in color, activists argued, with both African Americans and women subject to "despotic acts of legislation and false judicature," as Martin Delany put it.[7]

Nearly all black activists were confronting the woman question. In churches, despite elaborate efforts to keep women silent, cross-gender alliances put the licensing of female preachers on the agenda. At Ohio's Oberlin College, black students learned lessons in women's capacities and their claims as rights-bearing individuals. In antislavery circles, many men forged long-standing working relationships with women who increasingly held leadership positions and contributed to the success of abolitionism. These alliances brought African American activists to the earliest women's conventions in Seneca Falls and Rochester, where black women were likely spectators and black men provided support and leadership. By the fall of 1848, these influences were coming together to define the contours of a movement for women's rights among African Americans. In fraternal orders, women took the podium, claiming authority over their long-standing fund-raising work. In doing so they provoked proscriptive admonitions aimed at resisting any claims the women might make for rights. In church conferences, women called upon those men with a demonstrated commitment to women's rights to press forward on claims for women's religious authority. In black antislavery circles, quiet experiments in female leadership were given a new name, as activists came to understand them in women's rights terms.

Through this lens, the Cleveland convention of 1848 looks typical rather than novel. This chapter examines closely the debates at Cleveland to reveal how these many influences came together in the delegates' cheer for women's rights. Yet still unclear was the point of view of black women during Cleveland's national convention; not one was recorded as among the participants. How were black women thinking about their rights in 1848? One answer lies in the proceedings of subsequent conventions, where some black women insisted upon participating in the same manner as did men. Other women moved forward in more modest fashion, founding female associations through which they claimed a sort of public authority that also preserved their respectability.

From Female Influence to the Rights of Women

As the 1840s began, female influence was giving way to women's rights. Still, many commentators continued to frame their views about women's public endeavors in terms of female influence. Such ideas likely had a familiar, if not clichéd, ring. Domesticity and respectability were the well-worn tenets of ideological prescriptions that celebrated the home as woman's most exalted sphere and morality as her most powerful of tools. What had been a modest push at the boundaries of these precepts in the 1830s became a more deliberate refiguring in the 1840s. A defensive insistence on what women should *not* be and do emerged along with demands that women take responsibility for the collective well-being of African Americans. Female influence was increasingly set in opposition to ideas about women's equality. Was prejudice based upon sex analogous to that grounded in race, and should women's rights stand alongside claims for civil rights and against slavery? activists asked. By the late-1840s, some answered yes.

The female influence that dominated in the 1830s had not disappeared. Many activists continued to advocate this familiar idea. In the mind of Buffalo, New York's James Whitfield, this rubric took on an especially pointed tone when he set out precisely what women ought *not* to do. Whitfield addressed a local Sunday School Benevolent Society and "rejoiced" to see women foremost in supporting the work of benevolence. Such work had clear parameters, Whitfield explained, with women barred from "the turmoil of politics . . . the car of state . . . the intricate mazes of diplomacy . . . the rostrum and . . . the ensanguined field" of war. Women, Whitfield urged his listeners, had made crucial contributions to the community's well-being. They must, however, accept that positions of authority and leadership were the exclusive province of men.[8] Whitfield then complicated his formulation, explaining that society's "condition, prospects, and ultimate destiny" were measured by the standing of its women. Therefore, to find women active in benevolent endeavors reflected well on black Buffalo. Whitfield went on to assess the world's cultures. The degraded development of China and Turkey, ancient Egypt and Greece, and North America's "Indian tribes" resulted from women's inferiority, which reflected the "uncivilized" character of those cultures. Only societies of African and African-descended peoples merited praise. Among African tribes, Whitfield asserted, "woman is treated with a degree of courtesy and respect uncommon among barbarians, or, in fact, among any but the most enlightened nations." As applied to African Americans, Whitfield's logic was more pointed. Those subjected to slavery had risen quickly to a supreme level of civilization despite their profound oppression, and Whitfield charged women with sustaining such progress.

An untenable paradox had emerged. Whitfield's primary audience was black Buffalo's religious and mutual aid activists, many of whom likely took pride in his foregrounding of women's benevolent endeavors. Whitfield was a noteworthy native of the city; he had been politically active since sixteen when he addressed a political convention in Cleveland, and by twenty-two years of age he owned and operated a barbershop. The women whose work he praised lived among Buffalo's close-knit black residents, supporting at least a half dozen religious, literary, and benevolent societies.[9] The city's churches and political organizations tied Buffalo to a national African American public culture. When the city hosted, for example, the 1843 National Convention of Colored Citizens, ideas generated in Buffalo took on national significance. For African American activists generally, Whitfield presented a paradox. He charged black women with comporting their public lives in a constrained manner that would reflect well on their community's character. Yet he also deemed them the primary architects of public life. It was this tension, between domesticity and public responsibility, that invited a redefinition of womanhood.[10]

Some commentators distorted female influence nearly beyond recognition. If women bore responsibility for their communities' well-being, some posited, female influence might include women's activism in political circles. The commentary of Boston's William Nell, a Garrisonian activist and founding member of the Adelphic Union literary society, reflected this transformation. When he initially commented upon women's antislavery work, Nell deemed it within their "appropriate sphere." His thinking was shaped, in part, by a speech on the "influence of women" delivered to the Adelphic Union by Wendell Phillips.[11] Phillips had insisted on a distinct sphere for women, but it was an ambitious one: "When unrestrained by foreign dictation [to women was] to be attributed the success of every enterprise. . . . Impose upon her no restrictions—clip not the wings of her lofty aspiration for liberty. But let her do for her country and the world what seemeth to her good."[12] Phillips did not exempt women from respectability and domesticity, however, expecting that they would also bring to bear their superior moral sensibilities, "regenerating public sentiment by . . . sewing circles and fairs."[13] Nell initially concurred with Phillips, telling readers of the *Liberator* that women must be given "something to do" and with no "restrictions" imposed, an ideal that would unleash the full power of female influence.[14] But by 1848, Nell no longer subscribed to this view. Addressing a women's antislavery bazaar at Rochester, New York's Minerva Hall, Nell critiqued domesticity and advocated that women be released from "petty cares and groveling pursuits." The domesticity that had been central to the rhetoric of female influence was losing sway.

A new rhetoric of women's rights surfaced. As female influence lost coherence, this new set of ideas better explained the full range of expectations for black women, both in their homes and in public culture. This required a conceptual leap. Black activists began suggesting that the arbitrariness of prejudice grounded in race was similar to that grounded in sex. This view first emerged among black activists as they witnessed the challenges women activists such as Abby Kelley faced in the early 1840s. Might some challenge their right to political leadership because of race? they asked. As New Bedford, Massachusetts–based abolitionists Jeremiah Sanderson and Solomon Peneton put it, "Prejudice [as] its tendency is to exclude a large portion of the well-tried friends of the Slave, on account of their sex, we should not be surprised if its next step is to exclude another portion on account of colour."[15]

Perhaps race and sex prejudice were analogous, if not interrelated, ideas. Such was the view of Martin Delany, who transformed Sanderson's tentative query into a potent analysis.[16] In early 1848, just six months after joining the ranks of national antislavery lecturers, Delany embarked upon a "Western tour," during which he traveled between Pittsburgh, Columbus, Cincinnati, Cleveland, and Detroit, stopping in many smaller towns along the way. Delany's purpose was to solicit subscribers to the *North Star*, and he penned regular missives to Frederick Douglass back in Rochester.[17] Both African

Americans and women were, Delany explained, "generally oppressed and deprived of their rights by the despotic acts of legislation and false judicature."[18] Furthermore, women's autonomy and that of African Americans generally were mutually constitutive. As Delany expressed a desire to see black antislavery efforts become more self-supporting, women were critical to this objective. He called upon them to form "Anti-Slavery Societies, for the assistance of newspapers and competent lecturers among us." Delany placed the burden of enhancing African American independence upon women's shoulders. He urged that they follow the example of white female antislavery activists who "by their industry and perseverance, hold Fairs annually by which their newspapers and faithful lecturers are sustained." Black women's public work was similarly essential and, Delany remarked, "were it not for these efforts on the part of the ladies and societies, the Anti-Slavery papers . . . would have long since ceased to exist."[19] While, as literary historian Robert Levine suggests, Delany "operated within the conventional gender discourses," his ideas promoted women's intellectual and political development.[20] Delany called for black women's deeper engagement in politics.

Frederick Douglass marked this shift through the motto emblazoned on the masthead of his newspaper, the *North Star*. "Right is of no sex, truth is of no color, God is the Father of us all—and all we are brethren," was the credo that greeted Douglass's readers. Most of his biographers explain this position as a logical outgrowth of Douglass's associations with female antislavery activists. Such women were highly committed advocates, organizing, fundraising, and publishing. They risked bodily well-being and respectability by appearing alongside men on the speaker's circuit. As Waldo Martin explains, the *North Star*'s credo encapsulated Douglass's "ethical, civic, and political rationales for sexual equality" with a view that "the rights of woman and the rights of man are identical."[21] Yet, when placed in fuller context, Douglass's bold gesture is more complex; its meaning changed in the years immediately following the inaugural issue.

Douglass not only advocated the rights of women in 1848, he increasingly did so to an African American audience. The publication of the *North Star* marked an independent turn in Douglass's political evolution, and his overall effectiveness would require the cultivation of both black and white readers. The decision to publish his own newspaper was also a break from Douglass's position as protégé to William Lloyd Garrison. Douglass took a self-conscious turn toward African American public culture. The prospect of publishing a newspaper coalesced in Douglass's mind during an 1846–47 speaking tour of the British Isles during which he quietly amassed nearly $2,500, largely

North Star *masthead. Courtesy of the William L. Clements Library.*

collected by British female antislavery activists. Upon returning to the United States, Douglass dodged the Garrisonians' interest in what was rumored to be his plan to launch a newspaper, leading many of his long-standing allies to be taken aback when the *North Star*'s first issue appeared in December 1847.

Douglass was setting the terms of his own politics.[22] What were Douglass's expectations as he composed his provocative agenda? Certainly he believed this stance would secure a readership from among his white Garrisonian allies who shared a commitment to women's rights as well as antislavery. In this Douglass was correct. As historian Benjamin Quarles explains, five out of every six early subscribers to the *North Star* were white. However, as the itinerary of Martin Delany's western tour suggests, Douglass was anxious to attract a black readership as well. Less certain was how African Americans would respond to his assertion of parity between the rights of women and those of slaves and of black people.[23] Would African American public culture follow the *North Star*'s lead?

Black Public Culture without Regard to Color or Sex

The framing of the woman question in terms of rights reflected more than the radical ideas of a few men; Douglass and Delany were hardly alone in 1848. Black activists generally were striving for new common ground. They sought to expand their circles and bridge the divide between the East and the West. In print culture, as well as the realms of politics, religion, and education, the growth of communities and institutions was coupled with a self-conscious effort to establish a distinctly African American presence. A key dimension of this process was consideration of the woman question.

In churches, women's rights ideas collided with notions of female influence. Religious activists in Methodist churches debated whether women should be silent helpmeets or spiritual leaders. These denominations continued to expand throughout the 1840s, providing a sustained forum for reform activism, including antislavery and temperance. Church activists were seldom of one mind with those in secular circles. Indeed, the early 1840s had been marked by philosophical and tactical differences between religious and secular antislavery activists. Arising alongside these worldly matters were questions about internal institutional development. Westward migration and a spirit of competition spurred black Methodists to focus their attention on the establishment of new congregations and the nurturance of a new generation of ministers. In the AME Church, for example, the number of congregations more than doubled between 1836 and 1846, while the number of itinerant ministers grew by half.[24]

Ideas about women promised to reshape church structure and law. As black Methodist denominations moved into their second full decade of independence, church leaders began to scrutinize internal policies and practices. Among Methodists, the establishment of missionary societies, the support of common schools, and the creation of publishing houses occupied deliberations. These ambitions gave rise to questions about the sources and nature of religious leadership. What sorts of individuals were best suited for the ministry in an age of complex institutions and multifaceted agendas? Some promoted an educated ministry, eschewing those who came out of a local, self-taught tradition, preferring men with formal, often college or seminary training. Women's religious leadership surfaced within this discussion as well. The early struggles of preaching women like Jarena Lee and Julia Foote took on institutional significance as Methodists debated whether women should be granted licenses to preach.

Women's claims were situated in their work on behalf of the church. They had long raised an indispensable portion of denominational budgets, though this dependence upon women's work did not lead to a critical reconsideration of their authority. Instead, male church leaders generally labored to maintain a distinction between female support and male leadership through carefully orchestrated proceedings. For example, at the 1843 New York Annual Conference of the AME Zion Church, only when "regular proceedings" were "suspended" by the presiding officer did women enter the conference chamber. The United Daughters of Conference, represented by their officers, were "introduced" to the body, and they entered in procession "under the direction of their [male] Guardian." They were invited to sit "a few moments" and granted leave to "present their liberal and generous donation of fifty dollars." This interlude concluded with the women "treated" to "a short address, calculated to encourage them in their laudable enterprises."[25] Male church leaders regulated women in the conference chamber.[26] The public and authoritative nature of their fund-raising work was rendered invisible, and women's voices remained silenced. These highly structured encounters reinforced the divide between male and female standing within African American public culture, and this strategy frequently kept any discussion of churchwomen's rights off the table.

Advocates of change pushed ahead. Despite opposition in the form of carefully crafted rituals, they inserted women's rights into the agendas of church conventions, demanding the licensing of women to preach. Four years after Julia Foote's failed petition, the leadership of the AME Church again confronted the woman question. To overcome their marginalization within these tightly controlled public forums, women shrewdly called upon male allies. They were also organized, carrying a signed petition. The Reverend Dr. Nathan Ward, a missionary delegate and founding member of the church's Indiana Conference, acted as spokesperson, proposing to amend church law to permit the licensing of female preachers. Confronting the sixty-eight ministerial delegates in attendance, Ward spoke on behalf of forty "others," all signatories to the petition.[27] Among those present was Julia Foote, who later recounted the controversy that Ward's petition engendered: "This caused quite a sensation, bringing many members to their feet at once. They all talked and screamed to the bishop, who could scarcely keep order. The Conference was so incensed at the brother who offered the petition that they threatened to take action against him."[28] The petition met with defeat, but its very existence evidenced a new, collective point of view that differed from that of the previous decade. Struggles of extraordinary women, such as Jarena Lee and Julia Foote, became extensions of the aspirations of churchwomen generally. Ward's constituency sought not exceptions to, but fundamental alterations of, law that would have implications for all church activists.

Oberlin College was where some activists learned their first lessons about the rights of women. In that Ohio school, the presence of African American students fueled antislavery debates while the presence of young women stimulated women's rights agitation. Since its founding in 1833, Oberlin had been coeducational, admitting women and men. In 1835, through a set of negotiations generated by the admission of a group of radical antislavery defectors from Cincinnati's Lane Seminary, the trustees resolved to admit African Americans as well. Oberlin immediately became notorious for its radical mixing of the sexes and the races, but the school's climate was a moderate one. Black students never exceeded 5 percent of the student body in the pre–Civil War years, and most were enrolled in the preparatory department.[29] The presence of young women did not amount to an institutional endorsement of radical views on the rights of women. As historian Lori Ginzberg explains, Oberlin's female students withstood the competing expectations of female influence versus those of women's rights by immersing themselves in an evangelical, perfectionist worldview that generally eschewed engagement with politics.[30]

At Oberlin, a new generation of African American activists (young men—Oberlin would not admit its first black female students until the 1850s) was receiving its own education about the woman question. Enrolled in courses of study from the preparatory to the collegiate, Oberlin's black students came from cities and towns including New York, Pittsburgh, Washington, D.C., Louisville, and Cincinnati, the latter supplying a full one-third of the school's black students. Many brought with them a commitment to Garrisonian antislavery ideals, which by the 1840s included women's rights. This perspective conflicted with that of the school's leadership, which promoted the view that women were suited to work through a distinct sphere and barred them from speaking before promiscuous audiences.[31]

Oberlin's female students were powerful instructors on the woman question. Some openly challenged respectable strictures, generating a lively debate within the Oberlin community. Most controversial, perhaps, was Lucy Stone, one of the few women enrolled in the collegiate course in the 1840s. Stone organized a clandestine women's debating society and ultimately boycotted commencement exercises, refusing to have her graduation speech delivered by a male faculty member. Antoinette Brown Blackwell was Stone's ally. Blackwell similarly challenged gendered parameters by pursuing the theological course despite being refused formal enrollment. Stone went on to distinguish herself as a forceful antislavery and women's rights orator, while Blackwell became the first American woman to be ordained to the ministry.[32] Both women earned more detractors than they did allies during their years at Oberlin. Still, their refusal to conform to the school's model of respectable womanhood forced all members of the Oberlin community to refine their views about the standing of women in public life, particularly in politics and the church.

Across the nation, African American activists embraced Oberlin in all its complexity. There was, in their view, little to criticize. They appeared at ease with even the most radical implications of the school's integrated environment, lauding its egalitarian underpinnings and implicitly embracing the complexities that a cross-race and cross-gender student body generated.[33] The town itself was a popular stop on the lecture circuit, while those who could afford to do so educated their children there.[34] Commentators were sure to note the association whenever they encountered a former Oberlin student; having been at Oberlin was a marker of accomplishment and distinction.[35] Attendance at the school was held out as a hallmark of respectability, and its students were distinguished from those other young people who spent their time on frivolous and material pursuits.[36] By the late 1840s, Oberlin's black students were entering public culture; leading political organizations, churches, and schools; and bringing with them the complex sensibilities that time spent at Oberlin developed in its students.[37]

Alongside the Oberlin example, abolitionist activism remained a key setting in which ideas about the woman question were refined. During the 1839–40 split of the American Anti-Slavery Society, black activists had seen how the woman question could be divisive. Still, by the mid-1840s there were those black male activists who argued that public women were an asset. Such was the case with antislavery activist and AME Church minister Jeremiah Sanderson.[38] Sanderson wrote to his friend Amy Post, the Rochester-based Hicksite Quaker and antislavery activist, just after having attended the 1845 meeting of the American Anti-Slavery Society. Sanderson described how female abolitionists had enhanced the movement's capacity to attract audiences.[39] While having encountered many notables, including Phillips, Garrison, Douglass, Remond, and Abby Kelley, it was the remarks of a lesser-known woman, E. Jane Hitchcock, that most impressed him. Hitchcock's "nearly hour long" speech was "eloquent and logical," a style likely developed during her time touring with Abby Kelley on the antislavery lecture circuit.[40] "How strange," Sanderson reflected; "what a change has come over the face of the Society's character; a few years ago men in this city hissed at the mere idea of women's speaking in public in promiscuous assemblies; now men come to anti slavery convention[s] attracted by the announcements that women are to take part in the deliberations and they are often more desirous of hearing women than men." Public women like Hitchcock were, in Sanderson's estimation, an asset to antislavery gatherings, and their favorable reception signaled laudable changes. "Woman is rising up becoming free, the progress manifest at present of the idea of Woman's Rights in the public mind. . . . Man cannot be free, while the developer [of] his heart, soul, moral character or the maker of man in the highest sense—Woman is enslaved to conventionalisms."[41] With these remarks Sanderson sketched out a complex matrix of interests that many black activists would confront in the 1840s. Were the fates, or, more pointedly for African Americans, the *freedoms*, of men tied to those of women as he suggested? Did the "conventionalisms" of domesticity and respectable womanhood enslave women in the same sense that racism subjected all black people to bondage?

Sanderson was not alone in being influenced through cross-gender activism. Men, including Frederick Douglass, William Nell, Charles Remond, and William Wells Brown, confronted women's rights as they worked within organizations such as the Western New York Anti-Slavery Society (WNYASS). That society included women as full and equal members, and by 1847, WNYASS women raised funds, served on the executive committee, corresponded with antislavery papers, and traveled as delegates to national meetings.[42] Black male antislavery activists served as delegates alongside women in WNYASS conventions.[43] The minutes of these proceedings reveal little about how these activists experienced leadership shared across gender. The minutes do not reflect the likely awkward and even strained moments in these conventions, and the meanings black male activists took from these collaborations is not clear. Whatever their thinking, however, their interests in furthering the cause of abolitionism prevailed over any misgivings. Black men remained within these settings, experiencing firsthand the transition from the reserve of female influence to the assertiveness of women's rights.

These alliances explain how black men came to appear at the earliest women's rights conventions in 1848. Antislavery work has long been identified by historians as among the routes that antebellum-era women took to rights activism. The identities and political acumen that some women forged through antislavery work led them to resituate their interests in explicitly gendered terms and to manifest their political identities through outlets that were female dominated, both ideologically and administratively.[44] In 1848, antislavery women were among those who convened a meeting expressly for the consideration of women's rights. Their call for a convention at Seneca Falls proposed a discussion of the "social, civil and religious rights of women." The first day's proceedings were open to women exclusively, with the "public generally" invited to attend on the second day.

An asymmetry between male and female black activists was evident. No African American women took part in the formal proceedings at Seneca Falls, though historians suggest that black women were likely among the meeting's spectators. The role played by one black man, however, enjoys near-legendary status.[45] Frederick Douglass has long been venerated for being Elizabeth Cady Stanton's sole ally as she put forth a demand that the franchise be extended to women. Douglass not only supported Stanton's proposal; he committed to taking the floor and advocating for the measure. Strengthened by Douglass's alliance, Stanton persevered. And true to his word, Douglass brought his finely honed oratorical powers to bear on the assembled delegates, proclaiming, "The only true basis of rights, was the capacity of individuals."[46] Douglass exemplified the ultraist position on women's rights, expressing the view that he "dared not claim a right which he would not concede to women." Maintaining that women should be "elevated to an equal position with man in every relation of life," he told those gathered at Seneca Falls that "it need not be questioned whether she would use that right [to vote] or not," rather, "man should not withhold it from her."[47] This was the only resolution that did not pass unanimously, but the demand for women's right to the elective franchise was included in the Seneca Falls Declaration of Sentiments. The alliance between Stanton and Douglass has been lauded as a high point in antebellum political culture.[48]

This veneration of Douglass has obscured a full view of the woman question within black public culture in 1848. Douglass's gesture was neither exceptional nor a surprise. He was not the sole black male activist to take part in the early women's conventions. For example, two months later, at Rochester in August 1848, Douglass was joined by Jermain Loguen and William Nell. Loguen was a fugitive from Tennessee who settled in western New York during the late 1830s, attending the Oneida Institute and serving as an AME Zion minister and delegate to state and national black conventions. Loguen was appointed one of the convention's vice presidents and took the podium to speak in support of the women's objectives.[49] William Nell also addressed the gathering, praising the "energies and rare devotion of women in every good cause" while arguing that women were equal to men, such "that he should never cease to award the grateful homage of his heart for their zeal, in behalf of the oppressed class with which he stood identified."[50] These men arrived at the early women's conventions well-versed in the woman question. Since the late 1820s, African American activists had been grappling with questions about women's public authority highlighted by the Seneca Falls convention.

Those black activists who engaged with women at Seneca Falls and Rochester found their ideas challenged. Such was the case for William Nell, whose remarks in Rochester had reflected both female influence and women's rights understandings. Lucretia Mott openly objected to Nell's terming women "the better half of creation," warning that "man had become so accustomed to speak of woman in the language of flattering compliments, that he indulges in it unawares." Mott challenged Nell on his definition of equality, explaining that his view allowed for the possibility that women, like their male counterparts, might abuse their authority, remarking that she "also objected to calling man a tyrant, it is power that makes him tyrannical, and woman is equally so when she has irresponsible power."[51] Nell appeared to take Mott's critique to heart. His subsequent commentary on the women's conventions avoided simple dichotomies and eschewed domesticity. The women had "aimed a blow at prevailing despotic usages" and proved their "equality with man, exploding the absurd dogma of her incapacity to take care of herself," he advised the readers of the *Liberator*.[52] The early women's rights meetings served as an opportunity through which black activists, as both participants and observers of the proceedings, might further hone their ideas about the woman question.

1848 and the Woman Question in African American Public Culture

It would have been difficult to avoid a discussion of women's rights for a black activist in 1848. By late summer the question assumed a fine point: what were the implications of women's rights for African American public culture? A momentum was building, one that pressed for a reordering of power and authority in fraternal orders, churches, and political organizations. A deliberate and self-conscious network of activists pressed for the expansion of women's public standing, and a women's movement among African Americans was under way. Within some African American churches, discussion of the rights of women to preaching licenses took center stage, pressing the limits of female authority in the religious realm. In fraternal orders, perhaps the most exclusively male institutions, women were joining forces to share in the social capital generated in such spaces. In political conventions, the issue of women's rights was placed on the agenda, and women became members of these deliberative bodies. The women's rights issue took hold in black public culture. But such rights were measured by the standing of African American women relative to their black male counterparts rather than by abstract ideals or the rights claims of white women such as those set forth at Seneca Falls. Though these efforts secured only modest gains, by the close of 1848 African American activists could not deny the rights of women to be a key question confronting public culture.

Some campaigns were rhetorical. Activists aggressively recast long-standing questions in distinctly women's rights terms. Such was the case in

August 1848 when Frederick Douglass pointedly criticized the contradictions embodied in the practices of benevolent societies and churches. Such organizations, Douglass chided, heralded women as essential supporters of institutional life while denying them standing as members and leaders. This challenge was inspired by Cincinnati's United Colored American Association (UCAA), which Douglass singled out for praise when its female members took a prominent role in a public program. Fraternal orders were not public culture's sole offenders, and Douglass's critique was sweeping: "It is only necessary to give woman an equal opportunity, and she will prove herself an equal to man in all things. Why do the Sons of Temperance, Odd Fellows, masons, and other secret societies, solicit woman's aid in the furtherance of their objects, and yet deny them the privileges of their institutions?" In urgent tones, Douglass promised that the *North Star* would do its "duty . . . by reminding others of the importance of doing that which is right."[53]

Here was the woman question aimed at the heart of private, all-male fraternal orders. Such settings may seem like unlikely places in which to wage a campaign for women's rights. But Douglass knew that the Masons, for example, were popular and highly respected sites of associational life.[54] It was true that most secret societies had no formal place for women; only after the Civil War did they establish female auxiliaries, such as the Masonic Order of the Eastern Star.[55] Still, fraternal orders relied heavily upon women's fundraising and moral support to erect lodge halls and sponsor food drives, burial funds, cemeteries, and widows' pensions.[56] They also outdistanced political organizations in their capacity to attract large crowds. Douglass himself lamented with "the deepest mortification" that while only 2,000 black Americans attended political conventions in 1848 and a mere 1,500 subscribed to the antislavery press, a New York City Odd Fellows' celebration had attracted between four and five thousand people.[57]

Flattery was among the weapons Douglass used to further his views. His praise for the UCAA was genuine, even as it was intended to undercut the many more such organizations that did not invite women into their proceedings. Based in Cincinnati, the UCAA was one site of a public culture that included the Sons of Temperance, the Colored Orphan Asylum, five or six churches, primary and secondary schools, the United Daughters of the AME Church, and six "societies." The UCAA alone had some 300 members and several branches throughout the state.[58] The organization's reach extended deep into the lives of black Cincinnatians through, for example, its sponsorship of a cemetery and public ceremonies, such as the West Indian emancipation celebration. Douglass lauded the UCAA because it had included a woman, Anne Lee, among the speakers at a recent celebration. Lee had delivered an address before the "many hundreds" gathered and was commended for her "unsurpassingly neat and eloquent" style.[59] Douglass took the opportunity to recast the occasion in terms of women's rights, remarking: "And why not? [Why should a woman not speak at fraternal order meetings?] It is only necessary to give an equal opportunity, and she will prove herself equal to man in all things."[60]

Public women such as Anne Lee, Maria Stewart, and Julia Foote were remade through Douglass's words. For readers of the *North Star* who were encountering such female activists, Douglass explained their presence at the podium and the pulpit in the broadest woman question terms. He called upon his readers to ponder the place of women within public culture.[61] Why were women as a group denied the opportunity to exercise authority within churches, political conventions, and fraternal orders? Douglass's challenge captured the tension between the enormity of women's responsibilities and the constraints on their institutional standing. He took the contradictions implicit in the formulations of men like Theodore Wright, James Whitfield, and the like and questioned the contradiction they constructed.

Actual events in Cincinnati were not nearly as radical as Douglass's commentary suggested. Modesty cloaked Anne Lee's presence at the UCAA meeting, and her remarks never hinted at the radical remaking of gender conventions that Douglass called for. Lee took the podium to speak on behalf of the "twelve ladies" who "ascended the stage" along with the society's "six grand officers."[62] As an artifact, the text of Lee's actual remarks is rare. Such women were often memorialized only as silent attendees, and when they did speak, their words were summarized in the form of a resolution or mediated through the voice of a male ally. What makes Lee's remarks all the more interesting is that they avoided any overt challenge to the organization's gendered order. Lee praised the "onward and upward" course of the association, urging that it continue to bring "health to the sick—honor to the brave—success to the lover, and freedom to the slave." Lee used terms like "love" and "cherish" to convey the women's posture, without a hint of strain between the UCAA and its female allies.[63] What then was the source of Douglass's insight? The remarks of the man who followed Lee on the program conveyed the sense that questions about women's standing in public culture were circulating through the UCAA's proceedings.

Through the comments of George Brodie, who followed Lee on the program, we hear the event's woman question implications. Brodie was charged with replying to Lee and the "ladies."[64] Despite Lee's modest posture, she provoked a proscriptive retort from Brodie, one that reined in women's public authority. Brodie was a twenty-five-year-old porter and son of an AME Church minister who later became a minister himself. In a style which echoed that heard in black Methodist churches, Brodie thanked the women for their "splendid" gift and lauded their "labor indefatigable" and "zeal untiring." Signaling his self-conscious departure from the proceeding's agenda, he implored: "We ask your indulgence a few moments, whilst we disclose to you a few thoughts . . . in reference to the worth and character of woman." Brodie offered up respectable womanhood as an ideal, praising women's smiles, beauty, grace, benevolence, virtue, and constancy. In a properly ordered public life, Brodie argued, "the ladies, when called on, cheerfully assent to assist [the men,] if it be of a benevolent or charitable nature." The UCAA would "mount the rostrum of elevation," while its female associates would continue to offer much valued "encouragements."[65] His boldness contrasted with Lee's carefully chosen words. Black women, as they stepped into public culture in the 1840s, did so by striking a delicate balance between respectability and rights. This UCAA meeting took place on 20 July 1848, the very same day of the women's convention at Seneca Falls. For weeks Douglass had been publicizing those upcoming women's meetings in the *North Star*. We can only speculate that Lee and Brodie were aware of the confluence of events, but for the newspaper's readers, each event framed the other, helped along by Douglass's commentary.

Tensions within black Methodist churches were far more overt as women's rights ideas generated reconsideration of churchwomen's authority. At the year's AME Church General Conference, female activists who conducted fund-raising as the Daughters of Zion resurrected Rev. Nathan Ward's proposal of four years earlier, again advocating the licensing of women to preach. They confronted an imposing gathering of men from fourteen states, including 175 ministers and 375 male lay leaders.[66] They competed with an ambitious "official agenda" that included the election of a second bishop and a discussion of the structure of the church missionary society, the establishment of a book depository, a plan for common schools, and sanctions for divorce and remarriage. To overcome their exclusion from the formal proceedings, the female activists turned to a male ally, J. J. Gould Bias of Philadelphia, who agreed to sponsor their petition. Bias had been part of experiments in women's political leadership not only as a Garrisonian antislavery activist but also as a member of the American Moral Reform Society (AMRS), where he served in 1839 as a delegate alongside his wife, Eliza, and numerous other women.[67] The surviving conference reports do not say whether Bias couched his motion to license female preachers in language similar to that of the 1839 AMRS resolutions, which admitted persons "without regard to sex" and declared "that what is morally right for man to do, is morally right for woman." But the rhetoric put forth by the women's opposition suggests that such was the spirit of the proposal.

To put down such a resolution required powerful rhetoric in 1848. The task of defeating the Daughters of Zion proposal was given over to Daniel Payne, a Baltimore-based minister, later the denomination's senior bishop, who deployed a complex construction of black womanhood to defeat the Daughters of Zion.[68] Payne began by urging the church to tailor its laws to tenets of respectability and domesticity. The licensing of female preachers was "calculated to break up the sacred relations which women bear to their husbands and children," leading to the "utter neglect of their household duties and obligations," he warned.[69] Payne continued with a shrewdly crafted argument. First, he incorporated claims already made potent by antislavery and temperance advocates of the period. In his view, women's rights, like slavery, threatened the sanctity of African American family life. And, just as the consumption of alcohol led men to neglect their families, women might become similarly irresponsible if they bore the responsibilities for which being licensed to preach called. Payne's reasoning likely seemed flawed to the Daughters of Zion, who had long managed whatever tensions existed between their public responsibilities and their domestic obligations. Yet Payne correctly perceived that he would need to mobilize heavy ideological artillery if he and his church were going to withstand the force of the call for women's rights. Just three months after the issuance of his dissenting report, the call for the first of the women's movement conventions at Seneca Falls, New York, was issued.[70]

Antislavery circles were being similarly shaped by women's rights in 1848. There, these ideas bore fruit and expanded the way for female activists to assume authority alongside their male counterparts. Such was the case during the meeting of a Philadelphia-based African American antislavery society during October 1848. Called to generate support for the *North Star*, in substance this meeting centered around the charge that three of the city's African American churches were "pro-slavery," barring abolitionist lecturers from their pulpits, preaching only tepid antislavery ideas, and affiliating with denominations that failed to exclude slaveholders.[71] This provocative accusation generated a set of heated exchanges between activists on the local and national level.[72] Yet, as the controversy swirled through public meetings and the press, little attention went to the meeting's other provocative dimension: women served alongside men on the society's governing bodies.

Words were followed by deeds. As the Philadelphia meeting got under way, statements regarding the equal standing of men and women were followed by the seating of female officers. Charles Remond set the meeting's tone by couching the first resolution, one that called for a committee on the roll, in the suggestion that no "impediment" should prevent "any gentleman or lady who may desire to address the meeting" from doing so. With this, the proceedings were open to women, both black and white. Remond complimented the work of the nominating committee; two of the seven vice presidents were women, as were three of the nine business committee members. The related commentary suggests that the appointment of women to these positions of political leadership raised no questions among the delegates, and a closer look at some of the activists in attendance may help explain this easy acceptance. Among the female leadership were veteran political activists. Business committee members included Harriet Purvis, a founder of the Philadelphia Female Anti-Slavery Society and delegate to the Anti-Slavery Convention of Women in 1838 and 1839; Eliza Ann Bias, a Daughters of Temperance activist and 1839 AMRS officer; and schoolteacher Priscilla Stewart. Among the vice presidents were Harriet Smith, a leader of the local Women's Association of Philadelphia, and a woman noted as "Mrs. A. Reckless," likely Hetty Reckless, who had been a delegate to the 1839 Women's Anti Slavery Convention along with Harriet Purvis. These women's male allies likely helped pave their way. Present were Martin Delany, Frederick Douglass, Charles Remond, Robert Purvis, and J. J. Gould Bias, all of whom were already on record as accomplices in black women's efforts to secure standing in public culture.[73]

While quietly carried out, these innovations were nonetheless remarkable. Lucretia Mott was among the women in attendance and was well known to the black women delegates as their long-standing ally in the work of the Philadelphia Female Anti-Slavery Society. Mott conveyed her enthusiasm for the gender-inclusive character of the convention in a letter to Elizabeth Cady Stanton: "We are now in the midst of a Convention of the Colored people . . . all taking an active part—and as they include women—& white women too, I can do no less . . . than be present & take a little part." For Mott, who reported traveling to the meeting place despite the pouring rain, the significance of the meeting was the ambitious vision of its black activist leaders, one that embraced "the cause of the slave, as well as of women."[74]

"Three Cheers for Women's Rights":
The Cleveland National Convention of 1848

The 1848 cheer for women's rights at Cleveland now appears in its full context. Those who gathered for that national convention reflected debates already animating the fraternal orders, churches, and antislavery societies to which the delegates also belonged. The convention movement was once again at the center of black political culture. Gone were the rifts between moral suasionists on the one hand and political abolitionists on the other. Activists aimed for consensus around greater militancy, political engagement, and independence from white allies.

It was no coincidence that such a meeting took place in Cleveland. Leaders from eastern cities such as Philadelphia and New York were being challenged to incorporate activists from throughout the free states and territories into political culture. Many such challengers had come of age in the more remote cities and towns of the north and west. In his classic work, *The Burned-Over District*, Whitney Cross describes the region of New York State that lay west of the Catskill and Adirondack Mountains, invoking evangelist Charles Finney's characterization of the area as one burnt by "the fires of the forest and those of the spirit." Building upon Cross's insight, a subsequent generation of scholars extends the boundaries of this region west, to include parts of Pennsylvania and Ohio's Western Reserve.[75] The burning-over process, it is said, encouraged the growth of new ideas. The region was populated by people, mostly transplanted New Englanders, who were open to unusual religious beliefs, enthusiastic worship practices, and crusades aimed at the perfection of mankind and the attainment of millennial happiness.[76] Cross termed this phenomenon "ultraism," defined as a "combination of activities, personalities, and attitudes creating a condition of society which could foster experimental doctrines."[77] In the wake of Finney's revivals of the Second Great Awakening came Mormonism, Millerism, the Shakers, and the Oneida perfectionists.[78] The region was also home to abolitionists, temperance people, dress reformers, water cure enthusiasts, peace advocates, educational reformers, asylum-builders, and anti-tight-lacing societies.[79]

Women's rights also thrived in the Burned-over District. In her study of Rochester, New York, historian Nancy Hewitt explores the emergence of public women and women's rights in, what she terms, "the heart of the Burned-over District." In this city, the "fires of religious and reform enthusiasms" gave way to vivid expressions of social change and women's activism, and Hewitt situates this evolution firmly within the unique character of the region.[80] Hewitt's insights are supported by Judith Wellman's study of the signers to the 1848 Seneca Falls Declaration of Sentiments, which illustrates the decisive influence of two groups of Burned-over District women: political abolitionists from Seneca Falls and Ultraist Quakers from Waterloo and Rochester.[81]

Black activists were present in these ultraist scenes. Their migrations to Burned-over District locales reflected a particular interest—proximity to Canada.[82] Black settlements were scattered throughout this region—in locales including Syracuse, Rochester, Buffalo, Pittsburgh, Harrisburg, Columbia, and Cleveland, and farther west in cities like Detroit.[83] Burned-over District communities gave black Americans important access to the Canadian border, enabling them to avoid slave hunters and enjoy a less fettered freedom.[84]

Thus, to rethink the rights of women in Cleveland may not have been as radical a step as it would have in an eastern seaboard city. There, consensus was possible. What had been many isolated moments in the woman question debate of the 1830s and 1840s came together in a strident and unequivocal resolution that stated: "Whereas, we fully believe in the equality of the sexes, therefore, Resolved, That we hereby invite females hereafter to take part in our deliberations." The wording of this resolution reflected the state of African American public culture as a whole. In the realm of ideas, the resolution expressed a full *belief* in the rights of women, while in the material realm of institutional culture, it expressly altered the gendered dimension of the institution's structure. This moment was in part inspired by the women's conventions that had taken place just weeks earlier, but was also a product of a black public culture that had been forged in a variety of sites, from schools to fraternal orders and churches to antislavery societies, where women played vital roles.

The identities of the Cleveland convention delegates tells another part of the story. Frederick Douglass, for example, came to Cleveland after attending the women's conventions at Seneca Falls and Rochester. Douglass understood the degradations of color and sex as the by-products of equally arbitrary prejudices that he was committed to undoing. Martin Delany joined him in promoting the Cleveland resolution, and it was Delany who kept the issue alive when it might have died in committee. Earlier that year, Delany, writing to Douglass in the *North Star*, had suggested that African Americans and women were similarly oppressed.[85] If Delany repeated such sentiments to the Cleveland convention, they might have resonated strongly with the convention's male delegates, many of whom understood themselves to be victims of the arbitrary exercise of the state's power as expressed through black laws.

Oberlin College veterans shaped the debate. Charles Langston and William Howard Day were the two Ohio delegates who reminded the convention that women were "persons too" and thus equal participants in the conference's deliberations. Langston had attended Oberlin intermittently from the mid-1830s through 1843, and Day had graduated in 1847.[86] Langston and Day, who as African Americans were necessarily at the center of the school's most provocative innovations, absorbed a sophisticated range of thought on women's rights. Day remained an associate of both Lucy Stone and Antoinette Blackwell into the early 1850s.[87] These men's parsing of the language of the Cleveland resolution and their argument that the term "persons" included women marks them not as obstructionists but as men prepared to educate their fellow activists on the fine points of mid-nineteenth-century women's rights thought.[88]

Some delegates had just come from the summer's women's conventions in Seneca Falls and Rochester. There was Frederick Douglass, who had played a key role at Seneca Falls. In Cleveland, Douglass contributed the wording of the women's rights resolution. Through his authority as president, he ceded the floor to a white woman, Rebecca Sanford. Sanford had recently attended the western New York women's conventions, and she set forth the issues most salient to the nascent women's movement.[89] The right to vote and to marital property and a role in "making the laws" were her objectives, Sanford explained. Remarkably, however, she failed to address the matter that most immediately confronted the convention. Was the right of African American women to take part in such a gathering among those Sanford sought? Her silence on the point speaks volumes about the complex political terrain that black women were required to negotiate. On the one hand, Sanford's presence buoyed their claims for authority in the convention by reminding conference attendees that their deliberations were of interest to those active in allied social movements. However, black women's particular objectives might be overlooked if others spoke for them. Indeed, Douglass's choice of Sanford as the sole female speaker left black women's points of view indiscernible.

What of African American women? They were only the subjects of resolutions and the targets of sentiments of sisterhood. Although they were present during the proceedings, the meanings they associated with the debate remain a matter of speculation. Some insight into their views, however, may be gained from the following year's meeting of the State Convention of the Colored Citizens of Ohio. There, black female activists overtly claimed political rights. Their strategy was to ally themselves with the chair of that meeting's business committee, William Howard Day. Day presented a resolution authored by a woman known only by her name, Jane P. Merritt, that placed the issue of women's standing squarely before the state's African American leadership.[90] Merritt's resolution challenged women's exclusion from political authority: "Whereas the ladies have been invited to attend the Convention, and have been deprived of a voice, which the ladies deem wrong and shameful."[91] The women threatened to walk out of the proceedings, warning, "We will attend no more after tonight, unless the privilege is granted." Delegates who had been present at the national convention just four months earlier were already familiar with the arguments. John Watson, who had stood in favor of women's rights at Cleveland, spoke for the majority when he advocated a resolution "inviting the ladies to participate." The constituency that opposed Merritt's resolution paralleled that evident at the national meeting in Cleveland. The women finally prevailed, gaining admittance to the convention through their self-styled activism that included male allies. Ohio's African American women transformed their standing in the community's political life.[92]

The presence of black women at Cincinnati was not only a matter of form. They shaped the convention's deliberations. Seated as delegates, Ohio's women had the opportunity to weigh in on the convention's debates about female education, challenging their exclusion from female academies and seminaries, an issue that had drawn the attention of black political gatherings when Prudence Crandall's Connecticut school was attacked. In the late 1840s, Ohio's activists again took up this controversy when Frederick Douglass's daughter, Rosetta, was turned out of Seward Seminary in Rochester on account of her race. Rosetta, well prepared by her studies with the Mott sisters, had passed the school's entrance exam.[93] The objection of one parent, Horatio Warner, who wielded considerable influence as the editor and publisher of the *Rochester Courier*, persuaded the principal to uphold Rosetta's expulsion over Douglass's objections.[94] The Ohio delegates' resolution reveals that white women's activism continued to be a point of reference for African Americans. It began: "Whereas, the ladies of England, Scotland, Ireland and France have made strenuous efforts in behalf of right, liberty and equality . . . protesting against the contemptible conduct of that miserable wretch, H. G. Warner, in excluding from the Seminary in Rochester the child of the far-famed Frederick Douglass. . . ." The delegates praised those who had taken up Rosetta's cause: "Resolved, that the conduct of these ladies and gentlemen in this respect has our hearty approbation and united concurrence, and we hail it as an omen of the times when the world of mankind will be engaged on the side of outraged and oppressed humanity." The interconnectedness of the far-ranging realms of girls' education, civil rights, women's public work, and the antislavery movement was made manifest through young Rosetta's case.

Only from a public culture vantage point can the ascendancy of women's rights ideas be seen. By examining the diverse sites of African American associational life in a single frame, the connections between the decade's many conferences and conventions come into view. The bridges between fraternal orders, churches, and political organizations were built by activists whose lives were rarely limited to any one institution. Men and women moved from denominational conference to antislavery meeting and from college campus to fraternal celebration. By 1848, they were being regularly called upon to take up the woman question. Their sometimes warring words reveal how questions about women in public life were shaping institutions and knitting them together. In debating the merit of female influence versus women's rights, and then deciding upon what the latter might mean, activists gave public culture its meaning.

The year 1848 did not mark the advent of a simple consensus, however. While in some circles women's rights ideas reshaped the relationship of gender to power, in others this groundswell of change was kept at bay. Women were still called upon to fulfill domestic duties and conform to the constraints of respectable womanhood and to support such community institutions as burial societies, temperance groups, and orphanages.[95] In some settings the woman question seems not to have arisen, despite the excitement the issue was generating elsewhere. For example, at the Connecticut State Convention of Colored Men in September 1848, where the Reverend Amos G. Beman presided, not a word was said about the standing of women within the organization, even as "mothers" were implored to exercise their "duties" and their "influence" over the young.[96]

Black Women's Activism in a Post-1848 World

Black women's activism also turned inward in the wake of the Cleveland convention. Nearly two decades after Maria Stewart's inauspicious attempt to enter black politics, Stewart's daughters and sisters navigated a complex matrix of ideas and institutions. Some founded new women's organizations through which they put to use the lessons of the past years. These women deftly crafted a model of women's public work that encompassed race, responsibility, and respectability without any of the reticence that characterized some other women's assertions of public authority in the 1840s.

While refining their own identities and strategies as public women, these black female activists also educated the men in their midst. Their lessons were not those of white antislavery women but of African American women who were carefully navigating the terrain of rights while holding on to respectability, which they understood to be critical to their broader responsibilities.

Some of black public culture's most seasoned female activists turned their efforts toward female associations. In January 1849, for example, Sarah Mapps Douglass and her friends formed the Women's Association of Philadelphia.[97] Rooted in a spirit of race autonomy espoused by Martin Delany, this organization was distinct from the Philadelphia Female Anti-Slavery Society, though some women retained membership there. Delany was invited to speak at the association's inaugural meeting, and he "wrote and presented a constitution for the association, which the women adopted." An inaugural resolution reflected Delany's ideas: "Whereas, Believing Self-Elevation to be the only true issue upon which to base our efforts as an oppressed portion of the American people; and believing that the success of our cause depends mainly upon Self-Exertion. . . . Therefore we do agree to form ourselves into an Association, to be known as the Women's Association of Philadelphia, the object of which shall be, to hold Fairs or Bazaars for the support of the Press and Public Lecturers, devoted to the Elevation of the Colored People." Philadelphia's black women activists expressed their public autonomy not by joining a women's rights movement but by founding their own gender-specific and race-based organization, electing their own officers and organizing antislavery fairs to support the *North Star* while collaborating with men like Delany.[98]

Such organizations were not wholly deferential, but their claims on public authority were modest. In this spirit, the Philadelphia Women's Association published an announcement of its Christmas week fair, the proceeds from which would go to Frederick Douglass and the *North Star*. The primary objective was to lend support to Douglass's work. However, the announcement's authoritative tone suggests that Sarah Douglass and her colleagues saw themselves as far more than subordinate helpmeets. They boldly instructed readers of the *North Star* on their political obligations. The community should "sustain F. Douglass because his talents and correct principles demand your respect and confidence. Sustain him because it is right to do so," the women urged.[99] Philadelphia's black female reformers were willing to act as confident, authoritative voices in their city's public culture, raising funds while also offering guidance on what was "correct," what was "right," and what could be appropriately demanded of the community as a whole.

Women in other northern cities took up this task in the same vein. In Syracuse, Julia W. Garnet and her sisters formed a "Provisional Committee" to support the *Impartial Citizen*, a weekly newspaper published in the city by Samuel Ringgold Ward, an African American Congregationalist minister, American Anti-Slavery Society agent, and Liberty Party activist.[100] The committee included many western New York women who were familiar with the challenges of public life. Garnet herself had been raised in Boston, was educated at Prudence Crandall's school and the Noyes Academy, and taught in Boston before marrying Henry Highland Garnet in 1841.[101] Her colleague Caroline Storum Loguen, who had married Jermain Loguen in 1840, was active in providing aid and protection to fugitive slaves and as a public speaker at Syracuse events such as its First of August celebration.[102] These women announced their concerted entrance into public culture with a fair in September 1849 that promised to raise funds, educate, and entertain.[103] In January 1850, when the Buffalo Ladies Literary Progressive Improvement Society was formed, its broad mission statement suggested that women were self-consciously readying themselves for an expanded role in public life. The society endeavored to work toward the "moral, intellectual, political, and social advancement of its members, by endeavoring to promote, so far as possible, every branch of literature, art and science, and encouraging every political reform, which tends to secure human rights or elevate human character." Its solicitation requested "donations to support a reading room and library."[104]

To frame these women's organizations in the rhetoric of the Cleveland convention would be to posit them as a manifestation of an emerging rights consciousness. But when contrasted with the boldness of the claims made for the women at the Cleveland convention or the AME General Conference, this new wave of mutual aid societies appears modest. Despite all the excitement generated by calls for the rights of women in church conferences and political conventions, black women generally remained out of the fray. Women's forays into public culture and the controversy that greeted such moves had led their more visible white counterparts to construct a self-consciously autonomous women's rights movement.

Perhaps the best characterization for these late-1840s associations is sober. That is, black women's activism remained tempered by the particular brand of ridicule to which they were subjected. For black women, the lessons of the 1830s had been difficult. While they had been seasoned and steeled through antislavery activism, the public ridicule expressed in such commentary as Edward W. Clay's "Life in Philadelphia" shaped their sensibilities. Their efforts to embody rights, responsibility, and respectability demanded that black women activists master an artful dance. They shouldered responsibility for the material well-being of public culture along with a sense of collective esteem that relied upon their adherence to respectability's strictures.

However, after 1848, it was impossible to understand anything about black women's activism outside the frame of women's rights. Their exclusion from leadership positions, which would continue, could no longer be naturalized by the notion of a woman's sphere. Nor could the ideals of domesticity and respectable womanhood or a general disdain for manifestations of overt female public authority stand as unassailable norms. The emergence of the woman question exposed the extent to which black activists were making choices about the gendered character of institutional life, even though they were rarely of one mind. The stakes were indisputably high. Views about the rights of women could determine the capacities of institutions. The example of the American Anti-Slavery Society served as a cautionary tale. Women's rights principles might strengthen some alliances, as in the Western New York Anti-Slavery Society and at Seneca Falls, while simultaneously undermining others, as was the fear among many Methodists.

The 1850s would begin ominously. Black women found themselves navigating the same difficult terrain in a period fraught with crisis. The intransigence of slavery, the Fugitive Slave Act, the material challenges produced by general economic depression, intensified job competition with European immigrant labor, and fundamental challenges to the public standing of all free black people through pronouncements such as *Dred Scott v. Sanford* produced a climate in which free black activists felt themselves under siege. Public culture, which was already a complex terrain for black women, became further fraught. Ideas about women's rights would be recast as having no place inside the parameters of "race" organizations. By the mid-1850s, "three cheers for women's rights" had been displaced by a new refrain: "This is not a women's rights convention."

3

Not a Woman's Rights Convention
Remaking Public Culture in the
Era of Dred Scott v. Sanford

Mary Ann Shadd could not escape the woman question. During the winter of 1855–56, Mary Ann Shadd toured the United States promoting the emigration of African Americans to Canada. Her subject matter was provocative, yet Shadd found herself ridiculed for her womanhood as much as for her political point of view. Her travels brought her to the National Convention of Colored Citizens, where she sought delegate status and intended to make the case for Canadian emigration. Despite the efforts of a most influential ally, Frederick Douglass, the male delegates barred Shadd by a vote of twenty-three to three. When challenged to justify this determination, they resolved that the meeting was "not a woman's rights convention."[1] The tenor of her reception was the same when, just weeks later, she arrived at Philadelphia's Banneker Institute to debate one of its most prominent members, Isaiah Wears. Shadd's appearance was preceded by a pointed warning. She would be treated in the same manner as any "male opponent" because she was "too high spirited to crave any special favour or courtesy."[2] Shadd managed to carry the day on the emigration issue with the local three-judge panel voting her the winner over Wears. Still, the rhetoric that surrounded this public appearance had reframed its significance in terms of the woman question.

The Cleveland consensus of 1848 had been shattered. Women's rights, and the female publicity implicit in that notion, had been for a short time a point of convergence for African American political leaders. By the mid-1850s, the same ideas were feared and derided. In some sense, there had always been activists who expressed skepticism about the efficacy of a political agenda that embraced two radical sets of interests, those of race and sex. Starting with the passage of the Fugitive Slave Act in 1850, the pressures that bore down upon all black Americans were intense and unprecedented. Most activists turned inward, honing their political agenda and returning antislavery and civil rights to the fore. The fate of the early African American women's movement was bound up with these changes, and a general rethinking of political culture led to the marginalization of the women's rights issue.

For black activists, there was little optimism to go around in the 1850s. The climate only worsened over the course of the decade, with the Supreme Court's 1857 decision in *Dred Scott v. Sanford*, which declared black Americans noncitizens, a low point. In the realm of culture, minstrelsy gained newfound popularity and the ambitious political agenda of the late-1840s—one that embraced both race and sex issues—became raw material for cruel parodies that aimed to undercut the political standing of black Americans. Even some of the most outspoken black advocates of women's rights, such as Frederick Douglass, rethought their views. The result was that women's rights were put out of the realm of black politics. Activists no longer reached for the logic of female influence to support this posture and instead pointed to the need to restructure political culture. Black conventions simply were not forums for discussion of women's rights.

Shut out of politics, women's rights advocates adjusted their sights. In churches, the debates over female authority continued. In literary societies, the woman question often occupied center stage in debates and presentations. Fraternal orders worked harder than ever to persuade their female supporters that they should not press for greater access to secret societies. From the perspective of those who were advocating for the rights of black women, no venue was more fruitful than that of print culture. Since the late 1820s, women had been taking pen in hand and shaping the debates that swirled through their public lives. By the mid-1850s, their presence had grown in substance and style. Mary Ann Shadd began publication of the *Provincial Freeman*, extending the woman question debate into the realm of publishing while also creating a forum in which women's voices were being heard with unprecedented clarity.

A generational shift also shaped the decade. If women such as Maria Stewart, Jarena Lee, and Jane Merritt were representatives of the first generation of black women's rights activists, by the mid-1850s a new generation of young women was poised to join them. Raised under the influence of the century's early path breakers, young women were coming of age witnessing women at the podium, speaking before promiscuous audiences, editing newspapers, penning tracts and letters to the editor, organizing for church conferences, operating social and benevolent societies, and honing their skills in literary societies. Even through the degradations and disappointments of the 1850s, these new female activists continued to keep the question of their public lives on the agenda in African American public culture.

An Uneasy Alliance

Fissures deepened in the 1850s. But even in 1848, ambivalences about the turn toward women's rights had been present in black activist circles. This had been a muted opposition, however. For example, in 1849, when a group of Buffalo, New York's leading African Americans held a First of August celebration, concerns about the woman question, particularly women's rights, surfaced. West Indies Emancipation Day had been celebrated in many African American communities since 1834. Like other black freedom celebrations, such as January 1st, which marked the end of the international slave trade in Great Britain, Denmark, and the United States, and July 5th, New York State Abolition Day, August 1st celebrations were an opportunity for free African Americans to further the interests of the anti-slavery cause and reaffirm a sense of community.[3] These daylong affairs featured street processions, outdoor picnics, dances, and even steamboat excursions.[4] Women frequently played roles that mirrored their participation in church conferences, raising money, attending to male participants, and receiving praise for their "behind-the-scenes" efforts.[5]

Humor and bravado masked men's anxiety. As historian Mitch Kachun suggests, gender conventions were rarely challenged during such gatherings. They were, however, a forum in which men grappled with the implication of women's rights ideas.[6] Such was the case when activists in Buffalo, New York, staged an elaborate pageant that included a procession with a brass band and carriages with "beautiful and appropriate" banners. The day's events were followed by a banquet that concluded with "three hearty cheers or three times three, with a sip of pure cold water." The "regular toasts" honored the abolition of slavery in the West Indies. The "volunteer toasts" that followed included tributes to the star-spangled banner, the American eagle, and equality; others honored Gerrit Smith, Charles Remond, and the *North Star*.[7] These plaudits were topped off by Abner Francis's toast to "the ladies."[8] The proprietor of a clothing business, Francis had lived in western New York since the mid-1830s and had actively engaged the woman question through his work within the Western New York Anti-Slavery Society.[9] Francis had also been present at Cleveland's national convention the year before, and his toast was in the spirit of that gathering's women's rights resolution.

Francis condemned those forces that relegated women to a lesser standing:

"The Ladies—the almoners of the race of man, superior to the opposite sex in all the offices of benevolence and kindness, fully equal in moral, mental and intellectual endowments, in short, entitled to an equal participancy in all the designs and accomplishments allotted to man during his career on earth. May the accumulated evils of the past, and those of the present, which superstition and bigotry have prescribed for them as a test of inferiority, be buried forever."[10] Francis's toast was followed by cheers as enthusiastic as those for the "Star spangled banner" and the *North Star*. The unsettling nature of Francis's toast was made plain in a subsequent toast offered by James Whitfield. Whitfield paid homage to "the ladies," "the only tyrants whose chains can be borne without resistance." While Francis presented women as the victims of oppression, Whitfield turned the tables, positing women as "tyrants" and, by implication, men as their devoted servants. Here, in a carefully crafted celebration aimed at demonstrating the highest capacities of African Americans to exercise public leadership, anxieties about the woman question were aired.[11]

Out of abstract debates, real women increasingly stepped into public culture after 1848. Some, like Mary Ann Shadd, were emboldened and wore their public personas with a newfound indifference to respectability. Even the most principled male champions of women's rights were unsettled. Shadd, who would go on to have a long career as a journalist and advocate of Canadian emigration, began publishing her ideas in the late 1840s. Her father, Abraham Shadd, spent his life fighting for the equality and enfranchisement of black Americans. The elder Shadd believed that the best hope for free blacks was to improve themselves intellectually, morally, and socially, and he transmitted these ideals through the education and training of his children. Mary Ann's emergence into public life marked her, in a sense, as an inheritor of the activism of her father's generation.[12]

She was the female voice of racial uplift. In a long letter to Frederick Douglass, Shadd responded to his call for suggestions on how to improve the "wretched conditions" of free blacks in the North. Shadd did not bother to couch her comments in a timid, apologetic, or deferential tone, nor did she rely upon her father's reputation. Rather, she based her authority upon "ten years of teaching black children in all black schools." Shadd did not allow the public expression of her voice to depend solely upon the favor of male newspaper editors, either. She struck out on her own, publishing her developing theories about black self-help in a twelve-page pamphlet, *Hints to the Colored People of the North*. Shadd's tone was assertive, her demeanor strong-willed, and her intent openly political. Her goal was "to arouse her readers with a direct analysis of the condition of northern blacks, regardless of whether it might offend." Cloaking her condescension with the cover of personal experience and social obligation, she asserted that she wrote "as one who, by assent, if not by actual participation, has aided in this complexion of things."[13] Her forthrightness was as unsettling as her refusal to defer to male authority. When men like Douglass endorsed women having access to the press, they did not envision women using the press to criticize and challenge male leadership. They imagined a more complementary and compatible relationship between men and women. Shadd did not let them rest comfortably in this complacent anticipation.

Shadd did not fit any preexisting mold. A letter to the *North Star* sought to promote Shadd's endeavors and asked why Douglass had not yet commented on a "small pamphlet, containing twelve pages" authored by Mary Ann Shadd. The writer suggested that some deemed Shadd's writings objectionable and asked, "What think you of the language of this young sister . . . does she tell the truth or not! As one man I am sorry that I have to answer in the affirmative." The writer suggested that a deliberate effort to suppress Shadd's writings was afoot; while the pamphlet had been widely circulated in Philadelphia, local writers had not taken notice because Shadd's writings contained "too much truth."[14] Martin Delany praised Shadd's pamphlet as "an excellent introduction to a great subject, fraught with so much interest." But even Delany mixed his praise for Shadd with a hint of trepidation. She was, he remarked, "a very intelligent young lady, and peculiarly eccentric."[15] Delany's comments reflected male leaders' ambivalent view of Shadd. She was bright, and her assessments of the dilemmas facing free black people were on target. But she also stood out because of her uncompromising stance and her willingness to take on male leaders; Shadd was unique, out of place, and perhaps less than respectable.[16]

In politics, it was in women's rights conventions that activists first balked at the notion of an antislavery–women's rights platform. Some activists voiced concerns that their movement might be compromised by the inclusion of antislavery and civil rights issues. During the 1850 Women's Rights Convention at Worcester, Massachusetts, a resolution calling on the delegates to embrace "the million and a half of slave women at the South, the most grossly wronged and foully outraged of all women," sparked controversy. Wendell Phillips, its proponent, urged the adoption of an inclusive platform that would "bear in our heart of hearts the memory of the trampled womanhood of the plantation, and omit no effort to raise it to a share in the rights we claim for ourselves."[17]

Women's meetings were no place for questions of "color," some activists warned. After reviewing the proceedings of the Worcester convention, Jane Swisshelm, an abolitionist and editor of the *Pittsburgh Saturday Visiter*, strongly objected to any effort to link women's rights with abolitionism. She was "pretty nearly out of patience" with those, like Phillips, who "persist in their attempt to do everything at once."[18] Swisshelm drew a distinction between issues of race and those of gender, asserting that "in a Woman's Rights Convention, the question of color has no right to a hearing."[19] The women's movement was a demanding enough endeavor, and if it "paid right good attention to its own business, it would have had work plenty." Swisshelm reasoned that neither women nor slaves should further degrade their standing by linking their causes. While women might "aid the colored man . . . we would still lend him an oar or show him how to make one; but we do not want him in our boat. Let him row his own craft!" she urged.[20] As Swisshelm recast the issue, the interests of black women were absented from the women's movement. Erasing them within largely white women's rights circles, she also actively undermined claims they might have had to standing in race settings. White women's interests were juxtaposed against the concerns of the "colored" man, and black women were rendered politically invisible.[21]

Sex and color were emerging as the roots of two mutually exclusive political movements. Even those who defended the Worcester resolution did so in terms that reinforced the perception that issues of race and gender could not be adequately embraced by any one movement. Parker Pillsbury seized the opportunity presented by Swisshelm's critique to tutor reformers about the overlapping nature of the antislavery and women's rights causes. A native of New Hampshire, Pillsbury began his reform endeavors as a local antislavery lecturer and by 1850 was well-established as a staunch Garrisonian, national antislavery lecturer, and women's rights advocate.[22] Pillsbury supported Phillips's resolution, but he did so in a way that undermined the interconnectedness of the antislavery and women's rights movements. The pervasive nature of racial discrimination, Pillsbury explained, required that when any organization meant to include "the Ethiopian," it was necessary to "specify them whenever or wherever you mean to include them." Far from uncritical of the convention, he did take delegates to task for failing to include African Americans among its planners and participants, but he in effect marginalized race by making it subordinate to gender.[23] It was appropriate to speak, Pillsbury's argument went, only when demanding the rights of *all* women, "of sable as well as sallow complexion . . . of the carved in ebony as well as the chiseled in ivory."[24] Even as he endorsed the explicit inclusion of enslaved women's interests, Pillsbury made clear that theirs were issues of gender, not race. At Worcester, he clarified, "color was not discussed . . . it need not have been."[25]

One consensus emerged out of Worcester. Swisshelm and Pillsbury agreed on the need to define the parameters of two distinct causes. African American women might be included among those whose interests the women's movement might take up. But this was true only to the extent that black women's interests were *women's* interests. Concerns about "color" should find advocates elsewhere. African American women could be drawn as insiders or outsiders relative to either movement, depending upon how the significances of race and gender were understood. The intersectional character of black women's political identities opened the door to their marginalization in political culture.

Reconfiguring Public Culture, from the Fugitive Slave Act to Dred Scott

Uneasiness had turned into distress by 1850. Overly broad political agendas appeared doomed as national events rendered the prospects of all black Americans increasingly bleak. As the decade opened, black activists began rethinking the contours and capacities of their political culture and openly suggested that the issue of women's rights would have to be jettisoned in light of the new assault on civil rights and the renewed protections for slavery. Looking back from 1857, "Americus" bemoaned how law had been used to "ostrasize, degrade, and enslave the free colored population of the 'American Union'." For this commentator, an advocate of emigration to Canada, the Fugitive Slave Act of 1850 marked the beginning of a most tragic series of pronouncements from the nation's highest lawmakers. Congress had enacted the Kansas-Nebraska Act of 1854—what Americus termed the "Nebraska iniquity"—and then considered reopening the international slave trade. Finally, the U.S. Supreme Court had "denationalized" descendants of the African race. The results, he concluded, had been "ruinous" to the well-being and "posterity" of African Americans and there was no remedy in sight.[26] While his conclusion, that black people should abandon the United States, represented a minority view among activists, few could have disagreed with Americus that the decade had been distinguished by the enactment of unprecedented "oppression and disfranchisement."

African American public culture was under siege. Communities were shaken to their cores by the terms of the Fugitive Slave Act, that part of the congressional Compromise of 1850 that empowered slave owners to bypass state due process requirements and enlist the assistance of federal marshals when seeking to take alleged fugitives into custody.[27] The owner of a fugitive, or the owner's agent, was authorized to "pursue and reclaim such fugitive person" by procuring a warrant from a judge or commissioner "or by seizing and arresting such fugitive, where the same can be done without process." Commissioners appointed by the U.S. circuit courts or territorial superior courts had full authority to grant certificates of authorization, and U.S. marshals were deemed responsible for the return of fugitive slaves. The law established powerful enforcement mechanisms. Marshals were to be fined one thousand dollars if they refused to act and were liable for the slave's full value should the fugitive escape from custody. Owners or their agents could take the fugitive before a judge or commissioner, and, once the identity of the prisoner was established, the judge or commissioner was authorized to grant a certificate that would allow the removal of the slave "back to the State or Territory from whence he or she may have escaped." The use of "reasonable force or restraint" was permitted, and "any court, judge, magistrate, or other person whomsoever" was prohibited from interfering with the owner's action, thus denying fugitive slaves access to the writ of habeas corpus.[28] In the wake of the act's passage, thousands of black Americans fled for the safety of Canada, while those who remained in the United States, especially those who lived proximate to slave states, lived under threat of kidnapping and enslavement.

Political visions narrowed under the strain of the Fugitive Slave Act, and battles against slavery and for civil rights were held up as supreme.[29] These political tensions were felt in day-to-day life. Institutions were devastated as fugitives and their families fled to Canada hoping to avoid re-enslavement. Forty former slaves left Boston within sixty hours after the act became law, while Pittsburgh lost 200 people during the few days before the law was signed and another 800 after its enactment. Columbia, Pennsylvania, lost 487 of its 943 black residents over five years. This sudden and substantial exodus compromised institutional life. In Boston the AME Church lost 85 members; the AME Zion Church, 10; and the First Baptist Church, 40 of its 125 congregants. Buffalo's black Baptist Church lost 130 members, while the Negro Baptist Church of Rochester lost its pastor and all but 2 of its 112 worshippers.[30]

The Fugitive Slave Law of 1793 paled in comparison to the 1850 act. The former had permitted slave owners to apply to a federal judge for a certificate authorizing the return of a fugitive; the very small number of federal judges and their remote locations discouraged claimants who were required to travel extensively and at great expense. The new law provided for the appointment of an unlimited number of local commissioners who held all the powers of federal judges in fugitive cases and empowered slave owners to demand the assistance of federal marshals. The effects of the 1793 act had been mitigated by the passage of various state and local laws during the 1840s. Connecticut forbade its courts from hearing cases based upon the 1793 law; in Indiana, New York, and Vermont fugitives were explicitly afforded the right to a trial by jury; Pennsylvania and Ohio passed laws designed to prevent the kidnapping of fugitives. After a series of U.S. Supreme Court cases upheld the supremacy of the federal law, northern state legislatures were not dissuaded, enacting a new series of personal liberty laws designed to thwart the recovery of alleged fugitives. The legislatures of Massachusetts, Vermont, and Ohio in 1843, Connecticut in 1844, Pennsylvania in 1847, and Rhode Island in 1848 all passed statutes that enabled antislavery activists to challenge slaveholders in protracted legal proceedings, a tactic that often caused the cost of rendition to exceed the slave's value.[31] The 1850 act forged an unprecedented alliance between slaveholders and federal agents, enabling claimants to bypass state and local procedural requirements and generating a climate of confrontation and fear among all free African Americans.

Acquiescence characterized the northern response generally.[32] Only a small group of deeply committed antislavery activists responded, but they did so with dramatic militancy. Public meetings drew large crowds in Boston, Springfield, Worcester, Lowell, and Lynn, Massachusetts; in Syracuse, Rochester, and Cazenovia, New York; in Pennsylvania; in northern Ohio; and in Illinois and Wisconsin. In this open forum, antislavery activists expressed their outrage at the "diabolical spirit and cruel ingenuity" of the law. Meeting in secret, they went further, adopting new strategies designed to resist the enforcement of the act's provisions.[33]

Active resistance was the creed that shaped the African American response.[34] Fugitives who had been seized and detained were rescued by concerted mob action in the cases of Shadrach (Fred Wilkins) in Boston, William "Jerry" McHenry in Syracuse, John Price in Oberlin-Wellington, Moses Horner in Philadelphia, and James Hamlet in New York City. Other rescue attempts, such as those of Bostonians Thomas Sims and Anthony Burns, were unsuccessful but no less dramatic.[35] Among those who stood boldly against enforcement of the act were activists who had previously devoted their energies to women's rights. Jermain Loguen and Charles Langston participated in fugitive rescues.[36] Martin Delany and Robert Purvis spoke at mass gatherings and advocated self-defense, while Frederick Douglass and

Charles Remond organized Boston's African American community around a pledge of stern resistance.[37]

Congress did not stand alone in its denigration of the interests of free black Americans. The U.S. Supreme Court echoed the legislature's disregard of free black people. In successive decisions, the Court also constructed them as less than rights-bearing individuals.[38] The companion proceedings of *Smith v. Turner* and *Norris v. City of Boston*, which came to be known as the *Passenger Cases*, most graphically illustrated how the legal standing of free black people began to deteriorate over the course of the 1850s.[39] In a widely disseminated opinion, the Court reviewed the constitutionality of Boston's poor law and New York's quarantine law, which in both cases empowered local officials to prohibit allegedly undesirable immigrants from entering the United States through their ports. While principally concerned with Europeans, the opinion's broader discussion revealed that the need to regulate free African Americans was also a grave concern for the Court. Scholars often cite these cases as the origins of a constitutionally guaranteed right to interstate travel, pointing to Roger Taney's dissenting words: "We are one people, with one common country. We are all citizens of the United States; and, as members of the same community, must have the right to pass and repass through every part of it without interruption, as freely as in our own States."[40] Taney's use of the term "citizen," however, signaled that the right to travel was a qualified one. None of the seven justices who penned opinions in the *Passenger Cases* argued for an unfettered right to travel. Instead, they offered up a litany of exceptions: convicts, felons, vagabonds, paupers, the infirm, and slaves might all properly be excluded. None disagreed with the proposition that the exclusion of free African Americans was an unassailable right of the individual states.

The Court's analysis was suggestive of lived tensions. By the mid-1850s, the strife between African Americans and European immigrant workers who figured in the *Passenger Cases* was visible in cities from Boston and New York to as far south as Baltimore, Maryland. On the streets, white immigrants and African Americans lived side by side and competed in a tight labor market. African American communities were increasingly composed of freeborn people who saw in their status the basis for claims to citizenship and standing. White populations were augmented by significant numbers of foreign-born residents who also sought to secure their claims to rights and citizenship. Beginning in the late 1840s and accelerating in the early 1850s, German and Irish immigrants flooded seaport cities. Immigrant workers struggled to find employment and in many cases forged alliances with native-born white workers that brought about the nearly wholesale exclusion of African Americans from skilled and unskilled trades. Competition for employment led to escalating tensions. Commentators remarked that the degraded condition of free black Americans was due to "the sharp competition they have had to encounter with foreign labor, in some pursuits which were previously given up to them entirely."[41] Violence frequently accompanied these confrontations, and by the 1850s, it was an ordinary aspect of the everyday lives of black and white city-dwellers.

But it was its own anxieties that the Court foregrounded. No other justice disagreed with Roger Taney's conclusion that no scheme, be it a state regulation, an act of Congress, or an international treaty, could allow "Great Britain to ship her paupers to Massachusetts, or send her free blacks from the West Indies into the Southern States or into Ohio, in contravention of their local laws."[42] The Court was beginning to set the terms of a constitutional right to travel. The contours of such a right were, in part, being defined by setting forth free black people as among those whose travel would not be constitutionally protected.[43]

The *Dred Scott* decision was in many ways predictable. The animus toward free black people—implicit in the Fugitive Slave Act and openly expressed in the *Passenger Cases*—laid the groundwork. For nearly a decade legislation and litigation had pushed free black people beyond the protections of the U.S. Constitution. In *Dred Scott*, Taney's decision was again led by his thinking about free blacks and the necessity to limit their right to travel. In arguing that Scott, and by extension all African Americans, were never intended to be citizens of the United States, Taney warned that if African Americans were entitled to the "privileges and immunities" of citizens, then state black codes would be invalid. The result, Taney warned, would be to provide African Americans "the right to enter every other State whenever they pleased, singly or in companies, without pass or passport, and without obstruction, to sojourn there as long as they pleased, to go where they pleased at every hour of the day or night without molestation," a circumstance he deemed beyond the pale constitutionally and in practice.[44] Furthermore, free black people and slave owners stood on constitutionally distinct grounds, he argued. On the substance of Scott's claim, Taney rejected any inference that the right of slave owners to travel could be functionally limited. Invoking his reasoning in the *Passenger Cases*, Taney explained that the Constitution protected a slave owner's right to interstate travel—the right "to enjoy a common country"—such that movement between two states could not give rise to the deprivation of his property in persons.[45]

Americus pointed up a chilling continuity that few black activists could overlook. The *Dred Scott* decision prompted mass meetings and condemnation, such as in Philadelphia, where long-standing allies, including Charles Remond, William Still, Robert Purvis, and Lucretia Mott, condemned the Court's villainous act.[46] The *Scott* case did not reach immediately into the lives of free black people as the Fugitive Slave Act had, though it did set the stage for later disputes, including whether African Americans were entitled to U.S. passports.[47] But symbolically, *Dred Scott* was unparalleled. Taney's appropriation of the terms "citizen" and "rights," both of which had long been powerful rhetorical rubrics for black political activists, struck a deep blow. The legal degradations of the 1850s demanded a rethinking of African American political culture, and among the first matters up for reconsideration was the rights of women.

African American Women's Rights at the Political Margins

The times demanded a broad rethinking of politics. There was a great deal in the affairs in Congress and the Supreme Court that pressed black political activists to rethink their objectives and tactics. However, there was little on the face of these turns of events that insisted that women's rights presented a special problem. Certainly to deprive fugitive slaves of due process disproportionately affected men, who were overrepresented among fugitives, and litigation strategies in the *Dred Scott* case overlooked the arguably distinct claims of Scott's wife, Harriet, a decision that scholars argue had grave consequences for the Scott family.[48] While important, there is little evidence that these insights shaped a rethinking of African American political culture in the 1850s, particularly on women's rights. More directly relevant in this period was the emergence of new critiques in the realm of popular culture. Within minstrelsy, African American political culture—its leaders, its conventions, and its embrace of the rights of women—had become the direct target of a widely enjoyed mode of entertainment. Perhaps political respectability required a more narrowly drawn political agenda.

Minstrelsy was the "national art of its moment" in the 1850s. First through theatrical exhibitions and then through the dissemination of songsters, joke books, and sheet music, blackface humor was being consumed by the masses of urban, working- and middle-class white Americans.[49] Minstrelsy's overt targets included women, Irish immigrants, and the pretensions of European opera and theater. Its less apparent meanings were no less potent. As Eric

Lott argues in *Love and Theft*, minstrelsy had become a complex terrain upon which men constructed their whiteness and working-class status. Yet, for all its complexity, minstrelsy relied heavily upon actors who "were usually in blackface, speaking in a marked black dialect."[50] Racist and denigrating depictions of African Americans—through the wearing of burnt cork or grease paint, the adoption of faux dialect, and the substance of songs, jokes, skits, and stump speeches—pervaded this most popular form of nineteenth-century cultural expression. The claims that mid-nineteenth-century black activists made to respectability, particularly to a status based on education, erudition, and refinement, were minstrelsy's fodder. Caricatures that called the political competency of African Americans into question were enacted by performers, consumed by theatergoers, and disseminated into middle-class homes via popular literature.

Minstrelsy found humor in the coupling of black Americans with women's rights, particularly in the post–Seneca Falls era.[51] From black men's alliances with white women activists to black women's engagements with women's conventions and the "Bloomer" costume, midcentury minstrelsy produced a set of routines intended to undercut the legitimacy of African American public culture. Minstrelsy underscored the precarious position of African Americans as a group, but it particularly undermined African American women's rights.

Parodies of African American womanhood abounded. They were portrayed as "unsexed," or beyond the bounds of respectability. The effect was the usurping of black men within public culture. Typical was William H. Levison's character, Julius Caesar Hannibal. According to Levison's *Professor Julius Caesar Hannibal's Scientific Discourses*, Hannibal was a figure of some standing among African Americans, and the text memorialized his lectures on subjects ranging from "Noseology" and "De Rat" to "Future Punishment, or de Lass Day" and "Ass-tronomy." These lecture titles signaled the general thrust of Levison's caricature. Hannibal's use of nonstandard English exposed him as a man of little formal education, an impostor who exposed as dupes the black community that enthusiastically heard his lectures. This point was made vividly when, in chapter 22, Hannibal explained that his lecture on the "siance ob ABBOLITSHUN" came about at the "tickler inquest from Brudders Garrison, Seaweek, Abby Kelley, and odders of de same kidney," suggesting that black antislavery speakers were mere puppets of white activists.[52] The abolitionist movement, Hannibal told his audience, aimed to abolish black men and remove them from the country. Why? To give white men unfettered sexual access to black women. The goal of anti-slavery activism in Levison's parody was "amalgamation," particularly sexual relations between white men and seemingly willing black women.[53]

Unchaste black women could never claim respectability in the Hannibal "discourses." Levison, along with Edward Christy, also ridiculed black women's associations with women's rights politics. Such parodies undermined the political pretensions of black men and women while simultaneously undercutting the women's movement itself. Among the entries in Christy's 1858 *Ethiopian Joke Book* was a lecture "delivered" by an African American man, C. H. Fox, titled "Women's Rights." The lecture and commentary moved quickly to a condemnation of the "lords ob de creashun," of whom Fox rhetorically asked: "Who gib 'em de pribelege to use dat cognoblem? Wat did dey eber do to desarbe it? Did dey eber do anyting?"[54] As if his use of faux dialect were not sufficient to undermine Fox's intellect, Christy goes on to have Fox mis-tell the story of "creashun," or Genesis, explaining the fall as the fault of Adam rather than "Ebe." In his version of Genesis, Fox depicts humanity's fall from grace as the result of Adam's inattention to Eve. Adam stole apples with which Eve made a pie. Upon Adam's incarceration for thievery, Eve, finding herself unsupervised, took up public speaking: "Ebe gub up takin in washin, and went to work an gub lectures in the Metropolitan Hall, an got a party ob strong minded women to help her."[55] Fox concludes: "Ain't it led to Women's rights conwenshuns, sewin masheenes, baby jumpers, and Bloomer costumes? Don't de women wear trousers, an coats, an Panama hats. . . . Don't you hear de cry ob womans' rights trou de land?"[56] Here, gender relations among African Americans, both at home and in public culture, were inverted and, in Christy's presentation, perverted. Finally, the women's movement itself was undermined. Not only did it rely upon ill-equipped men for its champions, but it was also grounded in errors of literally biblical proportions.[57]

Only a small number of black activists openly took on the minstrelsy scene. In the late 1840s, Frederick Douglass commented indirectly upon the genre's ramifications. Reporting upon a performance by Gavitt's Original Ethiopian Serenaders, a troupe of African American actors in blackface, the editor of the *North Star* remarked that only when such performers "cease to exaggerate the exaggerations of our enemies" would they be "instrumental in removing the prejudice against our race." Although Douglass generally discouraged black artists from appearing before white audiences, he urged those who did to model respectability through "industry, application, and a proper cultivation of their taste."[58] Douglass pointedly criticized white performers. The

"Virginia Minstrels," "Christy's Minstrels," and the "Ethiopian Serenaders" were the "filthy scum of white society," he remarked in an editorial promoting an appearance by the abolitionist Hutchinson Family singers.[59] Black activists recognized the caricature of themselves in minstrelsy's images. As Lott explains, the stump speech genre in particular was based upon white observations of black churches and street oratory and parodied these goings-on in African American public culture. They built upon a kernel of lived experience: women's rights had emerged as a force in the shaping of African American public culture, and at stake in such expositions—real and imagined—were ideas about black women and their standing in public life.

How might black activists respond to the increasingly hostile climate of the 1850s? Ambivalences of the late 1840s pointed the way. For those who had remained at best uncomfortable with the rise of political women and the adoption of a women's rights platform, the disappointments of the 1850s presented an opportunity for retrenchment; their black political conventions were not women's rights meetings. For those who thought in tactical terms, the 1850s opened the door to a questioning of the capacity of any one movement—whether that seeking to abolish slavery and achieve civil rights, or that seeking to advance women's rights—to further both "race" and "sex" interests. Yet for others the challenges of the 1850s became an opportunity to affirm their political vision and the alliances they suggested.

Even Frederick Douglass faltered under the weight of the decade's degradations. In an 1855 speech before the Rochester Ladies' Anti-Slavery Society, Douglass reflected on the history of the movement and lamented its ineffectiveness. Abolitionism had taken on too many issues. He concluded in hindsight that "the battle of Woman's Rights should be fought on its own ground; as it is, the slave's cause, already too heavy laden, had to bear up under this new addition." It had been "a sad mistake" to allow the antislavery movement to be "rent asunder by a side issue," he lamented.[60] Douglass's retelling of the 1840 schism among antislavery activists was overly simple; the woman question was only one of several issues that divided activists. His remarks explained more about the political terrain during the 1850s. When he had adopted his motto, "Right is of no sex, truth is of no color," Douglass had intended it to stand both as a set of principles and as a model for political activism. By the mid-1850s this potent political ideal could no longer determine the shape of political culture.

Two distinct movements—one bound by "color" and the other by "sex"—emerged. The result was in some instances competition, as activists vied against one another for public consideration. For example, the Ohio State

Convention of Colored Men was denied an audience before the state legislature in 1854. John Mercer Langston, a recent Oberlin College graduate, had been charged with delivering an address to the state's political leadership titled "The Propriety and Justness of Extending the Elective Franchise to the Colored Men of the State." Langston reported that he had been refused the opportunity to speak, while the women who were present at the same time had been given the floor to discuss temperance and to deliver "a lengthy and elaborate address on women's rights." Langston affirmed that it was "fit and proper that [the] Senate should hear this address [concerning] women and her rights." It was, however, "equally fit and proper that I should be heard in behalf of the Colored People of Ohio, and their rights."[61] As the movements for civil rights and women's rights became distinct, they were received differently and competed with each other in politics.

Black women fit uneasily in this bifurcated political culture. Distinct agendas concerned with either race or sex left black women without a clear vehicle through which to articulate or make claims for their particular interests. They were being drawn as insiders or outsiders. The intersectional character of black women's identities confounded their standing within the public culture of the 1850s. In black convention circles, the very presence of black women came to suggest an endorsement of women's rights, causing female activists to be excluded from formal deliberations. In new political circles however, particularly that of the emerging emigration movement, women were welcomed as partners with their male counterparts during collective considerations of the future.

African American political conventions veered away from women's rights. In most instances they fell nearly silent.[62] Only on rare occasions was the presence of women even acknowledged. For example, by 1851 the women who participated in the State Convention of the Colored Citizens of Ohio were noted only as dispatching "a communication" to the assembled delegates and "pledging themselves to furnish means to publish the proceedings of this Convention."[63] Just three years earlier, Ohio's political gatherings had been foremost in support for women's rights, but by 1851 women were relegated to the position of silent supporters.

To advocate women's rights in black politics was to champion a lame horse. Women were pushed back into ancillary and subordinate roles in politics.[64] The argument had shifted, however. Ideas about women's equality were permitted to stand unchallenged. Instead, women's rights—indeed, women themselves—belonged in *women's* conventions, not antislavery and civil rights gatherings. By constructing women as sexed rather than raced individuals, male domination was permitted to reassert itself.

New York State's conventions became overtly hostile to women and their rights in this period. For example, at the 1853 Colored National Convention held in Rochester, New York, Frederick Douglass, serving as chair of the Committee on Declaration of Sentiments, advocated that Mary Jeffrey be seated as a delegate.[65] Jeffrey had been treasurer of the Syracuse Provisional Committee, the women's group organized to support Samuel Ringgold Ward's *Impartial Citizen* in 1849, and was president of the Geneva Ladies' Antislavery Society, which worked to support Douglass's antislavery lecture tours.[66] Her husband, Jason Jeffrey, was an abolitionist who took part in state and national conventions and in the campaign to expand black suffrage in New York. Mrs. Jeffrey's presence was met with a begrudging acceptance rather than the enthusiasm that had followed the call for women's rights at the 1848 convention. Noting this retrograde trend, Douglass conceded that the admittance of a female delegate had been "in advance of the times." His only solace was in the fact that "not a word of nonsense was talked . . . we had the good sense to make no fuss about it."[67]

Not all women's rights foes were so subtle as to remain silent. The 1854 meeting of the New York State Council of Colored People exposed the tensions that arose when African Americans were challenged to incorporate women's rights into an agenda centered on antislavery and civil rights. Jermain Loguen, representing the city of Syracuse, asserted the relevance of women's rights to black politics in what the conference secretary described as "an interesting speech titled 'Woman's Rights'."[68] But the conference president, William Rich, "earnestly objected" to Loguen's presentation. Rich did not condemn the substance of Loguen's remarks, argue for a more constrained vision of women's place, or mention women's special disabilities. Instead, he asserted flatly that women's rights were "irrelevant to the business of the Council," thus ruling the entire subject of Loguen's speech out of order. Rich understood women's rights concerns, irrespective of their merits, to be beyond the parameters of African American politics.

Even a concerted alliance could not shake Rich's influence. When Junius Morel of Philadelphia stepped forward to endorse Loguen's views, his urgings fell upon deaf ears.[69] Morel had been associated with Philadelphia's Garrisonians during the 1830s, but, impatient with the American Moral Reform Society (AMRS) leadership, he moved to Brooklyn, New York, by the mid-1840s. Explaining that he "warmly approved of the speech of Mr.

Loguen," Morel argued that claims for women's rights and civil rights shared a common basis: he "felt and believed that Human Rights were not to be defined either by sex or by complexion."[70] The marginalization of longtime leaders such as Loguen and Morel illustrates the increasing distinction drawn between race and sex organizations. Many black activists—male as well as female—continued to take part in the women's rights conventions of the 1850s, yet none were able to persuade black activists that the issue was a proper concern of civil rights and antislavery organizations.[71]

Women and their allies continue to press their point of view. Their effect was minimal, though it does suggest that the issue could not be killed even by years of frontal assault. By 1855, when Barbara Ann Steward sought to be seated at the Convention of the Colored People of the State of New York, held at Troy, she and her male allies must have known they were waging an uphill battle. The daughter of black abolitionist Austin Steward, Barbara Ann was a teacher and antislavery lecturer. Born in Canada West, she lived most of her life near Rochester, New York, and during the mid-1850s earned a reputation as an eloquent and persuasive speaker while touring western New York and New England. She was also recognized as a community leader: Ontario County's black citizens had selected Steward as one of their nine delegates to the 1853 black national convention in Rochester. Still, despite the support of allies, including Jermain Loguen and Frederick Douglass, Steward, the gathering's lone female delegate, was expelled from the convention "for no other reason than her sex," the *Troy Daily Times* reported.[72]

Steward's opponents constructed a careful logic. They objected to seating her, but not based upon claims of female incapacity or inferiority. It was the integrity of the proceedings, and by implication political culture, that was at stake. "This is not a woman's rights convention" became an often-repeated refrain during the 1850s.[73] The seating of a black female delegate had come to be understood as an endorsement of women's rights. Steward's womanhood determined her relationship to black political culture. According to this view, she must find her political home in the arena of women's rights and leave race issues to men.

Alternative perspectives did find at least one outlet, in the emigration politics that emerged in the 1850s. The Fugitive Slave Act reinvigorated African American interest in schemes to leave the United States permanently for Canada, South America, the Caribbean, or Africa, where people of African descent might secure freedom and full citizenship. For over thirty years, colonization schemes had been the target of pointed criticism; indeed, opposition to white-sponsored colonization societies had galvanized black and white antislavery thinkers into the abolitionist movement. During the earliest black political conventions, organized efforts to remove African Americans from the United States were uniformly condemned. In the 1850s, however, some African Americans embraced the prospect of making their lives over in a new land as a solution to the deepening degradation they endured in the United States.

In emigration conventions, women figured prominently. The 1854 meeting of the National Emigration Convention of Colored People was called for by Martin Delany.[74] Delany's Cleveland gathering called together "all colored men in favor of emigration out of the United States, and opposed to the American Colonization scheme of leaving the Western hemisphere."[75] The meeting crystallized one pronounced rift among black activists. Proponents of emigration, who were in the minority among black activists, were convinced that the situation in the United States was hopeless, while opponents insisted upon continuing their pursuit of rights in the land where they had been born and for which they had labored.

The contrast between women's role at Rochester in 1853 and their place in Cleveland was striking. At Cleveland, nearly one-quarter (39 of 171) of the "executive delegates" were women; Canadian activist Mary Bibb was elected a vice president, and four additional women served as members of the finance committee.[76] The gendered structure of this meeting paralleled that of the 1839 gathering of the AMRS. Most female delegates were in the company of male relatives, most often husbands, suggesting both that respectability demanded the presence of visible male escorts and that those same men endorsed the women's participation in political deliberations.

The nine-person Cleveland delegation included five women. Had they been present when that city hosted the 1848 National Colored Convention and heard Delany's bold call for women's equal participation in that gathering? Perhaps William Howard Day, who was also in attendance, told them what had transpired. In any event, the structure of Delany's 1854 convention embodied the ideals that he had urged upon black activist leaders six years earlier.

The past may explain how the emigration meeting was configured as it was. More interesting, perhaps, is imagining how ideas about women in politics, generated in the emigration context, may have reverberated throughout public culture. Delegates returned from Cleveland to a broad array of activist circles. Among the convention's officers were at least nine ministers, including Bishop William Paul Quinn, Rev. John A. Warren of Canada West, the

Reverends Augustus R. Green and William Webb of Pittsburgh, and Rev. William J. Fuller of Rhode Island from the AME Church; and Elder William Monroe of Detroit and the Reverend J. Theodore Holly of New York from the Baptist Church. Among the women were Elizabeth Briscoe, an AME Church activist, and Amelia Freeman, a female "Professoress" at Avery Institute, both of Pittsburgh, and Mary Bibb, a teacher, antislavery activist, and journalist from Canada West.[77] For every well-remembered participant in this emigration convention, there were at least two others who left little documentary evidence of their activism. Census records allow us but a momentary glimpse of these lives. Among these participants were Mary Blackson and her husband, Peter, a barber; Catherine Diary and her husband, Levi, a teamster; Mary Hawkins and her husband, Robert, a laborer; Rebecca Jackson and her husband, Henry, also a laborer; Lauretta Smith and her husband, Albert, a steward; and Arena Venerable and her husband, Samuel, a laborer.

Delany's convention was unequivocal evidence that women's rights had not disappeared from black politics. This was not, however, 1848. Women appeared in roles equal to those of men, but the conference minutes reveal nothing about how they took part in the proceedings. Delany's convention mirrored the meetings of the AMRS of the late 1830s, with women appearing to legitimize their political activities, in part, through close collaborations with male family members. However, the women in Delany's convention were distinct from those of the AMRS. In the latter instance, many were wives of working-class men and were likely working people themselves, though this is difficult to discern from the record. How these women understood the relationship between responsibility and respectability in the context of this emigration gathering is also difficult to discern. It is very likely that Delany himself, having long encouraged women to engage in respectable public activism, understood female convention delegates as affirming their standing and enhancing the esteem of the gathering overall. On the other hand, Delany had also expressed concern if not contempt for working women in an earlier period, and he may have viewed his convention as a vehicle by which working-class women were elevated to a more respectable standing. How the convention's female delegates thought about these questions cannot be fully discerned, but as they entered the convention hall they surely confronted the terms of the woman question debate already under way.

The public life of Sojourner Truth may hold some clues about working women's views generally. Truth is perhaps the best-remembered African American woman of the nineteenth century. However, her forays into antebellum public culture do not mesh neatly with those of the era's black public women generally. Instead, Truth's life presents an illuminating counternarrative. Nell Painter's insightful biography of Truth portrays a woman born enslaved who manumitted herself in the era of the North's gradual emancipation and then quickly emerged as a highly effective preacher and antislavery orator. Truth, in the 1840s still known as Isabella, shared many qualities with women like Maria Stewart, Jarena Lee, and Julia Foote that made them compelling and provocative public speakers. Yet she did not join the activist circles of African American public culture. Had the men who led public culture's institutions encountered Truth, Painter explains, they would have been "appalled" by her, a "powerful, middle aged, unlettered preaching woman." Truth's membership in unorthodox religious sects, disinterest in politics, and, most important, her failure to conform to respectability's tenets likely alienated her from those spaces, including the black convention movement, in which women were, more generally, challenging gendered proscriptions.[78] Painter's analysis suggests that it was no surprise that Truth was absent from such gatherings.

Even through her absence, Truth reveals something about the woman question in African American public culture. By the 1850s, the once enslaved Isabella had remade herself into Sojourner Truth, a public woman. Truth made her mark as an advocate of women's rights. Her reputation was earned through public speaking during events including the Ohio Women's Convention of 1851. There, Truth claimed women's rights to be grounded in three principles: in work women were the physical equals of men; differences in intellect did not justify the curtailment of rights; and men should esteem women just as Christ had done. Truth used her distinct presence as an unlettered, working-class, and formerly enslaved black women to draw in her audience. She did so with great effect.

At the same time, Truth was successfully remaking herself into a figure of respectability. Nell Painter demonstrates this through a careful reading of Truth's *cartes-des-visites*. The result was that little in Truth's person of the 1850s would have been off-putting to black activists generally. Why then did she not make her way onto the scene in African American political conventions much in the way she had in the women's movement? The answer is that her message was no longer welcome. In the late 1840s, Truth's women's rights ideas might have been compatible with a mainstream black political agenda (one can perhaps imagine her at Cleveland in 1848 or more likely in Cincinnati in 1849). But by the early 1850s, when Truth was entering public life, women and espousers of women's rights were generally unwelcome in black political circles. It was Truth's women's rights ideas and her femaleness that likely kept her away.[79]

Sustaining the Debate

Black Methodists continued to battle over licensing women to preach into the 1850s. For those church activists who had taken part in the era's emigration conventions, the contrast must have been striking. They were left to reconcile how women might serve as delegates to political bodies but could not be sanctioned as spiritual leaders. AME Church bishop William Quinn faced just this contradiction. Quinn presided over the denomination's 1852 General Conference at which the issue of female preachers again erupted. Quinn acknowledged that he had "given the subject some thought, but not enough to warrant him in expressing an opinion as to its merits."[80] Instead, he focused on the institutional implications of the matter, urging, "All that I ask is that something distinct may be done that will be satisfactory to all, and the question be put to rest." And so it was. Female activists secured a male ally, the Reverend Thomas Lawrence, to put forward their petition, but, according to Daniel Payne, it was "lost by a large majority."[81] In Payne's view, the question of the rights of churchwomen should be resolved not merely to further the orderly administration of church business but also to uphold the separate spheres that men and women were intended to inhabit. Payne believed that "man, strong in body and mind, is fitted by nature to execute what the weaker sex is incapacitated for, both physically and mentally." This view carried the day.[82]

For the moment, church debates were quashed. In contrast, literary societies entertained the question of women's public authority and incorporated it as a recurring theme in their proceedings. Women's issues were frequent topics taken up in lectures and debates during the 1850s, and women themselves pressed their standing forward by engaging their male peers on a variety of subjects.[83] Literary societies were well-established institutions within free black communities. As early as 1828, African Americans had come together to improve their "mental and moral condition," and during the 1830s and 1840s nearly forty such bodies were founded throughout the North and Upper South. These groups sought to fulfill their mission by the "stimulation of reading and the spreading of useful knowledge by providing libraries and reading rooms, the encouragement of literary efforts by providing audiences as critics, channels of publication for their literary productions and the training of future orators and leaders by means of debate."[84] Philadelphia's

Banneker Institute, according to its 1854 founding constitution, sought "primarily the mental improvement of its members by means of lectures, debates and the formation of such committees in the serious branches of knowledge [and] the diffusion of useful knowledge among all who may come within the pale of its influence."[85] With admission by invitation only, the group recruited its members primarily from the city's Institute for Colored Youth.[86] Led for much of its twenty-year existence by the young Jacob C. White Jr., the Banneker Institute was moderate, religious, and noncombative on race issues.[87]

The woman question surfaced regularly on the Banneker Institute's program. The rules governing the organization's debates and lectures provided that "every member shall be required to prepare and deliver a lecture in the order of the role, on any subject he may think proper."[88] The first lecturer of the 1855 season, Parker T. Smith, spoke to a full house on the "History of Women."[89] The "Question of Woman's Rights" was the topic of the October 1858 debate; eleven institute members took part in the exchange. In January 1860, the Reverend James Underdue, an abolitionist, Masonic lodge leader, and pastor of Philadelphia's First African Baptist Church, offered his interpretation of "The Mission of Woman."[90] Lauding the "true greatness" and intellectual capacities of women, Underdue pronounced woman "a suitable auxiliary for man" in the furtherance of her "moral and intellectual" mission. One commentator reported that Underdue's remarks were intended to challenge "false ideas" that he believed to be "entertained by many, and by a large portion of the gentler sex themselves."[91] The record does not make clear whether Underdue was arguing against those like Daniel Payne who saw women as suited only to the domestic realm or with those who advocated that women assume autonomous rather than merely auxiliary roles. Underdue discerned that both men and women were debating the proper position of women in public culture.

Underdue's voice was one in a chorus. In November 1858, when the Philadelphia Library Company of Colored Persons advertised its fall and winter exercises, the woman question was prominent. In contrast to the Banneker Institute, black Garrisonians, including William Still, William Whipper, and James McCrummill, ran the Library Company. The season's "opening address" was delivered by Samuel Smith on the subject "Woman." The scheduling of this event, just one month after the Banneker Institute's debate on women's rights, was a testament to the great interest black Philadelphians had in the woman question. And in this audience of Garrisonians, Smith surely found many who shared the pro–women's rights position proffered during the Banneker Institute debate. Too little evidence has survived about the substance of these meetings. Still, these fragments convey the extent to which the woman question occupied such public gatherings in the 1850s.

Women themselves began appearing at Banneker Institute meetings. Their presence made an explicit argument for the right of women to engage in public speaking and debate, even before mixed audiences. Their willingness to transgress gender conventions by lecturing and debating constituted as direct a challenge to a conventional definition of women's standing as anything they said. In October 1855, for example, Sarah Mapps Douglass addressed the Banneker Institute.[92] Douglass had been foremost among the women who, in collaboration with Martin Delany, formed the Woman's Association of Philadelphia in 1849. By 1852 she had become the first African American woman to attend the Female Medical College of Pennsylvania. Douglass gained experience as an orator in her work as a teacher of physiology and hygiene. She spoke with unquestionable authority on the subject of "Anatomy." Douglass's talk provoked the woman question, and community members asked whether such knowledge was "inconsistent with the delicacy of woman's character." One writer to the *Weekly Anglo-African* urged that women should not "shrink from the study of this great work. . . . An acquaintance with the structure . . . of the human system is necessary to those whose especial duty it is to protect the health of the young." By resituating Douglass's expertise in the domestic domain, such writers reinforced a limited view of women's proper intellectual pursuits.[93] No such rationale was offered on behalf of the male Banneker members who also attended Douglass's presentation; none was necessary. Although no one directly challenged the propriety of Douglass's actions, her talk required community members to reexamine their views about the parameters of women's education.

Women did not escape the expectation that they would raise funds for male-controlled enterprises, and they supported literary societies in this respect as well.[94] In 1856, when the Banneker Institute set out to finance the construction of a library, it turned not only to its close female associates but also to women in the larger community. The board resolved that "a committee of 5 be appointed with authority to circulate among the Ladies of our city subscription books for the purpose of aiding in collecting money."[95] The Subscription Committee reported that women held all but one of the "nine books issued." The following October, when the institute held its anniversary celebration, fourteen tickets were "given as complimentary to the ladies who have been assisting the Subscription Committee of the Institute in collecting money and books for our Library."[96] Literary societies such as the Banneker

Institute did not debate women's rights or engage female lecturers in a vacuum. The institute's recognition of the importance of women's material support appears in the proceedings directly alongside arguments about their standing within public culture.

Masons were also drawn into the woman question debate that swirled around them, though in less direct ways. While they restricted membership generally to men, the Masons, like churches and literary societies, relied upon the material support of women.[97] By the early 1850s, there were about thirty black Masonic lodges and ten Odd Fellows lodges in the United States.[98] At least one commentator, Martin Delany in an 1853 speech delivered before Pittsburgh's St. Cyprian Masonic lodge, had openly questioned the practice of excluding women from Masonry, arguing that among "nations of the ancients, priestesses were common."[99] Consistent with this view, women associated with fraternal orders challenged their circumscribed standing.

There were structural hurdles to overcome in fraternal orders. Women associated with the Felix Lodge of the Colored Masonic Fraternity of Washington City, D.C., tested the waters during the Grand Demonstration of 1854. In the Masonic order, as in African Methodist churches, women's participation was highly circumscribed through the imposition of complex rituals.[100] When the Felix Lodge invited one of its female supporters to address the group, the woman question was placed squarely before the order.[101] The program called for "the young ladies" to bestow a gift upon the lodge. They were "escorted into the church by a committee of the Craft" and "seated upon the platform." The proceedings then departed from the typical ritual as a woman—known to us only by her name, Ann M. Dade—was introduced to the audience and made a "concise and beautiful address" on behalf of her female associates. Her remarks, however, conveyed the sense that not all was well between the Felix Lodge and its female supporters. Dade began by presenting the women's gift, a banner that depicted a "weeping virgin" with "Time, standing behind her, with his hands infolded in the ringlets of her hair." The banner was, Dade explained, an emblem of the "love, high regard and esteem . . . of the daughters of 1854." She then proposed that the lodge "inscribe some glorious motto thereupon" that would inspire the "rising generations." In conclusion, Dade expressed her hope that the completed banner, through its imagery and words, would compel those who beheld it to cry out, "Is there no help for the rising daughters of Ethiopia?"[102]

The full meaning of Dade's final plea is not clear. Did she intend the banner to generate sympathy for what she saw as women's plight? Or did she intend it to serve as a call to arms, a symbol that might inspire others to act on women's behalf? Was it an expression of hopelessness that underscored some long-standing indifference to women's oppression? Or was it intended to convey women's exasperation with Masonic men? Who, indeed, would champion black women's interests? Whatever her intention, male Masonic leaders responded sharply as if Dade had publicly questioned Masonry's gendered order. In doing so, she drew previously silent activists into the woman question debate.

The duty of responding to Dade's challenge fell upon John Costin, a Washington, D.C., barbershop owner and founding member and former Grand Master of the Felix Lodge.[103] His opening remarks thanking the women for their gift were routine. But provoked by Dade's remarks, Costin quickly departed from this script. Costin offered an extended justification for women's exclusion from the Masonic order. He began by setting forth his own interpretation of the banner's imagery. In sharp contrast to Dade, he said that the scene of the virgin and Time conveyed the notion that "time, patience and perseverance will accomplish all things." This was, perhaps, Costin's admonition to those women who had grown impatient with their relationship to the order.

Costin drew upon the rhetoric of female influence that had been so influential in the 1830s. He began by flattering his female hearers: "It is a remark, as old perhaps as the formation of our species, that a lovely woman is the loveliest production of Nature." Women's minds were "formed of softer materials" and their bodies of a "finer texture." Costin took "delight in acknowledging their superiority in tenderness and personal beauty" and expressed confidence that women would "cheerfully acknowledge" men's "energy and strength of mind." Women's "timidity and feebleness . . . endear them more to us, perhaps, than any other quality they possess," and obliged men's "favourite passion, by looking up to us for that protection which we are always willing to afford." Men, on the other hand, were "formed for bold and arduous undertakings," with "weak minds and strong bodies." Their tempers would likely lead them to much unhappiness were it not for "the softening and cheering influence of a milder and more timid sex." Their ambitious, competitive spirits left them ill-prepared for failures, and they tended to blame others for their misfortune. "The rancor [men] produced," which led "to the misery and bloodshed" of history, was the best evidence of their shortcomings.[104]

Finally, Costin directly addressed the women in his audience, audaciously "reminding" them that they were not, in fact, curious about the secrets of

Freemasonry at all. Women were—or should be—content with "the lovely sphere that a kind Providence has assigned to them," where they might shed "the rays of domestic love and happiness." Costin's words laid bare the extent to which the woman question had become a point of contention. He responded to the critique implied by Dade's remarks: "Believe me, my gentle hearers, Masonry does not exclude you from her sanctuary, because she is indifferent to your welfare." Women were excluded from the order because "alive to the happiness of the whole human family [Masonry] imposes it as a special duty upon her votaries, to protect you," in battle, in war, and in politics.[105] There was, indeed, help for the "Daughters of Ethiopia," and it would come from male Masons. By the 1850s, when men like Costin were forced to debate the woman question, they did so in terms that echoed exchanges in other venues. Costin was a rising ministerial leader in the AME Church, and his ideas echoed those being espoused by the denomination's recently elected bishop, Daniel Payne.

The woman question debate animated the pages of the black press much as it did the platforms of public gatherings.[106] Cities such as New York and Washington, D.C., Cleveland and Boston, Rochester and San Francisco, Toronto and Philadelphia all supported weekly newspapers. Their readership extended throughout free black communities. Whether sponsored by antislavery societies, churches, or entrepreneurs, newspapers conveyed news and ideas to the remotest settlements. They facilitated debate by reprinting articles from rival sources and welcoming letters to the editor. The woman question played out dramatically within this medium.

Men no longer dominated print culture by the mid-1850s. Newspapers had become sites of power shared, if somewhat reluctantly, across gender lines. Mary Ann Shadd's *Provincial Freeman*, published in Canada West, is particularly noteworthy. Historian Jane Rhodes describes how Shadd, who had endured sustained attacks on her femininity and virtue, adopted a strategy employed by many public women of her time, allying herself with sympathetic male activists. Motivated to found a newspaper by her pointed disagreements with fugitive slave and emigration activist Henry Bibb and his paper, *Voice of the Fugitive*, Shadd brought two men into her "editorial group," and the first issues of the *Provincial Freeman* listed Samuel Ringgold Ward as its editor. The tasks of "writing, editing, and production" were in Shadd's hands through the *Freeman's* nearly four-year run. Shadd navigated the perilous terrain of gender while exercising substantial influence on African American intellectual and political culture.[107]

Shadd's paper was no special-interest vehicle aimed at promoting the rights of women. Her weekly covered topics of broad interest to African American communities throughout North America, including the emigration movement and abolitionism. The richness and complexity of the woman question was graphically captured on its pages. In 1854 and 1855 alone, scores of articles related to this debate were published reflecting a variety of questions and concerns. Essays on women's rights were featured alongside advice columns on courtship and marriage.[108] The history and labors of women's rights leaders were chronicled; married women's legal rights, the content of women's education, and proper avenues for women's work were debated.[109] Women's accomplishments in the public realm, especially female "firsts," were celebrated, and noted thinkers like Jane Swisshelm held forth on issues ranging from women's mission to men's sphere.[110] The *Freeman* never failed to highlight the public endeavors of African American women. Shadd's own grueling lecture schedule, along with the orations of the "eloquent and talented" poet Frances Ellen Watkins and "the fine literary and artistic attainments" of educator and emigration activist Amelia Freeman, were prominently featured.[111]

Read as a whole, the *Freeman* set forth an ambitious array of rights to which women were entitled. They included the right to speak and write in public, to control property, to hold elective office, to obtain an education, and to enter the professions. At the same time, it was mindful of the demands of respectability and domesticity, and the paper's boldest claims about the rights of women were coupled with a companion set of admonitions. Women were criticized for refusing chivalrous gestures, schooled in how to find a suitable mate, encouraged to adopt refined manners, and warned against petty jealousies. Even Shadd was praised for her "modest" manner, which was in strict keeping with woman's "sphere."[112] Aware of the tensions between women's rights, respectability, and domesticity, Shadd chose to distance her voice from conventional notions, using articles reprinted from other publications rather than her own editorial space when setting forth more constrained views of womanhood.

Women took up their pens to contribute to the *Freeman*, helping to shape the debate. In one exchange during the spring of 1854, "Henrietta W." wrote to the editor in response to an article on education. Her letter began with a cautious and apologetic tone: "I hope you will pardon the seeming boldness. . . . I have ventured to address you, with the view of ascertaining whether you will receive communications coming from one of my sex. . . . I have taken up my pen with a trembling hand and a fearful heart." Henrietta confessed that she did not possess even a "common school education," yet she ventured to offer her perspective, asserting that "the class of teachers under whom it has been our misfortune to be placed have been just a little better than none at all."[113] Henrietta made a bold claim for her standing in public culture, subordinating her misgivings to her interest in helping shape what she deemed to be an important discussion.

Henrietta's timidity met with fierce resolve. Dolly Bangs's reply in a subsequent edition of the *Freeman* expressed Bangs's fears: "I belong to 'that class styled the weaker sex' and . . . I can sympathize with [Henrietta] in her state of anxiety." Bangs also offered reassurance: "A writer need never fear of bringing down anything like ridicule upon herself . . . the only danger would be in her extreme modesty." Women need not hesitate to join the debate on education, or any other issue, for such an assertion of public authority was "hers by right."[114] Even in the face of concerns about respectability, their exclusion from politics, and the burdens of fund-raising and family, black women recognized themselves as at the center of an important debate. And that debate would, in part, determine their rights in public life.

Bangs's tone was neither modest nor shy. She claimed for women rights equal to those of men: "Would it not be preposterous to ask of man that which he has not the power to give?—he like woman, is but a creature dependant upon his Creator for his own rights." She argued that to discourage women from asserting public leadership "now, in the afternoon of the nineteenth century . . . seems ridiculous." The entire community, she maintained, had an interest in encouraging women's public endeavors to avoid squandering the "vast amount of latent talent which might be used." Yet women themselves must be the guardians of their own fate: "It is her right, as her duty, to press boldly forward to her appointed task, otherwise who is guilty of burying her talent?"[115] No reader of the *Freeman* could claim to be ignorant of the challenges of the woman question after reading Bangs's letter.

Coming-of-Age in the 1850s

A new generation of women was encountering the woman question everywhere they turned. Young black women of the 1850s were coming of age in a precarious but promising climate. Their relationship to public culture was intimate and engaged, forged as it was in reform politics, education, and the examples of their mothers' pioneering activism. In the pages of her diary, Charlotte Forten drew a picture of the climate in which young female activists came of age. Between 1854 and 1862, while working for much of this period as a schoolteacher in Salem, Massachusetts, Forten diligently recorded her quiet but highly observant presence at scores of the decade's reform gatherings. She attended dozens of public antislavery gatherings, during which she heard luminaries such as Garrison, Phillips, Remond, and William Cooper Nell, among others. The era's female speakers, black and white, especially inspired her 1856 ambition: "to be—an Anti-Slavery lecturer." She donned a "Bloomer" costume, read newspapers published by women, and practiced her debating skills in a local literary society. Forten's life was one of relative privilege, and she would go on to develop close associations with many of the era's most noteworthy reform activists. But the climate in which she came of age was not exclusively hers, belonging instead to an entire generation of young women in the free states and territories, many of whom certainly sampled some of the possibilities in which Charlotte Forten was steeped. To be a young African American woman in the 1850s was to glimpse an opening into public culture and perhaps to wonder what one might make of it.

At Oberlin College, young black women had joined the student body. There they, too, grappled with the woman question. The school's female graduates were steeped in the terms of the woman question debate and poised to grapple with its consequences. Lucy Stanton, the daughter of a Pittsburgh barber, graduated from Oberlin in 1850. She later assisted her husband, William Howard Day, with the publication of Cleveland's *Aliened American* and became a teacher in the South.[116] Stanton's classmate, Frances Williams, married Peter Clark, an antislavery activist, school administrator, and politician in Cincinnati.[117] In 1855, Ann Hazle, the daughter of a blacksmith, completed her studies and became a teacher in Ohio. The class of 1856 included four young black women. Sarah Woodson was the daughter of a farmer and became a teacher and then a professor at Wilberforce College while married to AME minister Jordan Early.[118] Louisa Alexander, the daughter of a tavern keeper, taught in the South. Sarah K. Wall became a Chillicothe, Ohio, schoolteacher. And Emma J. Gloucester published her ideas in the pages of the *Anglo-African Magazine*. The class of 1860 included Blanche Harris and Susan Reid. Harris was the daughter of a cook and a carpenter, while Reid was the daughter of a merchant, but (their class differences notwithstanding) both taught among the freed people in the postwar years. Mary Patterson, the daughter of a mason, completed her studies in 1862 and served as a school administrator in Washington, D.C.[119]

The character of the woman question debate was transformed over the course of the 1850s. While generally off the agenda in political gatherings, the debate was invigorated in fraternal orders, literary societies, and the press, and women were almost as likely as their male counterparts to define its terms and set its parameters. These changes in African American public culture had significant consequences during and after the Civil War. Young women played an unprecedented part in public life, organizing relief efforts, speaking publicly, and teaching freed people in the South.

Younger women were coming of age under the tutelage of a generation of female activists, many of whom had long navigated the simultaneous demands of public activism, domesticity, and respectability. They were schooled by necessity in the possibilities and the challenges of women's rights. To envision their sensibilities, we can imagine how Maria Stewart might have reflected upon the changes that had taken place during these decades. After leaving Boston, Stewart taught in schools from New York City to Baltimore and Washington, D.C. A brief newspaper piece in the *Weekly Anglo-African* in 1862 noted that Stewart had sponsored an "exhibition" that featured her students at Baltimore's St. Thomas Church School. Stewart had also shared "an interesting account of her early life." The article then went on to discuss a meeting of the Baltimore Lyceum. Two young women, Misses Davidge and Turockmorton, had debated what one commentator deemed a "somewhat unusual" question: "Have women a right to learn and practice the art of public speaking?" Following a "sharp and interesting discussion, the judges rendered a decision in favor of the affirmative." Imagine Maria Stewart's satisfaction upon reading this article, for its affirmation, through the Davidge-Turockmorton debate, of her early endeavors.[120] Although Stewart had felt herself much alone in her claims to public authority and autonomy, she and other activist women ensured that their daughters would understand such aspirations for public life as part of the broader changes that swept African American public culture during the Civil War and Reconstruction.

4

Something Very Novel and Strange

Civil War, Emancipation, and the Remaking of
African American Public Culture

On St. Helena Island, Charlotte Forten's sense of duty was forever transformed. Forten was among the first African American teachers to venture South and work with black refugees behind Union army lines. When she arrived at St. Helena Island, South Carolina, in 1862, she was twenty-five years old. Forten was reared in the midst of Philadelphia's reform community. Her grandfather, James Forten, was an adviser and financial supporter of Garrison's *Liberator*, a manager of the American Anti-Slavery Society (AASS), and an officer of the American Moral Reform Society (AMRS). Her grandmother Charlotte, her mother, Mary Virginia Woods, and three of her aunts—Margaretta, Sarah, and Harriet—were founding members of the interracial Philadelphia Female Anti-Slavery Society. In 1853, Charlotte was sent to Salem, Massachusetts, to complete her studies, living with family friends Charles and Amy Remond. There she fell under the influence of Charles's sister, Sarah Parker Remond, a lecturer for the AASS. Forten acknowledged her admiration for Sarah Remond's activism in the pages of her diary: "Last night Miss R. entertained me with an account of her tour, and of the delightful day she spent with Mr. [Wendell] Phillips. . . . I listened with most unwearied attention until the 'small hours of the morn' stole upon us."[1]

Forten's private writings reflect a naive passion. In the summer of 1862, with teaching experience in Salem and Philadelphia, Forten set out to teach among contraband slaves, of whose "sad . . . sufferings" she had heard moving accounts. This undertaking, she related, would offer the "delights of travel" while enabling her to find her "highest happiness" in doing her "duty."[2] Through the auspices of the Port Royal Relief Association, the young teacher secured a position on St. Helena Island, where she remained until poor health and her father's death drew her back to Philadelphia in late 1864.[3]

Womanhood's past and future were colliding within Forten. In the pages of her diary, Forten recorded how she survived a treacherous sea voyage, learned to defend herself with a gun, traveled alone or with other women, and ministered to the wounded of the much-celebrated Fifty-fourth Massachusetts regiment.[4] Forten understood that on the Sea Islands her presence, along with that of many other northerners, provoked the woman question. In a December 1862 letter to William Lloyd Garrison, she related the public events surrounding the issuance of General Rufus Saxton's Thanksgiving Day proclamation. It was a day of "thanksgiving and praise," and following the general, "Mrs. Frances D. Gage . . . spoke for a few moments very beautifully and earnestly."[5] Forten imagined the freed people's reaction to Gage: "It was something very novel and strange to them, I suppose, to hear a woman speak in public, but they listened very attentively, and seemed much moved by what she said."[6]

"Novel and strange" encounters were commonplace. The Civil War brought together northerner and southerner, black and white, male and female, formerly enslaved and formerly free people. Forten herself represented a cross-generational history of northern free black public culture and, coming of age in the 1850s, was raised navigating the turbulent waters of women's rights, responsibility, and respectability.[7] Frances Dana Gage brought to her Sea Island work many years of women's rights activism, through which she became a seasoned reformer, public speaker, and journalist. General Rufus Saxton, one of the earliest Union army officers to command African American troops, took part in the transformation of black manhood through military service. Perhaps Forten exaggerated the novelty of seeing women speaking in public to the "people of Port Royal" who gathered that day. But her insight reminds us that, as freed people entered the civic institutions that constituted public culture, they joined lively debates about the standing of women in public life.

Standing on St. Helena Island, Forten could not foresee the transformations that lay just over the horizon. From her vantage point at the earliest moment of Reconstruction, the end of slavery and the remaking of the nation as an interracial democracy (at least for a time) were faint glimmers. But the possibilities were breathtaking. For all black Americans, be they from the northern formerly free states or from the South's slave society, this was a moment long hoped for, an opportunity to remake life in the realms of family, labor, associational life, church, and politics. Woven through what quickly emerged as a complex and multifaceted agenda was the woman question.

The era's sea changes opened the door to broad rethinkings of the meanings of manhood and womanhood for black Americans. Activists, male and female alike, found openings in the era of the Civil War and early Reconstruction that invited a redefinition of their relationships and standing in public culture.

It was military service that redefined manhood. Time spent in the trenches and on the battlefield became the building blocks of new claims for freedom, citizenship, and civil rights. Women found openings in the exigency of war. At first glance, their efforts as soldier and contraband relief workers may have appeared to be a mere extension of a sort of benevolent domesticity that women, whether in northern towns and cities or in southern slave communities, had long performed. But benevolence demanded a great deal more than locally based good work in the Civil War era, and black women developed complex, national relief networks that evidenced a sophisticated sense of the political terrain within which their work transpired. Relief work also demanded that women do more than organize among themselves. Soon they were drawn into public speaking. Women learned how to command the podium, making the case for the value of their work but also aiding in the recruitment of soldiers and sustaining their morale throughout months and years of hard labor and personal risk. Women like Charlotte Forten joined the war effort as teachers among freed people, a task that in name appeared to be a simple extension of the work that some, mostly northern women, had done before the war. But as Forten's journal makes clear, to teach African Americans in the South during the Civil War and early Reconstruction bore little resemblance to the work of New England schoolteachers. Female teachers became fund-raisers, construction contractors, bookkeepers, nurses, and recruiters. They traveled without male escorts, alone or in the company of other women, carried guns, and endured scare tactics and assaults at the hands of southerners who hoped such women would abandon their posts.

Womanhood retained its salience, however. Parameters persisted and nowhere more so than in the realm of politics. Early Reconstruction did see some important experiments in cross-gender political culture, in settings dominated both by those who were formerly free—such as formal conventions—and by those who were formerly enslaved—such as mass meetings. The woman question was muted in politics. But it had not disappeared. By the late 1860s, black women would continue the work of Reconstruction-era politics in the institution that had always stood at the center of their public lives, the church.

Civil War, Emancipation, and the Remaking of Public Culture

To work for the war was to claim freedom and citizenship. African Americans in the free states greeted the Civil War as the final crisis in their long struggle to abolish slavery. For those fugitives who had lived in fear of a return to enslavement, the war held the promise of reunion with family, friends, and the places of their birth. Service to the Union cause promised to bolster African Americans' claims for civil rights. Through sacrifice in support of the war effort, black Americans in the North might prove themselves equal to those who already enjoyed the privileges of citizenship. Enslaved African Americans also contemplated military service and imagined a life beyond slavery's degradations and exploitations. Many took advantage of the disruptions of war to claim their freedom in practice even before it was recognized in principle or law. Black southerners sought to control their own labor, keep their families intact, and govern their own communities. Many imagined taking part in a rich public culture—schools, political organizations, social institutions, and churches—in which they would exercise a level of public autonomy and authority that had been denied them under slavery. These ideas moved African Americans to take part in the work of war. Their active participation—escaping to Union lines, serving the army as soldiers and laborers, and working to feed, clothe, and nurse these men and other runaways—transformed the war's objective from the preservation of the Union to the abolition of slavery. They made their cause into a national mission, rather than a sectional conflict or a mere racial issue.[8]

What ideas did former slaves bring to the woman question debate? Deborah Gray White draws a vivid picture of the distinct experiences of enslaved women, particularly in the antebellum decades. The organization of enslaved people's work, largely determined by slaveholders, tended to separate women and men, reserving skilled tasks and those requiring travel for men. Some women were recognized for their special skills, particularly seamstresses and cooks, while only women assumed the additional burden of childbearing and child rearing. This separation of women from men also extended to social activities, leading enslaved women to develop female networks of cooperation and independence along with affirmative definitions of who and what black women might be. These sensibilities, generated out of female networks, were a critical dimension of enslaved women's survival strategies as they confronted the myths of Jezebel and Mammy.[9]

Did slaves debate the woman question? Steven Hahn suggests that this is a difficult to answer question. In his examination of enslaved people's political culture, Hahn emphasizes that community among enslaved people was difficult to achieve in light of slaveholders' domination. Under these circumstances, institutions were "shaky" enterprises. Still, Hahn arrives at some conclusions about the relative authority of men and women. Those plantation elders who exercised power and authority were disproportionately male. But slave society did not mirror the gender conventions of the white world by which they were surrounded and some enslaved women achieved "places of honor," maintaining family and kinship networks; performing field and domestic work; teaching children; feeding and clothing community members; and serving as midwives, nurses, healers, and folk doctors.[10]

Religion may have been a site of gender tensions for the enslaved. Hahn concludes that it is difficult to know the extent to which enslaved women were subordinated to their male counterparts, if at all, but he generally finds no evidence of a patriarchal ideology in law or custom in enslaved communities. The one arena in which Hahn goes so far as to offer some specific conclusions is that of religion; and in doing so, he points up what may have been a shared concern among female religious activists, both formerly enslaved and formerly free, in the era of emancipation. Women had long been among the spiritual leaders in enslaved communities, Hahn explains. However, by the late antebellum period, as Christianity spread, such opportunities for women narrowed, seeming to suggest that as enslaved people entered Christianity's more formal worship structures, women continued to serve as spiritual guides but did not enter the ranks of preachers and congregation leaders. Hahn does not go so far as to say that this shift was the source of tension or debate among enslaved religious activists, but he leaves open the possibility that the debates about gender and religious authority already under way in some northern black Christian circles may have resonated with some freed people.[11]

Questions about gender, power, and public culture influenced these sea changes. Activists from the free states and territories, as they turned their attention to the work of war and the challenges of emancipation, continued the debates begun during the antebellum decades. Their field of discussion was greatly expanded, however, as they engaged with formerly enslaved people in military service, relief work, and the building of institutions. As Steven Hahn explains, former slaves were not mere passive recipients of northern culture; they came to the Civil War era with existing sensibilities about work, family, culture, and politics. Indeed, contests between these two perspectives were the fodder for institutional wranglings over ideology and practice for decades to come. Even in the earliest moments of their meetings, as Charlotte Forten's memories suggest, former slaves and the formerly free began to ask how women's rights and responsibilities might shape community life.

The Civil War redefined both manhood and womanhood for African Americans. Concerns with "becoming and behaving like a man" preoccupied African Americans during the war. Many black men were eager to enter military service even when they were officially barred from fighting. The Emancipation Proclamation of January 1863 opened the floodgates for black enlistment, and by the end of the war approximately 180,000 black men had served in the U.S. armed forces. Union recruiters, including Frederick Douglass, Martin Delany, and Mary Ann Shadd Cary, drew upon ideas about manhood to encourage enlistment.[12] During a rally in New Bedford, Massachusetts, for example, the Republican congressman Thomas Eliot challenged the men in the crowd to disprove racist stereotypes: "They tell us with fear and trembling that the colored men cannot fight. They say you have not the courage to fight, that you are not manly enough." Men who would not "prove" their willingness to fight opened themselves up to profound humiliation: "If you do not, the women will [do it] for you, for he [Lincoln] had no doubt but that if they had had the charge it would have been crushed out by this time." Black men who did not volunteer were not merely unmanly. In Eliot's view, they stood to threaten the gendered social order by inviting women to take charge.[13]

Military service furthered material and symbolic objectives. Historian Jim Cullen explains that black men were eager to enlist not only to liberate black people from slavery but also to dispel notions of enslaved people as dependent children. As Frederick Douglass put it: "Slavery never admitted our manhood. It always called us 'boys' and its whole machinery was so managed as to keep us 'boys.' "[14] Combat became a definitive marker of manhood, and black men participated in widely noted battles that did much to validate—and valorize—their masculinity.[15] John Mercer Langston rhetorically equated combat with manhood, arguing that black men were entitled to the vote "because they were men." Men had earned the vote through military service, having rushed "out into the arena, and demand[ed] before all the people their rights as native born inhabitants and men." Once again women were the "straw men," as it were. Langston argued that women, like boys, could not claim the same rights because they had not been called into combat: "They had not called women to the battlefield, they had not called boys to the battlefield, and the negro had fully proven his manhood there before God and before the nation."[16]

Women contributed to this developing discourse, echoing concerns about manhood, martial valor, and citizenship rights. Louisa Jacobs, daughter of author and reformer Harriet Jacobs, while reporting on relief efforts in Washington, D.C., emphasized that black soldiers had earned women's assistance. The "colored man . . . proved his claim to manhood, his valor commanding respect, even from his enemies." His willingness "to bleed and die to brave perils and hardships" made him worthy of support. She lamented that the nation itself did not wholly acknowledged this claim: "The heart of America has yet to grow larger. She sees only the shade of the face, not the merit that stamps the worth of man."[17] Other women saw the war, and particularly the prospect of military service, as a definitive test of black manhood. Lucinda Blue exhorted black men: "Arise then ye whose bodies are tainted with African blood; shake off the lethargy that centuries of oppression have bound to you. Prove that you are men capable of enjoying and appreciating the civil and political rights of man."[18]

Womanhood, too, was being remade. This intensely charged connection between notions of manhood and the performance of military service had contradictory consequences for women. On the one hand, it reinforced ideas about differences between the sexes. Women's formal disqualification from military service, which remained unquestioned, became more salient in wartime, and the presumption that military service was a qualification for active citizenship had ominous implications for women's rights. On the other hand, as manhood became more closely tied to military service, it became less dependent upon men's domination of other realms of public culture or the exclusion of women from such activities as public speaking. Women were allowed to make independent decisions in a climate that welcomed rather than feared their assertions of public standing. Of course, the absence of men from many civil institutions meant that the women who took soldiers' places were not regarded as interlopers but as fulfilling their patriotic duty.

Freedwomen were quickly confronted with questions about gender, sex, and kinship. Ex-slave women reconstructed their identities as wives and mothers while negotiating issues of marriage, paternity, child custody, and labor.[19] They wasted little time before becoming part of associational life. In an emerging public culture, freedom took on a lived dimension through access to material resources and spiritual sustenance. It was also in the same churches, political organizations, and various self-help and benevolent societies that freedwomen ran head on into a tangle of women's rights, responsibilities, and respectability. The challenges they faced were suggested in Harriet Jacobs's 1861 narrative, *Incidents in the Life of a Slave Girl*.[20] Jacobs's saga chronicled how she escaped enslavement to become a free woman in the North. Like many fugitive narratives, hers was intended as a tool in the antislavery cause and recounted the myriad evils of slavery, from uncompensated labor to the breakup of families. In a bold departure from the conventional narrative, Jacobs told firsthand of the particular degradation that enslaved women faced, that of sexual assault. In *Incidents* we learn that as a young woman, Jacobs, in an attempt to avoid the unwanted sexual overtures of one white man, entered into a consensual sexual liaison with another, hoping this might increase the likelihood of winning her freedom.

Jacobs was steeped in a trepidation that many formerly enslaved women likely shared. She was reluctant to publish her narrative and thereby subject herself to public scrutiny. Most compromising, in Jacobs's view, were the details of her sexual life. She could not know how readers, who did not share her experience, would judge her circumstances. But there were few reassurances for formerly enslaved woman who feared being judged for their less-than-respectable pasts.

While penning her text, Jacobs was a working woman and a reform activist in the North. In letters to friends, she expressed the fear that her northern friends and supporters would reject her when they learned of her children's parentage.[21] Jacobs was not purely a victim of her master; she was also an agent who negotiated her sexual relationships, although not under conditions that she controlled. She feared that, if judged by the standards of white womanhood, her moral standing would be fatally compromised. Jacobs's dilemma illustrates that, while their sexual exploitation made enslaved women dramatic symbols of the evils of slavery and valuable tools for the antislavery cause, their sexual histories also set them apart from respectable womanhood. For freedwomen, respectability resonated on a register that was distinct from that of their northern counterparts and made their entry into public culture all the more complex.

Minstrelsy continued to shaped the atmosphere in which black women made their public lives. The genre rarely distinguished between formerly free and formerly enslaved women. African Americans' espousal of women's rights continued to be the subject of stump speeches and jokes, with faux dialect, malapropisms, and mistaken tellings of history all mobilized to undercut black claims to public authority. Political cartoons pointedly mocked those black women who were women's rights activists. One example from *Harper's Weekly*, titled "Woman's Rights Convention," singled out black female activists. This three-panel cartoon lampooned women's rights advocates, including Mrs. O'Flarity, who took "the Chair" while her husband had

WOMAN'S RIGHTS CONVENTION.

THE COLORED SOROSIS.

Pages 127–29: "*Woman's Rights Convention,*" Harper's Weekly, *May 29, 1869. Courtesy of the William L. Clements Library.*

FURTHER PROCEEDINGS OF THE CONVENTION.
"Mrs. O'Flarity takes the Chair, and Mr. O'Flarity has the Floor!"

"There goes Mrs. Boggs to the Convention with my
only pair of Pants. Now I'll *have* to stay Home with
the Baby any how."

"the floor," and Mrs. Boggs, who wore her husband's "only pair of Pants" to "the Convention," thus requiring him "to stay Home with the baby." The power of these jests lay in the visual: Mrs. O'Flarity was depicted lifting a chair with one muscular arm while her husband lay flat on his back. Mr. Boggs, clad only in a nightshirt, stood in a window watching his wife head down the street in a man's suit.

A black woman occupied the first panel. She was not given a name, and her image was not accompanied by a humorous caption. She was merely dubbed "The Colored Sorosis," likely a reference to the Sorosis, an organization of white women excluded from men's professional associations. The parody lay entirely in the image, which spoke in a visual language first articulated by artists such as Edward Clay in the 1820s. The cartoon's African American "professional" woman was depicted with ill-proportioned clothes, a less than graceful posture, a dull expression, and flies swarming around her head. This hostile popular climate greeted black women, formerly free and formerly enslaved alike, as they entered post–Civil War public life.

Recrafting Womanhood's Terrain

Women also took part in the work of war. Mindful of the forces arrayed against their claims to respectability, indeed to womanhood itself, they used war work to recraft their standing in public culture. Women, both northern and southern, became teachers, public speakers, and organizers. Formerly enslaved women reconstructed their families and redefined their work while participating in the creation of a whole array of black institutions. These two groups met primarily in the church, where they created a new domain of public activity.

The war placed many African Americans in dire circumstances. Freed people were the first to endure the brunt of its hardships. Later, the young men who served in the military endured deplorable conditions in camps and on battlefields. As news spread about conditions in contraband camps and on the front lines, African American women in the North felt it their duty to facilitate the relief efforts. Whether they were displaced by an incursion of Union troops or had fled across Union lines, black southerners by the thousands turned themselves into refugees from slavery. Private relief work was essential because military commanders had not anticipated their presence. The numbers were staggering. For example, in 1862, Washington, D.C., was home to at least 400 destitute fugitives; by 1863, there were 10,000, with an additional 3,000 across the Potomac River in Alexandria, Virginia. Freedmen's Village in Alexandria housed 7,000 by 1864. By the war's end in 1865, an estimated 40,000 refugees were camped in the District of Columbia.[22]

Black women stepped into what they deemed a critical breach. The Union army had not anticipated the part that African Americans would play in the military, either. When finally permitted to become members of the Union forces, black soldiers had to campaign to receive uniforms, weapons, provisions, and wages on par with their white counterparts. They suffered horrendous conditions in the field, where disease and combat took a deadly toll. And they faced the risk of enslavement (or, for some, re-enslavement), given the Confederacy's refusal to regard them as prisoners of war. Despite these conditions, black men joined the Union's ranks in significant numbers. By the war's end, 180,000 African American men had fought on behalf of the Union, a figure that represented 10 percent of the Union forces, and just over 20 percent of black men between the ages of eighteen and forty-five.[23]

No one questioned the propriety of black women's war work. The transition appeared unremarkable at first: black women redirected their benevolent and fund-raising work to the interests of refugees, freed people, and soldiers. The continuity between the benevolent work of the antebellum years and war work is illustrated by the activities of Philadelphia's black female reformers. In the 1830s, women like Harriet Smith and Eliza Ann Bias had entered public culture through their affiliations with the AASS and the AMRS.[24] In the late 1840s, through the Philadelphia Women's Association, Sarah Mapps Douglass and her colleagues had raised funds to support "the press and public lectures."[25] By April 1863, these same women reorganized themselves into the Ladies Sanitary Association of St. Thomas's African Episcopal Church and engaged in soldiers' aid and refugee relief work.[26]

Old skills were deployed to new ends. The networking and organizing acumen that women had gained in benevolent societies were brought to bear. They expanded the missions of old organizations and founded new ones, forming sewing circles, conducting fairs, giving bake sales, and selling personal narratives. These organizations first emerged in major cities, including New York, Philadelphia, Boston, Washington, Chicago, and Baltimore. These were rapidly joined by organizations in smaller and more remote cities and towns. In Cleveland, San Francisco, Bridgeport, Syracuse, Pittsburgh, New Haven, and Worcester, women organized to raise funds, distribute clothing and food, nurse the ill and wounded, and lift soldiers' morale.[27] Women brought diverse experiences to this work. For some, like Mary Ann Shadd Cary and Frances Ellen Watkins Harper, war work was an extension of their previous public endeavors. For others, like Oberlin College's recent graduates, it was their first chance to act upon their developing ideas about women in public life. For most African American women, war work presented a first opportunity to take part in a public culture of national scope.

Women earned high praise from the start. For example, "Jamaica" reported on the "energetic ladies" of Victoria, Canada, whose black community was comprised largely of California emigrants who had fled the state in 1858 after its legislature attempted to pass a harsh bill prohibiting black immigration.[28] The women had organized themselves into the "Daughters of Victoria" and had been "engaged collecting money . . . for the relief of the suffering contrabands." Jamaica went out of his way to make these women's accomplishments known to African Americans on the West Coast through the San Francisco–based *Pacific Appeal*.[29] He deemed such work an extension of women's natural sphere. Women were, he explained, "better adapted for any such movement" than their "sterner friends"; no one could "shun a smiling ring for money, when emanating from nature's noblest daughters." The women's success was the strongest evidence for his claim. They raised nearly $430 through a bazaar and concert. Expressing the common consensus on women's war work, Jamaica wished the organization "God-speed."[30] Similarly, when a group of women in Beaufort, South Carolina, announced their plan to hold a fair "to aid the destitute freedmen on Edisto Island," the editor of the *Anglo-African* cheered, "Go on Ladies. You are Right."[31]

A self-conscious rethinking of womanhood followed. The challenge of situating women's war work in an ideological frame was captured by Philadelphia's William Forten in a resolution offered at the annual meeting of the Pennsylvania Equal Rights League. The state's women, he explained, had gone beyond the traditional boundaries of womanhood, exerting themselves in "superhuman" ways "hardly to be expected from those who bear the name of the tender sex." In "distributing clothing and comforts" to black soldiers, "whose sufferings . . . would have passed unheeded and not relieved," women braved "the storms of winter, the exhausting heat of summer; risked disease in hospitals, and faced uncomplainingly the insults and indignities of our heartless enemies." Forten, who had long allied himself with public women, also termed this work "disinterested and self sacrificing," straining to reconcile the authority and autonomy evidenced through these endeavors with ideals of feminine domesticity.[32]

These changes provoked careful thinking. No matter how self-sacrificing, as women's work took them further into public culture, men took notice. Some women's groups operated under the cover of older institutional structures, functioning as female auxiliaries to male-controlled institutions. Others stood apart from existing institutions yet incorporated male authority into their governance structures. But many new organizations were conceived, led, and operated entirely by women. These groups developed a network of affiliations that foreshadowed the black women's club movement that emerged a quarter of a century later.[33] Women's relationships to public culture were transformed as they exhibited greater authority, autonomy, and visibility. In wartime, unlike earlier periods, when they challenged long-standing limits, women were encouraged not criticized.[34]

Some worked autonomously. Washington, D.C.'s Contraband Relief Association (CRA), founded in 1862, was typical of these independent women's organizations. The CRA brought many women into public culture for the first time. Elizabeth Keckley headed the organization. Keckley had been enslaved in Missouri prior to purchasing her freedom; she then moved to Washington, D.C., and became a modiste to Mary Todd Lincoln.[35] Keckley's associates included Annie E. Washington, a schoolteacher, and Emma V. Brown, a recent Oberlin College graduate.[36] The CRA sponsored public events and spoke before large assemblies. For example, at the August 1863 ceremony in honor of the First U.S. Colored Infantry, Keckley presented the regiment's commander with a banner designed to "inspire with zeal and courage those who were to go forth and battle with the enemy." She explained that this was the women's "duty" to the war effort. If men were to "go forth in defence of Union and liberty . . . it is the least we can do to sympathize with, encourage and assist them."[37]

The CRA also had a national dimension. The organization coordinated the relief work of auxiliary organizations and, in so doing, developed a female-led relief network. CRA auxiliaries included the Young Ladies' Relief Associations of Baltimore and Washington, D.C., and the Fugitive Aid Society of Boston, organized by Joy Street Baptist Church members Octavia Grimes, wife of the pastor, and Sarah Martin, wife of the Reverend J. Sella Martin. The CRA network extended to other churches in Boston, including the Twelfth Baptist, where twenty-year-old Josephine St. Pierre Ruffin sewed clothing for refugees and learned lessons in women's organizing that served her well as a leader of the club movement during the 1890s.[38] Like Keckley, CRA member Louisa Slade extended the parameters of women's benevolent work to include public speaking as she traveled to promote the cause of freed people's relief. Slade visited Cleveland, Ohio, in August 1865. There she addressed a meeting of the Soldiers' Aid Society, presenting a "most moving picture of the [freed people's] privations and sufferings during the past winter."[39]

The CRA worked alongside similar though less autonomous women's organizations. Under the auspices of the Union Bethel Church, a freedmen's aid organization, the United Relief Association was established. While the membership was overwhelmingly female, men dominated the leadership.[40] Union Bethel maintained sex-segregated seating well into the 1870s.[41] But, even while working under the nominal supervision of men, these Methodist women extended the network within which they operated, serving as an umbrella organization for women's relief associations in Elmira, New York, and Baltimore, Maryland.[42]

Women were sometimes turning the tables and supervising the work of men. The Reverend James Gloucester reported on the anniversary exercises of the Female Benevolent Society of Troy, New York, noting that a woman of "rare accomplishments" had produced the well-written annual report for the occasion. He then described how the women had overseen the work of two other organizations, one of which was the male Society of St. Augustine.[43] Similarly, the women of Beaufort, South Carolina, arranged for the assistance of a man in their freed people's aid work. While holding fairs locally, they engaged John Jackson of Newport, Rhode Island, to act as their agent by collecting money and goods in the North. In this case, it was women who doled out praise as they lauded Jackson's contribution, noting that he was "giving freely of his time" and "lending all his energies" to their enterprise.[44]

Curiosity and confusion sometimes resulted as men took notice of women's independence. Identifying himself only as "Spy," a "gentleman" wrote about a First of August gathering in Harlem, New York, at which "the gentlemen were far less numerous than roosters in a barnyard." A number of the city's black women elected to mark the anniversary of emancipation in the West Indies with a "private picnic." Spy confessed that he had gone to some lengths to locate a "nice little nook" where he could "see without being seen." The discomfort generated by a female-directed gathering was evident in his description. At first he seemed deferential to a sense of propriety and declined to reveal the precise "spot" on which the picnic was held or the names of the ladies in attendance. However, he went on to offer details that were no doubt sufficient to identify them for the readers of the *Weekly Anglo-African*. "Madama M. of 17th St. and Madama O. of 11th Street" were at the "head of the affair," and "Miss McQ. of Florida" was one of the afternoon's speakers, he reported. Spy underscored his ambivalence as he remarked, "Two of the dear creatures turned orators on the occasion."[45] Did becoming an orator negate a woman's standing as a "dear creature," or augment it?

An easy acceptance generally greeted female public speakers in this period. Women were speaking in public in unprecedented numbers. They addressed large, mixed audiences on issues ranging from the home and benevolent work to the war effort and party politics. The trepidation that some women felt as they ascended to the podium was not entirely extinguished, but they were encouraged by the tacit acceptance they received. More experienced women regularly spoke at the most important of public gatherings. Younger women took up public speaking as a deliberate endeavor, finding courage by sharing the stage with their more experienced sisters.

Seasoned women were on the scene. They included veterans of ante-bellum reform movements for whom the war years created new opportunities. Sarah Mapps Douglass continued to lecture on health, physiology, and education in Philadelphia while serving as vice chair of the Women's Pennsylvania Branch of the American Freedmen's Aid Commission and as head of the Institute for Colored Youth's Preparatory Department.[46] Sarah Parker Remond, former vice president of the Salem Female Anti-Slavery Society, spent the war years in Great Britain, where she lectured on temperance, slavery, the cause of the Union, and the standing of African Americans as "freedmen and soldiers" while collecting funds for relief.[47] Sojourner Truth and Barbara Ann Steward were also prominent among those who lectured in support of emancipation, the war effort, and freed people's relief.[48]

Poet Frances Ellen Watkins Harper took to the podium and evidenced a newfound independence. Harper had done a modest amount of public speaking in the prewar era, supported by influential patrons. Among them had been William Watkins, a former American Moral Reform Society member who was also Harper's "father, teacher and political mentor" in the 1850s. William Still had promoted Harper's earliest speaking engagements in the pages of Mary Ann Shadd's *Provincial Freeman*.[50]

At the war's end, Harper struck out on her own. She shared platforms with some of the most notable men of the day, including John Mercer Langston, J. Sella Martin, Charles Remond, and Frederick Douglass. She received invitations from a broad range of civic, religious, political, and antislavery organizations and in 1867 undertook a two-year tour of South Carolina, Georgia, Alabama, and Tennessee, where she lectured on "Literacy, Land, and Liberation."[51] A broadside issued by Philadelphia's Social, Civic and Statistical Association emphasized Harper's competence and her effectiveness with white listeners: "The marked impression made by Mrs. Harper wherever she has spoken, leaves no room to doubt that she is qualified by her wonderful eloquence, pathos and earnestness to remove prejudice, convince objectors, and stir generally, the hearts of her audiences." Harper's standing was, however, still qualified by her sex, as the broadside noted that her abilities rose "to a degree unsurpassed by any female advocate of Freedom of the present day, on this continent."[52] Harper traveled extensively, addressing audiences on subjects including the folly of "Lincoln's Colonization Scheme," the abolition of slavery as the "Mission of the War," and "Reconstruction" as the "nation's great opportunity."

When addressing freedwomen, Harper delivered a pointed message. Here were another set of novel and strange encounters, with Harper coming together with freedwomen to create a shared conversation about women's public roles. Note that Harper lectured "privately" to women, however. Was this gesture intended to mitigate any discomfort her female audience members might have had in a promiscuous gathering? It is likely that women had a particular set of issues to contend with. According to an account that thinly veiled her allusions to sexual matters, Harper "talked with them about their daughters and about things connected to the welfare of the race." Harper encouraged all women to join in the work of uplift, urging, "Now is the time for our women to begin to try to lift up their heads and plant the roots of progress."[53] These sort of moments between formerly free and formerly enslaved women point up that the risks associated with assuming public roles presented particular challenges for freedwomen. Their sexuality and that of their daughters might easily become the fodder of political punditry and popular amusement.

Young women poured into public culture. Encouraged by female activists of the antebellum generation, they took up public speaking with great purpose. From Baltimore's Mental and Moral Improvement Society to Williamsburg, New York's Lyceum, from the Utica, New York, literary society to Washington, D.C.'s Israel Lyceum, black women developed their oratorical skills.[54] When a young woman "delivered a most excellent address on mental improvement" to the Philadelphia Library Company for Colored Persons, she did so in the well-established tradition of Sarah Mapps Douglass.[55] These women did not simply model the possibilities for public women; they used the power of the podium to frame the terms by which their actions were understood. Rebecca Taylor employed this strategy on a winter evening in 1863, when she shared the podium at the Israel Lyceum with Col. C. Fayette Bingham of Ohio. While her very presence asserted her right to speak in public, Taylor's address on the subject of women's rights made the connection between such ideas and her public undertakings explicit. Her speech was deemed noteworthy enough to be recommended for publication in the *Christian Recorder*.[56] The Baltimore Lyceum provided a forum where women could exercise leadership; in 1862 Elizabeth Conick was elected vice president.[57]

Public speaking and benevolent work became closely linked. Mary Buchanan of New Bedford, Massachusetts, embodied this connection. In 1863, Buchanan joined a newly formed women's organization devoted to "the benefit of the sick and wounded soldiers of the 54th and 55th Mass. regiments vol[unteer]s."[58] Buchanan allied herself with a reform community in which women were speaking in public as well as conducting fund-raising. Earlier that fall a number of her fellow officers had participated in a "Festival held in City Hall attended by 500 persons." New Bedford's black women provided the festival's focal point, with "Mrs. Castle and Mrs. Chapman" reading "compositions upon the question of the emigration of people of color, and Miss Jacobs a composition on home."[59] That winter, Buchanan herself was among the women at the podium.[60] Two summers later, in 1865, the *Anglo-African* reported her to be "preparing to appear as a public reader," an undertaking it enthusiastically endorsed in light of Buchanan's "talents of a high order."[61] The following month, Buchanan was featured among the speakers at a "Reception of the Toussaint Guards" in New Bedford. City hall was "filled, every seat being occupied and many persons including ladies were compelled to stand." The mayor offered the opening remarks, and then Buchanan was introduced. Her "address of welcome was beautifully conceived and handsomely delivered; it was a success and drew forth repeated manifestations of applause." Only then were this budding public speaker's remarks followed by the speeches of seven men.[62]

Young women like Buchanan were taking center stage. They ventured well beyond the relatively cloistered settings of literary societies and benevolent groups to spaces in which their skills were on full display. This upcoming generation of female orators was maturing in a climate of encouragement, less burdened by opposition than had been women in the antebellum era.[63]

Edmonia Highgate tested the waters at the National Convention of Colored Men in 1864. Highgate, who was on leave from her work as a teacher in Norfolk, Virginia, traveled to Syracuse, New York, hoping to share her views of the convention's objectives.[64] Black suffrage was the central issue at this gathering, and the convention's resolutions included a call that African Americans be granted the elective franchise throughout those states that remained in the Union, as well as in those that would rejoin the Union thereafter.[65] Steven Hahn points up this gathering as another of the early "novel and strange" encounters, as men from southern states, many of them former slaves, were among the delegates.[66]

Highgate wondered aloud whether "she would not be quite in her place perhaps, if a girl as she should tell the Convention what they ought to do."[67]

Highgate rightly understood the enormity of her undertaking as she stood side by side with some of the era's most accomplished male orators, including John Mercer Langston and the Reverend J. Sella Martin, both of whom followed her that day. Highgate's confidence was likely buoyed by the presence of mentors and allies, including Frances Ellen Watkins Harper and Jermain Loguen.[68]

There was nothing new in black women's work as teachers. They had labored in northern classrooms for decades before the war. It was what it meant to teach that was new. Teaching freed people in the South demanded fortitude and self-reliance. These women were encouraged, supported financially, and celebrated by their communities. Education was understood to be the cornerstone of freedom, and adults and children alike eagerly sought out any opportunity to learn.[69]

Many schools began through the efforts of local black communities. In 1861, for example, Virginia's Mary Peake, the daughter of a free black mother and an English father, established the first school for African Americans in Hampton, Virginia. Peake had for many years been active in Norfolk's black Baptist church and had founded a women's benevolent society, the Daughters of Zion.[70] Most teachers were middle-class white women sent south by northern aid societies, but many African Americans like Peake were among those who taught freed people.[71] In her study of the American Missionary Association (AMA), Clara DeBoer identifies scores of black men and women who taught in schools throughout the Upper South.[72] Between 1867 and 1870 the proportion of teachers and missionaries supported by the AMA who were black rose from 6 percent to 20 percent. During these same years, 54 percent of the teaching staff employed by the Presbyterian Committee on Freedmen was black.[73] Many of these teachers were veterans of the antebellum debates over women's education.

Training in the North was brought to bear in the South. Sara Stanley, teacher to the refugees in Norfolk, Virginia, had taught in Cleveland prior to the Civil War.[74] Sarah Woodson left her teaching position at Wilberforce University to teach for the Freedmen's Bureau in Hillsboro, North Carolina.[75] Mary J. R. Richards, an instructor at St. Mary's, Georgia, had taught in Liberia for four years. Mary Still and Susan L. Waterman, both teaching in Florida, had experience in Philadelphia and New Jersey prior to the war.[76] Lucy Stanton Day, a teacher in Buxton, Canada West, was sent by the Cleveland Freedmen's Association to Georgia in 1866, and then to Florence, Mississippi, where she taught school.[77] Priscilla Stewart, a member of Philadelphia's Garrisonian antislavery community, was also a veteran of the antebellum era's cross-gender political bodies, having served on the business committee of a Philadelphia antislavery convention in 1848. Stewart left her position as a primary school teacher in San Francisco in July 1865 to go "to some of the Southern States and endeavor to ameliorate the condition of the Freedmen."[78] Her community of activists marked the occasion with a public tribute and presented Stewart with a "pair of gold spectacles, as a testimony of their esteem for her moral worth, philanthropy and Christianity."[79] That same summer, Addie Semby left Washington, D.C., to assist in a Petersburg, Virginia, school for freed people. She was "cheerfully recommended" to her new community and wished success "in her new field of labor."[80] AME minister John M. Brown, working for the AMA in Norfolk, Virginia, encouraged the recruitment of women in a letter to AMA officials: "Pardon this suggestion but I think the ladies named will greatly aid in this good cause and should you decide to [illegible] them, and can send a few more of the same kind, you will greatly strengthen the good in this region."[81]

Even seasoned teachers sometimes were daunted. Many were leaving family, friends, and familiar communities for the first time. Mary Still, a member of Philadelphia's Garrisonian antislavery community, wrote to an AMA secretary: "I am about ready I shall be in New York on Thursday though my heart is very sad I think that I have decided hastily upon going so far from home alone." Mary Still, the sister of activist William Still, was in her midforties when she applied to the AMA and was placed first in Beaufort, South Carolina, and then in Jacksonville, Florida, where she taught primary classes. She later related the challenging conditions under which she worked: "My labors have in the house been from early morn until two From then I teach until six in the evening; and then . . . teach until nine." Still felt her "health failing" from the heat and from the burden of teaching and domestic duties. However, her confidence was eventually restored and Still renegotiated the terms of her contract, explaining to the AMA that she thought it best to forgo domestic chores in favor of occupying her time teaching. "I suppose my salary will go on the same," she added. Even with the demands of teaching, Still found time to advocate on behalf of local women who sought teaching positions with the AMA and to coordinate freedmen's relief work as vice president of the "Ladies' Fair of Beaufort."[82]

Oberlin College graduates were among the first to migrate south. Sara Stanley was among the earliest of these northern-trained teachers. She was freeborn in New Bern, North Carolina, and had attended Oberlin in 1852 and became a teacher in Norfolk, Virginia.[83] Stanley was a seasoned teacher and public speaker, having delivered, for example, the address of the Ladies'

Anti-Slavery Society of Delaware, Ohio, to an 1856 gathering of "disfranchised citizens of Ohio."[84] Like Stanley, Lucy Stanton Day, Blanche V. Harris, Louisa Alexander, and Sarah Jane Woodson all left their homes to teach among the refugees and freed people.[85] These women were joined by a younger generation of Oberlin women, many of whom were beginning their studies when the war began. For many of these young women, teaching was a transformative experience that reshaped their ideas about their roles as women. For example, twenty-four-year-old Oberlin student Clara Duncan wrote to her AMA supervisor, Professor Woodbury, from her post in Norfolk, Virginia, regarding the "unpleasant atmosphere" of the Mission House in which she lived. Duncan began by affirming her respect for and faith in Woodbury: "I respect you highly and love you dearly." "To suffer and be silent" was how Duncan described her "lot thus far" and her "duty." But the challenges of life in Norfolk led Duncan to reconsider her place. With her "heart and soul" still committed to the work of teaching, Duncan defended her right to challenge her working conditions. "Now I don't think duty demands silence," she explained.[86] Thus, while female teachers of the Civil War era were engaged in a task that women had long performed, the meaning of this work changed as young women began to see themselves as more than silent helpmeets.

The Multiple Sites of African American Politics

Law continued to be a bellwether for African American public culture. In the early Reconstruction years, the debates that surrounded the Fourteenth and Fifteenth Amendments to the U.S. Constitution brought black activists back to questions about women in politics. The final wording of each amendment reintroduced the terms of the sex versus color debate that had occupied activists in the antebellum decades. The Fourteenth Amendment introduced gender into the Constitution for the first time, imposing upon the individual states a penalty for depriving male citizens of the vote while leaving them free to exclude women from the franchise. The Fifteenth Amendment, which also concerned voting rights, explicitly prohibited the state and federal governments from denying or abridging the right to vote to any citizen "on account of race, color, or previous condition of servitude." Again, the rights of men, here African American men in particular, were deemed generally inalienable, while the exclusion of women of all races from the franchise remained permissible.

Black activists found a great deal to celebrate in the Reconstruction amendments. Their terms were a victory in their long-standing battles against slavery and civil rights. Yet the terms of these amendments cut against the assumptions that had supported the alliances between antislavery, civil rights, and women's rights activists. Long sought after political rights, which previously many had called for in universal terms, were being realized only in fractured form. Allies of the prewar period reconvened in the mid-1860s under the umbrella of the Equal Rights Association. There debates over the right to vote—who should enjoy it and under what terms—were framed in terms that pitted the interests of black men against those of white women. While few among these veteran activists abandoned the principal of universal suffrage—that is, suffrage for men and women, black and white—factions quickly emerged over how such a goal should be realized in the present climate. One view was reflected in Wendell Phillips's declaration, "This hour belongs to the Negro." This remark signaled acquiescence to the perceived limits of Reconstruction-era politics as well as an acceptance of a gendered political order in which only men would exercise formal authority, at least for the present. Elizabeth Cady Stanton captured the essence of the competing faction when she decried the possibility that white women could be made into the political inferiors of black men who were "unwashed" and "fresh from the slave plantations of the South." Perceived differences between the interests of white women and African American men, which were held at bay generally in the 1850s, erupted.

Black women moved in from the margins during this debate, offering their unique perspective. They insisted that an intersectional analysis, one that simultaneously took up race and gender, was required if organizations such as the Equal Rights Association expected to move forward in the postemancipation era. Black women activists urged that their lives, which were lived at the nexus of sex and color, should define political culture. Frances Ellen Watkins Harper's vision, the very one that this book borrows for its title, was that all the activists present were "bound up together" submerged in a cauldron. As historian Rosalyn Terborg-Penn illustrates, by 1870, African American activists, male and female, would split along the same lines that split apart the Equal Rights Association.[87] But, as Nell Painter explains through the examples of Frances Ellen Watkins Harper and Sojourner Truth, black women activists appeared to be of one mind during the debates over the terms of the Fourteenth and Fifteenth Amendments, even while lamenting their gendered limitations.

Bitterness and division were not the only outgrowths of this debate. Women's rights activism continued, but it also split along a racial divide. The long-standing if fragile alliance between black abolitionists and white women's rights advocates was wrenched apart. Many white woman suffrage advocates abandoned any commitment they still held to interracial political alliances. But, for African Americans, these debates were not such a sharp point of demarcation. The fissures that the debate exposed predated the Civil War; these divisions originated in the early 1850s when black activists and white women's rights leaders carved up the terrain of reform politics into separate spheres of race and sex.

This postwar debate and shift in strategy did not lead African Americans to abandon women's rights or the question of women's public standing. Throughout black public culture, women's rights remained a salient issue in the Civil War–era, meriting debate while dictating the gendered parameters of institutional life.[88] Indeed, after the adoption of the Fifteenth Amendment, many African American activists continued to work alongside white middle-class women's rights leaders on the issue of woman suffrage, joining organizations such as the American Woman Suffrage Association and the National Woman Suffrage Association.[89]

However, full consideration of the intersection of race, gender, and politics in this period requires an examination of women's rights within African American political culture more broadly. Among black political activists, both in mass settings and in the most visible of black political bodies, a different point of view was manifest, one that challenged any characterization of politics as an exclusively male realm.

Women's rights activism continued within black activist circles in much the same manner as it had before the war. The primary question continued to be one about the rights of women within African American life and culture. In popular politics, women's relationship to political culture was in flux. Historian Elsa Barkley Brown recounts how African Americans in Richmond, Virginia, both men and women, took part in the mass meetings associated with the state's 1867–68 constitutional convention. Black delegates, Brown argues, were significantly influenced by the views expressed in community meetings and by the African American presence in the convention galleries, both of which included women. Women also took part with men in political meetings held in other areas of Virginia, South Carolina, Louisiana, and Arkansas. This moment of political crisis, when women took an active part in political decision-making, was short-lived, though women throughout the Reconstruction-era South continued to participate actively in public political gatherings alongside their husbands.[90]

This was not an exclusively southern phenomena. In San Jose, California, the issue of women's political standing arose during a meeting to discuss a recent election of delegates to an upcoming black state convention. Objections had been lodged to the election of local barbershop owner Charles Mercier some two weeks earlier, the most controversial of which was that "the ladies assisted in the election."[91] To quell the dissent, Mercier withdrew and a new slate of delegates was proposed. These voting women had a male ally in the room, however, the meeting's chair, Peter Cassey. Cassey was a migrant from Philadelphia, where he had been raised in one of that city's most prosperous activist families. His political education included exposure to his father's leadership in education, antislavery, the press, and African American politics, where he served as a delegate to national conventions, including those of the AMRS. Cassey's mother, Amy, was a political activist in her own right as a member of the Philadelphia Female Anti-Slavery Society and Sarah Mapps Douglass's Philadelphia Women's Association.[92] Cassey moved that the "ladies be allowed to vote" as they had before, and chaos erupted. Secretary A. J. White bolted from the chamber, followed by "one dozen braves who are opposed to ladies voting for delegates to a State Convention."[93] Cassey congratulated the audience "upon the exit of these relics of a past age," and Mercier was reelected unanimously. This moment of women's political empowerment was brief, however. Within just a week another meeting was convened, and this time the audience included an "unusually large number of adult males." The outcome of the previous meeting was declared "null and void" because "women and boys" had participated in the election. This crowd resolved that "women and children are not entitled to the exercise of the elective franchise in matters pertaining to the body politic," and a new slate of delegates was elected.[94]

This was dubbed the "free speech crushing meeting." But despite this less than flattering characterization of the local black political scene, efforts to suppress women's activism persisted. A note to the San Francisco *Elevator* sought to clarify the matter. Women had, it seemed, continued their attempts to vote at the meeting, despite the many men who opposed them. The scene was chaotic. "There were seven females present, three of whom jumped up whenever the head fugleman or 2d lieutenant gave the signal" to vote. The women's attempts were met with "exclamations . . . from the male portion of them to sit down." The writer reassured the *Elevator*'s readers that social order, which was rooted in a gendered hierarchy, had been reestablished. The women were mistakenly "counted in only once" by a drill sergeant, but the man had been immediately replaced by "more reliable tellers" who, without question, "omitted the ladies."[95] In an ironic turn, which

"The Fifteenth Amendment. Celebrated May 19th 1870." Baltimore. Courtesy of the Library Company of Philadelphia.

Details of "The Fifteenth Amendment. Celebrated May 19th 1870."

ELECTIONEERING AT THE SOUTH.—Sketched by W. L. Sheppard.—[See Page 467.]

"Electioneering in the South," Harper's Weekly, *July 25, 1868.*
Courtesy of the William L. Clements Library.

underscored the vexed relationship of women to the political realm, the meeting ended with three women, along with three men, appointed to a finance committee charged with raising funds for the delegates' expenses.[96]

Women's political aspirations continued to make themselves visible in national black political conventions. The National Convention of Colored Men met in Washington, D.C., in January 1869, the same month in which the Fifteenth Amendment was proposed in Congress. Three hundred delegates were in attendance, and many were reported to be supporters of women's rights. Among those who certainly created this impression were the antebellum activists in attendance, including J. Sella Martin, Henry Highland Garnet, William Wells Brown, Robert Purvis, George T. Downing, and Frederick Douglass.[97] The seating of a female delegate, Harriet C. Johnson, principal of the Female Department of Avery College, met with some opposition, however. It was reported that the opposition came from "mainly southern delegates," while the delegates from New York, Philadelphia, and Baltimore were all in support. But the voices of those who opposed her seating were all but drowned out by a vote of 188 to 26.[98] Thus, even as many African Americans were contemplating the difficult compromise that the Fifteenth Amendment represented, many activists continued to advocate women's empowerment within black political culture.

In other settings female activists secured a similar hearing. At the December 1869 Colored National Labor Convention, for example, principles with their origins in the late 1840s shaped the proceedings. Speaking on behalf of the Committee on Address, John Mercer Langston reported that "in our organization we make no discrimination as to nationality, sex, or color."[99] Mary Ann Shadd Cary, representing Detroit, served as chair of the Committee on Female Suffrage. Cary was provided with an opportunity to address the convention on the "rights of women and the justice of their recognition by the sterner sex." The gathering then adopted a resolution proposed by Cary's committee that affirmed the organization's position on the woman question: "That as unjust discrimination in the departments of labor is made against women, and as the organization of associations for the protection of said interest among the colored people of the United States is in its incipiency . . . that colored women be cordially included in the invitation to further and organize cooperative societies." Just months after activists had split over the Fifteenth Amendment, African American political institutions still affirmed a commitment to including women as leaders and in the rank and file.

Black political leaders put women's suffrage on the agenda in the era's constitutional conventions and state legislatures. William Whipper, a delegate to the South Carolina Constitutional Convention of 1868, called for that body to enfranchise black women as well as men.[100] Men like Whipper acted as allies to their female counterparts. The following year, Louisa Rollin, his sister-in-law, who belonged to the American Woman Suffrage Association, urged the South Carolina House of Representatives to support universal suffrage.[101] This conjunction demonstrated how women continued to use antebellum-era tactics, such as relying upon male allies, to get their issues upon the agenda in spaces from which they were formally excluded. Whipper's ties to antebellum reforms were even more direct. His father, Philadelphia activist William J. Whipper, had been one of the founding members of the AMRS, the black political organization that, some thirty years before, had included women among its delegates, one of the earliest experiments in black women's political empowerment. But the Whipper-Rollin alliance also represented what was new about the postwar period: women were getting themselves onto the agenda and thereby inserting their own voices into the debate.

Black public culture did not end at politics. While formal authority in politics may have been largely ceded to men, black activist women stood poised for a rights campaign of their own making. Churchwomen used the opportunities offered in wartime to resurrect debates that had been quiet since the early 1850s. The proceedings of an 1863 AME Zion conference suggested that the woman question was once again emerging in religious circles. In a well-worn ritual, the Daughters of Conference were introduced for the purpose of donating the funds they had raised for the denomination. But rather than receiving the conventional vote of thanks, the women were "feelingly addressed" by Wilbur Strong, a teacher and Sunday school superintendent who soon became a missionary in Florida, on the subject of "woman in her sphere."[102] Strong's topic suggests that he felt moved to defend the institution against the challenges that were brewing in his and other black Methodist churches.

The licensing of female preachers was back on the table in the AME Church by 1864. The proposal was made by the Reverend Henry Davis of Burlington, New Jersey. The minutes do not identify Davis's female coconspirators, but his daughters probably played a role behind the scenes. Davis's daughter Rachel, then twenty-one years old, would ten years later became the assistant secretary to the church's first female missionary society, the Women's Parent Mite Missionary Society.[103] And his daughter Emily, then nineteen, would sign on to a petition for universal suffrage sponsored by Philadelphia's Banneker Institute in 1866.[104] Had his daughters encouraged Davis to re-inject the woman question into church deliberations? Perhaps the influence ran in the other direction, with Davis encouraging his daughters' public aspirations. More likely these were mutual influences, and we are left to imagine family exchanges in the Davis household, where across generations there were many answers to the woman question: preaching licenses, missionary societies, and the vote.

Davis's proposal was not a radical one. The hand of a female correspondent to the AME Church's *Christian Recorder*, Martha King, related for the first time the substance of such a petition. King's report revealed the limitations, as well as the innovativeness, of Davis's proposal. Yes, church law would be amended to license women "to exhort and to preach," but their activities would be carefully monitored by several layers of male church leaders. A woman would need to secure a "recommendation from the class of which she is a member," pass an examination, obtain a "majority of votes" in a special meeting, and then be examined by the Quarterly Conference's presiding elder. Once issued, a female preacher's license would require renewal once every year.[105] Even though this proposal was couched in a scheme that kept female preachers subject to an imposing system of oversight by male church leaders, it was once again defeated. Still, it signals to us that the woman question debate had been reinvigorated in the church. By the late 1860s, this debate was being fueled by ideas generated in politics as black Methodists asked themselves, Should churchwomen have the right to vote?

5

Make Us a Power
*Churchwomen's Politics and the
Campaign for Women's Rights*

In 1876, African American women won the right to vote. Through a broad campaign that began before the Civil War, black women secured the right to choose leaders, serve as representatives, and decide on legislation. Their campaign was waged by a multigenerational cadre of women; some gained their political acumen in the antebellum abolitionist movement, and others came of age in the tumult of the Civil War and Reconstruction. Male allies who advocated the extension of public authority to women offered essential support to the campaign. This victory was not entirely revolutionary, however; the advent of female suffrage did not automatically produce equality of representation in practice. At the close of the nineteenth century, although many more black women voted, few had been elected to high office.

Black women voting and holding office in the 1870s? At first, this scene may read like Octavia Butler meets *The History of Woman Suffrage*, a science fiction version of the nineteenth-century women's rights saga.[1] Or perhaps it is a parable authored by legal scholar Derrick Bell, returning to the "Geneva" chronicles and deploying the fantastical to make a point about race, law, and power in America.[2] The explanation lies, however, not in the realm of fiction but in the annals of African American women's history. In 1876, female members of the African Methodist Episcopal Zion (AME Zion) Church won the right to vote and to hold office within their denomination.[3]

The timing of this important moment of enfranchisement suggests how the periodization of political history does not always map well onto the history of women's politics. This chapter follows the emergence of black churchwomen's political culture from the early 1870s through the late 1880s, a period during which a sustained campaign for the rights of female church members transformed the relationship of gender to power for millions of

African American religious activists. Rights most often associated with the realm of party and state-sponsored politics—electing representatives and holding office—were at the core of what churchwomen sought in their communities' most powerful institutions.

Churchwomen began their campaign with a call for gender-neutral church law; they sought the removal of any barrier to their voting for local church officials. But the rhetoric that undergirded this seemingly modest objective had a greater force than many anticipated. Soon the same arguments, borrowed from the period's political contests, were being used to buttress claims for the creation of female offices, the founding of female missionary societies, and the seating of women as delegates in decision-making bodies. Churchwomen's rights claims also radiated outward, influencing debates among white religious activists, paralleling claims made by secular women's suffrage advocates, buttressing black men's claims to public influence, and reshaping allied organizations, including fraternal orders. If black women had largely ceded the reigns of party politics to their male counterparts, they simultaneously took up a new campaign grounded in the politics of race, as well as sex, to redefine their public standing.

Recentering the Debate, from Politics to Church

Ideas about women in politics continued to circulate in black activist circles, though they did not give rise to a distinct movement for women's political rights. An outspoken minority called for women's full political empowerment. Frederick Douglass advised black women to continue developing their political acumen in anticipation of the passage of "a sixteenth amendment," which would remove "their disability" and grant them the vote.[4] "Mater Familias," adopting a witty moniker that in itself inverted the gendered order by putting a woman at the head of a household, expressed regret that so few women took an active interest in politics: "While I do not object to a lively interest in the bustle subject [that is, to debates about fashion], I think a woman's mind is wide enough to accommodate other and more profitable subjects for reflection." She sought to encourage women's political activism: "While most people disapprove of women taking an active part in politics, few will deny that it is better for them to have the widest intelligence in regard to the vital questions before the country, than to be ignorant of them."[5]

Opponents could be equally vocal. An editorial commenting on Mater Familias's letter retorted: "One of [our] most intelligent and educated ladies gives us elsewhere her ideas about her sex taking an active interest in political matters, and reading political speeches. We agree . . . with the writer in the general idea that a lady's mind ought to grasp in its range of thought, political subjects. Her field, however, is the domestic circle, not the public stage."[6] Some women endorsed a conservative vision, insisting that politics were the province of men. In an essay titled "Woman's Power" published in the *Planet*, Georgetown, South Carolina's weekly newspaper, Alice King noted that the issue of women's suffrage had made "many women's pens and . . . tongues red hot."[7] Still, King argued that "it seems to us very likely that woman if she reaches her object will lose much more than she will gain." Women's influence was most effective when exerted through "indirectness" as they "spoke a word or two, which appeared to be dropped carelessly," a tactic that never failed to influence the votes of husbands and sons alike, in King's assessment. Women also stood to wield great influence through the pen, a vehicle that held more far-reaching promise than "so comparatively small a privilege as the suffrage." King warned against woman "lowering her dignity, crying out so widely for a thing which, after all, cool, common sense seems to point out to be more man's business." Rosetta Coakley echoed King's perspective in "Our Stumbling Blocks," a presentation to Washington, D.C.'s Bethel Literary Society. Coakley argued that women "can do more good by properly attending to their domestic duties, training up their children to be men and women of worth, than they can by troubling their brains with women's rights, so called." Her sentiments were seconded by the editor of the *People's Advocate*, who endorsed Coakley's essay as "replete with sound logic and good suggestions."[8] Forthright calls for women's political empowerment were met in part by invocations of the ideal of domesticity.

Coakley's resoluteness was misleading. A closer examination of her public life suggests that her ideas were far more complex than her remarks allowed for. Born a slave in Virginia, Coakley was educated in Washington, D.C.'s schools and became a teacher and administrator, duties that were arguably consistent with the ideal of female domesticity she espoused. However, Coakley then went on to serve as a national organizer for the Woman's Christian Temperance Union and was among those who called for the first meeting of the National League of Colored Women in 1895. If Coakley eschewed "women's rights, so called," her definition of domesticity was such that it permitted women to travel, lecture, and perform as leaders with national standing.[9] This formulation was something other than the restricted notion of female influence that had animated thinking during the antebellum decades.

There was no clear sacred-secular divide in black public culture. While operating pursuant to distinct structures, rules of governance, and, in some cases, leaders, the distance between political conventions and church conferences was a short one during the postwar decades. The agendas within these settings often reflected the overlapping interests of activists, many of whom moved nimbly between the sacred and the secular. Black churches rivaled political organizations as the most important sites of African American public culture. In his 1903 study of black churches, W. E. B. Du Bois reported that 2.7 million of the nation's 12 million African Americans were active church members—that is, nearly one out of every four to five people. Of these, 95 percent lived in the South, a statistic that illustrated the transformation of the black church from a northern- to a southern-based institution during Reconstruction.[10] Black Methodists numbered 1.2 million in 1903; by the turn of the twentieth century, one out of every ten African Americans belonged to a black Methodist denomination, a tenfold increase over the immediate postwar decades.[11]

Spiritual community was one identity among many for black churches. These public venues sponsored civil rights campaigns and lyceums, as well as mutual aid associations and widows' funds. They financed educational institutions, from elementary schools to theological seminaries and normal training institutes. Their sanctuaries, often the largest local gathering place, hosted political conventions, fraternal order celebrations, temperance rallies, and schools. Ministers often served as political leaders, emboldened by the moral and financial support of their denominations that somewhat insulated them from the retributions of whites. By one estimate, of the nearly 2,000 black male officeholders during the Reconstruction era, 276, or nearly 14 percent, were ministers. Such men exercised tremendous authority within black Methodism. In the African Methodist Episcopal (AME) Church, Bishop Richard Cain served as congressman from South Carolina for two years, and Bishop Theophilus Steward was a Republican Party activist in Georgia. In AME Zion, Bishop James Hood served as president of the North Carolina Colored Convention of 1865 and later as the state's assistant superintendent of education.[12] Consequently, during the proceedings of church conferences, spiritual matters and institutional business shared the agenda with party politics, civil rights, temperance, and education. These were vibrant and well-attended occasions, and their influence was extended by way of church publications. For many church leaders, politics and religion were compatible, even interdependent, and these men met little resistance as they moved between conferences and conventions.

Views about the rights of churchwomen were shaped through the intersection of religion and politics. Some saw a close connection between the movement for women's right to the vote and the power of spiritual forces. Benjamin Tanner, editor of the AME Church's weekly, the *Christian Recorder*, lauded the election of Methodist Episcopal Church (North) bishop Gilbert Haven as president of Boston's American Female Suffrage Association. Tanner remarked that a "good" movement appeared on its way toward seeking "success on the basis of a religion that honors God and Christ."[13] Tanner endorsed women's suffrage as among the century's "good" movements, an assessment more typically bestowed upon antislavery and temperance campaigns. Tanner went further, attributing the movement's likelihood of success to its reliance on religious leadership. This endorsement of the activism of Bishop Haven, a white Methodist, exemplified how African American leaders saw political interests as compatible with, and even enhanced by, their engagement with the church. Such confluences reinforced an incorporation of political tenets into church-based deliberations, especially those about the rights of churchwomen.

Black Methodist churches sat at Reconstruction's crossroads. Established institutions grew and were transformed by their extension into the South. The AME and AME Zion Churches, both of which originated in northern cities during the 1790s, expanded their memberships tenfold and moved their centers of operation to the South. New institutions were born. The Colored Methodist Episcopal (CME) Church was created when the Methodist Episcopal Church, South, excluded those former slaves who worshipped in its sanctuaries. These institutions struggled for legitimacy in relation to their white counterparts, asking whether black churches would best distinguish themselves through conformity or innovation. The tensions associated with the coming together of formerly enslaved and formerly free people were evident in debates about the desirability of an educated ministry, the role of lay leaders, and styles of worship. Alongside these issues emerged questions about women's formal authority.

Law and the Remaking of Women's Rights

In churches, as in political culture, law was a touchstone. Changes in religious law, in turn, led to lasting transformations in practice. Prior to the 1870s, while black Methodist churchwomen had consistently performed essential fund-raising and benevolent work, they were not formally recognized in church law. After the Civil War, women gained formal authority within Methodist bodies. By the early 1880s, they voted and held office in decision-making bodies, served as officers of home and foreign missionary societies, oversaw local church governance as stewardesses, and spread the gospel as duly licensed preachers. These innovations resulted from shifting views about women's rights in the church, and in practice they transformed women's relationships to the rituals, deliberations, and administration of religious bodies. Women were granted authority and autonomy in religious institutions long before they secured these rights in politics writ large.

The *Doctrines and Discipline* were the first target of churchwomen's campaign for rights. The result was that during the 1870s, both the AME and the AME Zion Churches amended their governing texts to delete formal distinctions between men and women. The issue first came before the AME General Conference in 1872, when Rev. Thomas Henderson, a member of the Missouri delegation, proposed that the law be amended such that "the word 'male' wherever it occurs as a qualification of electors be struck from the Discipline."[14] Henderson had been educated at Oberlin College, where he likely encountered debates about the rights of women. He was active in Republican Party politics while living in Kansas and likely followed the debate surrounding the language of the Fourteenth and Fifteenth Amendments.[15] Henderson's proposal was extended by a subsequent motion that declared all church members over the age of twenty-one, regardless of sex, be permitted to vote for local trustees. Four years later, gender qualifications were struck from all provisions related to Sunday school personnel.[16] In the AME Zion Church, similar revisions were taken up in 1876 when the General Conference voted to "strike out the word male in the Discipline."[17] Apparently, this directive was not fully implemented, and in 1880 a group of Boston churchwomen successfully petitioned "to strike out the words 'man' and 'men' in the *Discipline*," specifying those sections of the church law that had not already been so amended.[18]

There was remarkably little debate. Churchwomen gained the right to vote without a hint of opposition. Perhaps some did not anticipate how gates of power were opening to women. But the political rhetoric in which these changes in church law were couched at least invited questions. As religious activists criticized the appearance of the words "male" and "men" in church law, their positions echoed those women's rights advocates had uttered during debates surrounding the Fourteenth and Fifteenth Amendments. There was an interpretive link between campaigns to change church law and claims for women's rights in politics. As one Boston-based group of AME Zion Church petitioners put it, they sought to give "women the same rights in the church as men." This was no discrete campaign to give local women modest decision-making power. Proponents of gender-neutral church laws had more sweeping, though perhaps not fully articulated, objectives in mind.[19]

There was an explicit link between churchwomen's activism and campaigns being waged by women in the professions. In law, American women confronted bans upon their admission to the bar. The example of Charlotte Ray, a black woman who was one of the first American women to be licensed to practice law, illustrates how professional women's struggles, particularly the excision of restrictions such as "male" or "men" from the relevant rules, resonated with those of women in churches. Ray entered the Howard University Law School class of 1869. While her admission to law school was remarkable, Ray's future was uncertain; American courts, including those of the District of Columbia, had yet to admit women to practice. Teaching during the day at Howard's Normal and Preparatory Department, Ray studied commercial law in the evening and graduated in 1872, the sole woman in a class of fifteen.[20] By the time Ray completed law school, her professional prospects had changed. The District of Columbia's chief judge, David Cartter, had overseen an amendment to the laws related to the admission of attorneys in the district, such as to "strike out the word 'male.'"[21] A door once closed was opened, and in April 1872, Ray was admitted to the bar of the Supreme Court of the District of Columbia.[22] She went on to have a brief though remarkable stint as a practitioner, but finally returned to teaching.[23]

Changes in law opened doors to authority and leadership. This was true in sacred and secular circles. Intriguing connections suggest that it was significant that both in the church and in law, female activists had important links to antebellum public culture. In black Methodist churches, women such as Eliza Gardner drew upon their experiences in prewar antislavery politics. Charlotte Ray, while born in 1850, had the experience of her parents, Charles and H. Cordelia, by which to frame her aspirations. In both settings, women strategically drew upon male allies to further their interests. Churchwomen had long used sympathetic men to get their petitions before all-male governing bodies. Ray turned to one of her law professors, Alfred Riddle, to move her admission to the bar. Riddle was a likely ally; he had been an antislavery activist, Republican congressman, and women's rights advocate since the 1850s.[24] Finally, as churches served as public sites for rethinking of the woman question, Howard Law School appears to have served a similar purpose. In the late 1860s and early 1870s, the faculty, which included Albert Riddle, was led by John Mercer Langston, the 1849 Oberlin College graduate who had taken part in the early antebellum black political conventions that admitted women. Among Ray's classmates were Mary Ann

Shadd Cary, who would work alongside Ray as a National Woman Suffrage Association activist, and D. Augustus Straker, who, like Dean John Mercer Langston, would by the early 1870s become an outspoken advocate of women's suffrage.[25]

The Rights of Churchwomen

Debates surrounding the office of the stewardess exposed that gender neutrality did not prevail in Methodist churches. In 1872, at the same General Conference that granted women the right to vote for trustees, AME Church leaders created the office of the stewardess, authorizing local congregations to designate between three and nine women to sit as a board.[26] In 1876, the AME Zion Church followed suit, though in that denomination the stewardesses were to be appointed by the quarterly, or regional, conference.[27] In the CME Church, the first time the office was proposed in 1882 it was reported to have "produced laughter," which was punctuated by the tabling of the matter.[28] Three General Conferences over the course of eight years deliberated the issue before the proposal was finally approved.[29]

Ambivalence about women's religious authority shaped the final terms by which stewardesses were recognized. While the title might suggest that the office was equivalent to the long-standing office of steward, the authority extended to women was hardly equivalent to that of their male counterparts. Stewards were, by church law, aids to local ministers, while stewardesses were assigned to work "in assisting the preacher's steward in providing the necessary comfort for the minister."[30] They were envisioned as assistants to the minister's assistants or a sort of ladies' auxiliary to the stewards.[31] In some cases, their appointments could not be made locally, requiring confirmation by a quarterly conference; in others, women were made accountable to the stewards, who could "confirm or reject the nomination of the stewardesses; and hold them responsible for a faithful performance of their duty."[32] Such strictures delimited women's authority within the church. Still, the establishment of the office of the stewardess gave women formal recognition for the work they had long performed in local congregations. It enhanced their visibility, increased their authority, and, for some, raised questions about where these changes in women's roles might lead.

Despite the careful crafting of church law, some commentators feared unintended change. For example, the AME Church's *Christian Recorder* published a commentary asking whether offices such as that of stewardess would ultimately lead to a political end—woman suffrage—or to women "taking hold" and "speaking" in religious gatherings.[33] When attempting to appoint a board of stewardesses in a local congregation, the Reverend Henry McNeal Turner recognized the ambivalences expressed both in the wording of the new law and in the commentary that surrounded it. The stewards in his congregation refused to approve his female nominees until he threatened the men with removal. For the women, Turner had nothing but praise. They were "worth more than all the male officers put together," he offered, a remark that hinted at the feared consequences of such an innovation.[34] While men might retain the authority to pass on the selection of stewardesses, once appointed, women might prove themselves to be equally effective, or even superior, leaders.

Female missionary societies faced similar challenges. At the fore of this change was the AME Church, which created the Women's Parent Mite Missionary Society in 1874.[35] The AME Zion Church founded the Ladies' Home and Foreign Missionary Society in 1880,[36] and the CME Church authorized its Women's Missionary Society in 1890.[37] Like the stewardesses, female missionary leaders remained subject to male oversight. In some cases, members were elected from among those women who were perceived to be most loyal to the male leadership, the "wives and daughters of our bishops and elders, and other influential ladies of our churches." Other churches deprived women of a final say over missionary affairs. Governing boards, comprised of male ministers, oversaw women's work, or bylaws required the election of men to governing boards.[38]

Missionary societies were a double-edged sword for women seeking religious authority. The terms by which the societies were founded recognized the work women had long performed while extending women's control over fund-raising and outreach work. This expansion of the church's hierarchy was a tribute to women's church contributions and offered them an unprecedented opportunity to exercise leadership and independence. One AME Church commentator termed such societies the "woman movement" of the church, conveying the political sensibilities that were embodied in church practices.[39] However, the terms under which missionary societies were constituted also reflected ambivalence about the claims women were making on church authority. Women could for the first time serve as officers, speak from the podium, and preside over the proceedings at church conferences. They could conduct fund-raising and relief work pursuant to a constitution and bylaws, rather than at the discretion of male leaders. Yet the very constitutions and bylaws that guaranteed their authority also ensured the work of female missionary societies would remain subject to male supervision.

Not all divisions were between men and women in such matters. Women clashed with one another, revealing history's fault lines that were drawn between North and South. It was not the woman question itself that divided women but rather tensions that grew out of divisions between those from the North and those from the South. In the AME Church, for example, women initially operated under the auspices of the Women's Parent Mite Missionary Society. Northern women dominated the work of this organization and increasingly directed its work toward foreign, non-U.S. missions. By the early 1890s, the South's female church activists sought to counter this foreign mission agenda and to renew the church's effort to address the needs of African Americans in their region. They had the assistance of a male ally, Henry McNeal Turner, who paved the way for the founding of the Women's Home and Foreign Missionary Society. The women in Turner's family, all southerners, emerged as leaders in this competing missionary society and successfully established branches throughout the denomination in the coming years.[40]

It is unlikely that many churchwomen were surprised to encounter resistance as they began to vote, hold office, and take part in deliberative bodies. Little was new about that given the opposition they had encountered historically. There was something new, however. Women now operated pursuant to law and claimed their new roles as part of their rights as religious activists. They did not yet possess "the same rights in the church as men." Still, churchwomen used the new laws to insert themselves into the deliberations of decision-making bodies and withstand assaults on their authority.

Challenges multiplied going into the 1880s. No longer mere subjects of proceedings, being thanked for serving a meal or raising funds, churchwomen were regularly serving as conference delegates. For example, Amanda Beatty served as a secretary of the AME Zion West Tennessee and Mississippi Conference in 1884.[41] Beatty's service in her local conference led to her election as a "fraternal delegate" to the church's regional meeting held in Memphis the following year. While the conference minutes reported that it was a male ally, "Brother W. L. Carr," who nominated Beatty to her new post, among those present during her election were female allies: Nannie Riddick, who had earlier in the year been elected conference clerk, and the officers of the Ladies' Home and Foreign Missionary Society.[42]

The combination of law and well-placed male allies mattered. For example, controversy ensued when, during an 1885 meeting of the AME Zion Church Baltimore District Conference, Presiding Elder William Howard Day appointed Selena Bungay of Washington, D.C., to the committee that would determine the presiding elder's salary. Bungay's opponents insisted that, as a mere Sabbath school delegate, she should be "rejected from being appointed on any business of the conference." Day defended Bungay's right to sit on the committee, reasoning that his action was fully in accordance with church law, though when he finally prevailed, it was by way of a sarcastically worded resolution: "We bow with humble submission to the decision of the Presiding Elder and beg him to appoint sister Selena Bungay."[43] Changes in church law enabled duly appointed female officers and their allies to resist challenges to women's leadership.

Missionary society leadership opened the door to seats as conference officers. As early as 1880, officers of the AME Church's Mite Missionary Society appeared as conference officers delivering reports on their endeavors.[44] Female missionary society leaders soon returned to the conferences that had authorized their endeavors pleading for ministerial support. The women reported meeting with deeply held indifference, and even some outright hostility, from ministers, much of which was attributable to lingering hostility to the women's new authority. Their assessment was confirmed by male leaders, such as AME Zion's Bishop Singleton Jones, who told his General Conference that female missionary societies "were greatly hindered last year in consequence of a want of cooperation on the part of the brethren . . . that is, to come down to plain English, they did not encourage their sisters in their praiseworthy effort."[45] Jones's alliance with the female activists likely stemmed, in part, from his marriage to Mary Jane Talbert Jones, the society's first president.[46] Women's reliance upon male allies was a well-proven strategy. Yet the newfound power of women's standing as conference officers gave them access to the podium, where they made their own case for the value of female missionary work.

Some women adopted a deferential posture. Such was the case with Catherine Thompson, who was born in the 1840s in Lehigh County, Pennsylvania, and married to the Reverend Joseph Thompson. As treasurer of the AME Zion Ladies' Home and Foreign Missionary Society, Thompson beseeched the ministers: "Help us! Help us! dear brethren, by your cooperation, and we will try, under God, to do what we can to make the missionary work of our church a grand success."[47] Others, like AME Zion vice president Jane Hamer, offered reassurances to those who might misunderstand the women's assertions as somehow disloyal to the church. "I am for Zion," she pledged.[48] Still others lay the blame for the limited success of missionary work at the feet of uncooperative male ministers. In the AME Church, Mrs. S. C. Watson of the New Jersey Conference offered her analysis of the situation: "I do not blame the ladies for this. The fault is with the ministers. They do not like to have the society organized in their charges. . . . I hope brethren you will get out of the ladies' way and let them work."[49] Watson's solution was to ask the bishops to "make it binding on every minister to be compelled to see to it that this society is organized in this charge."[50]

It was ill-advised to leave the fate of missionary societies in the hands of men in the view of Eliza Gardner. Cloaked in discouragement, Gardner stepped to the podium at her church's 1884 General Conference to champion women's missionary endeavors. Earlier in the session, she had witnessed an effort to limit the rights of churchwomen. Two ministerial delegates had put forth a proposal that read: "Resolved, That females have all the rights and immunities of males, except the rights of orders and of the pastorate. They may be licensed as evangelists."[51] Though this measure failed, it prompted Gardner to craft a response that was neither deferential nor reassuring. Gardner made explicit the political underpinnings of women's quests for religious authority: "I do not think I felt quite so Christian-like as my dear sisters. I come from old Massachusetts, where we have declared that all, not only men, but women, too, are created free and equal, with certain inalienable rights which men are bound to respect." The rights of churchwomen were bound up with equality and freedom, as provided for in the constitution of her home state, and they were an extension of the "inalienable rights" provided for in the Declaration of Independence. In a twist on Supreme Court justice Roger Taney's notorious pronouncement in *Dred Scott v. Sanford*, Gardner claimed for churchwomen rights that "men *were* bound to respect."[52]

Female missionary societies were but one chapter in the great history of African Americans and their churches, Gardner urged. The struggle for women's rights had been born alongside "other good movements" dear to black Methodists, including "temperance reform and the antislavery cause." Here she cast churchwomen's struggles as part and parcel of the "good" cause of women's rights. A wrong outcome would put the church's standing in broader circles at risk, she explained: "If I would go back to Boston and tell the people that some of the members of this conference were against the women, it might have a tendency to prejudice our interests in that city with those upon whom we can rely for assistance." She concluded by proposing a bargain in which women would promote the good standing of the church in return for the support and respect of male leaders: "If you will try to do by us the best you can . . . you will strengthen our efforts and make us a power; but if you commence to talk about the superiority of men, if you persist in telling us that after the fall of man we were put under your feet and that we are intended to be subject to your will, we cannot help you in New England one bit."[53] Gardner cast these disputes not in terms of influence or rights but in terms of power. By the mid-1880s, churchwomen like Gardner understood their struggles to be part of black women's broader claims for public power and authority. The tenor of the woman question debate was shifting, with conciliation and ambivalence often replaced by confrontation and acrimony.

Gardner's threat was not an idle one. Black Methodist leaders knew well the case of Amanda Berry Smith, an itinerant preacher, who in the mid-1870s had left the ranks of the AME Church to work in support of white Christian endeavors. Smith was criticized for depriving black Americans, "those who need it most," of her skills and of her tremendous capacity to raise funds for AME missionary endeavors.[54] Gardner and other black female activists in New England were also organizing secular women's clubs.[55] As they met with resistance in religious institutions, black churchwomen helped construct alternative sites for their public ambitions. In turn, they used the confidence and collective sensibilities that grew out of secular organizations to assert their standing as religious leaders.

Black Baptist activists were confronting analogous changes. By the late 1870s, that denomination's female activists had emerged as visible participants in the formal proceedings of black Baptist associations. The Baptists' decentralized structure differed from more centralized and hierarchical Methodist bodies. Yet, at their core, the gendered struggles among African American Baptists in the 1870s and 1880s were the same as those of their Methodist counterparts: What would the relationship of women be to the denomination's sites of power and authority? In the immediate post–Civil War period, black Baptist leaders initiated a succession of statewide gatherings that grew into a discernible convention movement by the 1880s. Initially, women were shadowy figures in the records of these proceedings. They were objects of concern, as male leaders established widow's funds to support the wives and children of deceased ministers. By the late 1870s, black Baptist women were participating in conventions as missionary fund-raisers and public speakers. By the mid-1880s, female Sunday school teachers and missionary agents served as convention delegates, members of governing committees, and speakers.[56]

Two developments were key as Baptist women moved into previously all male spaces. The first, as historian Evelyn Brooks Higginbotham explains, was the development of a "female talented tenth." Women who were educated in the South's new institutions of higher learning, notably Spelman Seminary (later Spelman College) in Atlanta, operated mother's training schools and social service programs, taught Sunday school, raised funds, and in the process constructed women's networks among local congregations. At the same time, as historian Anthea Butler describes, poor and working women entered public culture through their associations with Baptist-sponsored Bible Bands. Begun by missionary activists, black and white, to bring literacy and Christianity to formerly enslaved women, the Bible Bands were vehicles for literacy, empowerment, and autonomy.[57] The women who appeared at state and regional conventions traced the roots of their activism to education, whether through higher learning or Bible study.

The form that their campaigns for rights took differed between Baptist and Methodist women. These distinctions reflected the denominations' contrasting institutional structures. Baptist women never appear to have made claims for formal office, such as licensed preacher, stewardess, or ordained minister. Perhaps they did not find it necessary to do so. Among Baptists, most authority, including that of electing pastors, resided with local congregations where women had long exerted significant influence. Among Methodists, power was situated in centralized and hierarchal bodies, and officeholding was often a prerequisite to power. Also, the tradition of preaching women, although unsanctioned, was much stronger among Methodist women than it was among Baptists. As Baptist women enjoyed a significant measure of power without asserting claims to formal office, Methodist women had reason to seek formal recognition.

In both denominations, women seeking to expand their roles within the church called upon influential male allies. William J. Simmons stands out among Baptists. A former slave, Reconstruction-era politician, author, and educator, Simmons encouraged and worked alongside the church's most visible female activists. Support of male leaders remained important when men who were uncomfortable with or felt threatened by women's new roles impugned their womanhood.[58]

Black churchwomen's identities as Baptists or Methodists meant that white churchwomen's activism was often a touchstone. They were *religious* activists, a view that linked them to their white counterparts. Debates about Methodist and Baptist polity and practice crossed racial lines, and in some cases these transracial denominational identities brought black and white activist women into contact. Historians have variously characterized these relations as cooperative, adversarial, and mutually dependent, and there is evidence enough to sustain each of these interpretations. However, as we explore the elements that shaped black women's ideas about their rightful place in the church, the fact rather than the quality of cross-racial contact is key. Black Baptist women encountered white Baptist women when the latter came to the South as missionaries.[59] Women of the CME Church knew their counterparts in the white Methodist Episcopal Church, South, through their shared home mission work.[60] Black and white women learned about one another's activities through the church-sponsored press. Black Methodist women may well have heard how two women designated to serve as associational delegates had been excluded from a Methodist Episcopal Church meeting in Arkansas.[61]

Churchwomen's Many Publics

The woman question debate cut dramatically across lines of race and religiosity. Black churchwomen did not need to look far to find echoes of their own struggles among white women in both church and politics. There was the debate within the white-led Methodist Episcopal Church (North) over the licensing of female preachers and the ordination of women, which culminated in the denial of women's right to sit as delegates in the General Conference in 1888. Most noted in this struggle by black Methodist activists was Maggie Newton Van Cott. The AME Church's *Christian Recorder* followed Van Cott's tribulations in the Methodist Church with an attention to detail that evidenced how black Methodists understood themselves to be, in part, Methodists across racial lines. The intersection of race and gender in Van Cott's case simultaneously transcended and reified the racial divide among Methodists. The *Recorder* noted, for example, that African Americans had been restricted to the sanctuary's galleries when Van Cott spoke at a New Orleans Methodist Church.[62] AME activists praised Van Cott—Bishop A. W. Wayman dubbed her "the great female evangelist."[63] Even as they were standing at the threshold of their own protracted contest over the same issue, AME activists expressed regret when the Methodist Episcopal Church (North) denied Van Cott's eligibility for the deaconate.[64] Black Baptist women likely saw threads of their own contests over gender and power as they observed Free Will Baptist women being ordained in the 1870s.[65] In all, African American churchwomen knew that their own struggles over the parameters of religious authority paralleled those being waged by their white counterparts.

Black churchwomen's demands sat uneasily alongside the demands of the National Woman Suffrage Association (NWSA) led by Susan Anthony and Elizabeth Stanton. During its January 1874 convention, the NWSA adopted a set of resolutions, the terms of which were a perverted take on the rights being sought by black churchwomen. The intersection of race and gender was complex. While urging the adoption of Charles Sumner's civil rights bill in Congress, the NWSA penned its own civil rights agenda, this one for women. Women's rights were awkwardly set up alongside the rights of African American men, and the convention called upon Congress to adopt "a civil rights bill for [women's] protection . . . that shall secure to them equally with colored men all the advantages and opportunities of life." This resolution may have struck a dissonant cord with black women, who likely heard the rights of black men being set up against the rights of women. However, the terms of the convention's fifth resolution likely elicited sympathy from black churchwomen. It demanded that women be "admitted to all theological seminaries on equal terms with colored men; to be recognized in all religious organizations as bishops, elders, priests, deacons; to officiate at the altar and preach in the pulpits of all churches, orthodox or heterodox; and that all religious sects shall be compelled to bring their creeds and biblical interpretations into line with the divine idea of the absolute equality of women with the colored men of the nation."[66] Here were expressly political white women, in a sense, signing on to much the same agenda as black female church activists. The rights of churchwomen were understood to be central to women's rights generally in this period, even among women such as Stanton and Anthony, for whom political enfranchisement was their first priority.

The reactions of male church leaders combined praise, lament, and denial. They were called upon to make sense of churchwomen's newfound authority as they represented their institutions in broader circles of church and state. Among such men was AME Church activist Benjamin Arnett, who eloquently grappled with his ambivalences. Arnett had spent his early years in Ohio, working as a teacher and itinerant minister. After the Civil War, his activism blossomed, encompassing a breadth of interests that few rivaled. Arnett rose to the station of bishop within the AME Church while extending his efforts far beyond religious institutions. Arnett took up politics, serving black state and national equal rights leagues and colored conventions, as well as the Republican Party. He was an ambitious organizer, helping to establish numerous benevolent, temperance, and fraternal societies, along with Sunday schools. By the mid-1880s, the woman question was frequently among his topics as he addressed a broad range of organizations.[67]

Arnett was a minister first, always cloaked as such by his garb or his honorific, Reverend. This performance of his standing and respectability enhanced the power and persuasiveness of his ideas. Arnett carried the church with him into a broad array of public venues. In doing so, he contributed to the cross-fertilization that shaped debates about the woman question. Through the 1870s and 1880s, Arnett attended the conferences at which black Methodists negotiated new roles for churchwomen, and, as a regular editor of conference minutes, he followed the related exchanges. As Arnett stepped to the podium in secular settings, the church debates in which he was involved echoed through his remarks.

Arnett always tailored his commentary to the character of his audience. For example, when speaking before a conference of white Methodist Episcopal Church (North) leaders in Baltimore, Arnett boasted about the innovations within his African American sect. His purpose that day was to encourage support for institutions of higher education for black women, and he used the new authority that churchwomen enjoyed in the AME Church to make his case. Arnett explained how his church had met the challenges of Reconstruction: "When we have no men to be officers of the church, we put in women. We have made them stewards, class-leaders, exhorters and [Bible] band leaders. Whenever they could be used for the good of the cause we have used them."[68] Here, Arnett promoted the enhancements in churchwomen's standing as proof of his denomination's resourcefulness and freedom from counterproductive gender conventions. Of course, Arnett was mindful that the white Methodist Episcopal Church leaders in his audience had confronted the same claims by their churchwomen. He implied that the AME Church leadership had deftly handled the woman question—a claim that was more hopeful than accurate, since a few years later the church divided over ordaining women to the ministry.

He took a different approach in political circles. As the elected representative from Green County, Arnett addressed the Ohio House of Representatives in 1886. He took the floor to call for the repeal of that state's "black laws."[69] African Americans in Ohio faced degradations in many forms, including separate railcars and schools and exclusion from the "jury box and the ballot box." In a speech that dramatically retold U.S. history as a long progression toward racial justice, Arnett urged the state's Republican leadership to do away with these remaining marks of slavery. One qualification was necessary, however: Arnett made clear that he was not advocating the right of African American men to marry white women, deflecting those who might brand him a miscegenationist. Nor, he continued, was he opening the door to white men who might "tamper with the virtue of our daughters." He "preferred" African American women, Arnett explained: "I have a pride for the women of my race." Here, we get a glimpse of Arnett's thinking about the churchwomen with whom he now shared leadership: they, like men, had endured all the degradations of enslavement. Arnett then shifted focus, directing his remarks to African American men: "My advice is to stand by our women, our sisters, our mothers, our daughters and our wives." Why? Because, he concluded, such devotions would produce "a generation of wise, intelligent, virtuous, industrious and loving women, who will be crowned jewels of the race, and models of womanhood in the commonwealth and christianity." In this setting, black churchwomen bolstered Arnett's claim that in seeking to have the "black laws" repealed, he was not acting out a desire for white women; black women were *women* enough for Arnett. Churchwomen were a source of race pride, demonstrating through their purity and virtue how far African Americans had already traveled from the degradations of slavery. Finally, Arnett set a course for the future. Through the production of "wise, intelligent, virtuous and loving women" the interests of the "race," the "commonwealth," and "christianity" would be served. Essential to Arnett's claim were women such as those of the AME Church; their public activism powerfully evidenced the qualities he most celebrated.[70]

Arnett had a third point of view to offer fraternal order leaders. When Arnett addressed Cincinnati's Grand United Order of Odd Fellows in 1884, he offered an analysis of a public culture in which authority was shared between the sexes. Only respectable women who conformed to his notion of "true womanhood" could expect to share in this collective enterprise, however. Arnett lauded the Odd Fellows for creating a female auxiliary, the Household of Ruth, in 1857, pronouncing this "modern invention" a "decided improvement." "We welcome the celestial intervention of women" who had proven themselves to be a "durable element of strength and success" and "an important adjunct to our order." (Arnett did not remark that it had taken his church two decades to avail itself of this source of "strength and success.") Arnett was deeply invested in female respectability and admonished the women present to follow the "illustrious examples" of biblical women such as Rebekah, Manoah, Sisera, Hannah, Naomi, Miriam, and Dorcas—modest, graceful, pious, devoted, zealous, courageous, self-sacrificing, noble, high-minded, generous, brave, and loving. These were, in Arnett's analysis, both "domestic and public virtues."[71] His tone suggested that the Odd Fellows' accommodation to women's public aspirations had been an easy and natural development, although we know that fraternal associations long excluded women from their ranks. In crafting an idealized fraternal past, Arnett sought to legitimate an ideal and impose it on the future. Respectability might enable black women to occupy visible positions in public culture, as officers of women's fraternal or religious auxiliaries, but he also hoped that respectability would minimize whatever tensions authority shared between men and women produced.

Fraternal orders had not escaped the woman question, Arnett's remarks demonstrate. Black Americans in secret societies were rethinking the relationship of gender to power. The Masons created a formal role for women with the founding of the Order of the Eastern Star in 1874. We know little about the circumstances under which these women's auxiliaries were established. What little we know about the 1874 founding of the Mason's Order of the Eastern Star has been gleaned from early institutional histories. Thornton A. Jackson established the first chapter of the order, the Queen Esther Chapter No. 1, in Washington, D.C., in August 1874. A barber, Howard University Medical College student, and lifelong Masonic activist, Jackson supported the proposal originated by Martha Welch and Georgiana Thomas, in whose home the first meeting was held. By 1890, statewide Grand Chapters of the Order of the Eastern Star had been established in North Carolina, Tennessee, California, Kansas, Louisiana, Kentucky, Ohio, Indiana, Michigan, Texas, Illinois, and Missouri. Many of the women associated with the order had religious affiliations, so innovations taking place in the church were connected to this development. White Masons and Odd Fellows had already founded female auxiliaries; white Odd Fellows founded the Daughters of Rebekah in 1851, and white Masons established the Order of the Eastern Star in 1868. Yet, as Theda Skocpol and Jennifer Oser suggest, the subsequent emergence of black women's auxiliaries was not imitative of white fraternal practices but demonstrated the distinct and "extraordinarily strong role" that women played in black fraternal groups.[72]

Were the forces that led to changes for black women in fraternal orders the same as those that had changed their standing in churches? It is difficult to say. There had long been anxiety in fraternal orders about the place of women. And religious activists certainly moved between churches and fraternal orders. Black women who supported the Masonic order had challenged the gendered conventions of fraternal orders by speaking at their gatherings and questioning their marginal standing even before the Civil War. As early as 1845, they had organized themselves into the Heroines of Jericho, a local women's auxiliary that operated in Philadelphia, Pittsburgh, and Chicago.[73] With the Civil War, this brand of female activism, like women's benevolent work, teaching, and public speaking, had become more visible. Henrietta Gilmour spoke "eloquently" at a Sharp Street Church gathering to honor a local Masonic lodge in 1866.[74] The Heroines of Jericho processed among the "various religious and moral associations" that marched in Pittsburgh's 1865 celebration of the Emancipation Proclamation, and were seated prominently "in front of the speaker's stand" while such luminaries as Lewis Woodson, Benjamin Tanner, and George Vashon expounded on the significance of the occasion.[75] In Chicago, Masonic women led public ceremonies at an 1865 gathering that "seemed to be entirely conducted by ladies." Women sold and collected the tickets, called the house to order, elected a woman, "Mrs. Blanks," president of the occasion, and produced a "beautiful silk flag" for the male members of the North Star Lodge. "Mrs. Sterrett" delivered the presentation speech. "Ruth," who reported on the occasion, noted with no hint of irony that the women "all seemed to understand themselves perfectly." Lest she leave the impression that the women were inattentive to more domestic concerns, Ruth concluded by noting that the evening closed with "sharp appetites . . . satisfied with the good things that had been bountifully provided by the ladies."[76]

The life of "Mrs. Blanks," who presided over the Chicago gathering, illustrates the multifaceted character of female activism in the post–Civil War years. Martha A. Blanks, who was often called Mrs. James Blanks, was born in Virginia around 1815. By 1850 she was living in Chicago with her husband, James, who was also from Virginia. As a free woman, Blanks operated a boardinghouse while her husband worked first as a laborer and by 1860 as a janitor. The Blanks were AME Church activists, making contributions to support the *Christian Recorder* and Wilberforce College while opening their home to visiting church dignitaries, leading one commentator to dub it "the minister's asylum."[77] Martha Blanks served as vice president of the Colored Ladies' Freedmen's Aid Society of Chicago and an officer of the Independent Order of Good Templars.[78] Women such as Martha Blanks, like the Reverend Benjamin Arnett, moved freely back and forth between religious and fraternal organizations.

Ambivalence continued to characterize the public face of male Masons on the woman question. The questioning was gentle. For example, an editorial in the *Christian Recorder* reported that Masons in the nation of Italy had welcomed women into the society's "memberships, its offices, and its honors" through "several Orders of Sister Masons, Venerables, and Great Mistresses." The brief item concluded with a curious query: "What will become of the 'secrets' of the system" if such reports were true? The comment suggested that women's admission to the order would undermine Masonry. Would female gossips fail to keep its secrets? Or were the secret rites so gendered that female members would necessarily destroy their coherence?

The prospect of new roles for women provoked the woman question in fraternal orders. Through their ambitions and through the openings that the Civil War offered, women like Martha Blanks modeled a version of female public activism that touched the lives of hundreds, if not thousands, of black activists in the post–Civil War era.[79]

Locating the Woman's Era

The 1890s have long been termed the "woman's era." The phrase was coined by African American women who promoted the idea within their own communities and eventually extended it to the nation as a characterization of their pubic lives. Among the first to publicly invoke this idea was Frances Ellen Watkins Harper, when commenting in 1893 upon the exclusion of African Americans from the World's Columbian Exposition in Chicago. Change was in the air, she informed her audience, and they should envision themselves as "on the threshold of woman's era."[80]

A great deal was new in the 1890s. When African American women in Boston joined together to form a club for the purpose of "uplifting" the race in 1893, they named their enterprise "The New Era Club." What was *new* about the era was manifest when the club began publishing its nationally circulated newspaper, the *Woman's Era*. The same spirit was evidenced by churchwomen who promoted this notion; for example, black Baptist women titled their magazine the *Baptist Woman's Era*.

To invoke the woman's era was also to speak of aspirations. For Frances Ellen Watkins Harper and her peers, it was a call for what might be. These women were, in a sense, visionaries. Scores of local women's clubs successfully joined together to form the National Association of Colored Women in 1896. Black Methodists sanctioned the ordination of women to the ministry in 1898. Black Baptist women founded their own national convention in 1900.

But all that was new and all that was yet to be had its start in the 1870s and 1880s. Before they were club women, temperance organizers, antilynching crusaders, or suffragists, most female activists learned to navigate issues of gender and power in churches and fraternal orders. Their daughters had come of age watching women command public authority as teachers, organizers, public speakers, preachers, deaconesses, and Masonic mistresses. By the mid-1880s, the woman's era was well under way.

6

Too Much Useless Male Timber
*The Nadir, the Woman's Era, and
the Question of Women's Ordination*

Heads bowed for the opening benediction at the First National Conference of the Colored Women of America. The voice of Eliza Ann Gardner, the meeting's chaplain, filled the hall. Seventy-three delegates from African American women's clubs in twenty-five states and the District of Columbia had come to Boston in 1895. Their purpose was to discuss "vital questions concerning our moral, mental, physical and financial growth and well-being." After spending three days deliberating an ambitious array of topics, including higher education, industrial training, justice, mental elevation, race literature, political equality, social purity, and temperance, the women resolved to meet again. This gathering laid the foundation for the National Association of Colored Women's Clubs.[1]

A female chaplain likely gave some delegates pause. Although preaching women were not unknown in black Christian circles, they rarely adopted such honorific titles as chaplain. Gardner's assumption of religious authority signaled the emergence of a cadre of assertive women at the highest levels of African American institutional life. Her own story chronicles the emergence of black women into public culture. Before the Civil War, Eliza Gardner learned female activism by example. Her mother was a committed church member, and the whole Gardner family joined the antislavery movement, opening their Boston home to fugitives and hosting many notable leaders, including William Lloyd Garrison, Wendell Phillips, and Frederick Douglass. Gardner's political sensibilities matured at the intersection of abolitionism and women's rights. A working woman, she supported herself as a dressmaker and later kept a boardinghouse.[2] Although Gardner worked for temperance reform, she made her mark in the church. As a young member of AME Zion's Daughters of Conference, she learned to navigate church politics under the tutelage of women of her mother's generation. In the post–Civil

War years, she garnered respect and admiration for her fund-raising abilities. Gardner spearheaded the movement that demanded licenses for female preachers, female leadership of missionary societies, the creation of the office of stewardess, and the ordination of women to the ministry. Eliza Gardner directly contributed to the transformation of black women's place in public culture. Her service as chaplain was a fitting culmination.[3]

Many and varied paths had led the women to Boston. Josephine St. Pierre Ruffin, who issued the meeting's call, entered public life during the Civil War, recruiting African American soldiers and working with the Contraband Relief Association out of her local Baptist church.[4] Ruffin embraced the movement for women's suffrage in the postwar decades as a member of the American Woman Suffrage Association and the Massachusetts School Suffrage Association. In the 1890s, she edited the *Woman's Era*, a monthly magazine.[5] Victoria Earle Matthews, church activist and delegate from Brooklyn, New York, was born a slave and had little formal education. Matthews initially worked as a domestic, but in the 1880s she embarked on a literary career as a freelance journalist.[6] Margaret Murray Washington was born in Macon, Georgia, in 1861, the daughter of a washerwoman (possibly an ex-slave) and an Irish immigrant whose name is unknown.[7] She attended Fisk University, where she edited the school paper and presided over more than one literary society. She became the lady principal at Tuskegee Institute, in Alabama, a position she held both before and after her marriage to the founding president, Booker T. Washington.[8]

These were the stories of black women's public culture. African American women came into their own in public life through active participation in reform movements, including antislavery, temperance, and women's rights. Education, be it in New England's public schools or the colleges of the Reconstruction-era South, was one of their key stepping stones. Through leadership roles in such institutions as churches, fraternal orders, and literary societies, they gained skills and earned the authority that their contributions demanded. Eliza Gardner might have been reluctant to admit how deeply these journeys were marked by hardship. Few black women entered public life free from the demands of work and family. They endured pointed ridicule, risked mob violence, and struggled to defend their respectability.

Both the "nadir" of race relations and the "woman's era" frame the outlines of this chapter. The tensions between these companion points of view on the 1890s led to new confrontations over gender and power. In churches, male activists looked to regain the measure of public authority they had formerly exercised in the political realm. Women's ambitions were once again tied to broader trends. The victories won in the preceding decades would come under assault, while their remaining aspirations, such as ordination to the ministry, would be thwarted as the optimism of Reconstruction was replaced by the disappointments of Jim Crow. Once again, ideas about manhood and womanhood were being constructed in relation to one another, and while men aggressively debated the woman question, they revealed their new anxieties about the nature of manhood in a world shaped by disfranchisement, segregation, and violence. Women emerged from the rancorous debates within churches into the club movement, creating new sites for autonomy and authority, and in turn reconfiguring African American public culture into a realm of deliberation and leadership shared by male and female activists.

The Rights and Wrongs of the Woman's Era

The disappointments of the nadir and the optimism of the woman's era were entangled with one another in the lives of African American activists.[9] The list of degradations was long. The collapse of Reconstruction, the imposition of white supremacy by legal and extralegal means, and the institutionalization of Jim Crow pushed African Americans to the margins of political power and the bottom rail of the social order. The disfranchisement plan that Mississippi adopted in 1890 served as a model for the rest of the South. Literacy tests, poll taxes, and other state election laws, along with economic sanctions and actual or threatened violence, forced black Americans out of the nation's political life. Black men lost the ballot and many other civil rights that the constitution and federal civil rights laws had briefly protected: the right to hold public office, to sit on juries, and to allocate tax dollars for schools and social services. Southern states imposed discriminatory laws that routinized the separate and inferior status of black citizens. Violence intimidated African Americans; more than 2,500 lynchings were recorded between 1884 and 1900. Segregation increasingly ordered employment, housing, public accommodations, schools, hospitals, and even cemeteries. In 1883 the Supreme Court declared unconstitutional the federal Civil Rights Act of 1875, a law prohibiting racial discrimination in places of public accommodation, and in 1896 gave its sanction to the "separate but equal" doctrine in *Plessy v. Ferguson*. In this hostile environment, black communities turned inward, no longer looking to the federal government for protection. Independent African American churches reemerged as key settings for discussion and debate.[10]

The spirit of the woman's era was optimism and accomplishment. American women heralded the removal of legal and attitudinal barriers to women's property rights, education, and the suffrage. Black women worked together in religious associations, secular women's clubs, missionary societies, and fraternal auxiliaries, gaining independence and influence. Indeed, the impetus for women's increasingly public activism came out of an express desire to combat pointed attacks on African American womanhood.[11]

If the nadir was the problem, the woman's era was the solution. In an essay titled "A Woman's View on Current Topics," AME Zion Church member May Brown discussed the "race problem" and queried, "What will the Negro of the United States do to gain just and merited recognition?" As Brown aptly characterized the situation, "Affairs are now reaching a climax. The whites are struggling to retain the supremacy. The Negroes are struggling for right and justice." But if the problem, as Brown saw it, lay in the deterioration of race relations, the solution would be found through the ethos of the woman's era. "The women cannot, must not, dare not be idle," she urged. Brown delivered an ambitious charge to her "own women," who must prepare to "read, to study, to keep . . . abreast with the thoughts of the day . . . take part in the social, religious, philanthropic and intellectual subjects which have never been found so exacting or so diffuse as now."[12] Writing in 1891, Brown was still hopeful, seeing women's activism as a weapon in the battle against the "race problem." However, by the turn of the twentieth century, such optimism was tempered. As the power and authority of black men within public culture was increasingly constrained, it became more difficult for black women to imagine their lives as unfettered by gendered boundaries. Churchwomen, in particular, found their expanding authority challenged even as they were asserting decisive influence through the independent club women's movement.

By 1892, the sites of women's public work had increased many times over. They could pursue their interests in civil rights and racial uplift not only under the familiar auspices of churches and fraternal orders but also through local women's clubs.[13] From the 1895 founding of the Colored Women's League of Washington, D.C., the movement spread quickly through the nation. The organizational and leadership skills developed in women's church societies served as the building blocks of the club movement, as churchwomen came together by way of their preexisting networking and fundraising endeavors.[14]

A politics of racial uplift through collective self-help guided the club movement. Black club women came together in the belief that they could solve the "race problem." Some clubs focused on improving the skills and intellectual capabilities of their members, while others aimed their programs at poor and working-class black families, offering lessons in domestic skills and child rearing. Club members visited jails, conducted Sunday schools, ran children's picnics and parties, and helped with funeral expenses and the finding of new homes. They sponsored lectures, held cooking and sewing classes, ran night schools, and founded kindergartens. They battled gambling and liquor consumption and sponsored employment agencies and homes for young women.[15] Historian Stephanie Shaw describes these clubs as an extension of black women's Civil War–era voluntarism. But, in the woman's era, women who served the race increasingly sought independence from male authority.

Still, the origins of the club movement were in the degradations of the nadir. For too long black women's claims to respectable womanhood had been undermined by innuendo and invective. In their call for a convention in 1895, the women of Boston's New Era Club singled out James Jacks, then president of the Missouri Press Association, for his especially egregious attacks on black womanhood. Writing in the *Montgomery Standard*, Jacks had ridiculed Ida B. Wells and her antilynching campaign and then impugned all black women, branding them prostitutes, thieves, and liars.[16] The meeting's call declared that Jacks's letter demonstrated "how pressing is the need of our banding together if only for our protection."[17] Jacks's vitriol tied the "progress of the race to the morality of its women."[18] Black women had long suffered similar assaults on their respectability from male leaders.[19]

Black women continued to be the targets of derisive entertainment. The minstrelsy industry deployed well-worn tactics to draw audiences and garner sales for the publishing endeavors that it fed. *Brudder Gardner's Stump Speeches and Comic Lectures*, published in 1884, brought minstrelsy into the homes of those Americans who were kept away from the theaters by distance or by social propriety. This satirical book was credited to Thomas Carey, whose other works included collections of wit, humor, and puns and instruction manuals for recitation and debating, grammar, social and business writing, word usage, real estate, and law. Carey's parody of African American public culture featured "Brudder Gardner," a buffoon esteemed by black Americans. In a stump speech layered with social meanings, Carey portrayed Gardner declaring himself a woman—"bein' ez I am a woman myself"—and then delivering a speech on "Woman's Rights." Carey's intention here is not entirely transparent. Did his black male protagonist become a woman through taking up women's rights, or was he feminized by his racial oppression? Was the humor of the piece enhanced by having Gardner deliver his speech in drag? In any case, black women were implicated; perhaps their claim to rights as women undermined the masculinity of their male allies, or perhaps they were so unfeminine that they might be portrayed as men.

Minstrelsy's ideas had changed. Women's continued exclusion from politics occupied center stage, as Carey's invention lamented the exclusion of black women from "votin'," "the ballit," "Congris," "givernin'," and "'lechshun nite" festivities. He stated their aspirations pointedly: "I want to assoom thet speer wich nacher fitted me fur ekally with man, but from whch maskeline jellasy hez thus fur exclooded me." Brudder (Sister?) Gardner closed with a jab at the antebellum purveyors of such ideas: "Mrs. Swissheld; there's Lucy Stone, and Anna Dickinson; there's Lucretia Mott, and Mrs. Jinks, all uv whom showed thet women cood seese to be women, and be ez neer men ez nacher allowed them. Thet's what all our sex want—to be ez neer men ez possible."[20] This mean-spirited satire concluded with the view that black women who claimed such rights ceased to be women, a characterization wholly compatible with Jacks's argument.

Even respected members of the law and business communities were drawn into the production of minstrelsy's ideas. In *Shantytown Sketches* (1898), Anthony J. Drexel Biddle, a Philadelphian of property, standing, and privilege, dabbled in writing humor that rivaled Carey in ridiculing black activists. A wealthy publisher, lecturer, and evangelist, Biddle did not single out African Americans for special derision; they, along with European immigrants, constituted the "lower" rung of society, all suitable as targets of his humor. His stories were "told in the dialects of the various divisions of the lower five. . . . His Irish men are real Irishmen, and talk like Irishmen, and his Germans never for get where they came from." Despite his self-description as "a traveler and a man of science," Biddle adopted the conventions of minstrelsy with no hint of irony. Among Biddle's sketches was a caricature of an African American organization he dubbed the "Watermelon Patch Debating Society."[21]

Biddle lampooned women's rights through the images of "Brother Philander," a member of the Watermelon Patch Society, and "Mr. Speak Easy," a guest representing the "Anti-Blumer Club." For Biddle, as with many writers of the minstrelsy genre, faux dialect was only the beginning of the joke. These men's ignorance of English usage had serious consequences. When Philander recited a poem—"De woman's rights women. Dey has but one song: Dey wants all der rights, an' Dey want to right wrong"—Speak Easy objects to his opponent having changed the topic to penmanship: "Did I not understahn' mah worthy rival to say that the ladies possessed the desire to write wrong?" The reader is drawn into the joke through a "misunderstanding" that is made all the more plain through the written word. Do the women want to "right" wrong, or "write" wrong? In Biddle's view, the likely answer was both; that is, they might want to correct the injustices to which they were subjected, but they would also likely "write" just as "wrong" as their counterparts spoke. Black women were not spared from caricature. A "fat, old woman . . . nodded her wooly head approvingly," and numerous others in the audience "screamed in their enthusiasm and delight" upon hearing Philander's verse. Finally, on the brink of a melee, the chair explained, "yo' know de motto ob ouh society is 'Woman's Rights.' " Advising that "Ah reckon dat we can't keep calm," he finally persuades Speak Easy to "call de 'bating off fo' dis ebein'," and a semblance of order is restored. African American public culture was represented as peopled with individuals with empty, ridiculous pretensions toward middle-class respectability, echoing the criticism made seventy years earlier when artist Edward Clay parodied the manners and dress of free black Philadelphians.[22]

Much of the power of these pieces lay in the blurring of boundaries between black and white, high and low, city and country, North and South. The manipulation of ideas about manhood and womanhood was critical to their success. Men dressed as women and women behaved like men; women's rights wreaked havoc on a community that was already overreaching in its public aspirations. Black activists generally remained silent in the face of such imagery. Perhaps this turning away was a type of rebuke. Implicit in the club women's more direct challenge to men such as Jacks was a rebuke of minstrelsy's long-standing denigrations. Black women claimed respectability by donning authority in public culture.

Black activists also took up print culture of a different sort, hoping to advance their own view of the woman question. By the mid-1880s, under institutional and entrepreneurial auspices, black leaders published scores of histories, treatises, and collective biographies aimed at promoting an alternative view of black public culture that depicted its activists as learned, respectable, and effective. Church activists penned denominational histories; writers chronicled the black past; African American achievements in journalism, education, and business were enumerated; and authors memorialized the lives of "notable" and "distinguished" individuals.

These works offered a counternarrative about African American history and culture that challenged both the popular images and the political degradations of the early Jim Crow era. They served as vehicles for defining a distinctly African American public culture, as authors detailed the parameters, as well as the worth, of separate churches, schools, publications, social and fraternal organizations, and political culture. Although many of these texts drew upon writings produced over the preceding half-century, they were forward-looking enterprises intended to situate African American intellectual life among broader trends, including such emerging fields as history and ethnology.[23] These texts acknowledged that this was "the woman's era," featuring women as visible, authoritative leaders in a wide range of public roles. Gone were the days when men, because they dominated institutions, commanded the discussion. The words of African American women resounded through the pages of these publications.

Women had been represented quite differently in earlier writings about African American history and culture. AME Church bishop Benjamin Tanner's *An Apology for African Methodism*, published in 1867, wove together a history of Christianity and people of African descent that justified those who "dared to organize a Church of men, men to think for themselves, men to talk for themselves, men to act for themselves."[24] As these words from his preface suggest, Tanner saw this as largely a men's saga, but he devoted the book's final chapter to "Influential Women in Communion with the AME Church." Tanner offers a decidedly conservative view of female church activists. Many were lauded first and foremost for their work as Christian wives and mothers; their homes were elegant, their children well tended to, and their demeanor subdued. Unmarried women served as teachers, writers, musicians, and vocalists. Devotion to the church was universal: Tanner featured fund-raisers, Sabbath school workers, beneficial society leaders, "sisters band" members, and mother's association organizers. Situating them firmly within the ideals of domesticity and true womanhood, Tanner underscored churchwomen's piety, earnestness, intelligence, modesty, and sweetness. Tanner's treatise was remarkable for its elisions, particularly its failure to acknowledge preaching women and the debates over their eligibility for ministerial licenses that erupted in his own denomination during the 1840s and early 1850s. He did not hint at the changes in women's public roles brought on by the Civil War, or the controversies surrounding the terms of the Fourteenth and Fifteenth Amendments that were brewing while he was completing this book. Tanner distinguished himself from many of his contemporaries by including women in his work, but this gesture did little more than promote a constrained view of women's standing in public culture.

Later texts registered the expansion of black women's public roles during and after the Civil War. They celebrated women's endeavors as physicians, dentists, lawyers, teachers and founders of institutions of higher learning, journalists and editors, missionary society directors, stewardesses in the church, temperance organizers, and artists. Some books set aside special chapters for women, as Tanner had done. I. Garland Penn's 1891 *The Afro-American Press and Its Editors* included a chapter dedicated to "Afro-American Women in Journalism," and G. F. Riching's *Evidences of Progress Among Colored People*, first published in 1896, contained a distinct chapter titled "Prominent Colored Women."[25] Books devoted exclusively to women's accomplishments constituted a new genre, drawing attention to women's contributions to public culture. Lawson Scruggs's *Women of Distinction: Remarkable in Works and Invincible in Character* (1893) offered over one hundred individual and institutional profiles;[26] Monroe Majors included nearly four hundred women in his *Noted Negro Women: Their Triumphs and Activities* (1893).[27] Susie Shorter's *Heroines of African Methodism* (1891) reprinted the author's remarks at the celebration of Bishop Daniel Payne's eightieth birthday.[28] This generation of African American women took up the pen themselves and limned their own representations.

According to literary scholar Hazel Carby, this period was distinguished by the proliferation of black women's writing, including Anna Julia Cooper's *A Voice from the South* and Ida B. Wells's *On Lynchings* (both 1892) and Gertrude Mossell's *The Work of the Afro-American Woman* (1894).[29] Scores of other black women were publishing their ideas in tracts and newspapers. Increasingly, male editors and compilers drew upon women's own writings for their representations of public women.

James Haley's *Afro-American Encyclopedia* (1895) exemplifies this practice.[30] Haley's tome, as its subtitle indicates, chronicled the "Thoughts, Doings, and Sayings of the Race, Embracing Lectures, Biographical Sketches, Sermons, Poems, Names of Universities, Colleges, Seminaries, Newspapers, Books, and a History of the Denominations." Among the one hundred "wisest and best" black Americans were nearly twenty-five women, many of whom were represented throughout the text (rather than in a discrete chapter) by their own writings. Mary Phelps, a teacher at Haines Normal and Industrial Institute in Augusta, Georgia, argued in "The Responsibility of Women as Teachers" that although women were not yet included in politics, their experience as educators might prepare them for that eventuality. Mrs. M. A. McCurdy, editor of the temperance newspaper *Woman's World*, maintained in "Duty of the State to the Negro" that while she insisted upon the state "doing its duty to the Negro (males)," the "thousands of women who are pleading today for equal franchise" must not be forgotten. Lucinda Gamble of Omaha, Nebraska, explained that the "emancipation of women" led to their becoming doctors, druggists, journalists, writers of prose, musicians, artists, social workers, and teachers.

The women included in Haley's book were not of one mind about what the parameters of their public lives might be, however. Some emphasized domesticity and respectability. Fannie Barrier Williams, who heralded the "growing power of women," still argued that their "opportunities and responsibilities" should focus upon domestic duties, self-help, and women's organizations. Others, such as Lillie Lovinggood of Birmingham, Alabama, defined "women's work in the education of the race" as encompassing home duties, teaching, the reform of modes of dress, maintaining social purity, teaching in industrial schools, and "professional and literary work." During the 1890s, an expanding array of public roles was being offered to women, and women themselves directed much of the discussion of their history and prospects.

Much of this burgeoning literature on African American history and culture was produced by religious writers. The woman question had concrete implications for denominational structures. Some male leaders used their texts as vehicles to debate the meaning of the changes in church law implemented during the 1870s and early 1880s; activists continued to disagree about the sorts of authority that should be accorded churchwomen. Other men and women activists held out these innovations as markers of denominational superiority; the standing of a religious institution, like that of the nation, was measured by the standing of its women, so the argument went.

In some cases, such texts were an opportunity to boast. AME Zion bishop James W. Hood described his denomination's elevation of female church members as evidence of the "black church's" superiority in his 1895 book, *One Hundred Years of the African Methodist Episcopal Zion Church; or, The Centennial of African Methodism*: "In Zion the black minister has shown the height to which he can rise respecting the rights of women when he is where there is nothing to hinder him from following his best convictions." Born in Pennsylvania, Hood had been politically active in North Carolina during Reconstruction. Hood explained that the changes in church law allowed women to serve as class leaders, superintendents of Sabbath schools, trustees, conference delegates, exhorters, and preachers. He claimed that his church was the "first" Methodist sect to grant women such authority. He argued that these changes demonstrated the strength of independent black denominations, comparing the "agitation" in the white-controlled Methodist Episcopal Church (North) over such questions with his church's straightforward amendments to church law. In Hood's view, women's enhanced religious authority was one answer to what he termed "the woman question." Echoing the principles that were articulated during the antebellum period, he declared: "Our idea is that we should not be hindered from using such instrumentalities as God is pleased to raise up, on account of sex."[31] Despite the assured tone of Hood's words, he left a great deal unsaid. The changes in women's religious authority of which he boasted had been controversial, and the woman question within his church was not settled.

Disagreements over the woman question within the AME Church animated the writings of Bishops Daniel Payne and Henry McNeal Turner. Turner first discussed the issue in his 1885 book, *The Genius and Theory of Methodist Polity*, which was structured as a series of questions and answers for those seeking to understand the internal workings of the denomination. Turner began by placing the debate in historical perspective, explaining that, although in the past women had been excluded from the ministry, such restrictions were deemed by "great scholars to be more upon the ground of inexpediency than divine disfavor."[32] Current AME law permitted women to be local trustees, stewardesses, deaconesses, and jurors in church tribunals.[33] Turner did not go so far as to advocate women's full ordination, although he later supported that position. But he came down squarely in favor of female preachers in an exchange that appears to be drawn from a conference debate:

> Q. Then do you mean to say that the action of the General Conference of 1884 recognizes female preachers, and gives them a legal standing in the A.M.E. Church, the same as local preachers, when licensed and doing evangelistic work?
>
> A. Yes; the language of the resolution is emphatic, applying to those then holding license and to such as may be licensed in the future, provided they hold membership in some Quarterly Conference.[34]

The argumentative tone of this exchange suggests that the licensing of female preachers, while settled in church law, remained a contentious issue among activists.

Payne refrained from making direct comment on Turner when he published his *History of the African Methodist Episcopal Church* six years later. But he did take up the matter of licensing women to preach. Rather than reporting upon the recent changes in church law (over which he had presided), the bishop reached into the past to recount how he had successfully thwarted such an innovation early in his ministerial career. Through his careful, though selective, retelling of the proceedings at the general conferences during the 1840s and early 1850s, Payne reminded his late-nineteenth-century readers that he had dissented from the findings of a church committee that appeared ready to grant women preaching licenses in 1848. Payne then described his first accomplishment as a newly elected bishop in 1852: settling the woman question by silencing the advocates of licensing female preachers for nearly fifteen years.[35] Ruling the issue out of order did not resolve it, however. The next confrontation concerned women's ordination to the ministry.

Religious Confrontations

Churchwomen were up front in the development of secular clubs. These settings, independent of ministerial scrutiny, offered them an opportunity to exercise authority that was still denied them within their religious institutions. Eliza Gardner of Boston's New Era Club and Victoria Earle Matthews of the Women's Loyal League of Brooklyn, New York, were among the notable AME Zion activists who founded autonomous women's groups.[36] As chaplain, Gardner provided spiritual leadership at the 1895 national meeting. Delivering the opening prayer was a responsibility traditionally reserved for male clergy members not only within the church but also in many women's organizations, so her invocation represented a striking innovation.[37] In the National Association of Colored Women (NACW), Gardner found a forum in which she could exercise the type of authority she had sought without success within the church. Victoria Matthews found an outlet for her skills of oratory and persuasion the following year, at the inaugural meeting of the National Federation of Afro-American Women. This convention, held in Washington, D.C., elected Matthews chair of the executive board and subsequently sponsored her public speaking tours as the group's national organizer.[38]

Church publications hailed the emergence of women's clubs in terms that, while consistent with the ethos of the woman's era, nonetheless hinted at the confrontations to come. A fall 1896 article in the *A.M.E. Zion Quarterly Review* heralded the meeting as "one of the most significant gatherings of the year." "Some of the best brains in this country" were connected with the organization, including Zion's own Victoria Matthews. The author exhorted: "It is to our womanhood that the race must look largely, if we would right long indulged wrongs, have long denied liberties assured, and fully justify the sacrifices made in the past in defense of manhood equality." The unintended but obvious contradiction in this language pointed to a central problem: women were called upon to defend "manhood" equality, not their own civil rights. This tension was deeply felt within the church: How could a male-dominated institution become a vehicle through which women could take responsibility for meeting the challenges facing the community? Could women, indeed, be charged with protecting manhood?[39]

The discord that these question provoked in the 1890s had been foregrounded a few years earlier. By the mid-1880s, this tension was manifest in the AME Church with a controversy over female ordination, perhaps the most challenging woman question of the era. The question came to the floor of the AME General Conference when the ordination of Sarah Ann Hughes of the North Carolina Annual Conference was revoked by the denomination's supreme body. Hughes began her career as a freelance evangelist in the early 1880s and was licensed to preach in 1882.[40] While she held a number of pastorates in the region, Hughes's aspirations to the ordained ministry were frustrated until Bishop Henry McNeal Turner arrived to oversee the North Carolina Conference.[41] Turner spoke out in support of female preachers, and at the 1885 session of the conference he ordained Hughes to the ministry as a deacon. Dissenting voices were raised almost immediately, and at the 1887 session an opponent of women's ordination, Bishop Jabez Campbell, replaced Turner. Campbell ruled Hughes's ordination contrary to church law, and her name was summarily stricken from the list of deacons.[42]

The denomination's bishops squared off over the issue in the pages of the *A.M.E. Church Review*, the church's quarterly magazine, in 1886.[43] Bishop Campbell argued that the Bible did not permit the ordination of women. He grounded his case in the concept of separate spheres for men and women: "Man cannot do woman's work and fill her place under the divine economy, and women cannot do man's work and fill his place under the same divine economy. . . . Women always have been and are now recognized as helpers . . . for that is the will of the Lord."[44] Bishop John Mifflin Brown, Turner's mentor and a veteran of previous women's rights contests, not only argued in support of women's ordination but also made a case for women's right to vote, underscoring the ways in which religious and political ideas were related. Brown framed the dispute in woman question terms, pressing an analogy between the issues confronting women and those confronting African Americans generally: "Two questions have disturbed the public mind for some time. These are 1. What shall be done with the Negro? 2. What shall be done with the women?" Without directly addressing Hughes's case, Brown pointed to women whom he deemed to be among the leading thinkers of the day. In addition to Lucy Stone Blackwell and Olympia Brown, he named several AME churchwomen, including Jarena Lee, Martha Low, and Emily Rodney Williams, all of whom he praised as excellent "pastors." Brown argued that women needed a voice in politics and urged that their status in society be clearly defined so they could take part in public culture as voters, officeholders, and ministers.[45]

Presiding at the following year's General Conference was Bishop Daniel Payne, who, over his long career as leader of the AME Church, had steadfastly held that women's roles should be confined to the domestic sphere.[46] The 1888 conference affirmed Bishop Campbell's action and formally prohibited women's ordination, amending the *Doctrines and Discipline* expressly to direct that bishops "shall not ordain any woman to the order of Deacon or Elder in the AME Church."[47]

For a time it appeared that the AME Zion Church would avoid this fate. Indeed it would be nearly ten years before it would erupt into a dispute over female ordination, the rancor of which far exceeded that of the same dispute among AME activists. The 1890s began quietly enough. The publication of a new edition of the church law, the *Doctrines and Discipline*, reflected the gender-neutral language that had been previously agreed upon. The word "male" had been deleted from those provisions that set the qualifications for offices such as trustee, steward, and member of the Quarterly Conference.[48] Women stepped into these new roles at the General Conference of 1892. While the seating of Fannie Van Brounk generated some discussion, the delegates voted overwhelmingly to admit her, and she was joined by at least four additional women, all of whom had been elected delegates by their local quarterly conferences.[49] Once women were taking part in the General Conference, the church's highest decision-making body, Zion elevated women to the ministry. In 1894, without fanfare, Bishop James W. Hood ordained the San Francisco–based evangelist Julia Foote a deacon at the New York Annual Conference.[50] The following spring, Bishop Alexander Walters ordained Mary J. Small, wife of Bishop John B. Small, deacon at the annual meeting of the Philadelphia and Baltimore Conference.[51]

A "large number of female delegates . . . seven in all" had attended AME Zion's 1896 General Conference, according to John Dancy, editor of the *Quarterly Review*. The women had "represented their Conferences with a dignity, courage and ability that won for them respect and honor from everyone. . . . Their presence created no friction, no controversy and provoked no minority report protesting against their being seated. Zion church moves right on without sounding trumpets or unduly exciting the multitude."[52] The following year, Maggie Hood appeared "in a new role" at Zion's Centennial Jubilee—that of "presiding officer." Marking Zion's 100th anniversary, the jubilee attracted an imposing audience, including leaders of Methodist sects worldwide. Some had doubts about her ability to command the authority required of a presiding elder. "It was feared that she would be timid and subject to 'stage freight,' as most women are when first called to preside," the *Quarterly Review* noted. But Hood drew strength from the example provided by one of Zion's most public women: "Taking her cue from Miss Eliza Gardner she seized the gavel and appeared as much at home as Bishop Hood[,] that is, her husband himself."[53]

Bishop John Small placed Zion's law and its practice squarely within the woman's era in his *Code on the Discipline of the African Methodist Episcopal Zion Church*, the content of which had been approved by the board of bishops. Small affirmed that church law did not discriminate against female congregants. In the context of denominational disciplinary proceedings, he made clear women's judicial authority: "Not merely are female members entitled to vote, when persons are brought to trial before the society of which they are members, but they are eligible to be appointed as members of a committee for trial of such cases." This provision was grounded in a more fundamental and far-reaching principle: "The word male having been stricken from our discipline, females are eligible to fill any position of which they are capable."[54] All signs suggested that Zion's innovations on the woman question, from the amendment of church law through the ordination of female ministers, had become comfortably incorporated into the denomination's sense of itself.

By 1898, however, AME Zion was unable to sustain its commitment to women's empowerment in the church. In North Carolina, the post–Civil War era home of the AME Zion Church, the campaign to force African American men out of politics, which culminated in the Wilmington riot in November 1898, profoundly compromised the public standing of African American men, including many of Zion's most visible leaders. With men politically marginalized, gender relations within the church became fraught with tension. In this context, as the question of "manhood equality" became more salient, the woman question took on new significance within the church. Institutional allegiances to the principles of the woman's era as expressed in gender-neutral structures faced a full-fledged challenge as male leaders sought to reaffirm their manhood through the reassertion of religious authority.

Disfranchisement had come late to North Carolina. African American men had recaptured their political standing through a fusion victory of the Republican and Populist parties over white Democrats in the 1894 election. The city of Wilmington, in particular, enjoyed a reputation as a relatively hospitable place for African Americans. Compared to other southern cities, black and white Wilmingtonians more commonly walked the same streets, lived in the same neighborhoods, and patronized the same shops. African Americans also continued to hold considerable political power. In 1897, for example, three black men served on the ten-member board of aldermen, the city's most important elected body. Other black officials included a member of the powerful five-constituent board of audit and finance, a justice of the peace, a deputy clerk of court, a superintendent of streets, and a coroner. The city had two black fire departments, an all-black health board, and a significant number of black policeman and, in federal positions, the mail clerk and postal carriers.[55]

The most conspicuous of black federal appointees was John C. Dancy, named collector of customs at the Port of Wilmington in 1897. Dancy was also an influential lay member of AME Zion, serving as editor of the church's magazine, the *A.M.E. Zion Quarterly Review*.[56] A relative newcomer to Wilmington, Dancy had replaced a prominent white Democrat. Dancy's salary as collector of customs was approximately $4,000 per year, which, as conservative editors often reminded the white public, was $1,000 more than the annual salary of the state's governor. Many whites, as well as some local blacks, understandably resented an outsider who enjoyed an economic status far above that of most people in Wilmington. Thomas M. Clawson, editor of the Democratic Party's *Wilmington Messenger*, made a practice of referring to Dancy as "Sambo of the Customs House."[57]

Dancy's vice presidency of the newly formed National Afro-American Council illustrates the connections between black political power and a local race-based order. At its first meeting in Rochester, New York, the council adopted a resolution to "secure uniform marriage laws in all the states, and revision of the laws in the twenty four States where inter-marriage between whites and blacks is not allowed."[58] White Democrats saw this resolution as an attempt to undercut white supremacy and a declaration that black men desired to marry white women.[59] In Wilmington, white Democrats vilified Dancy and argued that the political success of the fusion ticket had given men like Dancy license to advocate their personal desires to marry white women.[60]

During the 1898 campaign, the state's Democratic leadership visited Wilmington to organize a local committee and white supremacy clubs. Their efforts took hold in August when Alexander Manly, an African American newspaper editor, responded to a call for white men to "lynch a thousand times a week if necessary" to protect white women from black men. Manly boldly countered with an incendiary charge: "If the alleged crimes of rape were . . . so frequent as is ofttimes reported, her plea would be worthy of consideration." But, he contended, not every white woman who cried rape told the truth, nor was every sexual contact between black men and white women coerced. In fact, many black men were "sufficiently attractive for white girls of culture and refinement to fall in love with them, as is well known to all." If white newspapers decried crime in general rather than attributing all criminality to black people, "they would find their strongest allies among the intelligent Negroes themselves," the editor insisted. "Tell your men that it is no worse for a black man to be intimate with a white woman than for a white man to be intimate with a colored woman."[61]

Manly's editorial gave white Democrats all the political cover required for their conspiracy to seize power in Wilmington. When the polls closed that November, the Democrats claimed a "glorious victory." The white men of Wilmington served notice that mere political supremacy would not satisfy them. A few days later, they issued a "White Declaration of Independence," urging employers to fire black help and ordering Manly out of the city. They demanded resignations from the chief of police and the Republican mayor, who had another year to serve, terrifying them into giving up their offices.[62]

When black leaders failed to respond to the ultimatum, 500 white men burned down the Love and Charity Hall, the black mutual aid society building that housed Manly's newspaper. Then an army of white men rampaged through the city. They strip-searched black women and hunted down prominent black leaders, including John Dancy, and white Republican officeholders and either shot them or chased them out of town. Democrats seized the mayor's office, demanded the "resignations" of Republican officeholders, and filled the positions themselves. The dead, all African Americans, were estimated at between twenty and ninety. Hundreds more left the city, huddling in the woods. In the next month, 1,400 black people left Wilmington. Six months later, prosperous African Americans were still departing by the score.[63]

North Carolina's white supremacy campaign and the Wilmington riot deeply affected the entire AME Zion denomination. North Carolina was home to the AME Zion Church; its publication department was located there, and Livingstone College, its institution of higher learning, was located in Salisbury. A number of Zion's bishops made their permanent homes in North Carolina while they traveled "the circuit" overseeing far-flung congregations. The events of 1898 most directly affected the denomination's cadre of young ministers, many of whom were North Carolina born and raised. From Cumberland, Wilkes, and Moore counties, and from cities including Fayetteville, Charlotte, Kinston, Lincolnton, and New Bern, these men had joined Zion Church and received an education; by 1898 they made up the majority of the denomination's ministers. When black North Carolinians were so violently and decisively pushed out of politics, robbed of this marker of manhood, black men within AME Zion saw not only their own aspirations but also those of their brothers and their sons dashed. Despite efforts to keep it at bay, the nadir had arrived.

The Man in the Woman Question

The matter of women's ordination to the ministry was addressed at a singularly inauspicious moment for AME Zionites. The arguments put forth by church members linked the debate within the church to the contemporary contest over the standing of women in public life. The controversy began in the spring of 1898, when Bishop Charles Pettey ordained Deacon Mary Small to the station of elder. Small now stood shoulder to shoulder with all of the church's male leaders, save the bishops. She was empowered to administer church ritual and to oversee her own congregation, where she exercised authority over male leaders, including deacons, preachers, trustees, and stewards. Most church members learned of this development through an item in the church's weekly newspaper, the *Star of Zion*. The initial notice sounds almost naive, given the furious debates it unleashed: "After a spirited discussion, Mrs. Mary J. Small, wife of Bishop J. B. Small, was, by a vote of 34 to 13, elected and ordained an elder. . . . Mrs. Small has the same rights now as the ministers. The way is open now for her to pastor a church and be a presiding elder and bishop. She is the first woman to be ordained an elder. We have a few more female preachers who are deacons who will doubtless follow Mrs. Small."[64]

A furor erupted over Pettey's ordination of Small. For six months, the denomination was consumed with a debate over the propriety of women's ordination. Nearly half of the pages in the church's weekly newspaper were devoted to this issue, with bishops, ministers, and laypeople, both male and female, weighing in. A debate over the shape of church policy ensued, and long-standing questions about the relationship of women to the church and to public culture were revisited.

Changes over the preceding decades had positioned women as influential members of AME Zion. When the debate over women's ordination erupted, the denomination's female members jumped into the fray. Seemingly without hesitation or fear of reprisal, churchwomen argued in favor of Small's elevation to the ministry. While they continued to perform the full range of the church-related work customarily allotted to women, including fund-raising and missionary endeavors, churchwomen overthrew those ideas that had limited their place. Evalina Badham asked rhetorically: "Could I place [woman] in one prescribed circle and say stay thou here, step not forward nor backward; swerve neither to the right nor left? No, I could not." Badham asserted that any role a woman took up under the influence of the "Holy Spirit" was fitting and proper. The list was long. Badham claimed for women authority as class leaders, missionaries, Sabbath school teachers, fund-raisers, trustees, stewardesses, deaconesses, and members of church societies.[65] Sarah Pettey, whose husband, Charles, had ordained Mary Small, explained in her "Woman's Column" that women's sphere included business, higher education, medicine, and even international affairs (commenting on such matters as Cuban independence).[66] Projecting themselves as entitled to power and authority within AME Zion, churchwomen set the tone for their forceful contributions to the 1898 debate over women's ordination.

The ordination debate aired a wide range of competing views. Church members exchanged ideas about women's relationship to the church and to public culture generally, and they touched upon issues ranging from women's rights, the equality of the sexes, and the nature of women's sphere to the worth of fund-raising work. Some declared their enduring commitment to ideals of women's equality, and they were joined in this general sentiment by the newest generation of young women; others argued for curtailing women's roles within the church.

Women's ordination, asserted the Reverend J. Harvey Anderson, was an action "based upon the 'equality of the sexes.'" Anderson, a Civil War veteran, argued that church law was grounded in a principle that imposed "no limit nor restriction . . . upon female membership . . . 'she' being entitled to the same immunities as the 'he,' from start to finish."[67] To the extent that this position was considered an anomaly among Methodist sects generally, the Reverend J. J. Adams explained that it was rooted in well-established political precedents. Adams maintained that when the church law was made gender-neutral, women had been given "equal rights in the 'political economy' of the church," because "taxation without representation was declared wrong from the foundation of our free American government and is nonetheless true in the church as well as state."[68]

Other proponents argued that women's ordination was not only proper as an abstract principle but also followed from women's long-standing contributions to the church and to public culture. Women had "earned" the right to be ordained through their unwavering support and tireless labors. Boston's Eliza Gardner lamented the tenor of the debate: "I have read with some pain some of the articles [against women's ordination] that have been sent to the *Star* vilifying woman." She pointed out the irony that, at the very moment when some church members would deny women the right of ordination, "a strong appeal was made to the women of the church to come to the rescue of some of its departments."[69] Women demanded the consideration of the church's male leadership. An anonymous woman wrote: "We form a majority of the membership; we furnish a large part of the spiritual life, and we collect most of the money of the church. We believe that this entitles us to share in the government of the Church; and whether the Church law provides for it or prohibits it, cuts no figure with us. We shall continue to claim our rights."[70]

Church members agreed that female ministers must be qualified on the merits. They must have served in the lower ranks and passed the requisite examinations, just as did male aspirants to the ministry. Beyond this, women's ordination was linked to ideas about women's rights that had long undergirded changes in women's religious standing. In the difficult climate of the late 1890s, even the Reverend R. A. Morrisey, an outspoken advocate of women's ordination, felt the need to qualify his position. He explained that there would never be "wholesale and indiscriminate" ordination of women and that only those with "special qualification and fitness . . . should be admitted to the ministry."[71] Clarissa Betties argued that it was Mary Small's "genuine calling" that rendered her fit to serve as a minister.[72] B. F. Grant, a layman who had voted in favor of Small's ordination, explained her qualifications in terms of church law: "After we ordained her a deacon in York, and she passed a creditable examination the other week in Baltimore, she had a right to receive orders. . . . She prepared herself . . . and of course she won her position by merit—no favor in it."[73]

The opposition was equally resourceful and vocal, resurrecting arguments that came close to reducing churchwomen to silent helpmeets. The Reverend S. A. Chambers made the sweeping assertion that "woman is not man's equal, and the claim is simply ridiculous."[74] An editorial in the *Star of Zion* considered the concept of qualifications quite differently, arguing that a woman was "not physically able to pastor a church. She is too timid and fearful to get up at one or two o'clock in the night, unless some man is with her, and go across the city to see the sick or pray with some one ready to die. . . . It would be too hot and dusty in the summer and too cold and slushy in the winter for her to walk ten, fifteen and twenty miles on a circuit in the country to try to preach the gospel."[75] Others, like S. A. Chambers, sounded the alarm, claiming that "the next thing it will be women pastors, presiding elders and Bishops, then we shall be 'into it' up to our necks."[76] Such men feared that, once granted access to the ministry, religious women would turn the church's gendered order upside down. In an editorial reprinted in the *Star of Zion*, C. H. J. Taylor, who was personally acquainted with Mary Small, argued that ordination took women beyond the limits of their place within the church and within society: "There is plenty of work for good women like Mrs. Small to do in this world, without unsexing them by making them elders. . . . There are mannish women who, by this example, will come forward and do God's church any amount of damage. A woman in a river baptizing men; a woman in the army acting as chaplain; a woman celebrating marriage and a woman in the pulpit divesting herself of wig and teeth, when under religious excitement, are sights that even angels would be shocked to see, much less men."[77] Taylor's concern about the "unsexing" of women in positions of authority may well have been shared by black female activists, though clearly they took a different view of how female ministers might be perceived by their peers. Indeed, it was the circulation of ideas that denigrated black women's sexuality that had led women like AME Zion's Eliza Gardner to establish the 1890s club movement and adopt respectability as a strategy by which to resist white supremacy.[78]

Taylor's remarks suggest the continuing connections between ideas circulating in both religion and politics. Despite his familiarity with the issues and his deep engagement with the controversy unfolding within AME Zion, Taylor had not earned his reputation through religious activism. Instead, by the late 1890s, Taylor, who had been born a slave in Alabama, was known in African American public culture primarily as a lawyer, journalist, and politician. In the wake of Reconstruction's collapse, Taylor generated controversy when, in a scheme to establish African American political independence, he broke ranks with Republicans and joined the Democratic Party. He achieved some personal success; Grover Cleveland appointed him the U.S. minister to Liberia in 1887. By 1898, however, Taylor's strategy had crumbled as white supremacy became the Democrats' defining tenet.[79] Men like Taylor turned their sights on the church as a critical site of African American resistance to the degradations of Jim Crow. Gender, or more to the point, male supremacy was central to many such men's visions as well. "If God had intended woman to do the work of a man along all lines, he would have made her a man and not a woman," Taylor remarked. Here was a rebuke of the principles of equality and rights that had repositioned women as religious leaders in the preceding decades.

One thing was new in this woman question debate. Tensions between male leaders, generated by the collapse of Reconstruction and the rise of Jim Crow, appeared to be driving the exchanges. Women's ordination became the terrain upon which men, both for and against this innovation, expressed differences with one another. Through the deployment of metaphors of combat and violence, through critiques of men's capacities as ministers, through challenges to the church's hierarchical structure, and through shows of intellectual prowess, AME Zion's male leaders vied with one another for what little public authority had been left to them. What began as a woman question during the optimistic climate of Reconstruction became, with the assaults of Jim Crow, a man question.

The deployment of metaphors of combat and violence hinted that churchmen had more at stake in the debate than the standing of women. An early *Star of Zion* editorial recast the controversy in terms suggestive of a physical confrontation, speculating that "a great war is expected."[80] Bishop John Small, husband of the new elder, interjected the notion of a physical challenge: "A man who strikes a woman is a coward, and I think I will commit no sin if I strike a coward for striking my wife."[81] This age-old defense of a woman's honor amounted to an assertion of manhood. The Reverend S. A. Chambers, a vocal opponent of women's ordination, was the most dramatic of these verbal combatants, describing one of his opponents as having "laid off his coat, rolled up his sleeves, threw aside his silk beaver, thrust his fingers through his hair, foaming at the mouth and came dashing at us with his eyes flashing fire, breathing out epithets peculiar only to himself, shouting, as he advanced, 'Shoo! Shoo! Begone! Begone!' trying to scare us off the warpath, but we have not given back one inch, and never intend to as long as there is the least scent of powder smoke in the air." Chambers extended the martial metaphor: "We have waged war against ordaining women to Holy Orders in the absence of Biblical authority and shall cease firing only long enough to wipe out our gun and sink something or be sunk. The brother fired at us with a 2-inch gun and dodged around the corner and peeped to see what effect it would have, but he missed his mark and his target [that is, Chambers himself] stands as before."[82] In anticipation of a reply, Chambers wrote, "We pause for a heavier shot."[83]

The debate devolved quickly into an opportunity to vent criticism of male ministers. One *Star of Zion* editorial complained that since there was already "too much useless ordained male timber lying around in all of our conferences," female ministers were unnecessary.[84] Clarissa Betties admonished the men to withdraw their objections because churchwomen like Mrs. Small were already more hardworking than male ministers: "She is doing what you won't do. I will be glad when the time comes that those men will find something to do and let Rev. Mrs. Small alone."[85] Mrs. Rev. W. L. Moore suggested that the opponents of women's ordination did not see "through the eyes of faith, but look at Sister Small with eyes of jealousy." The move to ordain female ministers was due, in part, to inept male leadership: "My dear brother, do not worry any more about the sisters, but help see after Zion's property more than you do, then we will not have to ordain women."[86] Small's supporters were not spared ridicule, and the men who had endorsed the adoption of gender-neutral church law were chided: "Kicking ministers, you made the law. Now take your own medicine."[87]

These debates offered an occasion for challenging the church hierarchy—in particular, the relationships between bishops, elders, and deacons—and criticizing the deference paid to highly placed leaders such as bishops by lesser ministers and laypeople. Some, like the Reverend J. Harvey Anderson, defended the ordination of Mrs. Small as a reasonable exercise of a bishop's authority: "In ordaining females, [they] have in no way transcended their authority nor antagonized the polity of the AME Zion Church." Critics of the bishopric would be ostracized and "vanish in queer glances at the General Conference," he warned.[88] Bishop Hood himself sought to silence his critics with words that revealed the profound extent to which he demanded deference: "I should like to know when the General Conference authorized any one to tell the Bishops how to discharge the duties of their office. The suggestion is not only presumptuous, but it also lacks wisdom. . . . I think it likely that a bishop would follow his own judgment regardless of any advice from those who are not authorized to advise him."[89] Others took up this invitation to counter the bishops' expectations. Rev. J. H. McMullen claimed the right to oppose the bishops, insisting that "our ministers don't feel that they must act without consulting their own minds simply because they are discussing a question in which a bishop's wife [that is, Mary Small] is involved."[90] In the majority, however, were ministers like Rev. F. M. Jacobs, who argued that "there is an amount of respect due a Bishop in advance of a clergyman in the lower sea. . . . The ministry and many of the young men have either lost their respect or have never received proper training."[91] In Jacobs's view, young men were using the occasion of the women's ordination debate to test the limits of the bishops' authority.

This debate furnished an opportunity for Zion's men to demonstrate their

intellectual capacities for interpreting church law, as well as their comprehensive knowledge of Zion's history. B. F. Grant explained that, while he was
generally opposed to women's ordination, his reading of church law had
obligated him to support it. "As a lay delegate, I voted for her ordination, not
so much for my belief in the ordination of women but because I did not see
anything against it. She [Mrs. Small] only asked for what [the General
Conference, the denomination's lawmaking body] said she could have if she
was competent," he reasoned.[92] Rev. F. M. Jacobs also felt legally bound to
support women's ordination: "I was opposed to the action at that time [that
is, in the 1870s when the law was made gender-neutral], as I am opposed to it
now, but since it is a woman's right to aspire to these high positions in the
church under the law as it now exists . . . I take the ground and position as a
defender of her rights only on account of the gap in the law."[93]

The issue of biblical interpretation became one of the bitterest aspects of
the debate. Bishops, ministers, and laymen engaged in lengthy exchanges
over the relevance and proper interpretation of numerous Bible passages.
Demonstrating their thorough knowledge of the scriptures, those on both
sides of the debate presented an exhaustive range of examples that were
intended to convey women's proper standing in religious life. This was also
a contest over who could demonstrate a superior intellect and education
through a facility with languages—English, Greek, and Latin—in the reading
of biblical texts. These were not polite academic disagreements about wom-
en's standing in the church or the meanings of biblical texts: the very standing and authority of male church leaders was being contested.

By the close of 1898, the debate had subsided. In its resolution were traces
of strategies employed by black women activists since the 1830s. Small, Foote,
and the others who advocated women's ordination had allied themselves
with some of the denomination's most powerful men. It was true that church
activists generally were concerned that the debate had become so rancorous,
bitter, and volatile that the church itself could not withstand the divisions,
and Zionites admonished one another to let the matter rest until the next
General Conference, scheduled for 1900, during which, they were assured,
rationality would prevail. Still, the decisive factor in bringing the debate to a
close was the united front presented by the bishopric. While they had never,
as a body, ruled directly on the propriety of women's ordination, their actions
and their general remarks strongly suggested that they were of one mind in
their support for the ordination of women, and in their defense of their own
authority to ordain whom they pleased.[94]

The bishops' consensus might not have surprised those who knew them well. Of the eight currently in office, three—Charles Pettey, James Hood, and Alexander Walters—demonstrated their views by personally ordaining Small and / or Foote. Among the others were men whose pasts suggested they would endorse this advancement of churchwomen's standing, if pressed. Bishop Joseph Clinton, for example, had lived in Philadelphia in the pre–Civil War years and had been closely affiliated with that city's community of Garrisonian antislavery activists, joining many of them on what was termed "The Anti-Colonization and Woman's Rights Ticket," a slate that sought to represent the state of Pennsylvania in an 1850s national black political convention.[95]

These men were supported by influential lay leaders, including William Howard Day. The Oberlin graduate and Ohio abolitionist and political activist in the prewar years, Day had delivered the opening oration at the 1865 national black convention and invoked the slogan that appeared on the masthead of Frederick Douglass's *North Star*: "Right is of no sex, truth is of no color, God is the Father of us all, and all we are Brethren." Day sat as a member of the 1869 convention's committee on business and committee on rules and oversaw the admission of women delegates to that body. That decision had been grounded in both secular and religious principles. The related nature of oppression grounded in race and that grounded in gender was expressed by delegate Isaiah Wears, who stated that "to exclude [women] from seats in this convention would be too much like the actions of the occupants of the White House, who had excluded the colored race for two hundred years." Delegate J. Sella Martin also supported the admission of women delegates, explaining that there was no scriptural prohibition against such a step; "the term 'men' in the Bible meant men and women."[96] By 1876, Day had emerged as an influential lay leader, elected general secretary to the AME Zion General Conference. While they had not, as a body, ruled directly on the propriety of women's ordination, informal polls and their related pronouncements suggested that the bishops, along with many highly placed male lay leaders, were of one mind in their support for the ordination of women.

In 1898, the eight men who comprised Zion's bishopric had come of age in the antebellum decades, then lived to gain influence within the post-Reconstruction-era church. By the close of the century, they, like other leaders of the antebellum generation, saw their reign being slowly eclipsed by a younger cadre of men, many of whom did not share their experience with or their sensibilities about the woman question. An exchange between two of the preeminent leaders of the antebellum generation, Frederick Douglass and George Downing, captured this dynamic. After having suffered a collapse, Douglass wrote to Downing: "I think that neither you nor I have any right to be other than thankful. Our lives have been long in the land and we have both, I hope, done something to leave the world better than we found it. I shall be seventy-five, if I calculate right next month and you are not far behind. We have both seen our children's children. We have seen nearly all who labored with us disappear and pass."[97] Within the church, the insight and influence of the antebellum generation's leaders were still much revered. John Dancy wrote in the pages of the *Quarterly Review*: "It is remarkable how the older leaders of the race hold their own against all rivals. Up to the time of his death no member of the race could dislodge the great Frederick Douglass from his place as leader, thinker and orator. The same is likewise true of Mrs. Frances Ellen Watkins Harper. We have been hearing her on the lecture platform for thirty years—when we were a small boy—and she had no real competitor then. She hardly has any now. No woman in the race is her superior as an orator."[98] For what was likely their final moment of unassailable influence, AME Zion's antebellum generation leaders helped shape the course of the woman question within the church and within African American public culture more generally.

Bishop Cicero Harris, as he weighed in on women's ordination, invoked the memory of antebellum African American public culture, calling upon Zion Church's history and tradition as he defended the ordination of women. At the close of the century, women's rights were—as they had been since before the Civil War—on par with the principles of antislavery and civil rights. Harris urged:

> For a hundred years we have been pleading for and demanding the equal rights of citizens, without regard to color. Is it any wonder that we recognize the fact that the same arguments which, as to the equality of rights [also] abolish the sex line; and that as a rule where a white man was an abolitionist he was per consequence an advocate of women suffrage? Fred Douglass was consistently an ardent advocate of both Negro and of woman suffrage. These lines are from his pen: Right is of no sex, Truth is of no color, God is our common Father, And all mankind are brothers. To me these words are not only epigrammatic, but immortal.[99]

Harris's rhetoric powerfully expressed one of the most salient dimensions of the debates among black Methodists about the woman question during the preceding two decades: the principle that ideas about women's rights in the political realm should also guide the definition of their standing in the religious realm. For activist churchwomen, Harris aptly recast church history to bring it into alignment with their vision of women's rights that transcended institutional boundaries and encompassed all of African American public culture.

All Bound Up Together: The Woman Question, the Age of Imperialism, and the Dawning of Civil Rights

Harris was shrewd. He deployed a powerful rhetoric of history and rights. He did so well aware that the challenges embedded in his church's debates had far-reaching consequences for the future of African American public culture and the rights of people of African descent in the United States and in the world. Harris stood at the threshold of two sea changes in the political landscape, the emergence of U.S. imperialism and the birth of secular civil rights organizing. In both cases, the woman question debates in which the AME Zion Church and others had been embroiled had a direct bearing on how black Americans would take up these new challenges. As African American religious leaders determined how they would take part in U.S. imperial projects throughout the world, the long-standing woman question debate forced them to negotiate the gendered aspect of new missionary endeavors. In domestic politics, as what would emerge as the National Association for the Advancement of Colored People (NAACP) in the twentieth century was prefigured in organizations such as the Afro-American League and the National Afro-American Council, black Methodist activists mobilized their understandings of the woman question, developed through debates in religious circles, to newly emerging spheres of African American politics. In the former case, women did not fare well and despite their protestations were generally excluded from the leadership of foreign missionary societies. But in the realm of domestic politics, black women activists, the inheritors of a nearly seventy-year-long woman question debate, joined their male counterparts to lead what would become arguably black public culture's most sustained political body, the NAACP.

In the 1890s, the focus of missionary work was being transformed by the expansion of American imperialism. During the Civil War and Reconstruction, black Methodists had raised funds and ministered to former slaves in the southern states while supporting a modest number of foreign missionaries in such places as Liberia and Haiti. At the turn of the twentieth century, black Methodist leaders aimed to extend their influence to the world's people of color. This was a profoundly masculine re-envisioning of the missionary project that sought to rescue African American manhood from the degradations of a domestic Jim Crow order. As the Civil War had been a proving ground for an earlier generation of men, so too U.S. imperialism furnished an opportunity for black religious leaders to reestablish themselves as men and as citizens.[100]

Churchwomen had an alternative vision: they sought to take unqualified control of the missionary societies they had long sustained through their labors. For women, missionary societies were sites for the expression of an idealized womanhood and represented the culmination of a four-decades-long struggle for the rights of women within the church. Their claims were familiar to church leaders, but the faces of the women at the forefront of this struggle were new. Female activists of the immediate postwar generation shared the podium with their daughters, young women who had come of age under the guidance of female voters, officers, delegates, and preachers.

First during AME Zion's centennial celebration in 1896, and again at the General Conference of 1900, female church leaders took advantage of their standing as officers to press their case for control of missionary societies. Mrs. Maggie Hood-Banks, daughter of Bishop James Hood, called attention to women's long-standing work as missionaries: "The great missionary cause of our Church has been in the hands of the women ever since it has been a department of the Church. They have toiled early and late, sacrificing time and money, to build up the work."[101] Also at stake was the church's commitment to women's equality. Should women not "take an equal part in all things that have a common interest for both, whether, politically, socially or religiously?" asked Sarah Janifer, a thirty-eight-year-old Washington, D.C., schoolteacher. Woman "must organize, originate and mould sentiment, and in fact, take her place on the broadening platform of equality and justice," Janifer urged.[102]

Janifer's remarks hinted at two important themes that register the context of the debate over the woman question at the end of the century. First, the places of women in the political, social, and religious realms were analogous to one another, and principles of equality should best guide women in their public work. Rosina Nickson pointed to the Woman's Christian Temperance Union (WCTU) as one model of female autonomy that African American activists might look to as they contemplated female control over missionary affairs.[103] The WCTU was an especially complex example. The temperance organization made its influence felt through a national network of local clubs with over 135,000 members by the late 1880s. The organization had been plagued by tensions between black and white activists that centered on the organization's position on lynching and the segregation of its southern affiliates. Yet among its national leadership cadre were prominent African American women activists, including Frances Ellen Watkins Harper and Sarah J. Early; the latter was an Oberlin College graduate of the 1850s and wife of AME Church minister J. W. Early, whose biography she had authored in 1894.[104] Club activist Mary Church Terrell suggested similar connections when she addressed a meeting of the National Woman Suffrage Association in 1900. While arguing for women's political enfranchisement, Terrell made clear that her objective was to remedy the fact that "the most honorable and lucrative positions in Church and State have been reserved for men."[105] For all of these female leaders, the church and the state each remained a critical site of power, and women's struggles within them were closely allied.

Janifer saw churchwomen's challenges as bound up with those faced by women in the realm of politics, and she saw their futures as connected with changes in the nature of missionary work. The "broadening platform of equality and justice" to which she referred increasingly included international settings through which African American Methodists hoped to extend their influence. The women's male allies also saw the significance of robust female missionary societies in the imperial age. J. N. Manly argued that the turn of the century, more so than any other moment in church history, required the harnessing of all that churchwomen had to offer to missionary endeavors: "To fail in giving women charge of the Missionary Department would be a great sacrifice to the spread of our Zion Methodism throughout the United States and the world."[106]

"The great object of our church is to disciple the world," Manly urged. The idea that black Methodists were charged with bringing their faith to people of color throughout the world, especially to those fields of interest that U.S. imperialism appeared to be opening up, was key to the debate. The question that faced black Methodists was the extent to which women would control or take part in such encounters. Missionary work not only had the potential to make African American churches "great"; it had the potential to restore to those men who found themselves suddenly and forcefully evicted from the realm of state authority a type of greatness that most were unwilling to share with their female counterparts.

At the AME Zion General Conference of 1900, the century's two final woman questions were put on the table. The first—may women be properly ordained to the ministry?—was answered in the affirmative. This victory secured the standing of a small number of women who sought out such duties in the early twentieth century. But the tenor of the times was better captured by the answer to the second question—should women be granted exclusive control over their missionary societies? To that question the answer was *no*. Ideas about politics and religion remained intertwined. In a world of Jim Crow limitations and imperial possibilities, the woman question was being redrawn. What should be women's standing in international missionary endeavors? As African American women, religious and nonreligious alike, mobilized through women's clubs to challenge state-sanctioned Jim Crow, they were confronting new questions about the possibilities and limits for women in public culture.[107] Developments in the realms of both religion and politics ensured that black Methodists would be debating the woman question for decades to come.

Church activists were hardly alone in responding to the changes that the rise of Jim Crow was inflicting upon African American public culture. And churches were not the only places to which religious activists looked to develop their response to the era's degradations, as the rise of the women's club movement suggests. Perhaps the most significant of the attempts to resurrect a distinctly African American political culture in the 1890s was that spearheaded by journalist T. Thomas Fortune. Already by the late 1880s Fortune was calling for direct political action by black activists in terms that presaged Cicero Harris's vision for the AME Zion Church. Fortune advocated the creation of a political organization that fashioned itself after the high moment in American political culture, the antebellum abolitionist movement. Fortune's vision initially took shape at the 1890 meeting of the Afro-American League. This entity was short-lived, but its personnel and tenets suggest how church-based debates about the woman question continued to work in tandem with those in politics. AME Zion leaders were prominent among those joining Fortune in his call for the league's national convention; they included Bishop Alexander Walters, who had been a close ally to Julia Foote; John Dancy, who would be run out of Wilmington by a mob; and Joseph Price, president of AME Zion's Livingstone College. Surely many of the league's founding precepts were compelling for these men, but one had particular resonances given the debates unfolding in their church community; Fortune forthrightly argued that the participation of women in the fledgling organization was essential to its success. Indeed, when the delegates, numbering between 140 and 200 from at least twenty states, finally convened in Chicago, their resolutions included a provision that the league was open to all, regardless of sex.

The league and its successor organization, the National Afro-American Council, were endorsed by some of African American public culture's most prominent female activists, including Ida B. Wells. The league's male leadership found itself doing a very careful dance with Wells, who over time spoke as supporter and detractor, and with the advent of the 1890s she could not be neglected in either respect. Women like Wells were influential politicians, and the meaning of Fortune's initial declamation was of its time. The league needed women not because they would host its delegates or raise funds for its coffers, though they might do just that. Women were needed as allies and collaborators in a public culture in which they wielded real influence. The standing accorded to the league did generate controversy. When Ida Wells was elected secretary to the newly formed Afro-American Council in 1899, a dispute ensued, but Wells and her supporters carried the day. Many league and later council activists were veterans of the woman question debate, with AME Zion activists always among them, and their strong alliances with club women reflected this. In 1899 the NACW and the Afro-American Council held their conventions back-to-back in Chicago. Council leaders attended the women's gathering and then commenced their own. Club women were included on the council program, and prominent among them was Josephine Silone Yates, who, along with AME Zion bishop George Clinton, presented a paper titled "The Best System of Moral Training." No controversy appears to have been generated by this collaboration between female and male activists, and were there opponents to this arrangement in the room, they were likely reluctant to voice such sentiments in the face of so many activists who were already on the record for having endorsed women's public authority in their churches and other public settings.[108]

Thus, as the century came to a close, the woman question continued to shape African American public culture. The nearly three-decades-long campaign for the rights of African American women in churches had reaped some formidable authority for female religious activists. But these church-centered debates, which had always drawn upon political ideas, were in turn shaping two of the era's most enduring sites of political contestation. In the realm of U.S. imperial projects, the woman question debate lessened the likelihood that African American women would take part in such endeavors as missionaries. And in the realm of civil rights, those organizations that laid the groundwork for the twentieth century's NAACP came into being through the close alliances forged between, among others, male church activists and club women. In neither instance could the outcomes be easily judged losses or victories for the African American women's movement. While women did not yet head missionary societies, they continued to wield important influence over their church's international affairs. In civil rights politics, while women remained important collaborators, such organizations would never reach anything close to the gender parity in leadership that Fortune and others might have initially imagined. As had been true since the earliest years of the woman question debate, the fates of black women's public lives remained bound up with the optimism and despair, the triumphs and the disappointments, of all African Americans.

Conclusion

In the summer of 1907, the Reverend J. W. Brown presided over the dedication of the newly constructed Memorial African Methodist Episcopal Zion Church in Rochester, New York.[1] Even prior to the opening ceremonies, Memorial Church was touted as black Rochester's grandest edifice. Among its outstanding features were four stained-glass windows, illustrating the causes to which Zionites had devoted themselves during the denomination's 120-year history. One window depicted Harriet Tubman, a member of Zion's Auburn, New York, congregation, who symbolized overt resistance to the institution of chattel slavery. Tubman famously shepherded enslaved African Americans northward via the Underground Railroad. Another window featured a likeness of Frederick Douglass, who began his oratory career as a Zion exhorter, represented the labors of ministers and laypeople alike in the abolitionist movement of the antebellum North.[2] A third window portrayed Dr. Joseph C. Price, an educator and the first president of Zion's Livingstone College, located in Salisbury, North Carolina. Price represented the church's commitment to the education and the welfare of freed people in the South after the Civil War.

It was, however, the face of a white woman in the fourth window—that of Susan B. Anthony—that might have caused the casual visitor to Memorial Church to pause.[3] The window included a portrait of Anthony along with her famous statement, "Failure is Impossible." Anthony was well known as a longtime Rochester resident and a zealous advocate of women's rights.[4] This tribute to Anthony's life and work was made possible through the efforts of Rochester resident Hester Jeffrey and her associates in the Susan B. Anthony Club, one of the hundreds of African American women's clubs of the early twentieth century.[5]

The images in the windows of Memorial Church were also a tribute to the African American woman question debate, encompassing many of its themes and principles. The images of Douglass and Anthony captured the rich cross-pollination of the antebellum antislavery and women's rights movements. The valorization, not of saints, but of nominally secular leaders in the windows of a religious sanctuary suggested the permeability of the religious-secular divide. The image of Price, a southerner, in a northern congregation, suggested the extent to which African American public culture traversed divisions between the nation's northern and southern halves. Women's agency was boldly affirmed, certainly through the image of Anthony, but also through the image of Tubman. And these women's divergent life stories pointed up the differing consequences that the dynamics of race and gender had for black and white women. The contests and the cooperation between generations were captured in the opposing images of Douglass, a product of the antebellum era, and Price, who came of age in the postwar era. Finally, each of the images in the window of Rochester's AME Zion Church was a reminder of the extent to which African American public culture was deeply embedded in the nation's social and political transformations. While each of the individuals memorialized held significance for AME Zion Church and the city of Rochester, their lives encompassed much more: the abolitionist and women's rights movements and fugitive slave reform movements of the antebellum era, and the struggles for education and civil and political rights of the postwar years.

But the distance that the African American woman question debate had traveled was best reflected not in this homage to late leaders but in the process by which the windows had come to be installed in the new sanctuary. A woman, Hester Jeffrey, oversaw this undertaking. Jeffrey, in a long-standing tradition, raised the necessary funds. But as a product of the woman's era, she also led the committee that oversaw the production of the windows and controlled the podium when her accomplishments were unveiled. Jeffrey was a living testament to the force of the nineteenth-century woman question debate.

Jeffrey was the wife of R. Jerome Jeffrey and the daughter-in-law of the Reverend Rosewell Jeffrey, an affluent and prominent political activist. An organizer and an activist in her own right, Hester Jeffrey was a member of the Political Equality Club, the Woman's Protective Club of Rochester, the Woman's Christian Temperance Union, the (Frederick) Douglass Monument Committee, and the National Afro-American Council. She founded or helped to organize a number of local African American women's clubs, including the Susan B. Anthony Club for African American women, the

Mrs. R. Jerome (Hester) Jeffrey. Courtesy of the Library Company of Philadelphia.

Climbers, and the Hester C. Jeffrey Club. She maintained an active membership in the AME Zion Church and served on various committees there. In 1905, Jeffrey represented the New York Federation of Colored Women at a New York State Woman Suffrage Association convention. Jeffrey was also a friend and associate of Susan B. Anthony and was chosen to give a eulogy at Anthony's funeral in 1906.

It might have been difficult to summon up the image of Maria Stewart in that sanctuary. The ridicule to which she had been subjected in the 1830s may have felt like a distant memory or remote happenstance. Indeed, in Rochester, New York, in 1908 it might have seemed that women had always exercised such visible and independent standing in African American public culture. Hester Jeffrey knew better. While she celebrated the moment and the distance that women like her had come in public culture, she also possessed the wisdom of the past. She likely remembered how her mother-in-law, Mary Jeffrey, had only been grudgingly admitted to the Colored National Convention a half-century earlier in Rochester. The church windows Hester Jeffrey put into place were a tribute to great leaders, but her life was also a tribute to all of those who had struggled before her in the woman question debate.

Notes

Introduction

1. Melba J. Boyd, *Discarded Legacy: Politics and Poetics in the Life of Frances E. W. Harper, 1825–1911* (Detroit, Mich.: Wayne State University Press, 1994), 114. This speech was one of many in which Harper emphasized what she viewed as the convergence of interests among nineteenth-century Americans, as explained in Shirley Wilson Logan's *"We Are Coming": The Persuasive Discourse of Nineteenth-Century Black Women* (Carbondale: Southern Illinois University Press, 1999), 57–60.

2. Bettye J. Gardner, "William Watkins: Antebellum Black Teacher and Writer," *Negro History Bulletin* 39, no. 6 (1976): 623 24; C. Peter Ripley, ed., *The Black Abolitionist Papers* (Chapel Hill: University of North Carolina Press, 1991) (hereafter *BAP*), 3:96–97 n. 6. Note: In general, when I cite editorial information from *The Black Abolitionist Papers,* as I do here, citations are to the books; when I cite the documents, I cite the microfilm version by reel and frame number.

3. This use of the term "movement" is intended to challenge the historiographic hegemony that the movement among white, middle-class women during the same period has enjoyed, obscuring our view of the nineteenth century's multiple movements. The invocation of the term "movement" is not merely descriptive but also strategic. The work of shaping our understandings of the nineteenth-century women's movement began just weeks after the 1848 women's rights convention at Seneca Falls, New York; participants pronounced the gathering the beginning of a "movement," even though they could not know what might follow that event. For those who came together in 1848, the term was at best an aspirational claim to a political

status yet to be realized. To label the early women's conventions a movement was to elevate them to a standing on par with existing reform movements, such as antislavery and temperance, which were already acknowledged to be important in public life. Use of the term "movement" also conveyed a set of underlying strategies, signaling that some women intended to follow the lead of temperance and antislavery activists by using conventions, petitions, mass meetings, and the printing press to make their case to the public. By the 1890s, leaders of this movement used the writing of history to make the case for a singular women's movement. The multivolume *History of Woman Suffrage* asserted this view and left little room for alternate understandings. Mid-twentieth-century women's historians picked up on this impressive, though incomplete history, further reifying the perspective that Stanton, Anthony, Gage, and Harper actively promoted.

4. The debate among African Americans was part of a more widespread woman question debate in the United States. Some scholars have suggested that the American and British debates were parts of a single discussion emanating from one community of letters. See the introduction to Elizabeth K. Helsinger, Robin L. Sheets, and William Veeder, eds., *Defining Voices, 1837–1883*, vol. 1 of *The Woman Question: Society and Literature in Britain and America, 1837–1883* (New York: Garland Publishing, 1983), xiii. Helsinger et al. date the advent of the "Victorian Woman Question" to 1837, arguing that concern with distinctive concepts including "woman's mission," "woman's sphere," and "woman's influence" ally the debates of the 1830s with those of the 1880s, rather than with the debates of the late eighteenth and early nineteenth centuries. Bibliographer Dennis Norlin asserts that the phrase "the Woman Question" appeared in print for the first time in October 1866 in an *Atlantic Monthly* article by F. Sheldon titled "Various Aspects of the Woman Question." See Dennis A. Norlin, "The Term 'the Woman Question' in Late-Nineteenth-Century Social Discourse," *Bulletin of Bibliography* 49, no. 3 (September 1992): 179–93.

5. To capture an African American public culture, this study relies upon the records of African American institutions, including those of various Methodist and Baptist organizations, the "colored" convention movement, fraternal orders, literary and historical societies, mutual aid organizations, and the press.

6. African American activists debated whether their institutions should be bounded by race. Some groups, such as the American Moral Reform Society of the mid-1830s, rejected all "distinctions of color or complexion." See Howard H. Bell, "The American Moral Reform Society, 1836–1841," *Journal of Negro Education* 27, no. 1 (Winter 1958): 34–40.

7. Most recently, John Stauffer's *The Black Hearts of Men: Radical Abolitionists and the Transformation of Race* (Cambridge, Mass.: Harvard University Press, 2001) portrays antebellum political culture as one in which some men were able to develop cross-racial alliances.

8. Thanks for sharing the notion of a community of interpretation goes to my colleague at the École des Hautes Études en Sciences Sociales, Jean Hébrard, who

explains that public culture is the means by which communities "share the meaning of a word, an expression, a text, or an event by dialogical negotiations" ("Peut-on faire une histoire des pratiques populaires de lecture à l'époque moderne? Les 'nouveaux lecteurs' revisités," *Matériaux pour une histoire de la lecture et de ses institutions* 17 [2005]: 105–40).

9. Works that take up the intellectual dimension of nineteenth-century African American culture include Mia Bay, *The White Image in the Black Mind: African American Ideas about White People, 1830–1925* (New York: Oxford University Press, 2000); David W. Blight, "In Search of Learning, Liberty, and Self-Definition: James McCune Smith and the Ordeal of the Antebellum Black Intellectual," *Afro-Americans in New York Life and History* 9, no. 2 (1985): 7–25; and Patrick Rael, *Black Identity and Black Protest in the Antebellum North* (Chapel Hill: University of North Carolina Press, 2002).

10. Numerous black antislavery activists were deeply engaged with the transatlantic dimension of the abolitionist movement. See Richard J. M. Blackett, *Building an Antislavery Wall: Black Americans in the Atlantic Abolitionist Movement, 1830–1860* (Baton Rouge: Louisiana State University Press, 1983), and Alan Rice and Martin Crawford, eds., *Liberating Sojourn: Frederick Douglass and Transatlantic Reform* (Athens: University of Georgia Press, 1999).

11. Steven Hahn, *A Nation Under Our Feet: Black Political Struggles in the Rural South from Slavery to the Great Migration* (Cambridge: Harvard University Press, 2004).

12. Thomas Bender, "Whole and Parts: The Need for Synthesis in American History," *Journal of American History* 73 (June 1986): 120–36.

13. Jürgen Habermas, *The Structural Transformation of the Public Sphere: An Inquiry Into a Category of Bourgeois Society*, trans. Thomas Burger with Frederick Lawrence (Cambridge, Mass.: MIT Press, 1991). Other scholars have argued that some nineteenth-century African Americans shared a sphere of deliberation through which they arrived at notions of the common good and challenged their standing vis-à-vis the state—a public sphere in Habermasian terms. See the Black Public Sphere Collective, *The Black Public Sphere* (Chicago: University of Chicago Press, 1995). More precisely, scholars have argued that African Americans constituted a subaltern counterpublic, borrowing Nancy Fraser's rereading of Habermas. See, for example, Evelyn B. Higginbotham, *Righteous Discontent: The Women's Movement in the Black Baptist Church, 1880–1920* (Cambridge, Mass.: Harvard University Press, 1993). Fraser, along with other feminist theorists, has critiqued Habermas for setting forth an idealized model of the public sphere that does not fully account for the extent to which race, class, and gender necessarily excluded some persons from liberal, bourgeois modes of deliberation, and thus from one aspect of democratic political practice. Fraser argues that beyond Habermas's idealized public sphere lay nonliberal, nonbourgeois, competing public spheres, one of which was created through the discursive practices of free black people during the antebellum period. See Nancy Fraser, "Rethinking the Public Sphere: A Contribution to the Critique of Actually Existing Democracy," in Craig Calhoun, ed., *Habermas and the Public Sphere* (Cam-

bridge, Mass: MIT Press, 1992), 109–42. This book argues that for nineteenth-century African Americans, this realm was constructed not merely through discursive practices but through the materiality of African American life, hence the adoption of the term "culture" rather than "sphere." While this study considers the discursive dimension of black publicity, it argues that the public engagement of African Americans was shaped through the conditions of everyday life—poverty, displacement, violence, labor, and law. For discussion of African Americans and the public sphere, see Thomas C. Holt, "Afterword: Mapping the Black Public Sphere," in Black Public Sphere Collective, *Black Public Sphere*, 325–28.

14. Mary Ryan, *Women in Public: Between Banners and Ballots, 1825–1880* (Baltimore: Johns Hopkins University Press, 1990), 4.

15. Among the works produced by the first generation of such historians are Hallie Q. Brown, *Homespun Heroines and Other Women of Distinction* (1926; New York: Oxford University Press, 1988); Benjamin T. Tanner, *An Apology for African Methodism* (Baltimore: s.n., 1867); Monroe A. Majors, *Noted Negro Women: Their Triumphs and Activities* (Chicago: Donahue and Henneberry, 1893; Freeport, N.Y.: Books for Libraries Press, 1971); Gertrude Mossell, *The Work of the Afro-American Woman* (1908; New York: Oxford University Press, 1988); and Benjamin G. Brawley, *Women of Achievement: Written for the Fireside Schools Under the Auspices of the Woman's American Baptist Home Mission Society* (N.p.: Woman's American Baptist Home Mission Society, 1919). Works of the civil rights generation include Gerda Lerner, ed., *Black Women in White America: A Documentary History* (New York: Vintage Books, 1973); Dorothy Sterling, ed., *We Are Your Sisters: Black Women in the Nineteenth Century* (New York: W. W. Norton, 1984); and Bert James Loewenberg and Ruth Bogin, eds., *Black Women in Nineteenth-Century American Life: Their Words, Their Thoughts, Their Feelings* (University Park: Pennsylvania State University Press, 1976). The most recent histories to seek out such women include Rosalyn Terborg-Penn, *African American Women in the Struggle for the Vote, 1850–1920* (Indianapolis: University of Indiana Press, 1998); Jualynne E. Dodson, *Engendering Church: Women, Power, and the A.M.E. Church* (Lanham, Md.: Rowman & Littlefield, 2002); Shirley J. Yee, *Black Women Abolitionists: A Study in Activism, 1828–1860* (Knoxville: University of Tennessee Press, 1992); Ella Forbes, *African American Women during the Civil War* (New York: Garland Publishing, 1998); and Clara Merritt DeBoer, *Be Jubilant My Feet: African American Abolitionists in the American Missionary Association, 1839–1861* (New York: Garland Publishing, 1994).

16. Higginbotham, *Righteous Discontent*; Deborah Gray White, *Too Heavy a Load: Black Women in Defense of Themselves, 1894–1994* (New York: W. W. Norton, 1999).

17. Glenda E. Gilmore, *Gender and Jim Crow: Women and the Politics of White Supremacy in North Carolina, 1896–1920* (Chapel Hill: University of North Carolina Press, 1996).

18. Stephanie Shaw, *What a Woman Ought to Be and to Do: Black Professional Women Workers during the Jim Crow Era* (Chicago: University of Chicago Press, 1996).

19. James O. Horton and Lois E. Horton. *Black Bostonians: Family Life and Community Struggle in the Antebellum North* (New York: Holmes & Meier, 1979), 57.

20. In this respect, the book is aligned with many recent works that also seek to disrupt the dominance of the "Stanton-Anthony" story of nineteenth-century women's history. See, for example, Nancy A. Hewitt, *Women's Activism and Social Change: Rochester, New York, 1822–1872* (Ithaca, N.Y.: Cornell University Press, 1984), and Nancy Isenberg, *Sex and Citizenship in Antebellum America* (Chapel Hill: University of North Carolina Press, 1998). Most recently Lori Ginzberg has suggested an alternative origin for a woman's rights movement in Stanton and Anthony's own upstate New York backyard. See *Untidy Origins: A Story of Woman's Rights in Antebellum New York* (Chapel Hill: University of North Carolina Press, 2005).

21. Elsa Barkley Brown, "African American Women's Quilting: A Framework for Conceptualizing and Teaching African American Women's History," *Signs: Journal of Women in Culture and Society* 14, no. 4 (Summer 1989): 921–29.

22. In adopting the notion of male "allies," I rely upon Estelle Freedman's analysis in *No Turning Back: The History of Feminism and the Future of Women* (New York: Ballantine Books, 2002).

23. See Hazel V. Carby, *Reconstructing Womanhood: The Emergence of the Afro-American Woman Novelist* (New York: Oxford University Press, 1990), and Judith Butler, *Gender Trouble: Feminism and the Subversion of Identity* (New York: Routledge, 1990). See also Michael Awkward, "A Black Man's Place(s) in Black Feminist Criticism," in *Representing Black Men*, ed. Marcellus Blount and George P. Cunningham (New York: Routledge, 1996), 3–26. Awkward's question was not intended to inform any historical analysis as much as it was intended as a challenge to the late-twentieth-century field of feminist literary criticism. His pointing up of the latent essentialism embedded within some feminist analyses is nonetheless a useful insight for historians.

24. Elsa Barkley Brown, "African-American Women's Quilting."

25. Rev. J. Harvey Anderson, *Biographical Souvenir Volume of the Twenty-Third Quadrennial Session of the General Conference of the African Methodist Zion Church* (1908), 29, 80.

26. Black Public Sphere Collective, *Black Public Sphere*.

27. Leon Litwack, *North of Slavery: The Negro in the Free States, 1790–1860* (Chicago: University of Chicago Press, 1961); James O. Horton, *Free People of Color: Inside the African American Community* (Washington, D.C.: Smithsonian Institution Press, 1993); William D. Piersen, *Black Yankees: The Development of an Afro-American Subculture in Eighteenth-Century New England* (Amherst: University of Massachusetts Press, 1993); Elizabeth R. Bethel, *The Roots of African-American Identity: Memory and History in Free Antebellum Communities* (New York: St. Martin's Press, 1997); Scott Hancock, "The Elusive Boundaries of Blackness: Identity Formation in Antebellum Boston," *Journal of Negro History* 84, no. 2 (Spring 1999): 115; Rael, *Black Identity and Black Protest*.

28. Joanne P. Melish, *Disowning Slavery: Gradual Emancipation and "Race" in New England, 1780–1860* (Ithaca, N.Y.: Cornell University Press, 1998).

29. Horton, *Free People of Color*, 103–4; Bureau of the Census, Department of Commerce, *Negro Population in the United States, 1790–1915* (New York: Arno Press, 1918), 45, 51. Even so, African Americans comprised just one percent of Ohio's population in 1830.

30. Horton, *Free People of Color*, 103.

31. Baltimore, because of the overwhelmingly free character of its black population (90 percent of black Baltimoreans were free by 1850) and because the city permitted the maintenance of black institutions, including schools, churches, fraternal orders, and political organizations, was well-integrated into the public culture that was otherwise limited to the free states and territories. In this regard, Baltimore was distinct from southern cities like Charleston and New Orleans. See Christopher Phillips, *Freedom's Port: The African American Community of Baltimore, 1790–1860* (Urbana: University of Illinois Press, 1997).

32. Leonard P. Curry, *The Free Black in Urban America, 1800–1850: The Shadow of the Dream* (Chicago: University of Chicago Press, 1981), 250.

33. Ibid., 15–22.

34. Horton, *Free People of Color*, 113–14.

35. Ibid., 116.

36. Julie Winch, *A Gentleman of Color: The Life of James Forten* (New York: Oxford University Press, 2002), 332–40; Janice Sumler-Lewis, "The Forten-Purvis Women of Philadelphia and the American Anti-Slavery Crusade," *Journal of Negro History* 66, no. 4 (Winter 1981–82): 281–88; Julie Winch, *Philadelphia's Black Elite: Activism, Accommodation, and the Struggle for Autonomy, 1787–1848* (Philadelphia: Temple University Press, 1988).

37. Horton, *Free People of Color*, 107.

38. John R. McKivigan and Jason H. Silverman, "Monarchial Liberty and Republican Slavery: West Indies Emancipation Celebrations in Upstate New York and Canada West," *Afro-Americans in New York Life and History* (January 1986): 7–15; William B. Gravely, "The Dialectic of Double-Consciousness in Black American Freedom Celebrations, 1808–1863," *Journal of Negro History* 67, no. 4 (Winter 1982): 302–17; Mitch Kachun, *Festivals of Freedom: Memory and Meaning in African American Emancipation Celebrations, 1808–1915* (Amherst: University of Massachusetts Press, 2003); Geneviève Fabre, "African-American Commemorative Celebrations in the Nineteenth Century," in *History and Memory in African-American Culture*, ed. Geneviève Fabre and Robert O'Meally (New York: Oxford University Press, 1994), 72–91; Alessandra Lorini, *Rituals of Race: American Public Culture and the Search for Racial Democracy* (Charlottesville: University Press of Virginia, 1999); Shane White, " 'It Was a Proud Day': African Americans, Festivals, and Parades in the North, 1741–1834," *Journal of American History* 81, no. 1 (June 1994): 13–50.

39. Emma Jones Lapsansky describes this process in " 'Since They Got Those Separate Churches': Afro-Americans and Racism in Jacksonian Philadelphia," *American Quarterly* 32, no. 1 (Spring 1980): 58.

40. Ira Berlin, *Slaves Without Masters: The Free Negro in the Antebellum South* (New York: New Press, 1974), 289–90; Daniel A. Payne, *History of the African Methodist Episcopal Church* (1891; New York: Arno Press, 1969), 45. For a discussion of the Vesey "conspiracy" as largely an invention of some white Charlestonians' imaginations rather than a real rebellion plot, see Michael P. Johnson, "Denmark Vesey and His Co-Conspirators," *William and Mary Quarterly* 58, no. 4 (2001): 915–76.

41. Loretta J. Williams, *Black Freemasonry and Middle-Class Realities* (Columbia: University of Missouri, 1980), 45; Theda Skocpol and Jennifer Lynn Oser, "Organization Despite Adversity: The Origins and Development of African American Fraternal Associations," *Social Science History* 28, no. 3 (Fall 2004): 367–438, especially 373–82.

42. Regarding the rise of anti-Masonry, see Loretta Williams, *Black Freemasonry*, 54–59. African American leaders did not generally take up anti-Masonic thought. Even highly placed religious leaders, including the AME Church's founding bishop, Richard Allen, were among the founders of black Masonic lodges. See Horton, *Free People of Color*, 126–28. In 1844, there was a short-lived effort to bar AME ministers from holding membership in "Free Masonry and other secret societies." This measure met with "much debate and rather unpleasant feeling" and was ultimately withdrawn by its proponents. See "General Conference Journal, 1844," reprinted in C[harles] S. Smith, *A History of the African Methodist Episcopal Church, Being a Volume Supplemental to a History of the African Methodist Episcopal Church, by Daniel Alexander Payne* (Philadelphia: Book Concern of the AME Church, 1922), 417–27. See also Don A. Cass, *Negro Free Masonry and Segregation* (Chicago: E. A. Cook, 1957); William H. Grimshaw, *Official History of Freemasonry Among the Colored People in North America; Tracing the Growth of Masonry From 1717 Down to the Present Day* (1903; New York: Negro Universities Press, 1969); and William A. Muraskin, *Middle-Class Blacks in a White Society: Prince Hall Freemasonry in America* (Berkeley: University of California Press, 1975).

43. Donald Yacavone, "The Transformation of the Black Temperance Movement, 1827–1854: An Interpretation," *Journal of the Early Republic* 8 (Fall 1988): 282–86.

44. Scholars who have recently examined African American intellectual culture in this period include Bay, *White Image in the Black Mind*, and Rael, *Black Identity and Black Protest*.

45. Carol George describes this concern among AME ministers, particularly Bishop Richard Allen, in *Segregated Sabbaths: Richard Allen and the Rise of Independent Black Churches, 1760–1840* (New York: Oxford University Press, 1973), 174–75.

46. Winthrop D. Jordan, *White Over Black: American Attitudes Toward the Negro, 1550–1812* (Chapel Hill: University of North Carolina Press, 1968); Jennifer L. Morgan, *Laboring Women: Reproduction and Gender in New World Slavery* (Philadelphia: University of Pennsylvania Press, 2004); Jennifer L. Morgan, " 'Some Could Suckle Over Their Shoulder': Male Travelers, Female Bodies, and the Gendering of Racial Ideology, 1500–1770," *William and Mary Quarterly* 54, no. 1 (January 1997): 167–92.

47. Deborah Gray White, *Ar'n't I a Woman? Female Slaves in the Plantation South* (New York: W. W. Norton, 1999), 27–61.

48. See Rael, *Black Identity and Black Protest*, chaps. 4 and 5, which examine black leaders' use of "the vocabularies of elevation and respectability."

49. "Life in Philadelphia," *Daily National Journal*, 25 April 1829. Thank you to Clayton Lewis at the Clements Library for his generous advice about Clay and "Life in Philadelphia."

50. For discussion of the "Life in Philadelphia" series, see Emma Lapsansky, " 'Since They Got Those Separate Churches' "; Phillip Lapsansky, "Graphic Discord: Abolitionist and Antiabolitionist Images," in *The Abolitionist Sisterhood: Women's Political Culture in Antebellum America*, ed. Jean F. Yellin and John C. Van Horne (Ithaca, N.Y.: Cornell University Press, 1994), 201–30; and Rael, *Black Identity and Black Protest*, 161, et seq.

51. Jean F. Yellin, *Women and Sisters: The Antislavery Feminists in American Culture* (New Haven, Conn.: Yale University Press, 1989).

Chapter One

1. Maria W. Stewart, "Lecture Delivered at the Franklin Hall (21 September 1832) [Reprinted in *Liberator*, 17 November 1832]," in *Maria W. Stewart, America's First Black Woman Political Writer: Essays and Speeches*, ed. Marilyn Richardson (Bloomington: Indiana University Press, 1987), 45. Catherine Brekus points out that female evangelical preachers had been speaking before mixed audiences since as early as the 1740s. See *Strangers and Pilgrims: Female Preaching in America, 1740–1845* (Chapel Hill: University of North Carolina Press, 1998), 197, 205, 223. Earlier, Frances ("Fanny") Wright had drawn the ire of Americans, speaking to promiscuous audiences in the late 1820s. See Celia M. Eckhardt, *Fanny Wright: Rebel in America* (Cambridge: Harvard University Press, 1984).

2. James O. Horton and Lois E. Horton, *Black Bostonians: Family Life and Community Struggle in the Antebellum North* (New York: Holmes & Meier, 1979), 1–8.

3. Leonard P. Curry, *The Free Black in Urban America, 1800–1850: The Shadow of the Dream* (Chicago: University of Chicago Press, 1981), 166. On African Americans in antebellum Boston, see Horton and Horton, *Black Bostonians*. The legality of slavery in Massachusetts was undermined by the Supreme Judicial Court in 1783, after which the state's free black citizens challenged their exclusion from public facilities and schools. See Joanne P. Melish, *Disowning Slavery: Gradual Emancipation and "Race" in New England, 1780–1860* (Ithaca, N.Y.: Cornell University Press, 1998), 64–65, 94–95.

4. Donald M. Jacobs, "William Lloyd Garrison's *Liberator* and Boston's Blacks, 1830–1865," *New England Quarterly* 44 (June 1971): 259–77; *Liberator*, 12 November 1831.

5. Marilyn Richardson, Preface to Richardson, ed., *Maria W. Stewart*, 1.

6. *Liberator*, 28 September 1833.

7. Maria W. Stewart, "An Address Delivered Before the Afric-American Female Intelligence Society of America [reprinted from *Liberator*, 28 April 1832]," in Richardson, ed., *Maria W. Stewart*, 55.

8. Maria W. Stewart, "Religion and the Pure Principles of Morality, The Sure Foundation on Which We Must Build. Productions from the Pen of Mrs. Maria W. Steward [*sic*], Widow of the Late James W. Steward, of Boston," reprinted in Richardson, ed., *Maria W. Stewart*, 31, 37.

9. Regarding the development of such ideas as they pertained to white women, see Barbara Welter, "The Cult of True Womanhood: 1820–1860," *American Quarterly* 18, no. 2, pt. 1 (Summer 1966): 151–74; Nancy F. Cott, *The Bonds of Womanhood: "Woman's Sphere" in New England, 1780–1835* (New Haven, Conn.: Yale University Press, 1977); Barbara Epstein, *The Politics of Domesticity: Women, Evangelism, and Temperance in Nineteenth Century America* (Middletown, Conn.: Wesleyan University Press, 1981); Linda K. Kerber, *Women of the Republic: Intellect and Ideology in Revolutionary America* (Chapel Hill: University of North Carolina Press, 1980); Mary Kelley, *Private Woman, Public Stage: Literary Domesticity in Nineteenth-Century America* (New York: Oxford University Press, 1984); and Carroll Smith-Rosenberg, *Disorderly Conduct: Visions of Gender in Victorian America* (New York: Oxford University Press, 1985). Regarding African American women, see Shirley Carlson, "Black Ideals of Womanhood in the Victorian Era," *Journal of Negro History* 77, no. 2 (Spring 1992): 61–73.

10. Regarding images of slave women, see Deborah Gray White, *Ar'n't I a Woman? Female Slaves in the Plantation South*, rev. ed. (New York: W. W. Norton, 1999), and Jennifer L. Morgan, " 'Some Could Suckle Over Their Shoulder': Male Travelers, Female Bodies, and the Gendering of Racial Ideology, 1500–1770," *William and Mary Quarterly* 54, no. 1 (January 1997): 167–92.

11. Stewart, "Lecture Delivered at the Franklin Hall," 48.

12. Stewart, "Religion and the Pure Principles of Morality," 38.

13. "Matilda," "For the Freedom's Journal," *Freedom's Journal*, 10 August 1827.

14. Stewart, "Religion and the Pure Principles of Morality," 37–38.

15. Maria W. Stewart, "Mrs. Stewart's Farewell Address to Her Friends in the City of Boston," in Richardson, ed., *Maria W. Stewart*, 69.

16. Stewart, "Religion and the Pure Principles of Morality," 37–38.

17. William C. Nell, *Liberator*, 5 March 1852, reprinted in Richardson, ed., *Maria W. Stewart*, 90.

18. Dorothy Sterling offers this view in her commentary on Stewart's writings, *We Are Your Sisters: Black Women in the Nineteenth Century* (New York: W. W. Norton, 1984), 157. This same interpretation is offered by Shirley J. Yee in *Black Women Abolitionists: A Study in Activism, 1828–1860* (Knoxville: University of Tennessee Press, 1992), 115.

19. Elizabeth McHenry, *Forgotten Readers: Recovering the Lost History of African American Literary Societies* (Durham, N.C.: Duke University Press, 2002), 69–79.

20. Jan Lewis, "The Republican Wife: Virtue and Seduction in the Early Republic," *William and Mary Quarterly* 44, no. 4 (October 1987): 689–721.

21. On female influence, see Patrick Rael's discussion of "women and character formation" in *Black Identity and Black Protest in the Antebellum North* (Chapel Hill: University of North Carolina Press, 2002), 150–55. Rael aptly describes a point of view among antebellum black activists, one that he terms the "bulk" or "weight" of opinion, that favored limiting women's roles to the realms of home and benevolence. Rael overlooks the extent to which, even by the late 1830s, female influence was a contested notion that would be rivaled by a women's rights point of view.

22. Garland, "Female Influence," *Colored American*, 21 November 1840.

23. C[harles] B. R[ay], "Female Education," *Colored American*, 18 March 1837; "Augustine" [Lewis Woodson], "The West—No. VI," *Colored American*, 26 June 1838. For a discussion of Ray's early activism, see M. N. Work, "The Life of Charles B. Ray," *Journal of Negro History* 4, no. 4 (October 1919): 361–71; and Anne M. Boylan, *The Origins of Women's Activism: New York and Boston, 1797–1840* (Chapel Hill: University of North Carolina Press, 2002).

24. "Woman's Eloquence," *Colored American*, 17 November 1838; "Female Temper," *Freedom's Journal*, 20 April 1827.

25. "An Interested Observer, Thoughts on Miss S. M. Grimké's Duties of Woman" (reprinted from the *Advocate of Moral Reform*), *Colored American*, 22 September 1838.

26. See, for example, "Matilda," "For the Freedom's Journal"; and "Beatrice," "Female Education," *Liberator*, 7 July 1832.

27. "Beatrice," "Female Education." Regarding the identity of "Beatrice," see Julie Winch, " 'You Have Talents—Only Cultivate Them': Philadelphia's Black Female Literary Societies and the Abolitionist Crusade," in *The Abolitionist Sisterhood: Women's Political Culture in Antebellum America*, ed. Jean F. Yellin and John C. Van Horne (Ithaca, N.Y.: Cornell University Press, 1994), 107–8.

28. "Matilda," "For the Freedom's Journal."

29. Ellen, "Female Influence," *Colored American*, 30 September 1837.

30. "D." [editor], "To the Females of Color," *Colored American*, 7 July 1837.

31. Women were not singled out in this respect, and concerns about how young men and young women were to be educated occupied activists' exchanges. Relatedly, they asked whether African Americans should seek admission into already existing institutions of learning or found separate schools.

32. McHenry, *Forgotten Readers*, 42–57. See also Dorothy B. Porter, "The Organized Educational Activities of Negro Literary Societies, 1828–1846," *Journal of Negro Education* 5, no. 4 (October 1936): 555–76.

33. "Ladies Literary Society of the City of New York," *Colored American*, 23 September 1837; "Philadelphia Female Literary Society," *Liberator*, 29 November 1834.

34. *Colored American*, 3 February 1838.

35. ["Minerva Society"], *Colored American*, 15 September 1838; ["Colored Female Literary Society of Providence"], *Liberator*, 1 June 1833. For a thoughtful exploration of the role that the practice of reading played in the development of black and white women in the antebellum United States, see Mary Kelley, *Learning to Stand and*

Speak: Women, Education, and Public Life in America's Republic (Chapel Hill: University of North Carolina Press, 2006). For another perspective on the significance of reading and writing upon women, see Erica R. Armstrong, "A Mental and Moral Feast: Reading, Writing, and Sentimentality in Black Philadelphia," *Journal of Women's History* 16, no. 1 (2003): 78–102.

36. R[ay], "Female Education."

37. "Augustine," "The West—No. VI." On Woodson, see C. Peter Ripley, ed., *The Black Abolitionist Papers* (Chapel Hill: University of North Carolina Press, 1991) (hereafter *BAP*), 3:259 n. 3; Gayle T. Tate, "The Black Nationalist-Christian Nexus: The Political Thought of Lewis Woodson," *Western Journal of Black Studies* 19, no. 1 (1995): 9–18; Gayle T. Tate, "Prophesy and Transformation: The Contours of Lewis Woodson's Nationalism," *Journal of Black Studies* 29, no. 2 (1998): 209–23.

38. "Augustine," "The West—No. VI."

39. "Beatrice," "Female Education."

40. For a brief biographical sketch of Forten, see *BAP*, 3:164 n. 1.

41. James Forten Jr., "An Address Delivered Before the American Moral Reform Society," *Minutes and Proceedings of the First Annual Meeting of the American Moral Reform Society: Held in Philadelphia, in the Presbyterian Church in Seventh Street, Below Shippen, from the 14th to the 19th of August, 1837* (Philadelphia: Printed by Merrihew and Gunn, 1837).

42. "Address to the Female Literary Association of Philadelphia, on their First Anniversary: by a Member," *Liberator*, 13 October 1832. Regarding the Female Literary Association, see Marie J. Lindhorst, "Politics in a Box: Sarah Mapps Douglass and the Female Literary Association, 1831–1833," *Pennsylvania History* 65, no. 3 (Summer 1998): 263–78.

43. "Ladies Department. Address to the Female Literary Association of Philadelphia," *Liberator*, 9 June 1832.

44. McHenry, *Forgotten Readers*, 68.

45. "Prudence Crandall. Principal of the Canterbury, (Conn.) Female Boarding School," *Liberator*, 20 July 1833.

46. James O. Horton and Lois E. Horton, *In Hope of Liberty: Culture, Community, and Protest Among Northern Free Blacks, 1700–1860* (New York: Oxford University Press, 1997), 217–18; Susan Stranc, *A Whole-Souled Woman: Prudence Crandall and the Education of Black Women* (New York: W. W. Norton, 1990).

47. In June of 1831, the delegates to the First Annual Convention of the Colored People had voted to raise funds to support a manual labor college in New Haven. See *Minutes and Proceedings of the First Annual Convention of the People of Colour, Held by Adjournments in the City of Philadelphia, From the Sixth to the Eleventh of June, Inclusive, 1831* (Philadelphia: Committee of Arrangements, 1831). Subsequent schemes would propose such a school be opened in New York or Philadelphia. See Hilary J. Moss, "Education's Inequity: Opposition to Black Higher Education in Antebellum Connecticut," *History of Education Quarterly* 46 (2006): 16–35, and "High School for Young Colored Ladies and Misses," *Liberator*, 2 March 1833.

48. George Putnam and James G. Barbadoes, "Public Meeting of the Colored Inhabitants of Boston and Vicinity," *Liberator*, 23 March 1833.

49. *Proceedings of the Third Annual Convention, for the Improvement of the Free People of Colour in These United States, Held by Adjournments in the City of Philadelphia, From the 3d to the 13th of June Inclusive, 1833* (New York: By order of the Convention, 1833), 13.

50. "Miss Crandall," *Liberator*, 12 April 1834.

51. "American Colored Convention," *Liberator*, 21 June 1834.

52. Strane, *Whole-Souled Woman*, 149.

53. "Prudence Crandall."

54. Nathaniel Paul, "To Andrew T. Judson, Esq.," *Liberator*, 23 November 1833. See also Nathaniel Paul, "Letter from Rev. Mr. Paul," *Liberator*, 12 April 1834.

55. "From the Editor," *Colored American*, 7 August 1841.

56. "Extract. From the Speech of the Reverend Theodore S. Wright, Delivered Before the State Anti-Slavery Society, at Its Last Anniversary," *Colored American*, 11 September 1837. On Wright see David E. Swift, *Black Prophets of Justice: Activist Clergy Before the Civil War* (Baton Rouge: Louisiana State University Press, 1989), chap. 4.

57. "Letter from C. Lenox Remond," *Colored American*, 3 October 1840; "On the Condition of the Free People of Color [reprint from the *Anti-Slavery Examiner*]," *Colored American*, 14 March 1840. See also Benjamin Quarles, *Black Abolitionists* (New York: Oxford University Press, 1969), 47–50.

58. "Address, Written by One of Miss Crandall's Scholars," *Liberator*, 3 August 1833; "Slavery," *Liberator*, 6 April 1833; "Literary. Persecuted Children's Complaint," *Liberator*, 11 January 1834.

59. For Julia Williams Garnet's obituary, see "Died," *Christian Recorder*, 22 January 1870.

60. Julia W. Garnet et al., "Fair in Aid of the Impartial Citizen," *Impartial Citizen*, 5 September 1849; *BAP*, reel 6, frame 128; Ella Forbes, *African American Women during the Civil War* (New York: Garland Publishing, 1998), 100.

61. Hallie Q. Brown, *Homespun Heroines and Other Women of Distinction* (1926; New York: Oxford University Press, 1988), 23–29.

62. Regarding African American Quakers generally, see Henry J. Cadbury, "Negro Membership in the Society of Friends," *Journal of Negro History* 21, no. 2 (April 1936): 151–213.

63. *BAP*, 3:117–18 n. 1; Zillah, "Reply to Woodby," *Liberator*, 18 August 1832; Zillah, "To a Friend," *Liberator*, 30 June 1832; "Ladies' Department. Mental Feasts," *Liberator*, 21 July 1832.

64. "Editorial Correspondence," *Colored American*, 2 December 1837.

65. Pease relied upon Sarah Grimké's "Letter on the Subject of Prejudice against Colour amongst the Society of Friends in the United States," which incorporated Douglass's experience. See Gerda Lerner, *The Grimké Sisters from South Carolina: Pioneers for Woman's Rights and Abolition* (New York: Schocken Books, 1967), 257; Sarah

Mapps Douglass to William Basset, December 1837, Weld-Grimké Family Papers, Clements Library, University of Michigan, Ann Arbor.

66. Sarah Mapps Douglass, ALS to Editor of the *Friend*, September 1840, Weld-Grimké Family Papers, Clements Library, University of Michigan, Ann Arbor.

67. Sarah Mapps Douglass to William Basset, December 1837, and Sarah Mapps Douglass, ALS to *Friend*, Editor of the, September 1840, Weld-Grimké Family Papers, Clements Library, University of Michigan, Ann Arbor.

68. Jualynne E. Dodson, *Engendering Church: Women, Power, and the A.M.E. Church* (Lanham, Md.: Rowman & Littlefield, 2002), 41–45.

69. Boylan, *Origins of Women's Activism*, 34, 38–39, 74, 142.

70. *Liberator*, 30 June 1832.

71. "Another Celebration!!!" *Freedom's Journal*, 15 August 1828.

72. Brekus, *Strangers and Pilgrims*. Regarding early African American preaching women, see also Jualynne E. Dodson, "Nineteenth-Century A.M.E. Preaching Women," in *Women in New Worlds*, ed. Hilah F. Thomas and Rosemary S. Keller (Nashville, Tenn.: Abingdon, 1981), 276–92; Elizabeth E. Grammar, "Female Itinerant Evangelists in Nineteenth Century America," *Arizona Quarterly* 55 (Spring 1999): 67–96; Catherine L. Peck, "Your Daughters Shall Prophesy: Women in the Afro-American Preaching Tradition," in *Diversities of Gifts*, ed. Ruel W. Tyson, James L. Peacock, and Daniel W. Patterson (Urbana: University of Illinois Press, 1988), 143–56; and Judith Weisenfeld and Richard Newman, eds., *This Far by Faith: Readings in African-American Women's Religious Biography* (New York: Routledge, 1996).

73. Jarena Lee, "The Life and Religious Experience of Jarena Lee, A Coloured Lady, Giving an Account of Her Call to Preach the Gospel," in *Sisters of the Spirit: Three Black Women's Autobiographies of the Nineteenth Century*, ed. William L. Andrews (Bloomington: Indiana University Press, 1986), 25–48.

74. Daniel A. Payne, *History of the African Methodist Episcopal Church* (1891; New York: Arno Press, 1969), 190.

75. On Beman, see Jennifer Lee James, "Jehiel C. Beman: A Leader of the Northern Free Black Community," *Journal of Negro History* 82, no. 1 (1997): 141; and Kathleen Houseley, "'Yours for the Oppressed': The Life of Jehiel C. Beman," *Journal of Negro History* 77, no. 1 (Winter 1992): 17–29. On Beman's AME Zion congregation, see Horton and Horton, *Black Bostonians*, 50.

76. *Minutes of the Yearly Conferences of the African Methodist Episcopal [Zion] Church in America, Held in the City of New York, May 19, 1838, and also in Philadelphia, in the Wesley Church June 2d, 1838*, Howard Gottleib Archival Research Center, Boston University.

77. For extended analyses of Foote's autobiography, see Joycelyn Moody, *Sentimental Confessions: Spiritual Narratives of Nineteenth-Century African American Women* (Athens: University of Georgia Press, 2001); Chanta M. Haywood, *Prophesying Daughters: Black Women Preachers and the Word, 1823–1913* (Columbia: University of Missouri Press, 2003); Beverly Guy-Sheftall, *Words of Fire: An Anthology of African-American Feminist*

Thought (New York: New Press, 1995); and C. Eric Lincoln and Lawrence H. Mamiya, *The Black Church in the African American Experience* (Durham, N.C.: Duke University Press, 1990).

78. Julia A. J. Foote, "A Brand Plucked from the Fire: An Autobiographical Sketch by Mrs. Julia A. J. Foote," in Andrews, ed., *Sisters of the Spirit*, 161–234. For discussion of the influence of Foote's religious calling on her literary strategies, see Haywood, *Prophesying Daughters*. Bettye Collier-Thomas considers the ideas expressed in two of Foote's extant sermons in *Daughters of Thunder: Black Women Preachers and Their Sermons, 1850–1879* (San Francisco: Josey-Bass, 1998), 57–68.

79. This phrasing, which echoes Roger Taney's infamous words in the 1857 decision of *Dred Scott v. Sanford*, serves as a reminder that Foote's memoir was written looking back over forty years. Writing in 1879, Foote likely knew that the AME Zion Church was finally affirming the legitimacy of her early ambitions. In 1876, the church began to eliminate all gendered distinctions in church law, opening the door to the licensing of female preachers, and Foote herself was ordained as the denomination's first female deacon and second female elder. See Chapter 6, herein.

80. Foote, "A Brand Plucked from the Fire," 161–234. Foote is likely referring to a meeting of the AME Church's Philadelphia Annual Conference in or around 1840. She only recounted these events years later in her 1879 memoir. It appears that there was no contemporaneous mention of this meeting in the local or antislavery press.

81. In many ways, Foote's story is parallel to that of Sally Thompson, a white female itinerant preacher of the 1820s who was excommunicated by the Methodist Episcopal Church after she refused to "be silent." Thompson published her recollections in an 1837 memoir, *Trial and Defense of Mrs. Sally Thompson, On a Complaint of Insubordination to the Rules of the Methodist Episcopal Church, Evil Speaking and Immorality* (West Troy, N.Y.: W. Hollands, 1837). Her story is recounted in Brekus, *Strangers and Pilgrims*, 267–71.

82. Grimké's "What Are the Duties of Woman at the Present Time?" is reprinted in Larry Ceplair, ed., *The Public Years of Sarah and Angelina Grimké* (New York: Columbia University Press, 1989), 257–64. See also Gerda Lerner, "The Grimké Sisters and the Struggle Against Race Prejudice," *Journal of Negro History* 48, no. 4 (October 1963): 277–91.

83. "An Interested Observer," "Thoughts on Miss S. M. Grimké's 'Duties of Woman,'" *Colored American*, 22 September 1838 [reprint from the *Advocate of Moral Reform*]. For an analysis of this essay, see "Women and Social Movements in the United States, 1600–2000," ed. Kathryn Sklar and Thomas Dublin, <http://www.alexanderstreet6.com.proxy.lib.umich.edu/wasm/wasmrestricted/fmrs/doc8.htm>(accessed 22 September 2004). On the Female Moral Reform Society, see Smith-Rosenberg, *Disorderly Conduct*, chap. 5.

84. Smith-Rosenberg, *Disorderly Conduct.*

85. James Forten, "An Address Delivered Before the Ladies' Anti-Slavery Society of Philadelphia," 14 April 1835, *BAP*, reel 1, frame 651.

86. W[illiam] P. Johnson, *Colored American*, 17 July 1841.

87. Editor, "Bring Your Wives," *Colored American*, 21 August 1841.

88. A Friend, "Shall Women Sign Our Petitions?" *Colored American*, 13 November 1841.

89. "Minutes of the Fifth Annual Convention for the Improvement of the Free People of Colour in the United States," *BAP*, reel 1, frame 585, reprinted in Howard H. Bell, ed., *Minutes of the Proceedings of the National Conventions, 1830–1864* (New York: Arno Press, 1969).

90. Howard H. Bell, "The American Moral Reform Society, 1836–1841," *Journal of Negro Education* 27, no. 1 (Winter 1958): 34.

91. *Colored American*, 13 May 1837.

92. James Forten et al. "Minutes of the American Moral Reform Society . . . ," *National Enquirer*, 24 August 1836, *BAP*, reel 1, frame 693.

93. *Minutes and Proceedings of the First Annual Meeting of the American Moral Reform Society.*

94. Howard H. Bell, *A Survey of the Negro Convention Movement, 1830–1861* (New York: Arno Press, 1969), 54; Bell, "American Moral Reform Society," 38.

95. Julie Winch, *Philadelphia's Black Elite: Activism, Accommodation, and the Struggle for Autonomy, 1787–1848* (Philadelphia: Temple University Press, 1988), 112, 120–21.

96. "Proceedings of the Third Annual Meeting of the American Moral Reform Society," *National Reformer*, September 1839; Bell, "American Moral Reform Society," 38.

97. Grimké wrote, "Men and women were CREATED EQUAL; they are both moral and accountable beings, and whatever is *right* for man to do, is *right* for woman" (Ceplair, ed., *Public Years of Sarah and Angelina Grimké*, 213 [emphasis in original]).

98. Yee, *Black Women Abolitionists*, 106. See also Ira V. Brown, "Cradle of Feminism: The Philadelphia Female Anti-Slavery Society, 1833–1840," *Pennsylvania Magazine of History and Biography* 102 (1978): 155; Winch, *Philadelphia's Black Elite*, 85–86; and Jean R. Soderlund, "Priorities and Power: The Philadelphia Female Anti-Slavery Society," in Yellin and Van Horne, eds., *Abolitionist Sisterhood*, 67–90.

99. Two nephews of the Bustill sisters were AMRS activists and were likely present at the 1839 meeting. See Yee, *Black Women Abolitionists*, 17–18.

100. Ibid., 98.

101. Regarding violence against antislavery activists in Philadelphia, see Emma Jones Lapsansky " 'Since They Got Those Separate Churches': Afro-Americans and Racism in Jacksonian Philadelphia," *American Quarterly* 32, no. 1 (Spring 1980): 54–78, and Julie Winch, *A Gentleman of Color: The Life of James Forten* (New York: Oxford University Press, 2002), 301–4.

102. Yee, *Black Women Abolitionists*, 108.

103. Ira Brown, "Cradle of Feminism," 155; Winch, *Philadelphia's Black Elite*, 85–86; Soderlund, "Priorities and Power," 67–90.

104. For one discussion of this debate, see Rael, *Black Identity and Black Protest*, 49–53.

105. Regarding white women's petitioning campaigns, see Susan Zaeske, *Signatures of Citizenship: Petitioning, Antislavery, and Women's Political Identity* (Chapel Hill: University of North Carolina Press, 2003), and Alisse Portnoy, " 'Female Petitioners Can Lawfully Be Heard': Negotiating Female Decorum, United States Politics, and Political Agency, 1829–1831," *Journal of the Early Republic* 23, no. 4 (Winter 2003): 573–611.

106. "Right of Petition," *Colored American*, 28 July 1838.

107. Editorial, "Massachusetts Legislature," *Colored American*, 25 April 1840.

108. David Swift discusses the petitioning campaigns of black New Yorkers in *Black Prophets of Justice*, 105–8.

109. D[avid] Ruggles, "Celebration of the 3rd Anniversary of British West Indies Emancipation," *Colored American*, 29 July 1837. Ruggles earned a reputation as an early advocate of "full civil rights and suffrage for all people, regardless of race or sex"; see *BAP*, 3:175–76 n. 5.

110. "New York Petitions to the Legislature," *Colored American*, 11 March 1837.

111. Donald R. Kennon, " 'An Apple of Discord': The Woman Question at the World's Anti-Slavery Convention of 1840," *Slavery and Abolition* [Great Britain] 5, no. 3 (1984): 244–66.

112. See Dorothy Sterling, ed., *Ahead of Her Time: Abby Kelley and the Politics of Anti-Slavery* (New York: W. W. Norton, 1991), and Henry Mayer, *All on Fire: William Lloyd Garrison and the Abolition of Slavery* (New York: St. Martin's Press, 1998), 281–83.

113. Swift, *Black Prophets of Justice*, 109–10; Carol V. R. George, "Widening the Circle: The Black Church and the Abolitionist Crusade, 1830–1860," in *African-American Religion: Interpretive Essays in History and Culture*, ed. Timothy E. Fulop and Albert J. Raboteau (New York: Routledge, 1997), 153–76; Quarles, *Black Abolitionists*, 44–45.

114. "Verdict of the Colored Citizens of Boston," *Colored American*, 11 April 1840.

115. Thomas Van Rensellaer, "The Anniversary of the Anti-Slavery Society," *Colored American*, 2 May 1840, *BAP*, reel 3, frame 405.

116. Regarding Morel, see *BAP*, 4:218–19 n. 5.

117. J[unius] C. Morel, "Letter to Charles B. Ray (16 May 1840, Harrisburg, Penn.)," *Colored American*, 30 May 1840, *BAP*, reel 3, frame 442.

118. Jeremiah B. Sanderson and Solomon Peneton, "[Meeting of the Colored People of New Bedford]," 25 May 1840, *BAP*, reel 3, frame 440.

119. A Colored Man (11 January 1841, New Bedford, Mass.), "[Letter to the Editor,] New Organization," *Liberator*, 22 January 1841, *BAP*, reel 3, frame 845.

120. Samuel E. Cornish and Theodore S. Wright et al., "Statement of the Executive Committee of the American and Foreign Anti-Slavery Society, in Relation to the Charges of the Executive Committee of the American Anti-Slavery Society, and

Their Agent, Mr. J. A. Collins," *Emancipator*, 25 February 1841, *BAP*, reel 3, frames 903–6.

121. "American Slavery," *Liberator*, 6 August 1841 [reprint from the *Ipswich Express*, 5 January 1841], *BAP*, reel 4, frame 142.

122. These incidents were reported in the African American press. See, for example, Philemon, "Intelligent Action of Our Colored Friends," *Colored American* [reprint from *The Emancipator*], 30 May 1840. On Remond's role at the World's Anti-Slavery Convention, see Quarles, *Black Abolitionists*, 131–33. In " 'Apple of Discord,' " Donald R. Kennon characterizes this event as "one of many interrelated developments" that fostered the "emergence of an organized, independent, full-blown women's rights movement," by which he means a movement among white women in the United States and Britain. For a different analysis of women at the World's Convention, see Kathryn Kish Sklar, " 'Women Who Speak for an Entire Nation': American and British Women Compared at the World Anti-Slavery Convention, London, 1840," *Pacific Historical Review* 59, no. 4 (1990): 454–99.

123. Remond noted the work of three women's organizations: the Bangor [Maine] Female Antislavery Society, the Portland [Maine] Sewing Circle, and the Newport [Rhode Island] Young Ladies Juvenile Anti Slavery Society. Remond publicly thanked the women for their support in a letter published in the *Liberator*: "[Letter to Juvenile Anti-Slavery Society of Newport, RI]," Newport, 22 May 1840, *BAP*, reel 3, frame 447. On women's roles in raising funds for antislavery efforts, see Beverly Gordon, *Bazaars and Fair Ladies: The History of the American Fundraising Fair* (Knoxville: University of Tennessee Press, 1998); Deborah B. Van Broekhoven, *The Devotion of These Women: Rhode Island in the Antislavery Network* (Amherst: University of Massachusetts Press, 2002); and Julie Roy Jeffrey, *The Great Silent Army of Abolitionism: Ordinary Women in the Antislavery Movement* (Chapel Hill: University of North Carolina Press, 1998).

124. C[harles] Lenox Remond, "Letter to Charles B. Ray," *Colored American*, 3 October 1840, *BAP*, reel 3, frame 641.

125. J[ohn] T. H[inton], "Arrival of Wm. Lloyd Garrison and N. P. Rogers from England," *Liberator*, 28 August 1840, *BAP*, reel 3, frames 584–88; Patrick T. J. Browne, " 'To Defend Mr. Garrison': William Cooper Nell: The Personal Politics of Antislavery," *New England Quarterly* 70, no. 3 (1997): 415–22; Robert P. Smith, "William Cooper Nell: Crusading Black Abolitionist," *Journal of Negro History* 55, no. 3 (July 1970): 182–99.

126. Charles L. Remond, "Letter to Thomas Cole (2 October 1840, Edinburgh, Scotland)," *Liberator*, 30 October 1840, *BAP*, reel 3, frame 677. See also Douglas H. Maynard, "The World's Anti-Slavery Convention of 1840," *Mississippi Valley Historical Review* 47, no. 3 (December 1960): 452–71; and Miriam L. Usrey, "Charles Lenox Remond, Garrison's Ebony Echo: World Anti-Slavery Convention, 1840," *Essex Institute Historical Collections* 106, no. 2 (1970): 112–25.

127. Kimberlé Crenshaw, "Demarginalizing the Intersection of Race and Sex: A

Black Feminist Critique of Antidiscrimination Doctrine, Feminist Theory and Anti-racist Politics," *University of Chicago Legal Forum* (1989): 139–67; Kimberlé Crenshaw, "Mapping the Margins: Intersectionality, Identity Politics, and Violence Against Women of Color," *Stanford Law Review* 43 (July 1991): 1241–99.

128. E[dward] S. Abdy, *Journal of a Residence and Tour in the United States of North America* (London: John Murray, 1835), 31–33.

129. "African Dorcas Association," *Freedom's Journal*, 15 February 1828; "Donation," *Liberator*, 10 January 1835.

130. Regarding Van Rensellaer, see *BAP*, 3:177–78 n. 9.

131. "Proceedings of the Annual Meeting of the A.A.S. Society. Resolutions on Political Action," *Colored American*, 30 May 1840. For one discussion of this incident, see Yee, *Black Women Abolitionists*, 106.

132. Ray, *Colored American*, 6 June 1840.

133. Thomas Van Rensselaer, "Letter to Joshua Leavitt," *Emancipator*, 25 June 1840, *BAP*, reel 3, frame 468.

Chapter Two

1. Howard H. Bell, "National Negro Conventions of the Middle 1840s: Moral Suasion vs. Political Action," *Journal of Negro History* 42 (October 1959): 259–60.

2. Shirley J. Yee, *Black Women Abolitionists: A Study in Activism, 1828–1860* (Knoxville: University of Tennessee Press, 1992), 144–45, citing Willie Mae Coleman, "Keeping the Faith and Disturbing the Peace. Black Women: From Anti-Slavery to Women's Suffrage" (Ph.D. diss., University of California, Irvine, 1982), 18.

3. *Report of the Proceedings of the Colored National Convention Held at Cleveland, Ohio, on Wednesday, September 6, 1848* (Rochester: Printed by John Dick, at the *North Star* Office, 1848), in C. Peter Ripley, ed., *The Black Abolitionist Papers* (Chapel Hill: University of North Carolina Press, 1991) (hereafter *BAP*), reel 5, frame 768, et seq.

4. Ibid.

5. ["Proceedings of the Colored Convention Held at Cleveland, Ohio, September 6, 1848"], *North Star*, 6 September 1848.

6. Benjamin Quarles (*Black Abolitionists* [New York: Oxford University Press, 1969], 178) points to this moment as the beginning of a period during which black political conventions "generally seated women, although sometimes the delegates needed prodding." Quarles overstates the case here, overlooking the exclusion of female delegates from conventions in the immediate post–Fugitive Slave Act period, as discussed in Chapter 3, herein. Shirley Yee (*Black Women Abolitionists*, 144–45) notes this as the first instance in which a black political convention considered a proposal for women's equality. She understands the debate to reflect how many black men had not yet considered "that black women might play more than an auxiliary role in the antislavery movement." Rosalyn Terborg-Penn concludes that some male delegates found Delany's resolution too "radical," giving rise to an opposition. See Rosalyn

Terborg-Penn, *African American Women in the Struggle for the Vote, 1850–1920* (Indianapolis: University of Indiana Press, 1998), 32–33. Finally, Patrick Rael examines the issue of labor politics as it was debated in this convention to illustrate the leadership split between long-standing "movement stalwarts" of national prominence and the "lesser lights" also in attendance. Rael suggests that elite leaders, like Delany and Douglass, exerted their authority through, in part, their control of the movement's agenda, though he does not consider how the alliance that emerged through the debate over women's rights—with Douglass and Delany from the older leadership and Langston and Day from the new generation—transcended such distinctions. See Patrick Rael, *Black Identity and Black Protest in the Antebellum North* (Chapel Hill: University of North Carolina Press, 2002), 35–36.

7. M[artin] R. D[elany], "Dear Douglass," *North Star*, 26 May 1848.

8. J[ames] M. Whitfield, "Address Delivered Before the Sunday School Benevolent Society of Buffalo, N.Y., by J. M. Whitfield," Amos Beman Scrapbook I, p. 64, Beinecke Library, Yale University, New Haven, Conn. Whitfield would later gain prominence as a poet and journalist. See Joan R. Sherman, "James Monroe Whitfield, Poet and Emigrationist: Voice of Protest and Despair," *Journal of Negro History* 57, no. 2 (Spring 1972): 169–76.

9. Monroe Fordham, "Origins of the Michigan Street Baptist Church, Buffalo, New York," *Afro-Americans in New York Life and History* 21, no. 1 (January 1997): 7–18, quotation on 7. Regarding African Americans in antebellum Buffalo, see Gwendolyn Greene, "From 'The Chapel' to the Buffalo Urban League," *Afro-Americans in New York Life and History* 21, no. 1 (1997): 44–46.

10. For a similar construction of female influence by Cleveland-based activist David Jenkins, see "Female Influence," *Palladium of Liberty*, 3 April 1844.

11. Established in 1838, it was one among scores of African American literary societies operating in northern cities, sponsoring debates and lectures while distinguishing itself because "at a time when women were generally excluded from public lectures, the predominantly black association opened its meetings to all, regardless of color or sex" (James O. Horton and Lois E. Horton, *Black Bostonians: Family Life and Community Struggle in the Antebellum North* [New York: Holmes & Meier, 1979], chap. 3). See also Leonard P. Curry, *The Free Black in Urban America, 1800–1850: The Shadow of the Dream* (Chicago: University of Chicago Press, 1981), 206, and Dorothy B. Porter, "The Organized Educational Activities of Negro Literary Societies, 1828–1846," *Journal of Negro Education* 5, no. 4 (October 1936): 555–76.

12. William C. Nell, "Adelphic Union—Mr. Phillips's Lecture," *Liberator*, 19 March 1847, *BAP*, reel 5, frame 395.

13. William C. Nell, "The Anti-Slavery Bazaar at Minerva Hall," *North Star*, 7 January 1848, *BAP*, reel 5, frame 549.

14. Nell, "Adelphic Union—Mr. Phillips's Lecture."

15. Jeremiah B. Sanderson and Solomon Peneton, ["Meeting of the Colored People of New Bedford, 25 May 1840"], *BAP*, reel 3, frame 440.

16. Regarding Delany, see Tolagbe Ogunleye, "Dr. Martin Robinson Delany, 19th-Century Africanist Womanist: Reflections on His Avant-Garde Politics Concerning Gender, Colorism, and National Building," *Journal of Black Studies* 28, no. 5 (1998): 628–49; and Robert M. Kahn, "The Political Ideology of Martin Delany," *Journal of Black Studies* 14, no. 4 (1984): 415–40. Delany's family had fled Virginia for Pennsylvania to avoid the state's prohibitions against educating free black people. He later migrated to Pittsburgh and studied under Lewis Woodson, eventually emerging as a local reformer and journalist. See Victor Ulman, *Martin R. Delany: The Beginnings of Black Nationalism* (Boston: Beacon Press, 1971).

17. Robert S. Levine, *Martin Delany, Frederick Douglass, and the Politics of Representative Identity* (Chapel Hill: University of North Carolina Press, 1997), 19–57.

18. Martin R. Delany, "Letter to Frederick Douglass (7 May 1848, Cincinnati, Ohio)," *North Star*, 26 May 1848, *BAP*, reel 5, frame 657.

19. Martin R. Delany, "Letter to Frederick Douglass (5 November 1848, Pittsburgh, Penn.)," *North Star*, 17 November 1848, *BAP*, reel 5, frame 827. Ogunleye ("Dr. Martin Robinson Delany") argues that Delany was an Africanist-Womanist, a term more commonly used to characterize women of African descent committed to the liberation of the entire family through a complementary rather than adversarial or competitive relationship with their male counterparts. Of Delany, Ogunleye says that he established "postsexist African American social and political institutions . . . distanced himself from European patriarchal attitudes[, and] dedicated his life to a gender-inclusive formation and/or restoration of Africana nationals, institutions, polity, history, and culture." Ogunleye further sees Delany's womanism as distinct from the protofeminism of men like Douglass, who were, in Ogunleye's assessment, more likely to be allied with white rather than black women. See "Dr. Martin Robinson Delany," 630. I argue that Delany's thought on the woman question was well understood within the spectrum of African American thought of the period.

20. Robert S. Levine, ed., *Martin R. Delany: A Documentary Reader* (Chapel Hill: University of North Carolina Press, 2003), 18–19.

21. Waldo E. Martin Jr., *The Mind of Frederick Douglass* (Chapel Hill: University of North Carolina Press, 1984), 145, quoting Frederick Douglass, "The Rights of Women." Douglass expressed these sentiments at the 1850 Worcester, Massachusetts, woman's rights convention. See "Woman's Rights Convention at Worcester, Mass.," *Frederick Douglass' Paper*, 30 October 1851.

22. Waldo Martin explains Douglass's vision at this moment as one that called for an "associated effort" that gave "unity and direction to 'individual effort' and 'political action,'" a sense of priorities that gave unity and direction both to a broad social reform ethos and to the competing demands for primacy among various social reform causes" (*Mind of Frederick Douglass*, 18).

23. Benjamin Quarles, *Frederick Douglass* (1949; New York: Da Capo Press, 1997), 89–90, 131–32.

24. W. E. B. DuBois, *The Negro Church. Report of a Social Study Made Under the*

Direction of Atlanta University; Together with the Proceedings of the Eighth Conference for the Study of the Negro Problems, Held at Atlanta University, May 26th, 1903 (Atlanta, Ga.: Atlanta University Press, 1903), 126.

25. *The Minutes of the Annual Conferences of the African Methodist Episcopal Church in America, Including the New York and Philadelphia Conferences, 1843*, Mugar Memorial Library, Special Collections, Boston University, Boston, Mass.

26. *Minutes of the Philadelphia Annual Conference [of the AME Zion Church]*, Mugar Memorial Library, Special Collections, Boston University, Boston, Mass.

27. Ward was one of the twenty-one ministers who founded the Indiana Conference in 1840. See Daniel A. Payne, *History of the African Methodist Episcopal Church* (1891; New York: Arno Press, 1969), 130, 167–81.

28. Julia A. J. Foote, "A Brand Plucked from the Fire: An Autobiographical Sketch by Mrs. Julia A. J. Foote." In *Sisters of the Spirit: Three Black Women's Autobiographies of the Nineteenth Century*, ed. William L. Andrews (Bloomington: Indiana University Press, 1986), 216.

29. James O. Horton, "Black Education at Oberlin College: A Controversial Commitment," *Journal of Negro Education* 54, no. 4 (1985): 477–99; Ellen N. Lawson and Marlene Merrill, "The Antebellum 'Talented Thousandth': Black Students at Oberlin Before the Civil War," *Journal of Negro Education* 52, no. 2 (Spring 1983): 143–46.

30. Lori D. Ginzberg, "Women in an Evangelical Community: Oberlin, 1835–1850," *Ohio History* 89 (Winter 1980): 78–88.

31. Horton, "Black Education at Oberlin College."

32. Andrea M. Kerr, *Lucy Stone: Speaking Out for Equality* (New Brunswick, N.J.: Rutgers University Press, 1992); Elizabeth Cazden, *Antoinette Brown Blackwell. A Biography* (Old Westbury, N.Y.: Feminist Press, 1983).

33. *Colored American*, 20 November 1841; *Colored American*, 4 April 1840; "Augustine" [Lewis Woodson], *Colored American*, 13 July 1839.

34. Charles Remond planned to stop in Oberlin on an 1849 antislavery speaking itinerary that included Buffalo, Cleveland, Pittsburgh, and Harrisburg. See *North Star*, 3 August 1849. Oberlin was also among the many stops on Martin Delany's 1847–48 "Western Tour." See *North Star*, 9 June 1848.

35. On more than one occasion during his western tour, Martin Delany remarked upon the contributions of Oberlin students to local communities. See *North Star*, 9 June and 7 July 1848.

36. M[artin] R. D[elany], *North Star*, 16 June 1848.

37. *North Star*, 12 and 26 January 1849.

38. Sanderson followed the abolitionist debate over women's rights in 1839 and 1840 and chaired a meeting during which black New Englanders condemned those who deprived women of their right to speak merely "on account of their sex" (Jeremiah B. Sanderson and Solomon Peneton, ["Meeting of the Colored People of New Bedford"], 25 May 1840, *BAP*, reel 3, frame 440).

39. Amy Post was an ally to black antislavery men including Frederick Douglass, Charles Remond, and William Nell. Her leadership in the Western New York Anti-Slavery Society placed Post among western New York's more radical activists, those historian Nancy Hewitt terms "ultraist." Hewitt singles out western New York's ultraist women from their counterparts in benevolent and perfectionist circles in part for their attempts to forge links with working-class and African American women. See Hewitt, *Women's Activism and Social Change: Rochester, New York, 1822–1872* (Ithaca, N.Y.: Cornell University Press, 1984). The roots of Post's acquaintanceship with Sanderson are unclear; perhaps the two met during Sanderson's antislavery lecture tour of western New York during the early 1840s. See Rudolph M. Lapp, "Jeremiah B. Sanderson: Early California Negro Leader," *Journal of Negro History* 53, no. 4 (October 1968): 321–33, 322.

40. *BAP*, 3:466 n. 6.

41. "Jeremiah B. Sanderson to Amy Post, 8 May 1845, [New York City]," *BAP*, reel 5, frame 2; *BAP*, 3:463.

42. The WNYASS constitution provided that "any person, by signing this Constitution, shall be constituted a member of the Society." See Hewitt, *Women's Activism and Social Change*, 130, 180 (citing *Liberator*, 6 January 1843).

43. "Annual Meeting of the Western New-York Anti-Slavery Society (28 December 1846, Rochester, New York)," *BAP*, reel 5, frame 358; Hewitt, *Women's Activism and Social Change*, 120–21. On Remond generally, see Dorothy B. Porter, "The Remonds of Salem, Massachusetts: A Nineteenth-Century Family Revisited," *Proceedings of the American Antiquarian Society* 95, no. 2 (1985): 259–95; see also William C. Nell and J. C. Hathaway, "Fourth Annual Meeting of the Western New York Anti-Slavery Society," *National Anti-Slavery Standard*, 27 January 1848, [reprint from *The North Star*], *BAP*, reel 5, frame 561. At the December 1848 meeting of the WNYASS, Douglass, Nell, and Abner Francis were in attendance. See William C. Nell, "Fifth Annual Meeting of the Western N. Y. Anti-Slavery Society (12 December 1848, Rochester, New York)," *North Star*, 29 December 1848, *BAP*, reel 5, frame 871; and W[illiam] C. N[ell], "New England Anti-Slavery Convention (3 May 1848, Boston, Mass.)," *North Star*, 16 June 1848, *BAP*, reel 5, frame 677.

44. Women had long labored in antislavery society ranks, forming, for example, the groundbreaking Philadelphia Female Anti-Slavery Society in 1833 immediately following the first meeting of the American Anti-Slavery Society. Similar organizations spread throughout New England and west through the Burned-over District of New York and the Ohio Reserve. See Blanche Glassman Hersh, *The Slavery of Sex: Feminist-Abolitionists in America* (Urbana: University of Illinois Press, 1978); Ellen DuBois, *Feminism and Suffrage: The Emergence of an Independent Women's Movement in America, 1848–1869* (Ithaca, N.Y.: Cornell University Press, 1978); Jean F. Yellin and John C. Van Horne, eds., *The Abolitionist Sisterhood: Women's Political Culture in Antebellum America* (Ithaca, N.Y.: Cornell University Press, 1994); and Judith Wellman, *The Road*

to *Seneca Falls: Elizabeth Cady Stanton and the First Woman's Rights Convention* (Urbana: University of Illinois Press, 2004).

45. Rosalyn Terborg-Penn, in *African American Women*, suggests that black women were likely in attendance at these early women's meetings, but evidence of such has yet to come to light.

46. Eleanor Flexner and Ellen Fitzpatrick, *Century of Struggle: The Woman's Rights Movement in the United States*, enl. ed. (Cambridge, Mass.: Belknap Press of Harvard University Press, 1996), 68–72; Benjamin Quarles, "Frederick Douglass and the Woman's Rights Movement," *Journal of Negro History* 25, no. 1 (January 1940): 35–44, citing *North Star*, 28 July 1848; Wellman, *Road to Seneca Falls*, 203. For a discussion of the evolution of Douglass's women's rights ideas that associates their radicalization with his relationship to Gerrit Smith and James McCune Smith in the 1850s, see John Stauffer, *The Black Hearts of Men: Radical Abolitionists and the Transformation of Race* (Cambridge: Harvard University Press, 2001), 224–32.

47. James O. Horton, *Free People of Color: Inside the African American Community* (Washington, D.C.: Smithsonian Institution Press, 1993), 117; "Woman's Rights Convention," *North Star*, 11 August 1848.

48. Flexner and Fitzpatrick, *Century of Struggle*, 77.

49. "Woman's Rights Convention," *North Star*, 11 August 1848; Carol M. Hunter, *To Set the Captives Free: Reverend Jermain Wesley Loguen and the Struggle for Freedom in Central New York, 1835–1872* (New York: Garland Publishing, 1993).

50. "Woman's Rights Convention," *North Star*, 11 August 1848.

51. Ibid.

52. William C. Nell, "Woman's Revolution (14 August 1848, Rochester, New York)," *Liberator*, 1 September 1848, *BAP*, reel 5, frame 761. Nancy Hewitt notes this dynamic in *Women's Activism and Social Change*, 129.

53. "U.C.A. Association," *North Star*, 25 August 1848.

54. Maurice Wallace describes fraternal orders as crucial spheres of masculine identification in "'Are We Men?' Prince Hall, Martin Delany, and the Masculine Ideal in Black Freemasonry, 1775–1865," *American Literary History* 9, no. 3 (1997): 396–424.

55. The black Order of the Eastern Star was founded in 1874. See Mrs. Joe S. Brown, *The History of the Order of the Eastern Star Among Colored People* (New York: G. K. Hall, 1997), 151. Regarding Prince Hall and the earliest black Masonic organizations, see James O. Horton and Lois E. Horton, *In Hope of Liberty: Culture, Community and Protest Among Northern Free Blacks, 1700–1860* (New York: Oxford University Press, 1997), 126–27. Other fraternal societies organized by antebellum blacks also functioned as moral reform or mutual aid associations, and groups like the Order of Good Samaritans and Daughters of Samaria, the Daughters of Africa, and the Heroines of Jericho offered black women the opportunity to participate in auxiliary sororal organizations. Recent research suggests that those fraternal orders with their

origins in African American communities, as contrasted with those that developed from white-led orders, tended to operate through more gender egalitarian structures. See Theda Skocpol and Jennifer Lynn Oser, "Organization Despite Adversity: The Origins and Development of African American Fraternal Associations," *Social Science History* 28, no. 3 (Fall 2004), and, generally, Don A. Cass, *Negro Free Masonry and Segregation* (Chicago: E. A. Cook, 1957); Mary Ann Clawson, *Constructing Brotherhood: Class, Gender, and Fraternalism* (Princeton, N.J.: Princeton University Press, 1989); Curry, *Free Black in Urban America*; and Ian R. Tyrell, *Sobering Up: From Temperance to Prohibition in Antebellum America, 1800–1860* (Westport, Conn.: Greenwood Press, 1979). See also *BAP*, 4:110–11 n. 2.

56. Wallace, " 'Are We Men?' "; Horton and Horton, *Black Bostonians*, 31.

57. "What Are the Colored People Doing for Themselves?" *North Star*, 14 July 1848.

58. M[artin] R. D[elany], "Dear Douglass," *North Star*, 9 June 1848.

59. "Communication. Presentation to the U.C.A. Association, Cincinnati," *North Star*, 25 August 1848.

60. "U.C.A. Association."

61. William S. McFeely points out that while the *North Star* had an international readership, the vast majority of subscribers were white rather than black activists. See *Frederick Douglass* (New York: W. W. Norton, 1991), 151–53. However, Frankie Hutton explains that while most antebellum black newspapers had circulations that ranged from 1,500 to 3,000, actual readership was considerably wider due to "shared-copy" distribution. See *The Early Black Press in America, 1827 to 1860* (Westport, Conn.: Greenwood Press, 1993), xiv–xv.

62. "Communication. Presentation to the U.C.A. Association, Cincinnati."

63. While the record of Lee's remarks does not note her having expressed trepidation, we are left to wonder if she anticipated the pointed "guidance" that subsequent male speakers would offer to her and the other women present.

64. In the *North Star's* reportage Brodie is variously referred to as "I. W. Broady" and "C. W. Broady."

65. Brodie's remarks were supplemented by those of the Reverend Dr. Garry, who closed the UCAA proceedings. Garry noted that Brodie had "anticipated" his "tribute to 'Woman' " and went on then to clarify the distinct natures of men and women: "Man has been formed for intellect, woman hears the palm for affections, if man for the efforts of the head, woman for the sentiments of the heart."

66. C[harles] S. Smith, *A History of the African Methodist Episcopal Church, Being a Volume Supplemental to a History of the African Methodist Episcopal Church, by Daniel Alexander Payne* (Philadelphia: Book Concern of the AME Church, 1922), 19–20.

67. See Chapter 1, herein.

68. David W. Wills, "Womanhood and Domesticity in the AME Tradition: The Influence of Daniel Alexander Payne," in *Black Apostles at Home and Abroad: Afro-*

Americans and the Christian Mission from Revolution to Reconstruction, ed. David W. Wills and Richard Newman (Boston: G. K. Hall, 1982).

69. B[enjamin] T. Tanner, *An Outline of Our History and Government for African Methodist Churchmen, Ministerial and Lay. In Catechetical Form. Two Parts with Appendix* (Philadelphia: Grant, Faires & Rodgers, Printers, 1844).

70. African Americans reported on the women's conventions at Seneca Falls and Rochester in the *Liberator* and the *North Star*. See Nell, "Woman's Revolution," and *North Star*, 8 August 1848.

71. F[rederick] D[ouglass], "Visit to Philadelphia," *North Star*, 13 October 1848. Douglass singled out Stephen Gloucester's Central Presbyterian Church, St. Thomas Protestant Episcopal Church, and "Large Bethel," presumably Bethel AME Church. See also "Proceedings of the Anti-Slavery Convention Held in Philadelphia," *North Star*, 10 November 1848.

72. See, for example, W[illiam] D[ouglass], "Communications," *North Star*, 27 October 1848; F[rederick] D[ouglass], "Colored Churches in Philadelphia," *North Star*, 27 October 1848; W[illiam] D[ouglass], "Communications," *North Star*, 24 November 1848; G. [Letter to Frederick Douglass"], *North Star*, 1 December 1848; and F[rederick] D[ouglass], "St. Thomas Church, Philadelphia," *North Star*, 8 December 1848.

73. J. J. Gould Bias et al., "Proceedings of the Anti-Slavery Convention Held in Philadelphia," *North Star*, 10 November 1848. On Purvis, see Margaret H. Bacon, "The Double Curse of Sex and Color: Robert Purvis and Human Rights," *Pennsylvania Magazine of History and Biography* 121, no. 1/2 (January/April 1997): 53.

74. Lucretia Coffin Mott to Elizabeth Cady Stanton, 3 October 1848, in Ann D. Gordon, ed. *In the School of Anti-Slavery*, vol. 1 of *The Selected Papers of Elizabeth Cady Stanton and Susan B. Anthony* (New Brunswick: Rutgers University Press, 2000), 126–28. Regarding antislavery alliances between black and white women, see Ira V. Brown, "Cradle of Feminism: The Philadelphia Female Anti-Slavery Society, 1833–1840," *Pennsylvania Magazine of History and Biography* 102 (1978): 143–66.

75. There are those who have successfully argued that the Burned-over District stretched as far west as southeastern Michigan. See Judith Wellman, "Crossing Over Cross: Whitney Cross's *Burned-Over District* as Social History," *Reviews in American History*, 17, no. 1 (March 1989) 159–74; and Merton L. Dillon, "Elizabeth Chandler and the Spread of Antislavery Sentiment to Michigan," in *Abolitionism and Issues of Race and Gender*, ed. John R. McKivigan (New York: Garland Publishing, 1999), 205–18.

76. Whitney Cross, *The Burned-Over District: Social and Intellectual History of Enthusiastic Religion, 1800–1850* (New York: Harper and Row, 1950), 3.

77. Ibid., 173.

78. David M. Ellis, "Conflicts Among Calvinists: Oneida Revivalists in the 1820s," *New York History* 71, no. 1 (1990): 24–44; Russell W. Irvine and Donna Z. Dunkerton, "The Noyes Academy, 1834–1835: The Road to the Oberlin Collegiate Institute and

the Higher Education of African-Americans in the Nineteenth Century," *Western Journal of Black Studies* 22 (Winter 1998): 260–73.

79. Regarding the Burned-over District's ultraist climate generally, see Wellman, "Crossing Over Cross," 159–74; Karen J. Kriebl, "From Bloomers to Flappers: The American Women's Dress Reform Movement, 1840–1920" (Ph.D. diss., Ohio State University, 1998); James L. McElroy, "Social Reform in the Burned Over District: Rochester, New York as a Test Case, 1830–1851" (Ph.D. diss., SUNY Binghamton, 1974); and Linda K. Pritchard, "The Burned Over District Reconsidered: A Portent of Evolving Religious Pluralism in the United States," *Social Science History* 8, no. 3 (1984): 243–66.

80. Hewitt, *Women's Activism and Social Change*.

81. Regarding the emergence of the women's rights movement in the Burned-over District generally, see Wellman, "Crossing Over Cross," xxi; Judith Wellman, "The Seneca Falls Women's Rights Convention: A Study of Social Networks," *Journal of Women's History* 3 (1991): 9–37; Nancy A. Hewitt, "The Social Origins of Women's Antislavery Politics in Western New York," in *Crusaders and Compromisers: Essays on the Relationship of the Antislavery Struggle to the Antebellum Party System*, ed. Alan Kraut (Westport, Conn.: Greenwood Press, 1983); Margaret H. McFadden, *Golden Cables of Sympathy: The Transatlantic Sources of Nineteenth-Century Feminism* (Lexington: University Press of Kentucky, 1999); Keith E. Melder, *The Beginnings of Sisterhood: The American Women's Rights Movement, 1800–1840* (New York: Schocken Books, 1977); Jerome Nadelhaft, "Subjects and/or Objects: Abolitionists and 'Utopian' Women," *Reviews in American History* 21, no. 3 (1993): 407–14; Louise M. Newman, *White Women's Rights: The Racial Origins of Feminism in the United States* (New York: Oxford University Press, 1999); Robert E. Riegel, "Women's Clothes and Women's Rights," *American Quarterly* 15, no. 3 (Autumn 1963): 390–401; and Judith Wellman, "Women and Radical Reform in Antebellum Upstate New York: A Profile of Grassroots Female Abolitionists," in *Clio Was a Woman: Studies in the History of American Women*, ed. Mebel E. Deutrich and Virginia C. Purdy (Washington, D.C.: Howard University Press, 1980).

82. See Sharon A. Hepburn, "Following the North Star: Canada as a Haven for Nineteenth-Century American Blacks," *Michigan Historical Review* 25 (Fall 1999): 91–126; Daniel Hill, *The Freedom Seekers: Blacks in Early Canada* (Toronto: Stoddart, 1992); and Robin W. Winks, *The Blacks in Canada: A History* (Montreal; Kingston: McGill-Queen's University Press, 1997).

83. Gerald G. Eggert, "Two Steps Forward, a Step and a Half Back: Harrisburg's African American Community in the Nineteenth Century," *Pennsylvania History* 58, no. 1 (1991): 1–36; Henry Lewis Taylor Jr., "On Slavery's Fringe: City-Building and Black Community Development in Cincinnati, 1800–1850," *Ohio History* 95 (Winter–Spring 1986): 5–33; Richard C. Wade, *The Urban Frontier: Pioneer Life in Early Pittsburgh, Cincinnati, Lexington, Louisville, and St. Louis* (New York: Negro University Press, 1959).

84. For a general discussion of the African American presence in western New

York, see Ena L. Farley, "The African American Presence in the History of Western New York," *Afro-Americans in New York Life and History* 14 (January 1990): 27–89; Musette S. Castle, "A Survey of the History of African Americans in Rochester, New York, 1800–1860," *Afro-Americans in New York Life and History* 13 (July 1989): 7–32; Myra B. Young Armstead, Gretchen Sullivan Sorin, and Field Horne, *A Heritage Uncovered: The Black Experience in Upstate New York, 1800–1925,* ed. Cara A. Sutherland (Elmira, N.Y.: Chemung County Historical Society, 1988); Jan DeAmicis, "The Search for Community: Utica's African Americans," in *Ethnic Utica,* ed. James Pula (Utica, N.Y., 1994); Jan DeAmicis, " 'To Them That Has Brot Me Up': Black Oneidans and Their Families, 1850–1920," *Afro-Americans in New York Life and History* 21, no. 2 (July 1997): 19–38; Kathryn Grover, *Make a Way Somehow: African-Americans in Geneva, New York, 1790–1965* (Geneva, N.Y.: Geneva Historical Society, 1991); Paula J. Priebe, "Central and Western New York and the Fugitive Slave Law of 1850," *Afro-Americans in New York Life and History* 15, no. 1 (1992): 19–29; Milton C. Sernett, "On Freedom's Threshold: The African American Presence in Central New York, 1760–1940," *Afro-Americans in New York Life and History* 19, no. 1 (January 1995): 43–91; Jason H. Silverman, *Unwelcome Guests: Canada West's Response to American Fugitive Slaves, 1800–1865* (Milwood, N.Y.: Associated Faculty Press, 1985); Jessie Thorpe, *An Introductory History of African Americans in Rome, New York* (Rome, N.Y.: Afro-American Heritage Association, 1994); Judith Wellman, "This Side of the Border: Fugitives from Slavery in Three Central New York Communities," *New York History* 79 (October 1998): 359–92; William Joe Trotter Jr., *River Jordan: African American Urban Life in the Ohio Valley* (Lexington: University Press of Kentucky, 1998); Wade, *Urban Frontier*; and Shirley J. Yee, "Gender Ideology and Black Women as Community-Builders in Ontario, 1850–70," *Canadian Historical Review* 75, no. 1 (March 1994): 53–73.

85. Martin R. Delany, "Letter to Frederick Douglass (7 May 1848, Cincinnati, Ohio)," *North Star,* 26 May 1848, *BAP,* reel 5, frame 657.

86. Catalogue and Records of Colored Students, 1834–1972, Secretary's Office IV, Alumni Records, 3, Minority Student Records, Oberlin College, Oberlin, Ohio; Catalogue and Records of Colored Students, 1834–1972, 1, Secretary's Office IV, Alumni Records, 3, Minority Student Records, Oberlin College, Oberlin, Ohio. Langston attended Oberlin during 1836, 1839, and 1841–43, and Day attended in 1843–47. See "Catalogue and Record of Colored Students, Oberlin College [1835–1862]," *BAP,* reel 1, frame 540; and Richard B. Sheridan, "Charles Henry Langston and the African American Struggle in Kansas," *Kansas History* 22, no. 4 (1999–2000): 268–83.

87. Day is mentioned by both Stone and Blackwell in the women's correspondence with one another. See Antoinette Brown Blackwell to Lucy Stone, Oberlin, Ohio, [late February 1850], and Lucy Stone to Antoinette Brown Blackwell, West Brookfield, Mass., 9 June 1850, reprinted in Carol Lasser and Marlene D. Merrill, eds., *Friends and Sisters: Letters Between Lucy Stone and Antoinette Brown Blackwell, 1846–1893* (Urbana: University of Illinois Press, 1987), 68, 74.

88. Among the black Oberlin students, current and former, in attendance were J. D. Patterson, Sabram Cox, John L. Watson, and Justin Holland. Also in attendance was David Jenkins, former editor of the *Palladium of Liberty*.

89. Douglass had written admiringly of Sanford's contributions to the August 1848 Women's Rights Convention in Rochester, referring to Sanford as a "a lady of high order of intellect" ("Woman's Rights Convention," *North Star*, 11 August 1848).

90. We know little more about Merritt, who she was or how she came to attend the Cleveland convention and sponsor the women's petition, though she was likely related to a male delegate identified as "T. J. Merritt." See Philip S. Foner and George E. Walker, eds., *New York, Pennsylvania, Indiana, Michigan, Ohio*, vol. 1 of *Proceedings of the Black State Conventions, 1840–1865* (Philadelphia: Temple University Press, 1979), 227.

91. James Horton, in his essay "Freedom's Yoke: Gender Conventions Among Free Blacks" (*Free People of Color*, 115–16), uses the example of the Columbus convention as evidence of how black women in antebellum public culture "could assert power within their community unparalleled among white women of the time." In *Black Women Abolitionists*, Shirley Yee reads the language of the Columbus resolution as reflecting how black women were on the one hand "demanding an equal voice," while on the other, holding on to "contemporary notions of femininity" as "ladies" (*Black Women Abolitionists*, 145).

92. Foner and Walker, eds., *New York, Pennsylvania, Indiana, Michigan, Ohio*, 227; Yee, *Black Women Abolitionists*, 145; Horton, *Free People of Color*, 115–16.

93. Douglass objected to Rosetta's treatment in a letter to Warner published in the *Liberator* on 6 October 1848. See "Letters to Antislavery Workers and Agencies [Part 5]," *Journal of Negro History* 10, no. 4 (October 1925): 749–74. Nancy Hewitt (*Women's Activism and Social Change*, 128) explains that the local debate surrounding Rosetta's schooling reflected the opposition to Rochester's ultraist activists with whom Douglass was associated.

94. McFeely, *Frederick Douglass*, 160–61.

95. A Subscriber, "Letter to Martin R. Delany and Frederick Douglass," 8 June 1849, *BAP*, reel 6, frame 11; Martin R. Delany, "Colored People of Cincinnati, Second Article," *North Star*, 22 June 1849, *BAP*, reel 6, frames 16–17; Sarah M. Douglass et al., "Appeal of the Philadelphia Association," *North Star*, 13 July 1847, *BAP*, reel 6, frame 43; Theodore S. Wright, "Second Anniversary of the States' Delavan Union Temperance Society of Colored People," Amos Beman Scrapbook II, p. 143, Beinecke Library, Yale University, New Haven.

96. *Proceedings of the Connecticut State Convention, of Colored Men, held at New Haven, on September 12th and 13th, 1849* (New Haven: William H. Stanley, Printer, 1849).

97. Marie J. Lindhorst, "Politics in a Box: Sarah Mapps Douglass and the Female Literary Association, 1831–1833," *Pennsylvania History* 65, no. 3 (Summer 1998): 263–78.

98. Yee, *Black Women Abolitionists*, 109.

99. Douglass et al., "Appeal of the Philadelphia Association." See also Barbara Davis, *A History of the Black Community of Syracuse* (Syracuse, N.Y.: Onondaga Community College, 1980).

100. See Ronald K. Burke, *Samuel Ringgold Ward: Christian Abolitionist* (New York: Garland Publishing, 1995).

101. Regarding Garnet generally, see William M. Brewer, "Henry Highland Garnet," *Journal of Negro History* 13, no. 1 (January 1928): 36–52.

102. *BAP*, 4:38 39.

103. Julia W. Garnet et al., "Fair in Aid of *The Impartial Citizen* (August 1849)," *The Impartial Citizen*, 5 September 1849, *BAP*, reel 6, frame 128.

104. Sydna E. R. Francis and Mary E. Weir, "To a Charitable Public (1 January 1850, Buffalo, New York)," *North Star*, 22 February 1850, *BAP*, reel 6, frame 407.

Chapter Three

1. Shirley J. Yee, *Black Women Abolitionists: A Study in Activism, 1828–1860* (Knoxville: University of Tennessee Press, 1992), 146.

2. C. W., "Interesting Discussion on Emigration to Canada Between Miss M. A. Shadd of Canada, on the Affirmative, and Mr. J. C. Wears, of Philadelphia, in the Negative," *Provincial Freeman and Weekly Advertiser*, 22 December 1855.

3. William B. Gravely, "The Dialectic of Double-Consciousness in Black American Freedom Celebrations, 1808–1863," *Journal of Negro History* 67, no. 4 (Winter 1982): 306. Gravely (p. 305) notes that there were those within the free black community who did not endorse the August 1st celebration, pointing out that the West Indian emancipation had compensated slaveholders as a condition for black freedom. Critics such as James McCune Smith proposed that African Americans instead celebrate the date of Demark Vesey's death or Nat Turner's rebellion. See also Leonard I. Sweet, "The Fourth of July and Black Americans in the Nineteenth Century: Northern Leadership Opinion Within the Context of the Black Experience," *Journal of Negro History* 61, no. 3 (July 1976): 270–72. See also John R. McKivigan and Jason H. Silverman, "Monarchial Liberty and Republican Slavery: West Indies Emancipation Celebrations in Upstate New York and Canada West," *Afro-Americans in New York Life and History* (January 1986): 7–15.

4. Gravely, "Dialectic of Double-Consciousness," 304–5.

5. Mitch Kachun, *Festivals of Freedom: Memory and Meaning in African American Emancipation Celebrations, 1808–1915* (Amherst: University of Massachusetts Press, 2003), 85.

6. Ibid., 86.

7. Zita Dyson, "Gerrit Smith's Efforts in Behalf of the Negroes in New York," *Journal of Negro History* 3, no. 4 (October 1918): 354–59; Lawrence Friedman, "The

Gerrit Smith Circle: Abolitionism in the Burned Over District," *Civil War History* 26 (1980): 18–38; Lawrence Friedman, *Gregarious Saints: Self and Community in American Abolitionism, 1830–1870* (New York: Cambridge University Press, 1982).

8. Born in New Jersey, Francis ran a clothing business in Buffalo and was active as a member of the Buffalo Library Association and as a frequent member of the Western New York Anti-Slavery Society business committee. He had coordinated the 1840 and 1841 New York State black conventions and had represented Buffalo at the 1843 and 1848 national gatherings. See C. Peter Ripley, ed., *The Black Abolitionist Papers* (Chapel Hill: University of North Carolina Press, 1991) (hereafter *BAP*), 4:106 n. 6.

9. *BAP*, 4:105–6.

10. Henry Bibb and George Weir Jr., "First of August Celebrated at Buffalo," *North Star*, 10 August 1849, *BAP*, reel 6, frames 72–73.

11. Patrick Rael, *Black Identity and Black Protest in the Antebellum North* (Chapel Hill: University of North Carolina Press, 2002), 61–65.

12. Jane Rhodes, *Mary Ann Shadd Cary: The Black Press and Protest in the Nineteenth Century* (Indianapolis: Indiana University Press, 1999), 23–24. Regarding Shadd generally, see Jim Bearden and Linda Jean Butler, *Shadd: The Life and Times of Mary Shadd Cary* (Toronto: NC Press, 1977). Regarding the black press in the nineteenth century generally, see Frankie Hutton, *The Early Black Press in America, 1827–1860* (Westport, Conn.: Greenwood Press, 1993).

13. Rhodes, *Mary Ann Shadd Cary*, 21–23.

14. J. B. Y., "Miss Shadd's Pamphlet (23 April 1849, Philadelphia, Penn.)," *North Star*, 8 June 1849, *BAP*, reel 6, frame 10.

15. Rhodes, *Mary Ann Shadd Cary*, 23, citing Martin R. Delany, *The Condition, Elevation, Emigration, and Destiny of the Colored People of the United States* (1852; New York: Arno Press, 1968), 131.

16. Rhodes, *Mary Ann Shadd Cary*, 23.

17. "Proceedings of the Woman's Rights Convention, Held in at Worcester, October 23rd & 24th, 1850" (Boston: Prentiss and Sawyer, 1851), National American Woman Suffrage Association Collection, American Memory Web site, Library of Congress, Washington, D.C., <http://memory.loc.gov/ammem/index.html>.

18. The *Visiter* was a weekly antislavery and women's rights organ. See Lester B. Shippee, "Jane Grey Swisshelm: Agitator," *Mississippi Valley Historical Review* 7, no. 3 (December 1920): 211–12. An abolitionist and women's rights moderate, Swisshelm had joined in the call for the 1850 convention after a two-year courtship by Elizabeth Cady Stanton. Until that point, Swisshelm had scorned such gatherings because women bore "whole armsful of Resolutions" that made them "look too independent attended them. And that is ground which never can be maintained." Swisshelm further objected to the discriminatory character of the women's conventions that at times excluded men. With the 1850 convention call modified to invite men to participate, Swisshelm agreed to endorse the gathering, reasoning that this would "modify" the sexual equalitarian "madness." Quoted in Peter Walker, *Moral Choices: Memory,*

Desire, and Imagination in Nineteenth-Century American Abolition (Baton Rouge: Louisiana State University Press, 1978), 157–58. See also Sylvia Hoffert, *Jane Grey Swisshelm: An Unconventional Life, 1815–1884* (Chapel Hill: University of North Carolina Press, 2004), 147.

19. Peter Walker (*Moral Choices*, 147–60) explains that while Swisshelm wrote extensively on both subjects, her writing about slavery was analytically rudimentary and contrasted with her original and carefully conceived program for the emancipation of women.

20. While the extreme nature of Swisshelm's remarks may have ensured that she would not be highly influential within the women's movement, she was not set wholly outside of its parameters—she would be invited to address the following year's convention at Akron, Ohio. See ibid., 158.

21. Numerous works have discussed racism in the women's movement, though generally in the period after the passage of the Fifteenth Amendment. See Barbara H. Andolsen, *"Daughters of Jefferson, Daughters of Bootblacks": Racism and American Feminism* (Macon, Ga.: Mercer University Press, 1986); Nancie Caraway, *Segregated Sisterhood: Racism and the Politics of American Feminism* (Knoxville: University of Tennessee Press, 1991); and Louise M. Newman, *White Women's Rights: The Racial Origins of Feminism in the United States* (New York: Oxford University Press, 1999).

22. Stacey M. Robertson, *Parker Pillsbury: Radical Abolitionist, Male Feminist* (Ithaca, N.Y.: Cornell University Press, 2000), 69–75.

23. In fact, African Americans, including Sojourner Truth and Frederick Douglass, were in attendance at Worcester. See Benjamin Quarles, "Frederick Douglass and the Woman's Rights Movement," *Journal of Negro History* 25, no. 1 (January 1940), citing *The Spy* (Worcester, Mass.), 22 October 1850; and "Proceedings of the Woman's Rights Convention, Held at Worcester, October 23d 24th, 1850."

24. Rosalyn Terborg-Penn, *African American Women in the Struggle for the Vote, 1850–1920* (Indianapolis: University of Indiana Press, 1998), 15.

25. Parker Pillsbury, "Woman's Rights Convention and People of Color," *North Star*, 5 December 1850. For a local perspective on the Worcester meeting, see Carolyn J. Lawes, *Women and Reform in a New England Community, 1815–1860* (Lexington: University Press of Kentucky, 2000).

26. Americus, "Correspondence. For the *Provincial Freeman*. Letter No. 1," *Provincial Freeman*, 25 April 1857.

27. Stanley W. Campbell, *The Slave Catchers: Enforcement of the Fugitive Slave Law, 1850–1860* (Chapel Hill: University of North Carolina Press, 1970), 23–24. For discussion of the impact of the Fugitive Slave Act of 1850 generally, see Leon Litwack, *North of Slavery: The Negro in the Free States, 1790–1860* (Chicago: University of Chicago Press, 1961), 248–52.

28. Stanley Campbell, *Slave Catchers*, 23–24.

29. The literature on the impact of the Fugitive Slave Act is extensive. See Litwack, *North of Slavery*, 248–52; Benjamin Quarles, *Black Abolitionists* (New York:

Oxford University Press, 1969), 198–215; James O. Horton and Lois E. Horton, *In Hope of Liberty: Culture, Community and Protest Among Northern Free Blacks, 1700–1860* (New York: Oxford University Press, 1987), 252–62; and James O. Horton, *Free People of Color: Inside the African American Community* (Washington, D.C.: Smithsonian Institution Press, 1993), 50. See also Jane H. Pease and William H. Pease, "Confrontation and Abolition in the 1850s," *Journal of American History* 58, no. 4 (March 1972): 923–37.

30. These figures may be exaggerated; because fugitives were less likely to be counted by census enumerators or listed in city directories (and never as such) their numbers in the free states and territories are difficult to evaluate. The key point is that their exodus, in whatever number, was debilitating to African American institutions. See Quarles, *Black Abolitionists*, 200; Fred Landon, "The Negro Migration to Canada After the Passage of the Fugitive Slave Act," *Journal of Negro History* 5, no. 1 (1920): 22–36; Jason H. Silverman, *Unwelcome Guests: Canada West's Response to American Fugitive Slaves, 1800–1865* (Milwood, N.Y.: Associated Faculty Press, 1985); and Robin W. Winks, *The Blacks in Canada: A History* (Montreal and Kingston: McGill-Queen's University Press, 1997).

31. Stanley Campbell, *Slave Catchers*, 9–15.

32. Ibid., 49; Thomas D. Matijasic, "The Reaction of the Ohio General Assembly to the Fugitive Slave Act of 1850," *Northwest Ohio Quarterly* 55, no. 2 (1983): 40–60.

33. Examples of such meetings include those in Syracuse and Cazenovia, New York. See Gerrit Smith, "Anti-Fugitive Slave Law Meeting," Gerrit Smith Papers, box 92-1, folder 1, Moorland-Spingarn Research Center, Howard University, Washington, D.C.; and "Cazenovia Fugitive Slave Law Convention, Cazenovia, New York," in Philip S. Foner and George E. Walker Jr., eds., *New York, Pennsylvania, Indiana, Michigan, Ohio*, vol. 1 of *Proceedings of the Black State Conventions, 1840–1865* (Philadelphia: Temple University Press, 1979), 43. See also Stanley Campbell, *Slave Catchers*, 49–79.

34. Horton, *Free People of Color*, 91. See also Earl Smith, "Document: William Cooper Nell on the Fugitive Slave Act of 1850," *Journal of Negro History* 66, no. 1 (Spring 1981): 37–40.

35. Quarles, *Black Abolitionists*, 200–214; Horton and Horton, *In Hope of Liberty*, 254–60; Jayme A. Sokolow, "The Jerry McHenry Rescue and the Growth of Northern Antislavery Sentiment during the 1850s," *Journal of American Studies* 16, no. 3 (December 1982): 427–45; Leonard W. Levy, "Sims' Case: The Fugitive Slave Law in Boston in 1851," *Journal of Negro History* 35, no. 1 (January 1950): 39–74.

36. Paul Thornell, "The Absent Ones and the Providers: A Biography of the Vashons," *Journal of Negro History* 83, no. 4 (Fall 1998): 284.

37. Quarles, *Black Abolitionists*, 200–203; Earl Smith, "Document: William Cooper Nell," 37–40.

38. *Moore v. Illinois*, 55 U.S. 13; 14 L. Ed. 306; 14 How. 13 (1852). The Court first questioned whether free black people had a right to travel in the 1841 case of *Groves v.*

Slaughter but did not express a clear point of view until the *Passenger Cases* were decided in 1849. See 40 U.S. 449; 10 L. Ed. 800 (1841).

39. *Smith v. Turner*, 48 U.S. 283; 12 L. Ed. 702; 7 How. 283 (1849).

40. *Smith v. Turner*, 48 U.S. 283, 492. "Opinions of the Judges of the Supreme Court of the United States in the Cases of 'Smith v. Turner' and 'Norris v. the City of Boston,'" *Southern Quarterly Review* 16, no. 32 (January 1850): 444–502. For one discussion of the significance of this wide dissemination of the case for nineteenth-century legal culture, see Alfred L. Brophy, "'A Revolution Which Seeks to Abolish Law, Must End Necessarily in Despotism': Louisa McCord and Antebellum Southern Legal Thought," *Cardozo Women's Law Journal* 5, no. 1 (1998): 33–77. See also Andrew C. Porter, "Comment: Toward a Constitutional Analysis of the Right to Intrastate Travel," *Northwestern University Law Review* 86 (Spring 1992): 820–57; and Christopher S. Maynard, "Note: Nine-Headed Caesar: The Supreme Court's Thumbs-Up Approach to the Right to Travel," *Case Western Reserve Law Review* 51 (Winter 2000): 297–352.

41. "Free Blacks," *Frederick Douglass' Paper*, 19 October 1855 (reprint from the *Baltimore American*).

42. *Smith v. Turner*, 647.

43. Regarding the relationship between ideas about European immigrants and African Americans, both enslaved and free, see Gerald L. Neuman, "The Lost Century of American Immigration Law (1776–1875)," *Columbia Law Review* 93 (December 1993): 1833–1901; Mary S. Bilder, "The Struggle Over Immigration: Indentured Servants, Slaves, and Articles of Commerce," *Missouri Law Review* 61 (Fall 1996): 743–824; and Paul Brickner, "*The Passenger Cases* (1849): Justice John McLean's 'Cherished Policy' as the First of Three Phases of American Immigration Law," *Southwestern Journal of Law and Trade in the Americas* 10 (2003/2004): 63–79.

44. *Scott v. Sanford*, 60 U.S. 393, 417.

45. Ibid., 528.

46. "Meetings at Philadelphia," *Provincial Freeman*, 18 April 1857.

47. *National Era*, 25 December 1856; *National Era*, 22 April 1858.

48. Lea VanderVelde and Sandhya Subramanian, "Mrs. Dred Scott," *Yale Law Journal* 106 (January 1997): 1033–1120.

49. Eric Lott, *Love and Theft: Blackface Minstrelsy and the American Working Class* (New York: Oxford University Press, 1993), 171, 209.

50. W. T. Lhamon Jr., "Core Is Less," *Reviews in American History* 27, no. 4 (1999): 569.

51. Lott, *Love and Theft*, 271 n. 44.

52. In standard English, the passage would read: his lecture on the "science of Abolition" came about at the "particular request from Brothers Garrison, [Seaweek], Abby Kelley, and others of the same opinion."

53. Julius Caesar Hannibal, *Professor Julius Caesar Hannibal's Scientific Discourses. Originally Published in the New-York Picayune* (New York: Stringer and Townsend, 1852).

The Library Company of Philadelphia has identified Julius Caesar Hannibal as the pen name of William H. Levison.

54. In standard English, the passage would read: his commentary moved very quickly to a condemnation of the "lords of creation," of whom he rhetorically asked: "Who gives them the privilege to use that cognomen? What did they ever do to deserve it? Did they ever do anything?"

55. In standard English this passage would read: "Eve gave up taking in washing, and went to work and gave lectures in the Metropolitan Hall, and got a party of strong-minded women to help her."

56. In standard English this passage would read: "Hasn't it led to Women's Rights conventions, sewing machines, baby jumpers and Bloomer costumes? Don't the women wear trousers, and coats, and Panama hats. . . . Don't you hear the cry of women's rights through the land?"

57. E. C. B., *George Christy's Ethiopian Joke Book. Containing All the Most Laughable Jokes, Dialogues, Stories, &c. as Told Only by This Son of Momus!* (Philadelphia: Fisher & Brother, 1858). Levison treats this same subject with less subtlety, directly ridiculing black women for wearing "Turkey" trousers and "Ingin" women's straw hats. See Hannibal, *Professor Julius Caesar*, 61.

58. F[rederick] D[ouglass], "Gavitt's Original Ethiopian Serenaders," *North Star*, 29 June 1849. Here, my reading of Douglass's commentary differs from that of Eric Lott, who sees in Douglass's remarks an appreciation for the "limitations" and "possibilities" of minstrelsy. See Lott, *Love and Theft*. In my reading, the only possibility that Douglass allowed for black performers was one that promoted the activist agenda of respectability and was thus devoid of the very things that marked a performance as within the genre of minstrelsy.

59. F[rederick] D[ouglass], "The Hutchinson Family.—Hunkerism," *North Star*, 27 October 1878.

60. Frederick Douglass, "The Antislavery Movement. A Lecture by Frederick Douglass, Before the Rochester Ladies' A.S. Society," *Frederick Douglass' Paper*, 23 March 1855.

61. John Mercer Langston, "Address to the Honorable the Senate of Ohio; The Propriety and Justness of Extending the Elective Franchise to the Colored Men of the State," John Mercer Langston Papers, box 3, folder 2, Fisk University, Nashville, Tenn.

62. Such meetings included those in Maryland in 1852, New York in 1851, and Ohio in 1851 and 1852. See John H. Walker, "Proceedings of the Convention of Free Colored People of the State of Maryland," *Journal of Negro History* 1, no. 3 (July 1916): 302 et seq.; "The Free Colored Person's Convention [of Maryland]," *Baltimore Sun*, 28 July 1852; "Minutes of the State Convention, of the Colored Citizens of Ohio, Convened at Columbus, January 15th, 16th, 17th and 18th, 1851," "Proceedings of the State Convention of Colored People Held at Albany, New-York, on the 22d, 23d, and 24th of July 1851," and "Proceedings of the Convention, of the Colored Freemen

of Ohio, Held in Cincinnati, January 14, 15, 16, 17, and 19, 1852," in Foner and Walker, eds., *New York, Pennsylvania, Indiana, Michigan, Ohio*, 54–75, 257.

63. "Minutes of the State Convention, of the Colored Citizens of Ohio," 257.

64. Regarding the black convention movement in the 1850s, see Charles A. Gliozzo, "The Black Convention Movement, 1848–1856," *Journal of Black Studies* 3, no. 2 (December 1972): 227–36.

65. *BAP*, 4:40 n.

66. She later served as the treasurer of the Ontario County auxiliary of the National Council of Colored Persons.

67. Quarles, "Frederick Douglass and the Woman's Rights Movement," 35–44.

68. A fugitive slave active in the Burned-over District, Loguen maintained a steadfast commitment to women's rights even after 1850; for example, he was elected a vice president at the Rochester Women's Rights Convention in 1853. See Carol M. Hunter, *To Set the Captives Free: Reverend Jermain Wesley Loguen and the Struggle for Freedom in Central New York, 1835–1872* (New York: Garland Publishing, 1993), 6–7.

69. Born in North Carolina of a planter father and a slave mother, Morel was educated in Philadelphia, where he began a long reform career in 1829. He and John P. Thompson had published the *Rights of All*. Morel was an advocate of black emigration to Canada and played a prominent role in the national conventions of the 1830s. A member of Philadelphia's Young Men's Anti-Slavery Society, he was highly critical of the more established leaders of the AMRS for their ineffectiveness and timidity, and his frustration with their conservatism led Morel to move to Harrisburg and then to Newark, New Jersey, before finally settling in Brooklyn, New York. See *BAP*, 4:218 19 n. 5. See also Howard H. Bell, "The American Moral Reform Society, 1836–1841," *Journal of Negro Education* 27, no. 1 (Winter 1958): 34–40.

70. "Proceedings of the New York State Council" (reprinted from *Frederick Douglass' Paper*, 3 February 1854), in Foner and Walker, eds., *New York, Pennsylvania, Indiana, Michigan, Ohio*, 80; Carol Hunter, *To Set the Captives Free*, 96.

71. Those African American activists noted in the proceedings of the women's conventions of the 1850s include Sojourner Truth, Frederick Douglass, and Lewis Ford Douglass at Worcester, Mass., in 1850; Sojourner Truth at Akron, Ohio, in 1851; Frederick Douglass in New York in 1852; Jermain Loguen, William J. Watkins, Frederick Douglass, and James McCune Smith at Rochester in 1853; Frederick Douglass in Cleveland in 1853; Sojourner Truth in New York City in 1853; Harriet Purvis, Margaretta Forten, Nancy Prince, and Robert Purvis in Philadelphia in 1854; Jermain Loguen in New York State in 1855; and Sarah Remond and Charles Remond in New York City in 1858. Many other African Americans were in attendance at these meetings, although their names are not recorded in the conference minutes or press reports. See Terborg-Penn, *African American Women*.

72. Maria Diedrich, " 'Self-Love and Social Be the Same': Afro-American Efforts to Create Communities in the Slave Narrative Before the American Civil War,"

Archiv fur Kulturgeschichte (West Germany) 67, no. 2 (1985): 389–415; *BAP*, 4:297; Yee, *Black Women Abolitionists*, 146, citing the *Troy Daily Times*, 6 September 1855, 2.

73. "State Convention of the Colored Citizens of New York, Albany, January 20, 1855," in Foner and Walker, eds., *New York, Pennsylvania, Indiana, Michigan, Ohio*, 91; "Meeting of Colored Citizens of Rochester," *Frederick Douglass' Paper*, 21 September 1955.

74. For an insightful reading of the gendered dynamics of this meeting, see Bruce Dorsey, "A Gendered History of African Colonization in the Antebellum United States," *Journal of Social History* 34, no. 1 (Fall 2000): 77–104.

75. M[artin] R. Delany, "Call for a National Emigration Convention of Colored Men," *Frederick Douglass' Paper*, 19 August 1853.

76. The minutes distinguish between the "Executive Delegates" and the "Mass Convention." The names of those in the mass convention were not recorded in the minutes. See *Proceedings of the National Emigration Convention of Colored People; Held at Cleveland, Ohio, on Thursday, Friday and Saturday, the 24th, 25th and 26th of August 1854* (Pittsburgh: A. A. Anderson, Print., 1854).

77. Regarding Mary Bibb, see Afua Cooper, "The Search for Mary Bibb, Black Woman Teacher in Nineteenth-Century Canada West," in *"We Specialize in the Wholly Impossible": A Reader in Black Women's History*, ed. Darlene Clark Hine, Wilma King, and Linda Reed (Brooklyn, N.Y.: Carlson Publishing, 1995), 171–85. Bibb was the wife of fugitive slave and emigration activist Henry Bibb, who had died just three weeks before the Cleveland emigration meeting.

78. Nell Irvin Painter, *Sojourner Truth: A Life, a Symbol* (New York: W. W. Norton, 1996), 70.

79. Ibid., 121–28.

80. C[harles] S. Smith, *A History of the African Methodist Episcopal Church, Being a Volume Supplemental to a History of the African Methodist Episcopal Church, by Daniel Alexander Payne* (Philadelphia: Book Concern of the AME Church, 1922), 24.

81. Daniel A. Payne, *History of the African Methodist Episcopal Church* (1891; New York: Arno Press, 1969), 27–73.

82. Ibid., 301.

83. On the early-nineteenth-century origins of black literary societies, see Dorothy Porter, "The Organized Educational Activities of Negro Literary Societies, 1828–1846," *Journal of Negro Education* 5, no. 4 (October 1936): 555–76; and Elizabeth McHenry, *Forgotten Readers: Recovering the Lost History of African American Literary Societies* (Durham, N.C.: Duke University Press, 2002).

84. Dorothy Porter, "Organized Educational Activities," 557.

85. Banneker Institute, "Constitution," American Negro Historical Society Collection, box 5G, folder 2, Manuscripts and Archives, Historical Society of Pennsylvania, Philadelphia (hereafter HSP).

86. Linda M. Perkins, *Fanny Jackson Coppin and the Institute for Colored Youth, 1865–1902* (New York: Garland Publishing, 1987).

87. Emma J. Lapsansky, " 'Discipline to the Mind': Philadelphia's Banneker Institute, 1854–1872," *Pennsylvania Magazine of History and Biography* 117, no. 1–2 (January/April 1993): 83–102; Harry C. Silcox, "Philadelphia Negro Educator: Jacob C. White, Jr., 1837–1902," *Pennsylvania Magazine of History and Biography* 97, no. 1 (January 1973): 75–98.

88. Banneker Institute, "Rules of the Committee on Debates & Lectures as Adopted by the Institute," American Negro Historical Society Collection, box 5G, folder 3, 1 June 1854, HSP.

89. Smith was an abolitionist and journalist who headed the *Anglo-African*'s Philadelphia Department and served as president of the institute. See Donald Yacovone, ed., A *Voice of Thunder: The Civil War Letters of George E. Stephens* (Urbana: University of Illinois Press, 1997), 8. See also "Banneker Institute," American Negro Historical Society Collection, reel 1, 10 January 1855, HSP; and Emma Lapsansky, " 'Discipline to the Mind,' " 98.

90. Banneker Institute, American Negro Historical Society Collection, box 5G, folder 16, 17 January 1860, HSP; Yacovone, *Voice of Thunder*, 4. Underdue served as chaplain of the Thirty-ninth United States Colored Troops during the Civil War. See Yacovone, *Voice of Thunder*, 4.

91. Banneker, "Our Philadelphia Letter," *Weekly Anglo-African*, 28 January 1860, American Negro Historical Society Collection, reel 1, HSP.

92. Jacob C. White Jr., "Banneker Institute Minute Book," American Negro Historical Society Collection, reel 1 [from the book entry for 3 April 1856], HSP; Emma Lapsansky, " 'Discipline to the Mind," 95–96. Regarding Sarah Mapps Douglass, see Marie J. Lindhorst, "Politics in a Box: Sarah Mapps Douglass and the Female Literary Association, 1831–1833," *Pennsylvania History* 65, no. 3 (Summer 1998): 263–78.

93. G., "Mrs. Douglass Lectures," *Weekly Anglo-African*, 23 July 1859, African American Newspaper and Periodical Collection, reel 5, Wisconsin Historical Society, Madison. In the 1820s Douglass had founded a school for African American girls in Philadelphia and in 1831 founded Philadelphia's Female Literary Association. She had been an active member of the Philadelphia Female Anti-Slavery Society and had represented that organization at the 1837, 1838, and 1839 national women's antislavery conventions. See Lindhorst, "Politics in a Box," 263–64.

94. Beverly Gordon, *Bazaars and Fair Ladies: The History of the American Fundraising Fair* (Knoxville: University of Tennessee Press, 1998).

95. Jacob C. White Jr., "Banneker Institute Minute Book."

96. Banneker Institute, "Report of the Committee on Anniversary Celebration," American Negro Historical Society Collection, box 5G, folder 6, HSP.

97. Maurice Wallace, " 'Are We Men?' Prince Hall, Martin Delany, and the Masculine Ideal in Black Freemasonry, 1775–1865," *American Literary History* 9, no. 3 (1997): 396–424.

98. Other black fraternal societies functioned as moral reform or mutual aid

associations. Groups like the Order of Good Samaritans and Daughters of Samaria, the Daughters of Africa, and the Heroines of Jericho offered black women the opportunity to participate in auxiliary sororal organizations. See Don A. Cass, *Negro Free Masonry and Segregation* (Chicago: E. A. Cook, 1957); Mary Ann Clawson, *Constructing Brotherhood: Class, Gender, and Fraternalism* (Princeton, N.J.: Princeton University Press, 1989); Leonard P. Curry, *The Free Black in Urban America, 1800–1850: The Shadow of the Dream* (Chicago: University of Chicago Press, 1981); and Ian R. Tyrell, *Sobering Up: From Temperance to Prohibition in Antebellum America, 1800–1860* (Westport, Conn.: Greenwood Press, 1979). See also *BAP*, 4:110–11 n. 2.

99. Martin R. Delany, "The Origin and Objects of Ancient Freemasonry: Its Introduction into the United States, and Legitimacy among Colored Men. A Treatise Delivered Before St. Cyprian Lodge, No. 13, June 24th, A.D. 1853–A.L. 5853," reprinted in Robert S. Levine, ed., *Martin R. Delany: A Documentary Reader* (Chapel Hill: University of North Carolina Press, 2003), 49–67.

100. Cass, *Negro Free Masonry and Segregation*; William A. Muraskin, *Middle-Class Blacks in a White Society: Prince Hall Freemasonry in America* (Berkeley: University of California Press, 1975).

101. Founded in 1846, the Felix Lodge was the city's second Masonic organization and was affiliated with the District Grand Lodge, along with lodges from nearby Maryland and Virginia.

102. "Masonic Celebration," *Christian Recorder*, 27 December 1854.

103. William H. Grimshaw, *Official History of Freemasonry Among the Colored People in North America: Tracing the Growth of Masonry from 1717 Down to the Present Day* (1903; New York: Negro Universities Press, 1969), 137–38.

104. "Masonic Celebration," 107.

105. Ibid.

106. Penelope I. Bullock, *The Afro-American Periodical Press, 1838–1909* (Baton Rouge: Louisiana State University Press, 1981); Hutton, *Early Black Press in America*.

107. Rhodes, *Mary Ann Shadd Cary*, 70–74.

108. "Woman's Rights," *Provincial Freeman*, 6 May 1854; "Woman's Rights," *Provincial Freeman*, 12 August 1854; "Commandments to California Wives," *Provincial Freeman and Weekly Advertiser*, 17 November 1855; "Female Prudishness," *Provincial Freeman*, 20 January 1855; "A Warning to Young Wives," *Provincial Freeman and Weekly Advertiser*, 17 January 1855; "Hints for Marriageable Ladies," *Provincial Freeman and Weekly Advertiser*, 26 May 1855; "A Word to the Ladies," *Provincial Freeman and Weekly Advertiser*, 22 August 1855 (reprint from *Prototype*); "Why Men Like Pretty Girls," *Provincial Freeman and Weekly Advertiser*, 21 June 1856 (reprint from the *Kentucky News*).

109. "Lucy Stone," *Provincial Freeman*, 24 June 1854; *Provincial Freeman and Weekly Advertiser*, 19 May 1855; T[homas] W[entworth] Higginson, "Marriage of Lucy Stone by Protest," *Provincial Freeman and Weekly Advertiser*, 12 May 1855 (reprint from *Worcester Spy*); Mrs. Norton, "One of Our Legal Fictions," *Provincial Freeman*, 10 June 1854 (reprint from *Household Words*); Henry F. French, "Make Your Girls Independent,"

Provincial Freeman, 4 November 1854; "Female Education," *Provincial Freeman and Weekly Advertiser*, 7 June 1856; Excelsior, "[Letter to the Editor]," *Provincial Freeman and Weekly Advocate*, 26 April 1856; "Female Character," *Provincial Freeman and Weekly Advertiser*, 24 May 1856 (reprint from *Selected*); "What Shall a Young Lady Read?" *Provincial Freeman and Weekly Advertiser*, 10 May 1856; "Employment of Women in France," *Provincial Freeman*, 2 September 1854; "Women in America," *Provincial Freeman*, 15 August 1857 (reprint from *Life Illustrated*).

110. Mrs. Swisshelm, "Woman's Mission," *Provincial Freeman*, 25 January 1854; Mrs. Swisshelm, "Man's Sphere," *Provincial Freeman*, 23 September 1854 (reprint from *Cleveland Herald*).

111. W. S., "[Letter to the Editor]," *Provincial Freeman*, 2 September 1854; "Miss Watkins," *Provincial Freeman and Weekly Advertiser*, 27 December 1856 (reprint from the *A.S. Standard*); [Miss Watkins], *Provincial Freeman*, 11 July 1857 (reprint from *Norstown Republic*); A Humanitarian, "[Letter to the Editor]," *Provincial Freeman and Weekly Advertiser*, 15 March 1856 (reprint from *New York Correspondent Daily Columnist*); M. A. Shadd, "A Short Letter," *Provincial Freeman and Weekly Advertiser*, 8 March 1856; S., "Notice," *Provincial Freeman*, 11 November 1854; Editor, "[Miss Amelia Freeman]," *Provincial Freeman and Weekly Advertiser*, 19 April 1856; Melba J. Boyd, *Discarded Legacy: Politics and Poetics in the Life of Frances Ellen Watkins Harper, 1825–1911* (Detroit, Mich.: Wayne State University Press, 1994).

112. "Female Prudishness," *Provincial Freeman and Weekly Advertiser*, 20 January 1855 (reprint from the *Cleveland Herald*); "Hints for Marriageable Ladies," *Provincial Freeman and Weekly Advertiser*, 26 May 1855 (reprint from the *London Punch*); "A Word to the Ladies," *Provincial Freeman and Weekly Advertiser*, 22 August 1855 (reprint from *Prototype*); "A Warning to Young Wives," *Provincial Freeman and Weekly Advertiser*, 17 November 1855.

113. Henrietta W— s, "[Letter to the Editor]," *Provincial Freeman*, 22 April 1854.

114. Dolly Bangs, "[Letter to the Editor]," *Provincial Freeman*, 29 April 1854.

115. Ibid.

116. *BAP*, 4:217 n. 2.

117. Ellen N. Lawson and Marlene Merrill, "The Antebellum 'Talented Thousandth': Black Students at Oberlin Before the Civil War," *Journal of Negro Education* 52, no. 2 (Spring 1983): 142–55. See also Lawrence O. Christensen, "Peter Humphries Clark," *Missouri Historical Review* 88, no. 2 (1994): 145–56; Philip S. Foner, "Peter H. Clark: Pioneer Black Socialist," *Journal of Ethnic Studies* 5, no. 3 (Fall 1977): 17–35; and Lawrence Grossman, "In His Veins Coursed No Bootlicking Blood: The Career of Peter H. Clark," *Ohio History* 86, no. 2 (1977): 79–95.

118. Ellen N. Lawson, "Sarah Woodson Early: 19th Century Black Nationalist 'Sister,'" *UMOJA* 2 (Summer 1981): 15–26.

119. James O. Horton, "Black Education at Oberlin College: A Controversial Commitment," *Journal of Negro Education* 54, no. 4 (1985): 477–99; "Catalogue and Record of Colored Students, Oberlin College [1835–1862]," *BAP*, reel 1, frame 540.

120. Major, "Letter from Baltimore," *Weekly Anglo-African*, 22 February 1862; *BAP*, reel 14.

Chapter Four

1. Brenda Stevenson, introduction to *The Journals of Charlotte Forten Grimké*, ed. Brenda Stevenson (New York: Oxford University Press, 1988); Charlotte Forten Grimké, Journal Two, 6 March 1857, in Stevenson, ed., *Journals*.

2. Charlotte Forten Grimké, Journal Three, 17 August 1862, in Stevenson, ed., *Journals*. See also Ray Allen Billington, "A Social Experiment: The Port Royal Journal of Charlotte L. Forten, 1862–1863," *Journal of Negro History* 35, no. 3 (July 1950): 233–64.

3. Stevenson, introduction to *The Journals of Charlotte Forten Grimké*, 37.

4. Charlotte Forten Grimké, Journal Three, 27 October 1862, and Journal Four, 13 April and 22 July 1863, in Stevenson, ed., *Journals*.

5. Carol Steinhagen, "The Two Lives of Frances Dana Gage," *Ohio History* 107 (Winter–Spring 1998): 22–38.

6. Charlotte L. Forten, "Interesting Letter from Miss Charlotte L. Forten (27 November 1862, St. Helena's Island, Beaufort, S.C.)," *Liberator*, 19 December 1862, in C. Peter Ripley, ed., *The Black Abolitionist Papers* (Chapel Hill: University of North Carolina Press, 1991) (hereafter *BAP*), reel 14, frame 618. See also Charlotte Forten Grimké, Journal Three, 27 November 1863, in Stevenson, ed., *Journals*.

7. Charlotte Forten Grimké, Journal Three, 27 October 1862, and Journal Four, 13 April 1863 and 22 July 1863, in Stevenson, ed., *Journals*.

8. Donald G. Nieman, ed., *The Day of Jubilee: The Civil War Experience of Black Southerners* (New York: Garland Publishing, 1994).

9. Deborah Gray White, *Ar'n't I a Woman? Female Slaves in the Plantation South*, rev. ed. (New York: W. W. Norton, 1999).

10. Steven Hahn, *A Nation Under Our Feet: Black Political Struggles in the Rural South from Slavery to the Great Migration* (Cambridge: Harvard University Press, 2004).

11. Ibid.

12. David W. Blight, *Frederick Douglass' Civil War: Keeping Faith in Jubilee* (Baton Rouge: Louisiana State University Press, 1989). Note that Mary Ann Shadd had married since the prewar period, changing her name to Mary Ann Shadd Cary.

13. Leonard A. Grimes, "War Meeting of the Colored Citizens of New Bedford," *National Antislavery Standard*, 21 March 1863, in *BAP*, reel 14, frame 768. See also Kathryn Grover, *The Fugitive's Gibraltar: Escaping Slaves and Abolitionism in New Bedford* (Amherst: University of Massachusetts Press, 2001).

14. Frederick Douglass, "Letter to William Whipper," American Negro Historical Society Collection, box 3G, folder 9, Manuscripts and Archives, Historical Society of Pennsylvania, Philadelphia (hereafter HSP).

15. On African American men in the Civil War, see Jim Cullen, " 'I's a Man Now':

Gender and African American Men in the Civil War," in *Divided Houses: Gender and the Civil War*, ed. Catherine Clinton and Nina Silber (New York: Oxford University Press, 1992), 76–91; Ira Berlin, Joseph P. Reidy, and Leslie Rowland, eds., *Freedom's Soldiers: The Black Military Experience in the Civil War* (New York: Cambridge University Press, 1998); Edward A. Miller Jr., *The Black Civil War Soldiers of Illinois: The Story of the Twenty-Ninth U.S. Colored Infantry* (Columbia: University of South Carolina Press, 1998); Noah A. Trudeau, *Like Men of War: Black Troops in the Civil War, 1862–1865* (Boston: Little, Brown, 1998); Donald Yacovone, ed., *A Voice of Thunder: The Civil War Letters of George E. Stephens* (Urbana: University of Illinois Press, 1997); William Seraile, *New York's Black Regiments during the Civil War* (New York: Routledge, 2001); Donald R. Shaffer, " 'I Do Not Suppose That Uncle Sam Looks at the Skin': African Americans and the Civil War," *Civil War History* 46 (June 2000): 132–47; and John W. Blassingame, "Negro Chaplains in the Civil War," *Negro History Bulletin* 27, no. 1 (1963): 23–24.

16. J. Mercer Langston, "[Lecture at the Cooper Institute, New York, 28 February 1865]," *Elevator*, 12 May 1865, *BAP*, reel 15, frame 885.

17. Ella Forbes, *African American Women during the Civil War* (New York: Garland Publishing, 1998), 95.

18. Lucinda Blue, "The Break of Day (15 December 1862, Sacramento, Calif.)," *Pacific Appeal*, 20 December 1862, *BAP*, reel 14, frame 622.

19. Laura F. Edwards, *Gendered Strife and Confusion: The Political Culture of Reconstruction* (Urbana: University of Illinois Press, 1997); Karin L. Zipf, "Reconstructing 'Free Woman': African American Women, Apprenticeship, and Custody Rights during Reconstruction," *Journal of Women's History* 12, no. 1 (Spring 2000): 8–31; Noralee Frankel, *Freedom's Women: Black Women and Families in Civil War Era Mississippi* (Bloomington: Indiana University Press, 1999); Leslie A. Schwalm, *A Hard Fight for We: Women's Transition from Slavery to Freedom in South Carolina* (Urbana: University of Illinois Press, 1997); Thavolia Glymph, " 'This Species of Property': Female Slave Contrabands in the Civil War," in *A Woman's War: Southern Women, Civil War, and the Confederate Legacy*, ed. Edward D. C. Campbell Jr. and Kim S. Rice (Richmond, Va.: Museum of the Confederacy, 1996), 55–72; Catherine Clinton, "Reconstructing Freedwomen," in *Divided Houses: Gender and the Civil War*, ed. Catherine Clinton and Nina Silber (New York: Oxford University Press, 1992), 306–19.

20. Nell Irvin Painter, introduction to *Incidents in the Life of a Slave Girl, Written by Herself*, by Harriet Jacobs (1861), ed. Nell Irvin Painter (New York: Penguin Books, 2000).

21. Jean F. Yellin, *Harriet Jacobs: A Life* (New York: Basic, Civitas Books, 2004).

22. Forbes, *African American Women*.

23. Berlin, Reidy, and Rowland, eds., *Freedom's Soldiers*, 16–20.

24. James Joshua Gould Bias, William Thomas Catto, and George W. Goines, "Proceedings of the Antislavery Convention Held in Philadelphia," *North Star*, 10 November 1848, *BAP*, reel 5, frame 824.

25. Sarah M. Douglass et al., "Philadelphia Woman's Association," *North Star*, 9 March 1849, *BAP*, reel 5, frame 996. Regarding Sarah Mapps Douglass, see Marie J. Lindhorst, "Politics in a Box: Sarah Mapps Douglass and the Female Literary Association, 1831–1833," *Pennsylvania History* 65, no. 3 (Summer 1998): 263–78.

26. Forbes, *African American Women*, 77.

27. Ibid., 66, 70–79.

28. Rudolph M. Lapp, *Blacks in Goldrush California* (New Haven, Conn.: Yale University Press, 1977), 240–41.

29. William J. Snorgrass, "The Black Press in the San Francisco Bay Area, 1856–1900," *California History* 60, no. 4 (1981–82): 306–17.

30. "Jamaica," "Jottings (12 April 1863, Victoria, V.I.)," *Pacific Appeal*, 25 April 1863, *BAP*, reel 14, frame 822.

31. Sarah Bram and Jennie Lynch, "A Great Movement in South Carolina. Go on Ladies, You Are Right. We'll Vouch for the President and Secretary (14 August 1865, Beaufort, S.C.)," *Anglo-African*, 26 August 1865, *BAP*, reel 16, frame 117.

32. William D. Forten et al., "Proceedings of the Annual Meeting of the Pennsylvania Equal Rights League, held in Harrisburg, August 9th and 10th, 1865," *Christian Recorder*, 25 November 1865, *BAP*, reel 16, frame 467.

33. See Eric Foner, *Reconstruction: America's Unfinished Revolution, 1863–1877* (New York: Harper and Row, 1988), 25, for a discussion of white women's transformation through war work.

34. Among the important treatments of white women's war work are Jeanie Attie, *Patriotic Toil: Northern Women and the American Civil War* (Ithaca, N.Y.: Cornell University Press, 1998); Nancy S. Garrison, *With Courage and Delicacy: Civil War on the Peninsula and Women and the U.S. Sanitary Commission* (Mechanicsburg: Stackpole, 1998); Judith Ann Ginsberg, *Civil War Sisterhood: The U.S. Sanitary Commission and Women's Politics in Transition* (Boston: Northeastern University Press, 2000); and Lyde C. Sizer, *The Political Work of Northern Women Writers and the Civil War, 1850–1872* (Chapel Hill: University of North Carolina Press, 2000).

35. In 1868, Keckley published her memoirs, *Behind the Scenes; or, Thirty Years a Slave and Four Years in the White House*; later she joined the faculty of Wilberforce University. See Hallie Q. Brown, *Homespun Heroines and Other Women of Distinction* (1926; New York: Oxford University Press, 1988), 147–49. See also Michael Berthold, "Not 'Altogether' the 'History of Myself': Autobiographical Impersonality in Elizabeth Keckley's *Behind the Scenes; or, Thirty Years a Slave and Four Years in the White House*," *American Transcendental Quarterly* 13, no. 2 (1999): 105–19; and Xiomara Santamarina, *Belabored Professions: Narratives of African American Working Womanhood* (Chapel Hill: University of North Carolina Press, 2005).

36. Washington had been in charge of the Boston School in Washington, D.C., when it opened in 1864, having previously conducted her own school in the city. After the Boston school closed in 1868, she worked in the public school system. See Forbes, *African American Women*, 144, and George W. Williams, *History of the Negro Race*

in America (New York: Arno Press, [1968]), 2:122. Brown taught in a Georgetown school that she founded; later she married the supervising principal of the Washington public schools, Henry P. Montgomery. See Forbes, *African American Women*, 68–69, and Clara Merritt DeBoer, *His Truth Is Marching On: African Americans Who Taught the Freedmen for the American Missionary Association, 1861–1877* (New York: Garland Publishing, 1995), 222.

37. Forbes, *African American Women*, 106.

38. Ibid., 70, 115.

39. "Rusticus," "Excelsior [Letter to Robert Hamilton, 2 August 1865, Cleveland, Ohio]," *Anglo-African*, 12 August 1865, *BAP*, reel 16, frame 51. Regarding Ruffin, see Maude T. Jenkins, "She Issued the Call: Josephine St. Pierre Ruffin, 1842–1924," *Sage: A Scholarly Journal on Black Women* 5, no. 2 (Fall 1988): 74–76. On the CRA, see G. K. Eggleston, "The Work of Relief Societies during the Civil War," *Journal of Negro History* 14, no. 3 (July 1929): 272–99, 285.

40. John W. Cromwell, "The First Negro Churches in the District of Columbia," *Journal of Negro History* 7, no. 1 (January 1922): 64–106; Forbes, *African American Women*, 71. Thomas Green, one of the Bethel group's leaders, was a local preacher to his Washington congregation and later served as a lay delegate to the 1880 AME General Conference. See Alexander W. Wayman, *Cyclopedia of African Methodism* (Baltimore: M.E. Book Repository, 1882), 70.

41. Union Bethel A.M.E. Church, "Minutes of the Board of Trustees, November 14, 1878," Simms Family Papers, box 89-2, folder 32, Moorland-Spingarn Research Center, Howard University, Washington, D.C.

42. Forbes, *African American Women*, 73.

43. J[ames] N. Gloucester, "Our Troy Letter (20 February 1859)," *Weekly Anglo-African*, 25 February 1860, *BAP*, reel 12.

44. "The Work Among the Freedmen of the South. The Fair to Be Held in Beaufort, S.C. Next Month," *Anglo-African*, 14 October 1865, *BAP*, reel 16, frame 311.

45. Spy, "The First of August, at Harlem, N.Y.," *Weekly Anglo-African*, 17 August 1861, *BAP*, reel 13, frame 696.

46. Forbes, *African American Women*, 67; G, "Mrs. Douglass Lectures," *Weekly Anglo-African*, 23 July 1859, reel 5; "Lecture at the Institute for Colored Youth," *Christian Recorder*, 16 March 1861; and "The Winter Lectures at the Institute for Colored Youth," *Christian Recorder*, 30 March 1861, all in African American Newspaper and Periodical Collection, Wisconsin Historical Society, Madison; Banneker, "Letter from Philadelphia," *Weekly Anglo-African*, 6 April 1861, *BAP*, reel 13; "Interesting Meeting at the Institute for Colored Youth," *Christian Recorder*, 6 April 1861, African American Newspaper and Periodical Collection, Wisconsin Historical Society, Madison.

47. Wendy H. Venet, *Neither Ballots nor Bullets: Women Abolitionists and the Civil War* (Charlottesville: University Press of Virginia, 1991), 65–66; Forbes, *African American Women*, 66, 84, 198; "New Year's Soiree of the Total Abstinence Society," *Scotsman*,

2 January 1861, *BAP*, reel 13, frame 170; "Miss Remond's Lecture," *Soulby's Ulverston Advertiser*, 19 January 1861, *BAP*, reel 13, frame 202; "Lecture on Total Abstinence (11 January 1861)," *Dumfries and Galloway Courier*, 22 January 1861, *BAP*, reel 13, frame 217; "Slavery in America [an Address by Sarah Parker Remond]," *Derbyshire Courier*, 13 April 1861, *BAP*, reel 13, frame 452; Sarah Parker Remond, *The Negroes and Anglo-Africans as Freedmen and Soldiers* (London: Published for the Ladies' London Emancipation Society by Emily Faithful, 1864), *BAP*, reel 15, frame 170; Sarah P. Remond, "Letter from Miss Sarah P. Remond [22 October 1864, Aubrey House, Notting Hill, London, England]," *Liberator*, 11 November 1864, *BAP*, reel 15, frame 595.

48. Sojourner Truth, "A Speech by Sojourner Truth (2–3 June 1863, Battle Creek, Mich.)," *National Antislavery Standard*, 11 July 1863, *BAP*, reel 14, frame 947; Editor, "Sojourner Truth," *Pacific Appeal*, 27 February 1864 (reprint from the *Anglo-African*), *BAP*, reel 15, frame 260; Forbes, *African American Women*, 68, 100; Barbara A. Steward, "Letter from Arlington," *Weekly Anglo-African*, 21 April 1860.

49. Melba J. Boyd, *Discarded Legacy: Politics and Poetics in the Life of Frances Ellen Watkins Harper, 1825–1911* (Detroit, Mich.: Wayne State University Press, 1994), 36; Bettye J. Gardner, "William Watkins: Antebellum Black Teacher and Writer," *Negro History Bulletin* 39, no. 6 (1976): 623–24; James Forten et al., "Minutes of the American Moral Reform Society," *National Enquirer*, 24 August 1836, *BAP*, reel 1, frame 693; Shirley J. Yee, *Black Women Abolitionists: A Study in Activism, 1828–1860* (Knoxville: University of Tennessee Press, 1992), 106; Howard H. Bell, "Proceedings of the Colored National Convention, Held in Franklin Hall, Sixth Street, Below Arch, Philadelphia, October 16th, 17th and 18th, 1855" (Salem, N.J.: National Standard, 1856), in Howard H. Bell, *Minutes of the Proceedings of the National Negro Conventions, 1830–1864* (New York: Arno Press, 1969).

50. Regarding Still and the Underground Railroad generally, see L. Gara, "William Still and the Underground Railroad," in *Blacks in the Abolitionist Movement*, ed. John Bracey, August Meier, and Elliott Rudwick (Belmont, Calif.: Wadsworth Publishing, 1971); and William A. Breyfogle, *Make Free: The Story of the Underground Railroad* (Philadelphia: Lippincott, 1958).

51. Boyd, *Discarded Legacy*, 120.

52. SC&SA, "[Broadside]," American Negro Historical Society Papers, reel 4, HSP.

53. Forbes, *African American Women*, 218.

54. Mifflin, "Our Baltimore Letter (20 December 1859)," *Weekly Anglo-African*, 7 January 1860, *BAP*, reel 12, frame 415; Types, "Williamsburg Lyceum," *Weekly Anglo-African*, 4 February 1860, *BAP*, reel 12, frame 475; James Theodore Holly, "Letter from Rev. J. T. Holly (20 February 1860, New Haven, Conn.)," *Weekly Anglo-African*, 25 February 1860, *BAP*, reel 12, frame 508.

55. Banneker, "Our Philadelphia Letter (21 January 1861)," *Weekly Anglo-African*, 26 January 1861, *BAP*, reel 13, frame 229.

56. Thomas H. C. Hinton, "Washington Correspondence (12 December 1863)," *Christian Recorder*, 26 December 1863, *BAP*, reel 15, frame 145.

57. Major, "Letter from Baltimore (27 January 1862)," *Weekly Anglo-African*, 1 February 1862, *BAP*, reel 14, frame 101.

58. E[zra] R. J[ohnson], "News from Home," *Pacific Appeal*, 12 December 1863, *BAP*, reel 15, frame 116.

59. Ezra R. Johnson, "Festival for the Benefit of the 54th Massachusetts Regiment in N. Bedford," *Pacific Appeal*, 10 October 1863, *BAP*, reel 15, frame 1.

60. J[ohnson], "News from Home."

61. R[obert] H[amilton], "What We've Seen While Drifting (New Bedford, Mass.)," *Anglo-African*, 26 August 1865, *BAP*, reel 16, frame 124.

62. Ezra R. Johnson, "Reception of the Toussaint Guards," *Anglo-African*, 16 September 1865, *BAP*, reel 16.

63. "S. Howard's Lecture," *Pacific Appeal*, 28 November 1863, *BAP*, reel 15, frame 78; P[hillip] A. Bell, "The Lecture and War Meeting (1 June 1863)," *Pacific Appeal*, 6 June 1863, *BAP*, reel 14, frame 897; L. A. Bell, "[War Meeting]," *Pacific Appeal*, 13 June 1863, *BAP*, reel 14, frame 915; [Editor], "Rev. T. Starr King (8 June 1863, Calif.)," *Pacific Appeal*, 31 October 1863, *BAP*, reel 15, frame 21.

64. *Proceedings of the National Convention of Colored Men, Held in the City of Syracuse, N.Y., October 4, 5, 6, and 7, 1864; with the Bill of Wrongs and Rights, and the Address to the American People* (Boston: J. S. Rock and Geo. L. Ruffin, 1864), in Howard Bell, ed., *Minutes of the Proceedings of the National Negro Conventions*.

65. Xi Wang, *The Trial of Democracy: Black Suffrage and Northern Republicans, 1860–1910* (Athens: University of Georgia Press, 1997), 11–12.

66. Hahn, *Nation Under Our Feet*.

67. Forbes, *African American Women*, 129.

68. *Proceedings of the National Convention of Colored Men* (1864).

69. Foner, *Reconstruction*, 96–97. See also James D. Anderson, *The Education of Blacks in the South, 1860–1935* (Chapel Hill: University of North Carolina Press, 1988); Donald G. Nieman, ed., *African Americans and Education in the South, 1865–1900* (New York: Garland Publishing, 1994); Ronald E. Butchart, *Northern Schools, Southern Blacks and Reconstruction* (Westport, Conn.: Greenwood Press, 1980); and Robert C. Morris, *Reading, 'Riting, and Reconstruction: The Education of Freedmen in the South, 1861–1870* (Chicago: University of Chicago Press, 1981).

70. Joe M. Richardson, *Christian Reconstruction: The American Missionary Association and Southern Blacks, 1861–1890* (Athens: University of Georgia Press, 1986), 4–5; DeBoer, *His Truth Is Marching On*, 27–29.

71. Foner, *Reconstruction*, 144. See also Jacqueline Jones, *Soldiers of Light and Love: Northern Teachers and Georgia Blacks, 1865–1873* (Chapel Hill: University of North Carolina Press, 1980); Sandra E. Small, "The Yankee Schoolmarm in Freedmen's Schools: An Analysis of Attitudes," *Journal of Southern History* 45 (August 1979); Jac-

queline Jones, "Women Who Were More Than Men: Sex and Status in Freedmen's Teaching," *History of Education Quarterly* 19 (Spring 1979): 47–50; Joel Perlmann and Robert A. Margo, *Women's Work? American Schoolteachers, 1650–1920* (Chicago: University of Chicago Press, 2001); and Richardson, *Christian Reconstruction*, 163–209. Regarding white women as freed people's teachers, see Jones, *Soldiers of Light and Love*.

72. DeBoer, *His Truth Is Marching On*. Regarding African American education in the postwar era, see Ray Allen Billington, "A Social Experiment: The Port Royal Journal of Charlotte L. Forten, 1862–1863," *Journal of Negro History* 35, no. 3 (July 1950): 233–64; Adam Fairclough, " 'Being in the Field of Education and Also Being a Negro . . . Seems . . . Tragic': Black Teachers in the Jim Crow South," *Journal of American History* 87 (June 2000): 65–91; Betty Mansfield, "The Fateful Crisis: Black Teachers of Virginia's Freedmen, 1861–1882" (Ph.D. diss., Catholic University, 1980); Linda Marie Perkins, *Fanny Jackson Coppin and the Institute for Colored Youth, 1865–1902* (New York: Garland Publishing, 1987); Perlmann and Margo, *Women's Work?*; James Anderson, *Education of Blacks in the South*; and Linda Marie Perkins, "Heed Life's Demands: The Educational Philosophy of Fanny Jackson Coppin," *Journal of Negro Education* 51, no. 3 (Summer 1982): 181–90.

73. Morris, *Reading, 'Riting, and Reconstruction*, 92.

74. Ellen N. Lawson and Marlene D. Merrill, comps., *The Three Sarahs: Documents of Antebellum Black College Women* (New York: Edwin Mellen Press, 1984), 53. Regarding Stanley, see Judith Weisenfeld, " 'Who is Sufficient for These Things?' Sara G. Stanley and the American Missionary Association, 1864–1868," in *This Far by Faith: Readings in African American Women's Religious Biography*, ed. Judith Weisenfeld and Richard Newman (New York, Routledge, 1996), 203–19.

75. Lawson and Merrill, *Three Sarahs*, 158.

76. DeBoer, *His Truth Is Marching On*; Forbes, *African American Women*; Morris, *Reading, 'Riting, and Reconstruction*.

77. Lawson and Merrill, *Three Sarahs*, 200.

78. Stewart had served on the business committee of the antislavery convention along with Robert Purvis, Charles L. Remond, Martin R. Delany, Eliza Ann Bias, and Harriet Purvis. See Bias, Catto, and Goines, "Proceedings of the Antislavery Convention Held in Philadelphia."

79. Shadrach Howard et al., "Correspondence [Letter to Priscilla Stewart]," *Elevator*, 4 August 1865, *BAP*, reel 16.

80. J. A. J., "Good Words From Washington. Hear What a Friend Says (16 August 1865, Washington, D.C.)," *Anglo-African*, 3 September 1865, *BAP*, reel 16, frame 149.

81. John Mifflin Brown, "Letter to George Whipple and M. E. Strieby," *BAP*, reel 16. Brown was an Oberlin College graduate who, as an AME Church bishop in the 1880s, championed women's right to ordination. See Rt. Rev. J. P. Campbell, D.D., and Rt. Rev. John M. Brown, D.D., "The Ordination of Women; What is the Authority for It?" *A.M.E. Church Review*, 2:351–61.

82. Mary Still, "Letter to M. E. Strieby," *BAP*, reel 15; Mary Still, "Letter to M. E. Strieby," *BAP*, reel 16; Bram and Lynch, "A Great Movement in South Carolina."

83. Her father was a Garrisonian abolitionist who participated in a Rhode Island Antislavery Society meeting in 1841, and her mother was a teacher in a family-sponsored school in New Bern. See Robert Purvis, "Report of the Sixth Annual Meeting of the Rhode Island State Antislavery Society," *BAP*, reel 4, frame 324; and Lawson and Merrill, *Three Sarahs*, 48, 49.

84. Lawson and Merrill, *Three Sarahs*, 50–51, 65–70.

85. Ellen N. Lawson, "Sarah Woodson Early: 19th Century Black Nationalist 'Sister,' " *UMOJA* 2 (Summer 1981): 15–26.

86. Clara C. Duncan to Professor Woodbury, 19 December 1864, in Lawson and Merrill, *Three Sarahs*, 246–47.

87. Rosalyn Terborg-Penn, *African American Women in the Struggle for the Vote, 1850–1920* (Indianapolis: University of Indiana Press, 1998); Nell Irvin Painter, *Sojourner Truth: A Life, a Symbol* (New York: W. W. Norton, 1996).

88. Ellen DuBois, *Feminism and Suffrage: The Emergence of an Independent Women's Movement in America, 1848–1869* (Ithaca, N.Y.: Cornell University Press, 1978).

89. See Foner, *Reconstruction*, 480, and Terborg-Penn, *African American Women*.

90. Elsa Barkley Brown, "To Catch a Vision of Freedom: Reconstructing Southern Black Women's Political History, 1865–1880," in *Unequal Sisters: A Multi-Cultural Reader in U.S. Women's History*, 3rd ed., ed. Ellen DuBois and Vicki Ruiz (New York: Routledge, 2000), 124–46.

91. Mercier was a successful barber from Louisiana. See Lapp, *Blacks in Gold Rush California*, 105.

92. *BAP*, 3:89–90 n. 5.

93. A. J. White, "Public Meeting in San Jose," *Elevator*, 15 September 1865, *BAP*, reel 16. Cassey was a schoolteacher in San Jose and an ordained deacon in San Francisco's Protestant Episcopal Church. After the war, Cassey established the Phoenix Institute, a high school for black students. See Lapp, *Blacks in Gold Rush California*, 166, 184.

94. William H. Harper, "Letter to the Editor [Philip A. Bell]," *Elevator*, 16 September 1865, *BAP*, reel 16. Harper was the owner of the Harper and West Hotel and had been an antislavery activist in the East. See Lapp, *Blacks in Goldrush California*, 97–98.

95. *Elevator*, 11 October 1865, African American Newspaper and Periodical Collection, reel 3, Wisconsin Historical Society, Madison.

96. John A. Barber and Shadrach Howard, "The Ratification Meeting (11 October 1865)," *Elevator*, 13 October 1865, *BAP*, reel 16, frame 306.

97. Regarding Purvis, see Margaret H. Bacon, "The Double Curse of Sex and Color: Robert Purvis and Human Rights," *Pennsylvania Magazine of History and Biography* 121, no. 1/2 (January/April 1997): 53. Regarding Garnet, see William M.

Brewer, "Henry Highland Garnet," *Journal of Negro History* 13, no. 1 (January 1928): 36–52.

98. Terborg-Penn, "Afro-Americans in the Struggle for Woman Suffrage," 84–85.

99. Herman D. Bloch, "Labor and the Negro, 1866–1910," *Journal of Negro History* 50, no. 3 (1965): 163–84. Regarding Langston, see William Cheek and Aimee Lee Cheek, *John Mercer Langston and the Fight for Black Freedom, 1829–1865* (Champaign: University of Illinois Press, 1996).

100. A. A. Taylor, "The Negro in South Carolina during the Reconstruction," *Journal of Negro History* 9, no. 4 (October 1924): 381.

101. Terborg-Penn, *African American Women*, 45.

102. "Seventh Day's Proceedings," *Christian Recorder*, 2 May 1883. Regarding Strong, see William J. Walls, *The African Methodist Episcopal Zion Church: Reality of the Black Church* (Charlotte, N.C.: A.M.E. Zion Publishing House, 1974), 186–87, 191–93.

103. "An Address to the Auxiliary Mite Societies and the Women in General, of the A.M.E. Church," *Christian Recorder*, 29 June 1876.

104. Jacob C. White Jr., Octavius V. Catto, and John W. Simpson, "Banneker Institute," *Christian Recorder*, 28 April 1866.

105. Martha King, "For the Christian Recorder," *Christian Recorder*, 18 June 1864.

Chapter Five

1. The author of ten novels and numerous short stories, Butler is best known for examining topics in African American history through the genre of science fiction. For a general discussion of her works, see Rebecca O. Johnson, "African American Feminist Science Fiction," *Sojourner: The Women's Forum* 19, no. 6 (February 1994): 12–14; Sandra Y. Govan, "Homage to Tradition: Octavia Butler Renovates the Historical Novel," *MELUS: The Journal of the Society for the Study of the Multi-Ethnic Literature of the United States*, 13, no. 1–2 (Spring–Summer 1986): 79–96; Dorothy Allison, "The Future of Females: Octavia Butler's Mother Lode," in *Reading Black, Reading Feminist: A Critical Anthology*, ed. Henry Louis Gates Jr. (New York: Meridian, 1990), 471–78; and Ruth Salvaggio, "Octavia Butler and the Black Science Fiction Heroine," *Black American Literature Forum* 18, no. 2 (1984): 78–81. Elizabeth Cady Stanton, Susan B. Anthony, Matilda Joslyn Gage, and Ida Husted Harper produced the six-volume *History of Woman Suffrage* over the course of forty-one years (New York: Fowler & Wells, 1881–1922). Historians long relied upon this collection as the premiere primary source for nineteenth-century women's history.

2. Through his fictional character, the African American civil rights lawyer Geneva Crenshaw, Bell explores law, history, and race through allegory, parable, and time travel to analyze contemporary issues of race and justice in the U.S. See Derrick A. Bell, *Faces at the Bottom of the Well: The Permanence of Racism* (New York: Basic Books, 1992) and *And We Are Not Saved: The Elusive Quest for Racial Justice* (New York: Basic Books, 1987).

3. William J. Walls, *The African Methodist Episcopal Zion Church: Reality of the Black Church* (Charlotte, N.C.: A.M.E. Zion Publishing House, 1974), 111.

4. Benjamin Quarles, "Frederick Douglass and the Woman's Rights Movement," *Journal of Negro History* 25, no. 1 (January 1940): 35–44.

5. "A Woman's Idea of Politics," *Elizabeth (New Jersey) Daily Journal,* John Mercer Langston Papers, box 60-1, Moorland-Spingarn Research Center, Howard University, Washington, D.C.

6. Ibid.

7. Alice King, "Woman's Power," *Georgetown Planet,* 31 May 1878. *The Georgetown Planet Weekly* began publication in 1873 with James A. Bowley and R. O. Bush as its editors.

8. C. D. Johnson, "Bethel Literary: An Essay and a Speech," *The People's Advocate,* 14 October 1882, John Mercer Langston Papers, box 60-1, Moorland-Spingarn Research Center, Howard University, Washington, D.C.

9. Elizabeth L. Davis, *Lifting as They Climb: An Historical Record of the National Association of Colored Women* (1933; New York: G. K. Hall and Co., 1996), 215–18; Lawson Scruggs, *Women of Distinction: Remarkable in Works and Invincible in Character* (Raleigh: L. A. Scruggs, 1893), 268–70.

10. W. E. B. DuBois, *The Negro Church. Report of a Social Study Made Under the Direction of Atlanta University; Together with the Proceedings of the Eighth Conference for the Study of the Negro Problems, Held at Atlanta University, May 26th, 1903* (Atlanta, Ga.: Atlanta University Press, 1903).

11. Ibid.

12. Eric Foner, *Freedom's Lawmakers: A Directory of Black Officeholders during Reconstruction* (Baton Rouge: Louisiana State University, 1996), xxi, 35–36, 108, 203–4.

13. "Bishop Haven Has Been Elected," *Christian Recorder,* 5 November 1874; "The Ballot for Women," *Christian Recorder,* 23 December 1875.

14. *The Fifteenth Quadrennial Session of the General Conference of the African Methodist Episcopal Church. Place of Session, Nashville, Tennessee. May 6, 1872,* New York Public Library, Schomburg Center for Research in Black Culture, New York, N.Y.

15. W[illiam] N[ewton] Hartshorn, *An Era of Progress and Promise, 1860–1910* (Boston: Priscilla Publishing Company, 1910), 440.

16. *The Sixteenth Session, and the Fifteenth Quadrennial Session of the General Conference of the African Methodist Episcopal Church. Place of Session, Atlanta, Georgia, from May 1st to 18th, 1876,* New York Public Library, Schomburg Center for Research in Black Culture, New York, N.Y.

17. Walls, *African Methodist Episcopal Zion Church,* 111.

18. Rev. Mark M. Bell, *Daily Journal of the Sixteenth Quadrennial Session of the General Conference of the AME Zion Church, of America, Held at Montgomery, Alabama, May, A.D., 1880* (New York: Book Concern of the AME Zion Church, 1880), 71.

19. Ibid.

20. Lois Baldwin Moreland, "Charlotte E. Ray," *American National Biography Online*

<http://www.anb.org.proxy.lib.umich.edu/articles/11/11-00995.html> (accessed May 4, 2006); J. Clay Smith Jr., "Black Women Lawyers: 125 Years at the Bar; 100 Years in the Legal Academy," *Howard Law Journal* 40 (Winter 1997): 365–97.

21. Belva A. Lockwood, "My Efforts to Become a Lawyer," *Lippincott's Monthly Magazine*, February 1888, 223.

22. Jill Norgren, "Before It Was Merely Difficult: Belva Lockwood's Life in Law and Politics," *Journal of Supreme Court History* 23, no. 1 (1999): 16–42. Norgren explains that while Belva Lockwood was the first woman to be admitted to the bar of the Supreme Court of the United States in 1880, Ray's 1872 admission to the District of Columbia bar preceded that of Lockwood by five months. Ray's case appears to contrast with that of Mary Ann Shadd Cary, who is reported to have withdrawn from Howard University Law School because she was prohibited from admission to the bar by the laws of the District of Columbia. See Rosalyn Terborg-Penn, *African American Women in the Struggle for the Vote, 1850–1920* (Indianapolis: University of Indiana Press, 1998), 38.

23. J. Clay Smith Jr., "Charlotte E. Ray Pleads Before Court," *Howard Law Journal* 43 (Winter 2000): 121–39.

24. In the pre–Civil War era, Riddle had helped repeal Ohio's black laws and defended Ohio abolitionists charged with forcible resistance to enforcement of the federal Fugitive Slave Act in the case of John Price, often termed the "Oberlin-Wellington rescue." See Richard L. Aynes, "The Bill of Rights, the Fourteenth Amendment, and the Seven Deadly Sins of Legal Scholarship," *William and Mary Bill of Rights Journal* 8 (February 2000): 407–35 n. 14; and Steven Lubet, "Symposium: Of John Brown: Lawyers, the Law, and Civil Disobedience: Slavery on Trial: The Case of the Oberlin Rescue," *Alabama Law Review* 54 (Spring 2003): 785–829, 798. In the postwar era, Riddle represented suffragists Victoria Woodhull, Susan Anthony, and Elizabeth Cady Stanton in a petition to Congress for the right to the vote. See Reva B. Siegel, "She the People: The Nineteenth Amendment, Sex Equality, Federalism, and the Family," *Harvard Law Review* 115, no. 4 (February 2002): 948–1046, 972. Riddle also moved Belva Lockwood's admission to the U.S. Supreme Court in 1879. See Mary L. Clark, "The Founding of the Washington College of Law: The First Law School Established by Women for Women," *American University Law Review* 47 (February 1998): 613–76 n. 45.

25. Catalogue and Records of Colored Students, 1834–1972, Secretary's Office IV, Alumni Records, Minority Student Records, Oberlin College, Oberlin, Ohio; "State Convention of the Colored Citizens of Ohio, Columbus, Ohio," Foner and Walker, eds., *New York, Pennsylvania, Indiana, Michigan, Ohio*, 227; *Proceedings of a Convention of the Colored Men of Ohio, held in the City of Cincinnati, on the 23rd, 24th, 25th and 26th days of November, 1858* (Cincinnati: Moore, Wilstach, Keys & Co., 1858); D. Augustus Straker, *Christian Recorder*, June 4, 1874; Terborg-Penn, *African American Women*, 50.

26. *The Fifteenth Quadrennial Session of the General Conference of the African Methodist Episcopal Church. Place of Session, Nashville, Tennessee. May 6, 1872.*

27. Walls, *African Methodist Episcopal Zion Church*, 111.

28. Othal H. Lakey, *The History of the C.M.E. Church* (Memphis, Tenn.: C.M.E. Publishing House, 1996), 272.

29. Ibid.

30. *Minutes, Eleventh Session, South Carolina Annual Conference, 1876*, cited in Walls, *African Methodist Episcopal Zion Church*, 111; Cicero R. Harris, *Zion's Historical Catechism* (Charlotte, N.C.: A.M.E. Zion Publishing House, 1922), 22.

31. Lakey, *History of the C.M.E. Church*, 272.

32. *The Fifteenth Quadrennial Session of the General Conference of the African Methodist Episcopal Church. Place of Session, Nashville, Tennessee. May 6, 1872*.

33. "Primitive Deaconate," *Christian Recorder*, 8 July 1875 (reprint from the *Christian Union*).

34. H. M. T., "Communications. How the Stewardesses System Operates in the AME Church," *Christian Recorder*, 15 May 1873.

35. Lawrence S. Little, *Disciples of Liberty: The African Methodist Episcopal Church in the Age of Imperialism, 1884–1916* (Knoxville: University of Tennessee Press, 2000), 10.

36. Walls, *African Methodist Episcopal Zion Church*, 376, 388.

37. Lakey, *History of the C.M.E. Church*, 303.

38. Walls, *African Methodist Episcopal Zion Church*, 376, 388; Little, *Disciples of Liberty*, 10.

39. "The Mite Missionary Society / Women's Missionary Society," *Christian Recorder*, 28 May 1874.

40. Stephen Angell, *Bishop Henry McNeal Turner and African American Religion in the South* (Knoxville: University of Tennessee Press, 1992), 219.

41. "West Tennessee and Miss. Conference," *Star of Zion*, 19 December 1884.

42. "Mississippi," *Star of Zion* 8, 24 October 1884. "Mississippi: Synopsis of the Minutes of the Second District Meeting," *Star of Zion*, 28 November 1874. Throughout the mid-1880s numerous women were reported as elected delegates, appointed agents, and speakers before black Methodist conferences at all levels.

43. "Baltimore District Conference," *Star of Zion*, 3 July 1885.

44. Rev. Benjamin W. Arnett, B.D., *Journal of the 17th Session and the 16th Quadrennial Session of the General Conference of the African Methodist Episcopal Church in the United States, Held at St. Louis, Missouri, May 3–25, 1880* (Xenia, Ohio: Torchlight Printing Company, 1882); *Minutes of the Thirteenth Session of the Georgia Annual Conference of the AME Church Held in Campbell Chapel, Americus, Georgia, January 21, 1880*, African Methodist Episcopal Church, Office of the Historiographer, Nashville, Tenn.

45. Quoted in Walls, *African Methodist Episcopal Zion Church*, 391.

46. Ibid., 402–3.

47. Quoted in ibid., 391.

48. Quoted in ibid., 392.

49. Rev. Joseph H. Morgan, *Morgan's History of the New Jersey Conference of the A.M.E. Church, from 1872 to 1887. And of the Several Churches, as Far as Possible from Date*

of Organization, with Biographical Sketches of Members of the Conference (Camden, N.J.: S. Chew, Printers, 1887).

50. Ibid.

51. Rev. C. R. Harris, *Daily Proceedings of the Seventeenth Quadrennial Session of the General Conference of the AME Zion Church in America, Held in New York City, May, 1884* (AME Zion Book Concern, 1884).

52. Walls, *African Methodist Episcopal Zion Church*, 392–93; *Scott v. Sanford*, 60 U.S. 393 (1857), 407. The Constitution of the Commonwealth of Massachusetts provided in pertinent part: "All men are born free and equal, and have certain natural, essential, and unalienable rights" (Article I). Thank you to Anne Boylan for pointing out this reference.

53. Quoted in Walls, *African Methodist Episcopal Zion Church*, 392–93.

54. Adrienne M. Israel, *Amanda Berry Smith: From Washerwoman to Evangelist* (Lanham, Md.: Scarecrow, 1998), 60.

55. National Association of Colored Women (U.S.), *A History of the Club Movement Among the Colored Women of the United States of America: As Contained in the Minutes of the Conventions, Held in Boston, July 29, 30, 31, 1895, and of the National Federation of Afro-American Women, Held in Washington, D.C., July 20, 21, 22, 1896* (1902), Records of the National Association of Colored Women's Clubs, 1895–1992 (Bethesda, Md.: University Publications of America, 1993–).

56. Evelyn B. Higginbotham, *Righteous Discontent: The Women's Movement in the Black Baptist Church, 1880–1920* (Cambridge, Mass.: Harvard University Press, 1993), 48–59, 68–70; *Minutes of the Thirty-Ninth Annual Meeting of the Consolidated American Baptist Missionary Convention, Held in the Zion Baptist Church, Cincinnati, Ohio, from Thursday, October 16th, to Wednesday, October 22nd, A.D., 1879* (Lexington, Ky.: Wilson & Zimmerman, 1880); *The Fifth Anniversary of the Baptist Educational, Missionary and Sunday School Convention of South Carolina, Held with the Pee Dee Union Baptist Church, Cheraw, May 4–8, 1881* (Columbia, S.C.: W. B. McDaniel, General Book and Job Printer, 1881); *Minutes of the Seventeenth Annual Session of the Jackson Missionary Baptist Association, Held with First Colored White Oak Baptist Church, Copiah County, Miss. September 3d, 4th and 5th, A.D. 1885* (Jackson, Miss.: Charles Winkley, Book and Job Printer, 1885).

57. Anthea D. Butler, " 'Only a Woman Would Do': Bible Reading and African American Women's Organizing Work," in *Women and Religion in the African Diaspora*, ed. Barbara D. Savage and R. Marie Griffith (Baltimore: Johns Hopkins University Press, 2006).

58. Higginbotham, *Righteous Discontent*, 68–71; Anthea Butler, " 'Only a Woman Would Do.' "

59. Higginbotham, *Righteous Discontent*.

60. Mary E. Frederickson, " 'Each One Is Dependent on the Other': Southern Churchwomen, Racial Reform, and the Process of Transformation," in *Visible Women: New Essays in American Activism*, ed. Nancy Hewitt and Suzanne Lebsock (Urbana: University of Illinois Press, 1993), 296–324.

61. Gregory Vickers, "Modes of Womanhood in the Early Woman's Missionary Union," *Baptist History and Heritage* 24 (1989): 41–53; Slayden Yarbrough, "The Southern Baptist Spirit, 1845–1995," *Baptist History and Heritage* 30, no. 3 (1995): 25–34.

62. *Christian Recorder*, 28 May 1874.

63. "Our New York Letter," *Christian Recorder*, 21 November 1878; Bishop A. W. Wayman, "Notes by the Way," *Christian Recorder*, 30 November 1876.

64. Rev. John O. Foster, *Life and Labors of Mrs. Maggie Newton Van Cott, the First Lady Licensed to Preach in the Methodist Episcopal Church in the United States* (Cincinnati: Hitchcock and Walder, for the author, 1872); William R. Phinney, *Maggie Newton Van Cott: First Woman Licensed to Preach in the Methodist Episcopal Church* (Rye, N.Y.: Commission on Archives and History, New York Annual Conference, United Methodist Church, 1969); Jacqueline Field-Bibb, *Women Towards Priesthood: Ministerial Politics and Feminist Praxis* (Cambridge: Cambridge University Press, 1991); Carolyn De-Swarte Gifford, ed., *The Debate in the Methodist Episcopal Church Over Laity Rights for Women* (New York: Garland Publishing, 1987); Carolyn DeSwarte Gifford, ed., *The Defense of Women's Rights to Ordination in the Methodist Episcopal Church* (New York: Garland Publishing, 1988).

65. James R. Lynch, "Baptist Women in Ministry through 1920," *American Baptist Quarterly* 13, no. 4 (1994): 304–18.

66. "Memorials Adopted by the National Woman Suffrage Association, [15 January 1874]," in Ann D. Gordon, ed., *Against an Aristocracy of Sex, 1866–1873*, vol. 2 of *The Selected Papers of Elizabeth Cady Stanton and Susan B. Anthony* (New Brunswick: Rutgers University Press, 2000), 32–34.

67. Horace Talbert, *The Sons of Allen: Together with a Sketch of the Rise and Progress of Wilberforce University, Wilberforce, Ohio* (Xenia, Ohio: Aldine Press, 1906), 182–85.

68. Benjamin W. Arnett, *Centennial Address on the Mission of Methodism to the Extremes of Society, Delivered by Rev. Benjamin W. Arnett, D.D., Dec. 16th, 1884, at the Centennial M.E. Church, Baltimore, MD*, Daniel Murray Pamphlet Collection, American Memory Web site, Library of Congress, Washington, D.C., <http://memory.loc.gov/ammem/index.html>.

69. Arnett served as a representative in the Ohio state legislature from 1885 to 1886.

70. B[enjamin] W. Arnett and J. A. Brown, *The Black Laws: Speech of Hon. B. W. Arnett of Greene County, and Hon. J. A. Brown of Cuyahoga County, in the Ohio House of Representatives* (Columbus, Ohio: Ohio State Journal, 1886), American Memory Web site, Library of Congress, Washington, D.C.

71. Benjamin W. Arnett, *Biennial Oration, Before the Second B.M.C. of the Grand United Order of Odd Fellows. Delivered by Rev. Benjamin W. Arnett, P. G. M., A Member of Messiah Lodge, No 1641, in Heuck's Opera House, Cincinnati, Ohio, October 10 1884* (Dayton, Ohio: Christian Publishing House, 1884), Daniel Murray Pamphlet Collection, American Memory Web site, Library of Congress, Washington, D.C.

72. Theda Skocpol and Jennifer Lynn Oser, "Organization Despite Adversity: The Origins and Development of African American Fraternal Associations," *Social Science History* 28, no. 3 (Fall 2004): 367–438.

73. One commentator, "Hannibal," reported to the readers of the *Christian Recorder* his attendance at the twentieth anniversary meeting of Pittsburgh's "Heroines of Jericho, of Naomi Court" in 1865. See "Letter from Hannibal," *Christian Recorder*, 7 October 1865.

74. "Masonic," *Christian Recorder*, 7 July 1866.

75. "Africana," "Letter from Pittsburg [*sic*]," *Christian Recorder*, 4 February 1865.

76. "Ruth." "Chicago Correspondence," *Christian Recorder*, 20 May 1865.

77. J. W. Malone, "Communications. A Voice From the Far North-West," *Christian Recorder*, 3 December 1870; Rev. E. Weaver, "Wayside Jottings. Our Visit to Chicago, Illinois," *Christian Recorder*, 22 September 1866; J. A. Shorter, "Contributions to Wilberforce College," *Christian Recorder*, 7 October 1865; "Acknowledgements," *Christian Recorder*, 9 February 1867; "Acknowledgments," *Christian Recorder*, 31 August 1861.

78. Frederic Myers. "Letter from Rev. Frederic Myers," *Christian Recorder*, 24 February 1866; Jos. W. Moore. "The Independent Order of Good Templars, of Chicago, Ill.," *Christian Recorder*, 9 February 1867.

79. Martha Blanks's life was not one of elite privilege, though in 1864 one commentator noted her husband as among black Chicago's "wealthier portion." Blanks spent most of her adult life operating a boardinghouse in the home she shared with her husband, James. By age sixty-four, however, she appears in the census as a woman alone and without an occupation in a boardinghouse operated by a white woman. That household's other boarders were also African Americans. See "Editorial Correspondence. Wealth Among the Colored People of Chicago," *Christian Recorder*, 2 September 1865.

80. May Wright Sewall, ed., *World's Congress of Representative Women* (New York: Rand McNally Company, 1894), 435. See also <http://columbus.gl.iit.edu/reed2 .html#12> (accessed 24 April 2003).

Chapter Six

1. Elizabeth L. Davis, *Lifting as They Climb: An Historical Record of the National Association of Colored Women* (1933; New York: G. K. Hall, 1996), 10–17.

2. Hallie Q. Brown, *Homespun Heroines and Other Women of Distinction* (1926; New York: Oxford University Press, 1988).

3. Brown, *Homespun Heroines*, 117–18.

4. Ella Forbes, *African American Women during the Civil War* (New York: Garland Publishing, 1998), 144.

5. Brown, *Homespun Heroines*, 152–53.

6. Ibid., 225–30.

7. The precise year of Washington's birth remains a bit of a mystery. While her

gravestone recorded her year of birth as 1865, which would establish her as having been born after emancipation, more recent histories set her year of birth as 1861, leaving open the question of whether she had been born enslaved or free. Hallie Quinn Brown, in *Homespun Heroines*, indicated that Washington was born in 1865, marking her as a freeborn woman.

8. Ibid., 208–16.

9. Rayford W. Logan, *The Negro in American Life and Thought: The Nadir, 1877–1901* (New York: Dial Press, 1954); Rayford W. Logan, *The Betrayal of the Negro: From Rutherford B. Hayes to Woodrow Wilson* (New York: Collier Books, 1965).

10. Evelyn Brooks Higginbotham, "The Black Church: A Gender Perspective," in *African American Religion: Interpretive Essays in History and Culture*, ed. Timothy E. Fulop and Albert J. Raboteau (New York: Routledge, 1997), 205–6. For a general discussion of race relations in this period, see Joel Williamson, *A Rage for Order: Black / White Relations in the American South Since Emancipation* (New York: Oxford University Press, 1986), 117–51; and Donald G. Nieman, ed., *Black Freedom / White Violence, 1865–1900* (New York: Garland Publishing, 1994).

11. Higginbotham, "Black Church," 214–15.

12. May M. Brown, "A Woman's Views on Current Topics," *AME Zion Quarterly Review*, 1891.

13. Deborah Gray White, *Too Heavy a Load: Black Women in Defense of Themselves, 1894–1994* (New York: W. W. Norton, 1999), 26–27.

14. Higginbotham, "Black Church," 217.

15. Deborah Gray White, *Too Heavy a Load*, 28–29.

16. Stephanie J. Shaw, "Black Club Women and the Creation of the National Association of Colored Women," *Journal of Women's History* 3, no. 2 (1991): 10–25. I agree with Shaw's argument that the club movement grew out of decades of black women's activism, but the club movement was also a response to the public degradations exemplified by Jacks's letter, especially among churchwomen.

17. Elizabeth Davis, *Lifting as They Climb*, 15.

18. Deborah Gray White, *Too Heavy a Load*, 23–24.

19. Ibid., 60.

20. T. J. Carey, *Brudder Gardner's Stump Speeches and Comic Lectures* (New York: Excelsior Publishing House, 1884). Translated from faux dialect into standard English: women protested their exclusion from voting, the ballot, Congress, governing, and election night festivities. He stated: "I want to assume that sphere which nature fitted me for equally with man, but from which masculine jealousy has thus far excluded me. . . . Mrs. Swisshelm; there's Lucy Stone, and Anna Dickinson; there's Lucretia Mott, and Mrs. Jinks, all of whom showed that women could cease to be women, and be as near men as nature allowed them. That's what all our sex want— to be as near men as possible."

21. Anthony J. Drexel Biddle, *Shantytown Sketches* (Philadelphia: Drexel Biddle, Publisher, 1898).

22. Ibid.

23. Mia Bay, *The White Image in the Black Mind: African American Ideas about White People, 1830–1925* (New York: Oxford University Press, 2000); John Hope Franklin, *George Washington Williams: A Biography* (Chicago: University of Chicago Press, 1985).

24. Benjamin T. Tanner, *An Apology for African Methodism* (Baltimore: s.n., 1867), 16.

25. I. Garland Penn, *The Afro-American Press and Its Editors* (1891; New York: Arno Press, 1969); G. F. Richings, *Evidences of Progress Among Colored People* (1896; Philadelphia: Geo. S. Ferguson, 1902).

26. L[awson] A. Scruggs, *Women of Distinction: Remarkable in Works and Invincible in Character* (Raleigh: L. A. Scruggs, 1893).

27. Monroe Majors, *Noted Negro Women: Their Triumphs and Activities* (Chicago: Donahue and Henneberry, 1893; Freeport, N.Y.: Books for Libraries Press, 1971).

28. Susie I. Shorter, *The Heroines of African Methodism* (Xenia, Ohio: Chew, 1891).

29. Hazel Carby, *Reconstructing Womanhood: The Emergence of the Afro-American Woman Novelist* (Oxford: Oxford University Press, 1990).

30. James T. Haley, *Afro-American Encyclopedia; or, The Thoughts, Doings, and Sayings of the Race, Embracing Lectures, Biographical Sketches, Sermons, Poems, Names of Universities, Colleges, Seminaries, Newspapers, Books, and a History of the Denominations, Giving the Numerical Strength of Each. In Fact, It Teaches Every Subject of Interest to the Colored People, as Discussed by More Than One Hundred of Their Wisest and Best Men and Women* (Nashville, Tenn.: Haley & Florida, 1895).

31. J. W. (James Walker) Hood, *One Hundred Years of the African Methodist Episcopal Zion Church; or, The Centennial of African Methodism* (New York: A.M.E. Zion Book Concern, 1895), 159.

32. Henry M. Turner, *The Genius and Theory of Methodist Polity* (Philadelphia: A.M.E. Publications, 1885), 18.

33. Ibid., 148, 166–69, 184.

34. Ibid., 99–101.

35. Daniel A. Payne, *History of the African Methodist Episcopal Church* (1891; New York: Arno Press, 1969), 268–79, 297–305.

36. Deborah Gray White, *Too Heavy a Load*, 27. See also Craig S. Wilder, *A Covenant with Color: Race and Social Power in Brooklyn, 1636–1990* (New York: Columbia University Press, 2000).

37. *A History of the Club Movement Among the Colored Women of the United States as Contained in the Minutes of the Conventions, held in Boston, July 29, 30, 31, 1895, and of the National Federation of Afro-American Women held in Washington, D.C., July 20, 21, 22, 1896* (n.p.: 1903).

38. Ibid.

39. *A.M.E. Zion Quarterly Review* 6, no. 3–4 (July–October 1896): 28.

40. Elizabeth E. Grammar, "Female Itinerant Evangelists in Nineteenth-Century America," *Arizona Quarterly* 55 (Spring 1999): 67–96; Jualynne E. Dodson, "Nine-

teenth-Century A.M.E. Preaching Women," in *Women in New Worlds*, ed. Hilah F. Thomas and Rosemary S. Keller (Nashville, Tenn.: Abingdon, 1981), 276–92.

41. Stephen Angell, *Bishop Henry McNeal Turner and African American Religion in the South* (Knoxville: University of Tennessee Press, 1992); John Dittmer, "The Education of Henry McNeal Turner," in *Black Leaders of the Nineteenth Century*, ed. Leon Litwack and August Meier (Urbana: University of Illinois Press, 1988), 253–74.

42. Stephen Ward Angell, "The Controversy Over Women's Ministry in the African Methodist Episcopal Church during the 1880s: The Case of Sarah Ann Hughes," in *This Far By Faith: Readings in African American Women's Religious Biography*, ed. Judith Weisenfeld and Richard Newman (New York: Routledge, 1996), 94–109. See also Dodson, "Nineteenth-Century A.M.E. Preaching Women," 276–89; Jualynne E. Dodson, "Power and Surrogate Leadership: Black Women and Organized Religion," *Sage: A Scholarly Journal on Black Women* 5, no. 2 (Fall 1988): 37–42; Jualynne E. Dodson and Cheryl T. Gilkes, "Something Within: Social Change and Collective Endurance in the Sacred World of Black Christian Women," in *Women and Religion in America: Volume 3: 1900–1968*, ed. Rosemary Radford Reuther and Rosemary Skinner Keller (San Francisco: Harper and Row, 1986), 80–89; Cheryl T. Gilkes, "The Politics of 'Silence': Dual-Sex Political Systems and Women's Traditions of Conflict in African American Religion," in *African American Christianity: Essays in History*, ed. Paul E. Johnson (Berkeley: University of California Press, 1994), 80–110; Catherine Peck, "Your Daughters Shall Prophesy: Women in the Afro-American Preaching Tradition," in *Diversities of Gifts*, ed. Ruel W. Tyson, James L. Peacock, and Daniel W. Patterson (Urbana: University of Illinois Press, 1988); and Jeanne B. Williams, "Loose the Woman and Let Her Go! Pennsylvania's African American Women Preachers," *Pennsylvania Heritage* 22, no. 1 (1996). 4–9.

43. J. P. Campbell and John M. Brown, "The Ordination of Women; What Is the Authority For It?" *A.M.E. Church Review* (April 1886).

44. Angell, *Bishop Henry McNeal Turner*, 183.

45. Campbell and Brown, "Ordination of Women," 454–55. Brown might also have had in mind the case of Margaret Wilson. Wilson had been called to the ministry in 1870 and served as a missionary until 1883, when Wilson was given the Haleyville Mission. In this capacity, Wilson had purchased a lot and a building. See Rev. Joseph H. Morgan, *Morgan's History of the New Jersey Conference of the A.M.E. Church, from 1872 to 1887. And of the Several Churches, as Far as Possible from Date of Organization, with Biographical Sketches of Members of the Conference* (Camden, N.J.: S. Chew, Printers, 1887), 51.

46. David W. Wills, "Womanhood and Domesticity in the AME Tradition: The Influence of Daniel Alexander Payne," in *Black Apostles at Home and Abroad: Afro-Americans and the Christian Mission from the Revolution to Reconstruction*, ed. David W. Wills and Richard Newman (Boston: G. K. Hall, 1982), 133–46; Charles Killiam, "Daniel A. Payne and the A.M.E. General Conference of 1888: A Display of Contrasts," *Negro History Bulletin* 32, no. 7 (1969): 11–14.

47. *The Doctrines and Discipline of the AME Church* (Philadelphia: A.M.E. Book Concern, 1912), 208; Lawrence S. Little, *Disciples of Liberty: The African Methodist Episcopal Church in the Age of Imperialism, 1884–1916* (Knoxville: University of Tennessee Press, 2000), 11.

48. *The Doctrines and Discipline of the African Methodist Episcopal Zion Church in America* (New York: A.M.E. Zion Book Concern, 1892; revised by the General Conference, Pittsburgh, Pa., 1892).

49. *[Proceedings of the General Conference for 1892]*, 1892, Livingstone College, African Methodist Episcopal Zion Church Archives, Salisbury, N.C.

50. William J. Walls, *The African Methodist Episcopal Zion Church: Reality of the Black Church* (Charlotte, N.C.: A.M.E. Zion Publishing House, 1974), 111.

51. Ibid.; George M. Miller, "This Worldly Mission: The Life and Career of Alexander Walters (1858–1917) [Part 1]," *A.M.E. Zion Quarterly Review* 97 (April 1985): 1, 10–18.

52. *A.M.E. Zion Quarterly Review* 6, no. 3–4 (July–October 1896), 33.

53. Ibid., 7, no. 1 (April 1897).

54. Bishop John B. Small, *Code on the Discipline of the African Methodist Episcopal Zion Church* ([York, Pa.]: York Dispatch Print, 1898).

55. Glenda E. Gilmore, "Murder, Memory, and the Flight of the Incubus," in *Democracy Betrayed: The Wilmington Race Riot of 1898 and Its Legacy*, ed. David S. Cecelski and Timothy B. Tyson (Chapel Hill: University of North Carolina Press, 1998), 79.

56. Walls, *African Methodist Episcopal Zion Church*, 358.

57. H. Leon Prather Sr., "We Have Taken a City: A Centennial Essay," in Cecelski and Tyson, eds., *Democracy Betrayed*, 16–17.

58. Gilmore, "Murder, Memory," 73–90.

59. The legal right to marry white women was probably not what this resolution meant to those present. Black delegates addressed an entirely different but very pressing issue for their constituents; their proposals sought to extend statutory protection to black women who were in long-term liaisons with white men. This was a common occurrence, particularly in the South. See ibid.

60. Ibid., 79–80.

61. Ibid., 79.

62. Ibid.

63. Prather, "We Have Taken a City"; Gilmore, "Murder, Memory."

64. *Star of Zion*, 2 June 1898, 2.

65. Evalina H. Badham, "Woman's Place in the Church," *A.M.E. Zion Quarterly Review* 7, no. 1 (April 1897): 21 et seq.

66. Mrs. Bishop C. C. [Sarah] Pettey, "Woman's Column: Signs of the Times," *Star of Zion*, 28 October 1897. See also Glenda E. Gilmore, "Gender and Jim Crow: Sarah Dudley Pettey's Vision of the New South," *North Carolina Historical Review* 68, no. 3 (July 1991): 261–85.

67. Rev. J. Harvey Anderson, "Searchlight Scenes: Ordination of Women and the General Conference," *Star of Zion*, 29 September 1898.

68. Rev. J. J. Adams, "Something Will Drop Yet," *Star of Zion*, 6 October 1898.

69. Eliza A. Gardner, "From Boston, Mass.," *Star of Zion*, 16 February 1899.

70. "Cannot Frighten Her," *Star of Zion*, 23 November 1899.

71. Rev. R. A. Morrisey, "Female Preachers: Objections Answered—Scripture Proofs," *Star of Zion*, 22 September 1898.

72. Mrs. Clarissa Betties, "Let Rev. Mrs. Small Alone," *Star of Zion*, 22 December 1898.

73. B. F. Grant, "A Few Sparks: No Use to Kick Because a Woman Has Been Ordained Elder," *Star of Zion*, 23 March 1898.

74. Rev. S. A. Chambers, "Cannon Balls: Reply to Rev. J. H. Gilmer, Jr.," *Star of Zion*, 21 July 1898.

75. "Physically Unfit," *Star of Zion*, 18 August 1898.

76. Rev. S. A. Chambers, "Redhot Cannon Ball: No Authority in Scripture for the Ordination of Women," *Star of Zion*, 16 June 1898, 1.

77. "Don't Need Women Elders," *Star of Zion*, 11 August 1898, 4.

78. Deborah Gray White, *Too Heavy a Load*.

79. Randall B. Woods, "C. H. J. Taylor and the Movement for Black Political Independence, 1882–1896," *Journal of Negro History* 67, no. 2 (Summer 1982): 122–35.

80. *Star of Zion*, 28 July 1898, 4, reprinted from the *Pee Dee (N.C.) Herald*.

81. Bishop J. B. Small, "Mrs. Small's Case: Bishop Small Speaks," *Star of Zion*, 16 June 1898, 6.

82. Rev. S. A. Chambers, "Cannon Balls: Reply to Rev. B. J. Bolding," *Star of Zion*, 28 July 1898, 2, 7.

83. Rev S. A. Chambers, "Cannon Balls: Reply to Rev. J. H. Gilmer, Jr.," 3.

84. "Physically Unfit," *Star of Zion*, 18 August 1898, 4.

85. Betties, "Let Rev. Mrs. Small Alone," 6.

86. Mrs. Rev. W. L. Moore, "Eyes of Jealousy," *Star of Zion*, 28 July 1898, 5.

87. Grant, "A Few Sparks," 6.

88. Anderson, "Searchlight Scenes," 1.

89. Bishop J. W. Hood, "Female Elders: Not Until There is a Call for Female Pastors Will There be a Necessity for Female Elders," *Star of Zion*, 27 October 1898, 5. See also John H. Satterwhite, "An Interpretation of History: Henry Evans, James Walker Hood, and Bishop James Wesley Wactor," *A.M.E. Zion Quarterly Review* 96, no. 3 (1984): 28–31.

90. Rev. J. H. McMullen, "Bishop Small Errs: The General Conference Never Dreamed of Women Elders," *Star of Zion*, 30 June 1898, 1.

91. Rev. F. M. Jacobs, "Topics of the Times: Star—Dream—Woman Ordination—Paul's Advice," *Star of Zion*, 21 July 1898, 1.

92. Grant, "A Few Sparks," 6.

93. Jacobs, "Topics of the Times," 1.

94. Anderson, "Searchlight Scenes," 1. Anderson reported after an informal poll of the bishops that four of the eight—Pettey, Walters, Small, and Hood—publicly endorsed women's ordination. Subsequent to his writing, two additional bishops—Lomax and Harris—publicly endorsed Mary Small's elevation to the station of bishop. See also Bishop T. H. Lomax, "Episcopal Visits," *Star of Zion*, 28 July 1898, 3; and Bishop C. R. Harris, "Episcopal Dots: Women Elders—Railroad Discrimination—Coleman Factory," *Star of Zion*, 4 August 1898, 2.

95. David H. Bradley Jr., *A History of the AME Zion Church, Part I, 1796–1872* (Nashville: Pantheon Press, 1956), 140–41; "Anti-Colonization and Woman's Rights Ticket. Members to State Council," American Negro Historical Society Collection, box 1G, folder 4, Manuscripts and Archives, Historical Society of Pennsylvania, Philadelphia (hereafter HSP). Among the other ticket members were progressives Robert Purvis and William Whipper, Columbia, Pa.; Samuel Van Brakle and Benjamin Clark, York, Pa.; Alphonso M. Sumner, James McCrummill, J. J. Gould Bias, Francis A. Duterte, and Edward Bennet, Harrisburg, Pa.; David B. Bowser and Rev. Lewis Woodson, Rev. A. R. Green, and John B. Vashon, Pittsburgh, Pa.; Samuel Williams, James Wilson, M.D., Benjamin B. Moore, and Joseph Gardner, Reading, Pa.; Rev. William Jackson, West Philadelphia; Prof. Charles L. Reason; and Rev. Joseph Clinton. Once elected to the bishopric, Clinton traveled extensively throughout the northeast and Canada, organizing twelve annual conferences in ten years and taking in hundreds of itinerant preachers. After the Civil War, Clinton oversaw the first AME Zion missionaries to the South and would serve as the president of the Freedmen's American and British Commission. See Walls, *African Methodist Episcopal Zion Church*, 185–86.

96. Philip S. Foner and George E. Walker, eds., *Proceedings of the Black National and State Conventions 1865–1900* (Philadelphia: Temple University Press, 1986), 12, 349–54.

97. Frederick Douglass, "Letter to George T. Downing," George T. Downing Papers, box 152–1, folder 23, Moorland-Spingarn Research Center, Howard University, Washington, D.C. Regarding Downing generally, see Lawrence Grossman, "George T. Downing and Desegregation of Rhode Island Public Schools, 1855–1866," *Rhode Island History* 36, no. 4 (1977): 99–105.

98. "[Editor]," *A.M.E. Zion Quarterly Review* 6, no. 3–4 (July–October 1896): 21.

99. Harris, "Episcopal Dots," 2.

100. Michele Mitchell, " 'The Black Man's Burden': African Americans, Imperialism, and Notions of Racial Manhood, 1890–1910," *International Review of Social History* 44 (1999): 77–99; Little, *Disciples of Liberty*; James T. Campbell, *Songs of Zion: The African Methodist Episcopal Church in the United States and South Africa* (New York: Oxford University Press, 1995).

101. Mrs. Maggie Hood-Banks, "The Missionary Department: Shall the Women or Men Control It," *Star of Zion*, 19 April 1900.

102. Miss S. J. Janifer, "A Woman's Plea: Let the Women Control the Missionary

and Church Extension Departments," *Star of Zion*, 23 November 1899; James Harvey Anderson, *Biographical Souvenir Volume of the Twenty-Third Quadrennial Session of the General Conference of the African Methodist Episcopal Zion Church* (n.p., 1908), 28.

103. Miss Rosina L. Nickson, "Our Girls and the Possibilities," *A.M.E. Zion Quarterly Review* 9, no. 4 (October 1899–January 1900).

104. Regarding racial tensions in the WCTU, see Carol Mattingly, *Well-Tempered Women: Nineteenth-Century Temperance Rhetoric* (Carbondale: Southern Illinois University Press, 1998), 75–95. Regarding Sarah J. Early, see Ellen N. Lawson and Marlene D. Merrill, comps., *The Three Sarahs: Documents of Antebellum Black College Women* (New York: Edwin Mellen Press, 1984); and Stephen W. Angell, "Early, Jordan Winston," American National Biography Online, <http://www.anb.org/articles/home .html> (accessed 4 January 2007).

105. Rosalyn Terborg-Penn, *African American Women in the Struggle for the Vote, 1850–1920* (Indianapolis: University of Indiana Press, 1998), 65.

106. Rev. J. N. Manly, "Let the Women Have the Missionary Department," *Star of Zion* (1900).

107. See Glenda E. Gilmore, *Gender and Jim Crow: Women and the Politics of White Supremacy in North Carolina, 1896–1920* (Chapel Hill: University of North Carolina Press, 1996). Gilmore's study, while principally focused on female activists in the secular realm, carefully examines black churchwomen's work within it. See also Glenda E. Gilmore, "Gender and Jim Crow," 261–85.

108. Among the male veterans of the woman question at the 1899 convention were Henry McNeal Turner of the AME Church, Cicero Harris and James Hood of the AME Zion Church, and Lewis H. Douglass, son of Frederick Douglass and veteran of women's suffrage campaigns of the 1860s and 1870s. For this discussion of the Afro-American League and the Afro-American Council I draw upon Shawn Alexander's very fine dissertation on the subject, " 'We Know Our Rights and Have the Courage to Defend Them': The Spirit of Agitation in the Age of Accommodation, 1883–1909" (Ph.D. diss., University of Massachusetts, 2004), as well as Patricia A. Schechter, *Ida B. Wells-Barnett and American Reform, 1880–1930* (Chapel Hill: University of North Carolina Press, 2001). See also Kevin K. Gaines, *Uplifting the Race: Black Leadership, Politics, and Culture in the Twentieth Century* (Chapel Hill: University of North Carolina Press, 1996).

Conclusion

1. Rev. Thomas James organized Memorial AME Zion Church in the early 1830s. James's antislavery activism, and that of congregation members Frederick Douglass, Harriet Tubman, and Jacob P. Morris, soon made it a common meeting place for Rochester's black leaders. Douglass briefly published the *North Star* in the church basement, and Tubman often hid fugitive slaves there. See C. Peter Ripley, ed., *The Black Abolitionist Papers* (Chapel Hill: University of North Carolina Press, 1991), 4:100;

and David H. Bradley Jr., *A History of the AME Zion Church, Part I, 1796–1872* (Nashville: Pantheon Press, 1956), 1:110–15.

2. Lenwood G. Davis, "Documents: Frederick Douglass as a Preacher, and One of His Last Most Significant Letters," *Journal of Negro History* 66, no. 2 (1981): 140–43; William L. Andrews, "Frederick Douglass, Preacher," *American Literature* 54, no. 4 (1982): 592–97.

3. William J. Walls, *The African Methodist Episcopal Zion Church: Reality of the Black Church* (Charlotte, N.C.: A.M.E. Zion Publishing House, 1974), 253; "Church in Rochester," *A.M.E. Zion Quarterly Review* [17] (1907): 120–21.

4. See Nancy A. Hewitt, *Women's Activism and Social Change: Rochester, New York, 1822–1872* (Ithaca, N.Y.: Cornell University Press, 1984), 61, 208–9.

5. <http://www.winningthevote.org/HJeffreys.html>.

Selected Bibliography

Full bibliography available at <http://hdl.handle.net/2027.42/4945b>.

Primary Sources
Manuscript Sources

Ann Arbor, Michigan
  University of Michigan, William H. Clements Special Collections Library
    Harriet deGarmo Fuller Papers
    Minute books of the United Sons of Salem Benevolent Society of the Free Sons
      of Ethiopia of Salem
    Weld-Grimké Family Papers
Berkeley, California
  Bancroft Library, University of California, Berkeley
    Jeremiah Burke Sanderson Papers, 1875–1912
Boston, Massachusetts
  Boston University, Mugar Memorial Library
    Edward Starr Afro-American Collection
    William Monroe Trotter Papers
  Massachusetts Historical Society
    William Lloyd Garrison Papers, 1833–82
Chicago, Illinois
  Newberry Library
    Everett Family Papers, 1820–1930
    The Nortnightly of Chicago, 1869–
    Pullman, Inc., Scrapbooks

Madison, New Jersey
  Drew University, United Methodist Church General Commission on Archives
    and History
    Methodist Periodical Collection
Madison, Wisconsin
  State Historical Society of Wisconsin
    African American Newspaper and Periodical Collection
Nashville, Tennessee
  A.M.E. Church, Office of the Historiographer
  Fisk University
    John Mercer Langston Papers, 1846–1930
  Southern Baptist Historical Society
    American Baptist Missionary Convention Records
New Haven, Connecticut
  Yale University, Beinecke Library
    Amos Beman Scrapbooks, I–IV, 1838–57
New York, New York
  Columbia University, Butler Library
    Black Abolitionist Papers
    Records of the National Association of Colored Women's Clubs, 1895–1992
  Morgan Library
    Gilder-Lehrman Collection
  New-York Historical Society
    Gerrit Smith Letters, 1834–74
  Union Theological Seminary
    Auburn Theological Seminary, Records, 1821–1970
Oberlin, Ohio
  Oberlin College Archives
    Ellen Lawson and Marlene Merrill Papers
    Letters Received by Oberlin College, 1822–66
    Marlene Deahl Merrill Papers
    Secretary's Office IV, Alumni Records 3, Minority Student Records
Philadelphia, Pennsylvania
  African Episcopal Church of St. Thomas
    African Episcopal Church of St. Thomas, Archives of the African Episcopal
      Church of St. Thomas, 1792–1996
  Historical Society of Pennsylvania, Manuscripts and Archives
    American Negro Historical Society Collection
    Mother Bethel African Methodist Episcopal Church of Philadelphia, Records,
      1822–1972
    Pennsylvania Society for Promoting the Abolition of Slavery

William Still Papers
Vigilant Committee of Philadelphia, Minutes book, 1839–44
Salisbury, North Carolina
Livingstone College, African Methodist Episcopal Zion Church Archives
Annual and Quadrennial Conference Proceedings
Washington, D.C.
Howard University, Moorland-Spingarn Research Center
Bustill-Bowser-Asbury Collection, 1732–1941
Mary Ann Shadd Cary Papers
Charles Chapman Papers
Anna Julia Cooper Papers
Frederick Douglass Papers
George T. Downing Papers, 1840–1930
Gregoria Fraser Goins Papers, 1877–1964
John Mercer Langston Papers
Ruffin Family Papers, 1753–1924
Simms Family Papers
Gerrit Smith Papers
Lewis Tappan Papers
Henry McNeal Turner Papers
Leigh R. Whipper Papers, 1864–1965
Jacob C. White Papers, 1857–1914
Library of Congress
Susan B. Anthony Collection
Frederick Douglass Papers, 1841–1964
Daniel Murray Pamphlet Collection, American Memory Website
National American Woman Suffrage Association Collection, American
Memory Website
National American Woman Suffrage Association Records, 1850–1960
Elizabeth Cady Stanton Papers, 1814–1946
Carter G. Woodson Collection, 1803–1936

Newspapers and Periodicals

The Abolitionist (New York, New York)
The Afro-American (Baltimore, Maryland)
The A.M.E. Church Review (Philadelphia, Pennsylvania)
The A.M.E. Zion Quarterly Review (Wilmington, North Carolina)
The Anglo-African (New York, New York)
Atlantic Monthly (New York, New York)
The Christian Recorder (Philadelphia, Pennsylvania)

The Colored American (Augusta, Georgia)
The Colored American (New York, New York)
The Colored American (Washington, D.C.)
The Elevator (San Francisco, California)
Frederick Douglass' Paper (Rochester, New York)
Freedmen's Bulletin (Chicago, Illinois)
Freedom's Journal (New York, New York)
The Liberator (Boston, Massachusetts)
Mirror of the Times (San Francisco, California)
National Baptist World (Wichita, Kansas)
The National Era (Washington, D.C.)
The New National Era (Washington, D.C.)
The New York Freeman (New York, New York)
The North Star (Rochester, New York)
Palladium of Liberty (Columbus, Ohio)
The Pennsylvania Freeman (Philadelphia, Pennsylvania)
The Provincial Freeman (Toronto & Chatham, Canada West)
The Rights of All (New York, New York)
Rochester Freeman (Rochester, New York)
Southern Christian Recorder (Atlanta, Georgia)
The Spy (Worcester, Mass.)
Star of Zion (Charlotte, North Carolina)
Weekly Advocate (New York, New York)
Weekly Anglo-African (later *The Anglo-African*) (New York, New York)

Published Primary Sources

Abdy, E[dward] S. *Journal of a Residence and Tour in the United States of North America*. London: John Murray, 1835.

Andrews, William L., ed. *Six Women's Slave Narratives*. New York: Oxford, 1988.

Aptheker, Herbert. "Report on the Condition of the People of Color in the State of Ohio (1835)." In *A Documentary History of the Negro People in the United States*, edited by Herbert Aptheker, 157–58. New York: Citadel Press, 1965.

Bell, Howard H., ed. *Minutes of the Proceedings of the National Negro Conventions, 1830–1864*. New York: Arno Press, 1969.

Brawley, Benjamin G. *Women of Achievement: Written for the Fireside Schools Under the Auspices of the Woman's American Baptist Home Mission Society*. N.p.: Woman's American Baptist Home Mission Society, 1919.

Brown, Hallie Q. *Homespun Heroines and Other Women of Distinction*. 1926. New York: Oxford University Press, 1988.

Brown, William Wells. *The Rising Sun; or, The Advancement of the Colored Race*. 1874. New York: Negro Universities Press, 1970.

Carey, T. J. *Brudder Gardner's Stump Speeches and Comic Lectures.* New York: Excelsior Publishing House, 1884.

Ceplair, Larry, ed. *The Public Years of Sarah and Angelina Grimké.* New York: Columbia University Press, 1989.

Coffin, Levi. *Reminiscences of Levi Coffin.* 1899. New York: Arno Press, 1968.

Davis, Lenwood G. "Documents: Frederick Douglass as a Preacher, and One of His Last Most Significant Letters." *Journal of Negro History* 66, no. 2 (1981): 140–43.

Delany, Martin R. *The Condition, Elevation, Emigration, and Destiny of the Colored People of the United States.* 1852. New York: Arno Press, 1968.

"Documents Relating to Negro Masonry in America." *Journal of Negro History* 21, no. 4 (October 1936): 411–32.

E. C. B. *George Christy's Ethiopian Joke Book. Containing All the Most Laughable Jokes, Dialogues, Stories, &c. as Told Only by This Son of Momus!* Philadelphia: Fisher & Brother, 1858.

Finkelman, Paul, ed. *Free Blacks, Slaves and Slaveowners in Civil and Criminal Courts.* 2 vols. New York: Garland Publishing, 1988.

Foner, Eric. *Freedom's Lawmakers: A Directory of Black Officeholders during Reconstruction.* Baton Rouge: Louisiana State University Press, 1996.

Foner, Philip S., and George E. Walker, eds. *New York, Pennsylvania, Indiana, Michigan, Ohio.* Vol. 1 of *Proceedings of the Black State Conventions, 1840–1865.* Philadelphia: Temple University Press, 1979.

Foote, Julia A. J. "A Brand Plucked from the Fire: An Autobiographical Sketch by Mrs. Julia A. J. Foote." In *Sisters of the Spirit: Three Black Women's Autobiographies of the Nineteenth Century,* edited by William L. Andrews, 161–234. Bloomington: Indiana University Press, 1986.

Forten, Charlotte L. *The Journals of Charlotte Forten Grimké.* Edited by Brenda Stevenson. New York: Oxford University Press, 1988.

Foster, Rev. John O. *Life and Labors of Mrs. Maggie Newton Van Cott, the First Lady Licensed to Preach in the Methodist Episcopal Church in the United States.* Cincinnati: Hitchcock and Walder, for the author, 1872.

Gordon, Ann D., ed. *In the School of Anti-Slavery.* Vol. 1 of *The Selected Papers of Elizabeth Cady Stanton and Susan B. Anthony.* New Brunswick: Rutgers University Press, 2000.

———. *Against an Aristocracy of Sex, 1866–1873.* Vol. 2 of *The Selected Papers of Elizabeth Cady Stanton and Susan B. Anthony.* New Brunswick: Rutgers University Press, 2000.

Haley, James T. *Afro-American Encyclopedia; or, The Thoughts, Doings, and Sayings of the Race, Embracing Lectures, Biographical Sketches, Sermons, Poems, Names of Universities, Colleges, Seminaries, Newspapers, Books, and a History of the Denominations, Giving the Numerical Strength of Each. In Fact, It Teaches Every Subject of Interest to the Colored People, as Discussed by More Than One Hundred of Their Wisest and Best Men and Women.* Nashville, Tenn.: Haley & Florida, 1895.

Hannibal, Julius Caesar. *Professor Julius Caesar Hannibal's Scientific Discourses. Originally Published in the New-York Picayune.* New York: Stringer and Townsend, 1852.

Harris, Cicero R. *Zion's Historical Catechism*. Charlotte, N.C.: A.M.E. Zion Publishing House, 1922.

Hartshorn, W[illiam] N[ewton]. *An Era of Progress and Promise, 1860–1910*. Boston: Priscilla Publishing Company, 1910.

Holsey, Lucius H. *Autobiography, Sermons, Addresses and Essays of Bishop L. H. Holsey, D.D.* Atlanta, Ga.: Franklin Printing and Pub. Co., 1898.

Hood, J. W. (James Walker). *One Hundred Years of the African Methodist Episcopal Zion Church; or, The Centennial of African Methodism*. New York: A.M.E. Zion Book Concern, 1895.

——. *Speech of the Rev. James W. Hood, of Cumberland County Court on the Question of Suffrage, Delivered in the Constitutional Convention of North Carolina, February 12, 1868*. Raleigh: W. W. Holden & Son, 1868.

Keckley, Elizabeth. *Behind the Scenes: Thirty Years a Slave, and Four Years in the White House*. Edited by Frances Smith Foster. Urbana: University of Illinois Press, 2001.

Lasser, Carol, and Marlene D. Merrill, eds. *Friends and Sisters: Letters Between Lucy Stone and Antoinette Brown Blackwell, 1846–1893*. Urbana: University of Illinois Press, 1987.

Lawson, Ellen N., and Marlene D. Merrill, comps. *The Three Sarahs: Documents of Antebellum Black College Women*. New York: Edwin Mellen Press, 1984.

Lee, Jarena. "The Life and Religious Experience of Jarena Lee, A Coloured Lady, Giving an Account of Her Call to Preach the Gospel." In *Sisters of the Spirit: Three Black Women's Autobiographies of the Nineteenth Century*, edited by William L. Andrews, 25–48. Bloomington: Indiana University Press, 1986.

"Letters from Negro Leaders to Gerrit Smith." *Journal of Negro History* 27, no. 4 (October 1942): 432–53.

Levine, Robert S., ed. *Martin R. Delany: A Documentary Reader*. Chapel Hill: University of North Carolina Press, 2003.

Lockwood, Belva A. "My Efforts to Become a Lawyer." *Lippincott's Monthly Magazine*, February 1888, 223.

Majors, Monroe A. *Noted Negro Women: Their Triumphs and Activities*. Chicago: Donahue and Henneberry, 1893; Freeport, N.Y., Books for Libraries Press, 1971.

McFarlin, Annjenette S., comp. *Black Congressional Reconstruction Orators and Their Orations, 1869–1879*. Metuchen, N.J.: Scarecrow Press, 1976.

Mohonk Conference on the Negro Question. *Proceedings*. Boston: G. H. Ellis, 1890–91.

Morgan, Rev. Joseph H. *Morgan's History of the New Jersey Conference of the A.M.E. Church, from 1872 to 1887. And of the Several Churches, as Far as Possible from Date of Organization, with Biographical Sketches of Members of the Conference*. Camden, N.J.: S. Chew, Printers, 1887.

Mossell, Gertrude. *The Work of the Afro-American Woman*. 1908. New York: Oxford University Press, 1988.

Nell, William C. *The Colored Patriots of the American Revolution*. 1835. New York: Arno Press, 1968.

"Opinions of the Judges of the Supreme Court of the United States in the Cases of 'Smith v. Tuner' and 'Norris v. the City of Boston.' " *Southern Quarterly Review* 16, no. 32 (January 1850): 444–502.

Paul, Susan. *Memoir of James Jackson: The Attentive and Obedient Scholar Who Died in Boston, October 31, 1833, Aged Six Years and Eleven Months, by His Teacher, Miss Susan Paul.* Edited by Lois Brown. 1835. Cambridge, Mass.: Harvard University Press, 2000.

Payne, Daniel A. *History of the African Methodist Episcopal Church.* 1891. New York: Arno Press, 1969.

Penn, I. Garland. *The Afro-American Press and Its Editors.* 1891. New York: Arno Press, 1969.

Porter, Dorothy B. "Early Manuscript Letters Written by Negroes." *Journal of Negro History* 24 (April 1939): 199–210.

Quarles, Benjamin. "Letters from Negro Leaders to Gerrit Smith." *Journal of Negro History* 27, no. 4 (October 1942): 432–53, 450–51.

Randolph, Peter. *From Slave Cabin to Pulpit.* Boston: J. H. Earle, 1893.

Richings, G. F. *Evidences of Progress Among Colored People.* 1896. Philadelphia: Geo. S. Ferguson, 1902.

Ripley, C. Peter, ed. *The Black Abolitionist Papers.* Chapel Hill: University of North Carolina Press, 1991.

Scruggs, Lawson. *Women of Distinction: Remarkable in Works and Invincible in Character.* Raleigh: L. A. Scruggs, 1893.

Shorter, Susie I. *The Heroines of African Methodism.* Xenia, Ohio: Chew, 1891.

Small, John B., Bishop. *Code on the Discipline of the African Methodist Episcopal Zion Church.* [York, Pa.]: York Dispatch Print, 1898.

Smith, C[harles] S. *A History of the African Methodist Episcopal Church, Being a Volume Supplemental to a History of the African Methodist Episcopal Church, by Daniel Alexander Payne.* Philadelphia: Book Concern of the AME Church, 1922.

Smith, Earl. "Document: William Cooper Nell on the Fugitive Slave Act of 1850." *Journal of Negro History* 66, no. 1 (Spring 1981): 37–40.

Smith, James L. "Letters to Antislavery Workers and Agencies (Part 5)." *Journal of Negro History* 10, no. 3 (July 1925): 444–68.

Stanton, Elizabeth C., Susan B. Anthony, and Matilda G. Gage, eds. *History of Woman Suffrage.* 6 vols. New York: Fowler & Wells, 1881–1922.

Sterling, Dorothy, ed. *Speak Out in Thunder Tones: Letters and Other Writings by Black Northerners, 1787–1865.* Garden City, N.Y.: Doubleday, 1973.

Stewart, Maria W. "Lecture Delivered at the Franklin Hall (21 September 1832) [Reprinted in *The Liberator,* 17 November 1832]." In *Maria W. Stewart, America's First Black Woman Political Writer: Essays and Speeches,* edited by Marilyn Richardson, 45–49. Bloomington: Indiana University Press, 1987.

———. "Religion and the Pure Principles of Morality, The Sure Foundation on Which We Must Build. Productions from the Pen of Mrs. Maria W. Steward [*sic*], Widow of the Late James W. Steward, of Boston." In *Maria W. Stewart, America's First Black Woman Political Writer: Essays and Speeches*, edited by Marilyn Richardson, 28–42. Bloomington: Indiana University Press, 1987.

Still, William. *Underground Railroad Records*. Philadelphia: Porter & Coates, 1872.

Swisshelm, Jane Grey. *Half a Century*. Chicago: Jansen, McClung & Company, 1880.

Talbert, Horace. *The Sons of Allen: Together with a Sketch of the Rise and Progress of Wilberforce University, Wilberforce, Ohio*. Xenia, Ohio: Aldine Press, 1906.

Tanner, Benjamin T. *An Apology for African Methodism*. Baltimore: s.n., 1867.

———. *An Outline of Our History and Government for African Methodist Churchmen, Ministerial and Lay. In Catechetical Form. Two Parts with Appendix*. Philadelphia: Grant, Faires & Rodgers, Printers, 1844.

Taylor, Susie K. *A Black Woman's Civil War Memoirs*. Edited by Patricia W. Romero and Willie L. Rose. Princeton: Markus Weiner Publishers, 1991.

Thompson, Sally. *Trial and Defense of Mrs. Sally Thompson, On a Complaint of Insubordination to the Rules of the Methodist Episcopal Church, Evil Speaking and Immorality*. West Troy, N.Y.: W. Hollands, 1837.

Turner, Henry M. *The Genius and Theory of Methodist Polity*. Philadelphia: A.M.E. Publications, 1885.

Walker, John H. "Proceedings of the Convention of Free Colored People of the State of Maryland." *Journal of Negro History* 1, no. 3 (July 1916): 302.

Washington, Booker T. *The Booker T. Washington Papers*. Urbana: University of Illinois Press, 1972–1989.

Wayman, Alexander W. *Cyclopedia of African Methodism*. Baltimore: M. E. Book Repository, 1882.

Williams, George W. *History of the Negro Race in America*. 2 vols. New York: Arno Press, [1968].

Woodson, Carter G., ed. *The Mind of the Negro as Reflected in Letters Written during the Crisis, 1800–1860*. Washington, D.C.: Associated Publishers, 1926.

———. *Negro Orators and Their Orations*. New York: Russell & Russell, 1969.

Yacovone, Donald, ed. *A Voice of Thunder: The Civil War Letters of George E. Stephens*. Urbana: University of Illinois Press, 1997.

Secondary Sources

Alexander, Shawn L. " 'We Know Our Rights and Have the Courage to Defend Them': The Spirit of Agitation in the Age of Accommodation, 1883–1909." Ph.D. diss., University of Massachusetts, 2004.

Allison, Dorothy. "The Future of Females: Octavia Butler's Mother Lode." In *Reading Black, Reading Feminist: A Critical Anthology*, edited by Henry Louis Gates Jr., 471–78. New York: Meridian, 1990.

Anderson, James D. *The Education of Blacks in the South, 1860–1935*. Chapel Hill: University of North Carolina Press, 1988.

Andolsen, Barbara H. *"Daughters of Jefferson, Daughters of Bootblacks": Racism and American Feminism*. Macon, Ga.: Mercer University Press, 1986.

Angell, Stephen [Ward]. *Bishop Henry McNeal Turner and African American Religion in the South*. Knoxville: University of Tennessee Press, 1992.

——. "The Controversy Over Women's Ministry in the African Methodist Episcopal Church during the 1880s: The Case of Sarah Ann Hughes." In *This Far By Faith: Readings in African American Women's Religious Biography*, edited by Judith Weisenfeld and Richard Newman, 94–109. New York: Routledge, 1996.

Armstead, Myra B. Young, Gretchen Sullivan Sorin, and Field Horne. *A Heritage Uncovered: The Black Experience in Upstate New York, 1800–1925*. Edited by Cara A. Sutherland. Elmira, N.Y.: Chemung County Historical Society, 1988.

Armstrong, Erica R. "A Mental and Moral Feast: Reading, Writing, and Sentimentality in Black Philadelphia." *Journal of Women's History* 16, no. 1 (2003): 78–102.

Attie, Jeanie. *Patriotic Toil: Northern Women and the American Civil War*. Ithaca, N.Y.: Cornell University Press, 1998.

Awkward, Michael. "A Black Man's Place(s) in Black Feminist Criticism." In *Representing Black Men*, edited by Marcellus Blount and George P. Cunningham, 3–26. New York: Routledge, 1996.

Aynes, Richard L. "The Bill of Rights, the Fourteenth Amendment, and the Seven Deadly Sins of Legal Scholarship." *William and Mary Bill of Rights Journal* 8 (February 2000): 407–35.

Bacon, Margaret H. "The Double Curse of Sex and Color: Robert Purvis and Human Rights." *Pennsylvania Magazine of History and Biography* 121, no. 1/2 (January/April 1997): 53.

Bardaglio, Peter W. *Reconstructing the Household: Families, Sex, and the Law in the Nineteenth-Century South*. Chapel Hill: University of North Carolina Press, 1995.

Bay, Mia. *The White Image in the Black Mind: African American Ideas about White People, 1830–1925*. New York: Oxford University Press, 2000.

Bearden, Jim, and Linda Jean Butler. *Shadd: The Life and Times of Mary Shadd Cary*. Toronto: NC Press, 1977.

Bederman, Gail. *Manliness & Civilization: A Cultural History of Gender and Race in the United States, 1890–1917*. Chicago: University of Chicago Press, 1995.

Bell, Derrick. *And We Are Not Saved: The Elusive Quest for Racial Justice*. New York: Basic Books, 1987.

——. *Faces at the Bottom of the Well: The Permanence of Racism*. New York: Basic Books, 1992.

Bell, Howard H. "The American Moral Reform Society, 1836–1841." *Journal of Negro Education* 27, no. 1 (Winter 1958): 34–40.

——. "National Negro Conventions of the Middle 1840s: Moral Suasion vs. Political Action." *Journal of Negro History* 42, no. 4 (October 1959): 247–60.

——. *A Survey of the Negro Convention Movement, 1830–1861*. New York: Arno Press, 1969.

Bender, Thomas. "Whole and Parts: The Need for Synthesis in American History." *Journal of American History* 73 (June 1986): 120–36.

Berkeley, Kathleen. " 'Colored Ladies Also Contributed': Black Women's Activities from Benevolence to Social Welfare, 1866–1896." In *The Web of Southern Social Relations: Women, Family, and Education*, edited by Walter J. Fraser, R. Frank Saunders Jr., and Jon L. Wakelyn, 181–203. Athens: University of Georgia Press, 1985.

Berlin, Ira. *Slaves Without Masters: The Free Negro in the Antebellum South*. New York: New Press, 1974.

Berlin, Ira, Joseph P. Reidy, and Leslie Rowland, eds. *Freedom's Soldiers: The Black Military Experience in the Civil War*. New York: Cambridge University Press, 1998.

Berthold, Michael. "Not 'Altogether' the 'History of Myself': Autobiographical Impersonality in Elizabeth Keckley's *Behind the Scenes; Or, Thirty Years a Slave and Four Years in the White House*." *American Transcendental Quarterly* 13, no. 2 (1999): 105–19.

Bethel, Elizabeth R. *The Roots of African-American Identity: Memory and History in Free Antebellum Communities*. New York: St. Martin's Press, 1997.

Bilder, Mary S. "The Struggle Over Immigration: Indentured Servants, Slaves, and Articles of Commerce." *Missouri Law Review* 61 (Fall 1996): 743–824.

Billington, Ray Allen. "A Social Experiment: The Port Royal Journal of Charlotte L. Forten, 1862–1863." *Journal of Negro History* 35, no. 3 (July 1950): 233–64.

Blackett, Richard J. M. *Building an Antislavery Wall: Black Americans in the Atlantic Abolitionist Movement, 1830–1860*. Baton Rouge: Louisiana State University Press, 1983.

The Black Public Sphere Collective. *The Black Public Sphere: A Public Culture Book*. Chicago: University of Chicago Press, 1995.

Blassingame, John W. "Negro Chaplains in the Civil War." *Negro History Bulletin* 27, no. 1 (1963): 23–24.

Blight, David W. *Frederick Douglass' Civil War: Keeping Faith in Jubilee*. Baton Rouge: Louisiana State University Press, 1989.

———. "In Search of Learning, Liberty, and Self-Definition: James McCune Smith and the Ordeal of the Antebellum Black Intellectual." *Afro-Americans in New York Life and History* 9, no. 2 (1985): 7–25.

Bloch, Herman D. "Labor and the Negro, 1866–1910." *Journal of Negro History* 50, no. 3 (1965): 163–84.

Blount, Marcellus, and George Cunningham, eds. *Representing Black Men*. New York: Routledge, 1996.

Bordin, Ruth. *Women and Temperance: The Quest for Power and Liberty, 1873–1900*. Philadelphia: Temple University Press, 1981.

Boyd, Melba J. *Discarded Legacy: Politics and Poetics in the Life of Frances E. W. Harper, 1825–1911*. Detroit, Mich.: Wayne State University Press, 1994.

Boylan, Anne M. *The Origins of Women's Activism: New York and Boston, 1797–1840*. Chapel Hill: University of North Carolina Press, 2002.

Bradley, David H., Jr. *A History of the AME Zion Church, Part I, 1796–1872*. Nashville: Pantheon Press, 1956.

Brekus, Catherine A. *Strangers and Pilgrims: Female Preaching in America, 1740–1845*. Chapel Hill: University of North Carolina Press, 1998.

Brewer, William M. "Henry Highland Garnet." *Journal of Negro History* 13, no. 1 (January 1928): 36–52.

Breyfogle, William A. *Make Free: The Story of the Underground Railroad*. Philadelphia: Lippincott, 1958.

Brickner, Paul. "*The Passenger Cases* (1849): Justice John McLean's 'Cherished Policy' as the First of Three Phases of American Immigration Law." *Southwestern Journal of Law and Trade in the Americas* 10 (2003 / 2004): 63–79.

Brophy, Alfred L. "'A Revolution Which Seeks to Abolish Law, Must End Necessarily in Despotism': Louisa McCord and Antebellum Southern Legal Thought." *Cardozo Women's Law Journal* 5, no. 1 (1998): 33–77.

Brown, Elsa Barkley. "African-American Women's Quilting: A Framework for Conceptualizing and Teaching African American Women's History." *Signs: Journal of Women in Culture and Society* 14, no. 4 (Summer 1989): 921–29.

———. "Negotiating and Transforming the Public Sphere: African American Political Life in the Transition from Slavery to Freedom." *Public Culture* 7 (1994): 107–46.

———. "Negotiating and Transforming the Public Sphere: African American Political Life in the Transition from Slavery to Freedom." In *The Black Public Sphere: A Public Culture Book*, edited by Black Public Sphere Collective, 111–50. Chicago: University of Chicago Press, 1995.

———. "Womanist Consciousness: Maggie Lena Walker and the Independent Order of Saint Luke." *Signs: Journal of Women in Culture and Society* 13, no. 3 (1989): 610–33.

Brown, Ira V. "Cradle of Feminism: The Philadelphia Female Anti-Slavery Society, 1833–1840." *Pennsylvania Magazine of History and Biography* 102 (1978): 143–66.

Browne, Patrick T. J. "'To Defend Mr. Garrison': William Cooper Nell: The Personal Politics of Antislavery." *New England Quarterly* 70, no. 3 (1997): 415–22.

Bullock, Penelope I. *The Afro-American Periodical Press, 1838–1909*. Baton Rouge: Louisiana State University Press, 1981.

Burke, Ronald K. *Samuel Ringgold Ward: Christian Abolitionist*. New York: Garland Publishing, 1995.

Butchart, Ronald E. *Northern Schools, Southern Blacks and Reconstruction*. Westport, Conn.: Greenwood Press, 1980.

Butler, Anthea D. "'Only a Woman Would Do': Bible Reading and African American Women's Organizing Work." In *Women and Religion in the African Diaspora*, edited by Barbara D. Savage and R. Marie Griffith, 155–78. Baltimore: Johns Hopkins University Press, 2006.

Butler, Judith. *Gender Trouble: Feminism and the Subversion of Identity*. New York: Routledge, 1990.

Cadbury, Henry J. "Negro Membership in the Society of Friends." *Journal of Negro History* 21, no. 2 (April 1936): 151–213.

Calhoun, Craig, ed. *Habermas and the Public Sphere*. Cambridge, Mass.: MIT Press, 1992.

Campbell, James T. *Songs of Zion: The African Methodist Episcopal Church in the United States and South Africa*. New York: Oxford University Press, 1995.

Campbell, Stanley W. *The Slave Catchers: Enforcement of the Fugitive Slave Law, 1850–1860*. Chapel Hill: University of North Carolina Press, 1970.

Caraway, Nancie. *Segregated Sisterhood: Racism and the Politics of American Feminism*. Knoxville: University of Tennessee Press, 1991.

Carby, Hazel. *Reconstructing Womanhood: The Emergence of the Afro-American Woman Novelist*. Oxford: Oxford University Press, 1990.

Carlson, Shirley. "Black Ideals of Womanhood in the Victorian Era." *Journal of Negro History* 77, no. 2 (Spring 1992): 61–73.

Cass, Don A. *Negro Free Masonry and Segregation*. Chicago: E. A. Cook, 1957.

Castle, Musette S. "A Survey of the History of African Americans in Rochester, New York, 1800–1860." *Afro-Americans in New York Life and History* 13 (July 1989): 7–32.

Cazden, Elizabeth. *Antoinette Brown Blackwell: A Biography*. Old Westbury, N.Y.: Feminist Press, 1983.

Cecelski, David S., and Timothy B. Tyson, eds. *Democracy Betrayed: The Wilmington Race Riot of 1898 and Its Legacy*. Chapel Hill: University of North Carolina Press, 1998.

Cheek, William, and Aimee L. Cheek. *John Mercer Langston and the Fight for Black Freedom, 1829–1865*. Champaign: University of Illinois Press, 1996.

Christensen, Lawrence O. "Peter Humphries Clark." *Missouri Historical Review* 88, no. 2 (1994): 145–56.

Clark, Mary L. "The Founding of the Washington College of Law: The First Law School Established by Women for Women." *American University Law Review* 47 (February 1998): 613–76.

Clawson, Mary Ann. *Constructing Brotherhood: Class, Gender, and Fraternalism*. Princeton, N.J.: Princeton University Press, 1989.

Clinton, Catherine. "Reconstructing Freedwomen." In *Divided Houses: Gender and the Civil War*, edited by Catherine Clinton and Nina Silber, 306–19. New York: Oxford University Press, 1992.

Coleman, Willie Mae. "Keeping the Faith and Disturbing the Peace. Black Women: From Anti-Slavery to Women's Suffrage." Ph.D. diss., University of California, Irvine, 1982.

Collier-Thomas, Bettye. *Daughters of Thunder: Black Women Preachers and Their Sermons, 1850–1879*. San Francisco: Josey-Bass, 1998.

Cooper, Afua. "The Search for Mary Bibb, Black Woman Teacher in Nineteenth-Century Canada West." In *"We Specialize in the Wholly Impossible": A Reader in Black*

Women's History, edited by Darlene Clark Hine, Wilma King, and Linda Reed, 171–85. Brooklyn, N.Y.: Carlson Publishing, 1995.

Cott, Nancy F. *The Bonds of Womanhood: "Woman's Sphere" in New England, 1780–1835*. New Haven, Conn.: Yale University Press, 1977.

Crenshaw, Kimberlé. "Demarginalizing the Intersection of Race and Sex: A Black Feminist Critique of Antidiscrimination Doctrine, Feminist Theory and Antiracist Politics." *University of Chicago Legal Forum* (1989): 139–67.

——. "Mapping the Margins: Intersectionality, Identity Politics, and Violence Against Women of Color." *Stanford Law Review* 43 (July 1991): 1241–99.

Cromwell, John W. "The First Negro Churches in the District of Columbia." *Journal of Negro History* 7, no. 1 (January 1922): 64–106.

Cross, Whitney. *The Burned-Over District: Social and Intellectual History of Enthusiastic Religion, 1800–1850*. New York: Harper and Row, 1950.

Cullen, Jim. "'I's a Man Now': Gender and African American Men in the Civil War." In *Divided Houses: Gender and the Civil War*, edited by Catherine Clinton and Nina Silber, 76–91. New York: Oxford University Press, 1992.

Curry, Leonard P. *The Free Black in Urban America, 1800–1850: The Shadow of the Dream*. Chicago: University of Chicago Press, 1981.

Dailey, Jane, Glenda E. Gilmore, and Bryant Simon, eds. *Jumpin' Jim Crow: Southern Politics from Civil War to Civil Rights*. Princeton: Princeton University Press, 2000.

Davis, Barbara. *A History of the Black Community of Syracuse*. Syracuse, N.Y.: Onondaga Community College, 1980.

Davis, Elizabeth L. *Lifting as They Climb: An Historical Record of the National Association of Colored Women*. 1933. New York: G. K. Hall and Co., 1996.

——. *The Story of the Illinois Federation of Colored Women's Clubs / Elizabeth L. Davis; The History of the Order of the Eastern Star Among Colored People / Mrs. Joe S. Brown*. 1922. New York: G. K. Hall, 1997.

DeAmicis, Jan. "'To Them That Has Brot Me Up': Black Oneidans and Their Families, 1850–1920." *Afro-Americans in New York Life and History* 21, no. 2 (July 1997): 19–38.

DeBoer, Clara Merritt. *Be Jubilant My Feet: African American Abolitionists in the American Missionary Association, 1839–1861*. New York: Garland Publishing, 1994.

——. *His Truth Is Marching On: African Americans Who Taught the Freedmen for the American Missionary Association, 1861–1877*. New York: Garland Publishing, 1995.

Diedrich, Maria. "'Self-Love and Social Be the Same': Afro-American Efforts to Create Communities in the Slave Narrative Before the American Civil War." *Archiv Fur Kulturgeschichte (West Germany)* 67, no. 2 (1985): 389–415.

Dillon, Merton L. "Elizabeth Chandler and the Spread of Antislavery Sentiment to Michigan." In *Abolitionism and Issues of Race and Gender*, edited by John R. McKivigan, 205–18. New York: Garland Publishing, 1999.

Dodson, Jualynne E. *Engendering Church: Women, Power, and the A.M.E. Church*. Lanham, Md.: Rowman & Littlefield, 2002.

——. "Nineteenth-Century A.M.E. Preaching Women." In *Women in New Worlds*, edited by Hilah F. Thomas and Rosemary S. Keller, 276–92. Nashville, Tenn.: Abingdon, 1981.

——. "Power and Surrogate Leadership: Black Women and Organized Religion." *Sage: A Scholarly Journal on Black Women* 5, no. 2 (Fall 1988): 37–42.

Dodson, Jualynne E., and Cheryl T. Gilkes. "Something Within: Social Change and Collective Endurance in the Sacred World of Black Christian Women." In *Women and Religion in America: Volume 3: 1900–1968*, edited by Rosemary Radford Reuther and Rosemary Skinner Keller, 80–89. San Francisco: Harper and Row, 1986.

Dorsey, Bruce. "A Gendered History of African Colonization in the Antebellum United States." *Journal of Social History* 34, no. 1 (Fall 2000): 77–104.

DuBois, Ellen. *Feminism and Suffrage: The Emergence of an Independent Women's Movement in America, 1848–1869*. Ithaca, N.Y.: Cornell University Press, 1978.

DuBois, W. E. B. *The Negro Church. Report of a Social Study Made Under the Direction of Atlanta University; Together with the Proceedings of the Eighth Conference for the Study of the Negro Problems, Held at Atlanta University, May 26th, 1903*. Atlanta, Ga.: Atlanta University Press, 1903.

Dumenil, Lynn. *Freemasonry and American Culture, 1880–1930*. Princeton, N.J.: Princeton University Press, 1984.

Dyson, Zita. "Gerrit Smith's Efforts in Behalf of the Negroes in New York." *Journal of Negro History* 3, no. 4 (October 1918): 354–59.

Eckhardt, Celia M. *Fanny Wright: Rebel in America*. Cambridge: Harvard University Press, 1984.

Edwards, Laura F. *Gendered Strife and Confusion: The Political Culture of Reconstruction*. Urbana: University of Illinois Press, 1997.

Eggert, Gerald G. "Two Steps Forward, a Step and a Half Back: Harrisburg's African American Community in the Nineteenth Century." *Pennsylvania History* 58, no. 1 (1991): 1–36.

Eggleston, G. K. "The Work of Relief Societies during the Civil War." *Journal of Negro History* 14, no. 3 (July 1929): 272–99.

Ellis, David M. "Conflicts Among Calvinists: Oneida Revivalists in the 1820s." *New York History* 71, no. 1 (1990): 24–44.

Epstein, Barbara. *The Politics of Domesticity: Women, Evangelism, and Temperance in Nineteenth Century America*. Middletown, Conn.: Wesleyan University Press, 1981.

Fabre, Geneviève. "African-American Commemorative Celebrations in the Nineteenth Century." In *History and Memory in African-American Culture*, edited by Geneviève Fabre and Robert O'Meally, 72–91. New York: Oxford University Press, 1994.

Fairclough, Adam. " 'Being in the Field of Education and Also Being a Negro . . . Seems . . . Tragic': Black Teachers in the Jim Crow South." *Journal of American History* 87 (June 2000): 65–91.

Farley, Ena L. "The African American Presence in the History of Western New York." *Afro-Americans in New York Life and History* 14 (January 1990): 27–89.

Field-Bibb, Jacqueline. *Women Towards Priesthood: Ministerial Politics and Feminist Praxis.* New York: Cambridge University Press, 1991.

Flexner, Eleanor, and Ellen Fitzpatrick. *Century of Struggle: The Woman's Rights Movement in the United States.* Enlarged ed. Cambridge: Belknap Press of Harvard University Press, 1996.

Foner, Eric. *Reconstruction: America's Unfinished Revolution, 1863–1877.* New York: Harper and Row, 1988.

Foner, Philip S. "Peter H. Clark: Pioneering Black Socialist." *Journal of Ethnic Studies* 5, no. 3 (Fall 1977): 17–35.

Forbes, Ella. *African American Women during the Civil War.* New York: Garland Publishing, 1998.

Fordham, Monroe. "Origins of the Michigan Street Baptist Church, Buffalo, New York." *Afro-Americans in New York Life and History* 21, no. 1 (January 1997): 7–18.

Frankel, Noralee. *Freedom's Women: Black Women and Families in Civil War Era Mississippi.* Bloomington: Indiana University Press, 1999.

Franklin, John Hope. *George Washington Williams: A Biography.* Chicago: University of Chicago Press, 1985.

Frederickson, Mary E. " 'Each One Is Dependent on the Other': Southern Churchwomen, Racial Reform, and the Process of Transformation." In *Visible Women: New Essays in American Activism,* edited by Nancy Hewitt and Suzanne Lebsock, 296–324. Urbana: University of Illinois Press, 1993.

Freedman, Estelle B. *No Turning Back: The History of Feminism and the Future of Women.* New York: Ballantine Books, 2002.

Friedman, Lawrence. "The Gerrit Smith Circle: Abolitionism in the Burned Over District." *Civil War History* 26 (1980): 18–38.

———. *Gregarious Saints: Self and Community in American Abolitionism, 1830–1870.* New York: Cambridge University Press, 1982.

Fulop, Timothy E., and Albert J. Raboteau, eds. *African-American Religion: Interpretive Essays in History and Culture.* New York: Routledge, 1997.

Gaines, Kevin K. *Uplifting the Race: Black Leadership, Politics, and Culture in the Twentieth Century.* Chapel Hill: University of North Carolina Press, 1996.

Gara, Larry. "William Still and the Underground Railroad." In *Blacks in the Abolitionist Movement,* edited by John Bracey, August Meier, and Elliott Rudwick, 44–52. Belmont, Calif.: Wadsworth Publishing, 1971.

Gardner, Bettye J. "William Watkins: Antebellum Black Teacher and Writer." *Negro History Bulletin* 39, no. 6 (1976): 623–24.

Garrison, Nancy S. *With Courage and Delicacy: Civil War on the Peninsula and Women and the U.S. Sanitary Commission.* Mechanicsburg: Stackpole, 1998.

Gates, Henry Louis, Jr., ed. *Reading Black, Reading Feminist.* New York: Meridian Books, 1990.

George, Carol V. R. *Segregated Sabbaths: Richard Allen and the Rise of Independent Black Churches, 1760–1840.* New York: Oxford University Press, 1973.

——. "Widening the Circle: The Black Church and the Abolitionist Crusade, 1830–1860." In *African American Religion: Interpretive Essays in History and Culture,* edited by Timothy E. Fulop and Albert J. Raboteau, 153–76. New York: Routledge, 1997.

Giesberg, Judith Ann. *Civil War Sisterhood: The U.S. Sanitary Commission and Women's Politics in Transition.* Boston: Northeastern University Press, 2000.

Gifford, Carolyn DeSwarte, ed. *The Debate in the Methodist Episcopal Church Over Laity Rights for Women.* New York: Garland Publishing, 1987.

——. *The Defense of Women's Rights to Ordination in the Methodist Episcopal Church.* New York: Garland Publishing, 1988.

Gilkes, Cheryl T. "The Politics of 'Silence': Dual-Sex Political Systems and Women's Traditions of Conflict in African American Religion." In *African American Christianity: Essays in History,* edited by Paul E. Johnson, 80–110. Berkeley: University of California Press, 1994.

Gilmore, Glenda E. "Gender and Jim Crow: Sarah Dudley Pettey's Vision of the New South." *North Carolina Historical Review* 68, no. 3 (July 1991): 261–85.

——. *Gender and Jim Crow: Women and the Politics of White Supremacy in North Carolina, 1896–1920.* Chapel Hill: University of North Carolina Press, 1996.

Ginzberg, Lori D. *Untidy Origins: A Story of Woman's Rights in Antebellum New York.* Chapel Hill: University of North Carolina Press, 2005.

——. *Women and the Work of Benevolence: Morality, Politics, and Class in the Nineteenth-Century United States.* New Haven, Conn.: Yale University Press, 1990.

——. "Women in an Evangelical Community: Oberlin, 1835–1850." *Ohio History* 89 (Winter 1980): 78–88.

Gliozzo, Charles A. "The Black Convention Movement, 1848–1856." *Journal of Black Studies* 3, no. 2 (December 1972): 227–36.

Glymph, Thavolia. " 'This Species of Property': Female Slave Contrabands in the Civil War." In *A Woman's War: Southern Women, Civil War, and the Confederate Legacy,* edited by Edward D. C. Campbell Jr. and Kim S. Rice, 55–72. Richmond, Va.: Museum of the Confederacy, 1996.

Gordon, Ann D., Bettye Collier-Thomas, John H. Bracey, Arlene V. Avakian, and Joyce A. Berkman, eds. *African American Women and the Vote, 1837–1965.* Amherst: University of Massachusetts Press, 1997.

Gordon, Beverly. *Bazaars and Fair Ladies: The History of the American Fundraising Fair.* Knoxville: University of Tennessee Press, 1998.

Govan, Sandra Y. "Homage to Tradition: Octavia Butler Renovates the Historical Novel." *MELUS: The Journal of the Society for the Study of the Multi-Ethnic Literature of the United States* 13, no. 1–2 (Spring–Summer 1986): 79–96.

Grammar, Elizabeth E. "Female Itinerant Evangelists in Nineteenth Century America." *Arizona Quarterly* 55 (Spring 1999): 67–96.

Gravely, William B. "The Dialectic of Double-Consciousness in Black American Freedom Celebrations, 1808–1863." *Journal of Negro History* 67, no. 4 (Winter 1982): 302–17.

Greene, Gwendolyn. "From 'The Chapel' to the Buffalo Urban League." *Afro-Americans in New York Life and History* 21, no. 1 (1997): 44–46.

Grimshaw, William H. *Official History of Freemasonry Among the Colored People in North America: Tracing the Growth of Masonry From 1717 Down to the Present Day.* 1903. New York: Negro Universities Press, 1969.

Gross, Bella. *Clarion Call: The History and Development of the Negro People's Convention Movement in the United States from 1817 to 1840.* New York: n.p., 1947.

Grossman, Lawrence. "George T. Downing and Desegregation of Rhode Island Public Schools, 1855–1866." *Rhode Island History* 36, no. 4 (1977): 99–105.

——. "In His Veins Coursed No Bootlicking Blood: The Career of Peter H. Clark." *Ohio History* 86, no. 2 (1977): 79–95.

Grover, Kathryn. *Make a Way Somehow: African Americans in Geneva, New York, 1790–1965.* Geneva, N.Y.: Geneva Historical Society, 1991.

Guy-Sheftall, Beverly. *Words of Fire: An Anthology of African American Feminist Thought.* New York: New Press, 1995.

Habermas, Jürgen. "Social Structures of the Public Sphere." In *The Structural Transformation of the Public Sphere: An Inquiry Into a Category of Bourgeois Society.* Translated by Thomas Burger with Frederick Lawrence, 27–56. Cambridge, Mass.: MIT Press, 1991.

Hahn, Steven. *A Nation Under Our Feet: Black Political Struggles in the Rural South from Slavery to the Great Migration.* Cambridge: Harvard University Press, 2004.

Hancock, Scott. "The Elusive Boundaries of Blackness: Identity Formation in Antebellum Boston." *Journal of Negro History* 84, no. 2 (Spring 1999): 115–29.

Harris, Cicero R. *Zion's Historical Catechism.* Charlotte, N.C.: A.M.E. Zion Publishing House, 1922.

Haywood, Chanta M. *Prophesying Daughters: Black Women Preachers and the Word, 1823–1913.* Columbia: University of Missouri Press, 2003.

Hébrard, Jean. "Peut-on faire une histoire des pratiques populaires de lecture à l'époque moderne? Les 'Nouveaux Lecteurs' revisités." *Matériaux pour une histoire de la lecture det de ses institutions* 17 (2005): 105–40.

Helsinger, Elizabeth K., Robin L. Sheets, and William Veeder, eds. *Defining Voices, 1837–1883.* Vol. 1 of *The Woman Question, Society and Literature in Britain and America, 1837–1883.* New York: Garland Publishing, 1983.

Hepburn, Sharon A. "Following the North Star: Canada as a Haven for Nineteenth-Century American Blacks." *Michigan Historical Review* 25 (Fall 1999): 91–126.

Hersh, Blanche Glassman. *The Slavery of Sex: Feminist-Abolitionists in America.* Urbana: University of Illinois Press, 1978.

Hewitt, Nancy A. "The Social Origins of Women's Antislavery Politics in Western

New York." In *Crusaders and Compromisers: Essays on the Relationship of the Antislavery Struggle to the Antebellum Party System*, edited by Alan Kraut, 205–33. Westport, Conn.: Greenwood Press, 1983.

——. *Women's Activism and Social Change: Rochester, New York, 1822–1872*. Ithaca, N.Y.: Cornell University Press, 1984.

Hewitt, Nancy, and Suzanne Lebsock, eds. *Visible Women: New Essays in American Activism*. Urbana: University of Illinois Press, 1993.

Higginbotham, Evelyn B. "African American Women's History and the Metalanguage of Race." *Signs: Journal of Women in Culture and Society* 17 (Winter 1992): 251–74.

——. "Beyond the Sound of Silence: Afro-American Women in History." *Gender and History* 1 (Spring 1989): 50–67.

——. "The Black Church: A Gender Perspective." In *African American Religion: Interpretive Essays in History and Culture*, edited by Timothy E. Fulop and Albert J. Raboteau, 201–26. New York: Routledge, 1997.

——. *Righteous Discontent: The Women's Movement in the Black Baptist Church, 1880–1920*. Cambridge, Mass.: Harvard University Press, 1993.

Hill, Daniel. *The Freedom Seekers: Blacks in Early Canada*. Toronto: Stoddart, 1992.

Hine, Darlene Clark. *Hine Sight: Black Women and the Re-Construction of American History*. Brooklyn, N.Y.: Carlson Publishing, 1994.

——. "Rape and the Inner Lives of Black Women: Thoughts on the Culture of Dissemblance." In *Hine Sight: Black Women and the Re-Construction of American History*, edited by Darlene Clark Hine, 37–47. Brooklyn, N.Y.: Carlson Publishing, 1994.

Hine, Darlene Clark, and Christie Anne Farnham. "Black Women's Culture of Resistance and the Right to Vote." In *Women of the American South: A Multicultural Reader*, edited by Christie Anne Farnham, 204–19. New York: NYU Press, 1997.

Hine, Darlene Clark, and Kathleen Thompson. *A Shining Thread of Hope: The History of Black Women in America*. New York: Broadway, 1998.

Hine, Darlene Clark, Wilma King, and Linda Reed, eds. *"We Specialize in the Wholly Impossible": A Reader in Black Women's History*. Brooklyn, N.Y.: Carlson Publishing, 1995.

Hodes, Martha E. *White Women, Black Men: Illicit Sex in the Nineteenth Century*. New Haven, Conn.: Yale University Press, 1997.

——, ed. *Sex, Love, Race: Crossing Boundaries in North American History*. New York: New York University Press, 1999.

Hoffert, Sylvia. *Jane Grey Swisshelm: An Unconventional Life, 1815–1884*. Chapel Hill: University of North Carolina Press, 2004.

Hopkins, Leroy T. "Spiritual Fatherland: African American Intellectuals and Germany, 1850–1920." *Yearbook of German-American Studies* 31 (1996): 25–35.

Horton, James O. "Black Education at Oberlin College: A Controversial Commitment." *Journal of Negro Education* 54, no. 4 (1985): 477–99.

———. *Free People of Color: Inside the African American Community*. Washington, D.C.: Smithsonian Institution Press, 1993.

Horton, James O., and Stacy Flaherty. "Black Leadership in Antebellum Cincinnati." In *Race and the City: Work, Community, and Protest in Cincinnati, 1820–1970*, edited by Henry L. Taylor Jr., 70–95. Urbana: University of Illinois Press, 1993.

Horton, James O., and Lois E. Horton. *Black Bostonians: Family Life and Community Struggle in the Antebellum North*. New York: Holmes & Meier, 1979.

———. *In Hope of Liberty: Culture, Community and Protest Among Northern Free Blacks, 1700–1860*. New York: Oxford University Press, 1997.

Houseley, Kathleen. "'Yours for the Oppressed': The Life of Jehiel C. Beman." *Journal of Negro History* 77, no. 1 (Winter 1992): 17–29.

Hunter, Carol M. *To Set the Captives Free: Reverend Jermain Wesley Loguen and the Struggle for Freedom in Central New York, 1835–1872*. New York: Garland Publishing, 1993.

Hunter, Tera. *To 'Joy My Freedom: Southern Black Women's Lives and Labors After the Civil War*. Cambridge, Mass.: Harvard University Press, 1997.

Hutton, Frankie. *The Early Black Press in America, 1827 to 1860*. Westport, Conn.: Greenwood Press, 1993.

Ihle, Elizabeth L. "Black Women's Education in the South: The Dual Burden of Sex and Race." In *Changing Education: Women as Radicals and Conservators*, edited by Joyce Antler and Sari Knopp Biklen, 69–80. Albany: State University of New York Press, 1990.

Irvine, Russell W., and Donna Z. Dunkerton. "The Noyes Academy, 1834–1835: The Road to the Oberlin Collegiate Institute and the Higher Education of African Americans in the Nineteenth Century." *Western Journal of Black Studies* 22 (Winter 1998): 260–73.

Isenberg, Nancy. *Sex and Citizenship in Antebellum America*. Chapel Hill: University of North Carolina Press, 1998.

Israel, Adrienne M. *Amanda Berry Smith: From Washerwoman to Evangelist*. Lanham, Md.: Scarecrow, 1998.

Jacobs, Donald M. "William Lloyd Garrison's *Liberator* and Boston's Blacks, 1830–1865." *New England Quarterly* 44 (June 1971): 259–77.

James, Jennifer Lee. "Jehiel C. Beman: A Leader of the Northern Free Black Community." *Journal of Negro History* 82, no. 1 (1997): 133–57.

Jeffrey, Julie Roy. *The Great Silent Army of Abolitionism: Ordinary Women in the Antislavery Movement*. Chapel Hill: University of North Carolina Press, 1998.

Jenkins, Maude T. "She Issued the Call: Josephine St. Pierre Ruffin, 1842–1924." *Sage: A Scholarly Journal on Black Women* 5, no. 2 (Fall 1988): 74–76.

Johnson, Michael P. "Denmark Vesey and His Co-Conspirators." *William and Mary Quarterly* 58, no. 4 (2001): 915–76.

Johnson, Rebecca O. "African American Feminist Science Fiction." *Sojourner: The Women's Forum* 19, no. 6 (February 1994): 12–14.

Jones, Jacqueline. *Labor of Love, Labor of Sorrow: Black Women, Work, and the Family from Slavery to the Present*. New York: Basic Books, 1985.

——. *Soldiers of Light and Love: Northern Teachers and Georgia Blacks, 1865–1873*. Chapel Hill: University of North Carolina Press, 1980.

——. "Women Who Were More Than Men: Sex and Status in Freedmen's Teaching." *History of Education Quarterly* 19 (Spring 1979): 47–50.

Jordan, Winthrop D. *White Over Black: American Attitudes Toward the Negro, 1550–1812*. Chapel Hill: University of North Carolina Press, 1968.

Kachun, Mitch. *Festivals of Freedom: Memory and Meaning in African American Emancipation Celebrations, 1808–1915*. Amherst: University of Massachusetts Press, 2003.

Kahn, Robert M. "The Political Ideology of Martin Delany." *Journal of Black Studies* 14, no. 4 (1984): 415–40.

Kelley, Mary. *Learning to Stand and Speak: Women, Education, and Public Life in America's Republic*. Chapel Hill: University of North Carolina Press, 2006.

——. *Private Woman, Public Stage: Literary Domesticity in Nineteenth-Century America*. New York: Oxford University Press, 1984.

Kennon, Donald R. " 'An Apple of Discord': The Woman Question at the World's Anti-Slavery Convention of 1840." *Slavery and Abolition* [Great Britain] 5, no. 3 (December 1984): 244–66.

Kerber, Linda K. *Women of the Republic: Intellect and Ideology in Revolutionary America*. Chapel Hill: University of North Carolina Press, 1980.

Kerr, Andrea M. *Lucy Stone: Speaking Out for Equality*. New Brunswick, N.J.: Rutgers University Press, 1992.

Killiam, Charles. "Daniel A. Payne and the A.M.E. General Conference of 1888: A Display of Contrasts." *Negro History Bulletin* 32, no. 7 (1969): 11–14.

Kriebl, Karen J. "From Bloomers to Flappers: The American Women's Dress Reform Movement, 1840–1920." Ph.D. diss., Ohio State University, 1998.

Krowl, Michelle A. " 'Her Just Dues': Civil War Pensions of African American Women in Virginia." In *Negotiating Boundaries of Southern Womanhood: Dealing with the Powers That Be*, edited by Janet L. Coryell, Thomas H. Appelton Jr., Anastatia Sims, and Treadway Sandra Gioia, 48–70. Columbia: University of Missouri Press, 2000.

Lakey, Othal H. *The History of the C.M.E. Church*. Memphis, Tenn.: C.M.E. Publishing House, 1996.

Landon, Fred. "The Negro Migration to Canada After the Passage of the Fugitive Slave Act." *Journal of Negro History* 5, no. 1 (1920): 22–36.

Lapp, Rudolph M. *Blacks in Gold Rush California*. New Haven, Conn.: Yale University Press, 1977.

——. "Jeremiah B. Sanderson: Early California Negro Leader." *Journal of Negro History* 53, no. 4 (October 1968): 321–33.

Lapsansky, Emma J. " 'Discipline to the Mind': Philadelphia's Banneker Institute,

1854–1872." *Pennsylvania Magazine of History and Biography* 117, no. 1–2 (January/April 1993): 83–102.

——. " 'Since They Got Those Separate Churches': Afro-Americans and Racism in Jacksonian Philadelphia." *American Quarterly* 32, no. 1 (Spring 1980): 54–78.

Lapsansky, Phillip. "Graphic Discord: Abolitionist and Antiabolitionist Images." In *The Abolitionist Sisterhood: Women's Political Culture in Antebellum America*, edited by Jean F. Yellin and John C. Van Horne, 201–30. Ithaca, N.Y.: Cornell University Press, 1994.

Lawson, Ellen N. "Sarah Woodson Early: 19th Century Black Nationalist 'Sister.' " *UMOJA* 2 (Summer 1981): 15–26.

Lawson, Ellen N., and Marlene Merrill. "The Antebellum 'Talented Thousandth': Black Students at Oberlin Before the Civil War." *Journal of Negro Education* 52, no. 2 (Spring 1983): 142–55.

Lerner, Gerda. "The Grimké Sisters and the Struggle Against Race Prejudice." *Journal of Negro History* 48, no. 4 (October 1963): 277–91.

——. *The Grimké Sisters from South Carolina: Pioneers for Woman's Rights and Abolition.* New York: Schocken Books, 1967.

Lerner, Gerda, ed. *Black Women in White America: A Documentary History.* New York: Vintage Books, 1973.

Levine, Robert S. *Martin Delany, Frederick Douglass, and the Politics of Representative Identity.* Chapel Hill: University of North Carolina Press, 1997.

Levy, Leonard W. "Sims' Case: The Fugitive Slave Law in Boston in 1851." *Journal of Negro History* 35, no. 1 (January 1950): 39–74.

Lewis, Jan. "The Republican Wife: Virtue and Seduction in the Early Republic." *William and Mary Quarterly* 44, no. 4 (October 1987): 689–721.

Lhamon, W. T., Jr. "Core Is Less." *Reviews in American History* 27, no. 4 (1999): 566–71.

Lincoln, C. Eric, and Lawrence H. Mamiya. *The Black Church in the African American Experience.* Durham, N.C.: Duke University Press, 1990.

Lindhorst, Marie J. "Politics in a Box: Sarah Mapps Douglass and the Female Literary Association, 1831–1833." *Pennsylvania History* 65, no. 3 (Summer 1998): 263–78.

Little, Lawrence S. *Disciples of Liberty: The African Methodist Episcopal Church in the Age of Imperialism, 1884–1916.* Knoxville: University of Tennessee Press, 2000.

Litwack, Leon. *North of Slavery: The Negro in the Free States, 1790–1860.* Chicago: University of Chicago Press, 1961.

Litwack, Leon, and August Meier. *Black Leaders of the Nineteenth Century.* Urbana: University of Illinois Press, 1988.

Loewenberg, Bert James, and Ruth Bogin, eds. *Black Women in Nineteenth-Century American Life: Their Words, Their Thoughts, Their Feelings.* University Park: Pennsylvania State University Press, 1976.

Logan, Rayford W. *The Betrayal of the Negro: From Rutherford B. Hayes to Woodrow Wilson.* New York: Collier Books, 1965.

——. *The Negro in American Life and Thought: The Nadir, 1877–1901*. New York: Dial Press, 1954.

Logan, Shirley W. *"We Are Coming": The Persuasive Discourse of Nineteenth-Century Black Women*. Carbondale: Southern Illinois University Press, 1999.

Lorini, Alessandra. *Rituals of Race: American Public Culture and the Search for Racial Democracy*. Charlottesville: University Press of Virginia, 1999.

Lott, Eric. *Love and Theft: Blackface Minstrelsy and the American Working Class*. New York: Oxford University Press, 1993.

Lubet, Steven. "Symposium: Of John Brown: Lawyers, the Law, and Civil Disobedience: Slavery on Trial: The Case of the Oberlin Rescue." *Alabama Law Review* 54 (Spring 2003): 785–829.

Lynch, James R. "Baptist Women in Ministry through 1920." *American Baptist Quarterly* 13, no. 4 (1994): 304–18.

Mack, Kibibi V. *Parlor Ladies and Ebony Drudges: African American Women, Class, and Work in a South Carolina Community*. Knoxville: University of Tennessee Press, 1999.

Mansfield, Betty. "The Fateful Crisis: Black Teachers of Virginia's Freedmen, 1861–1882." Ph.D. diss., Catholic University, 1980.

Martin, Waldo E., Jr. *The Mind of Frederick Douglass*. Chapel Hill: University of North Carolina Press, 1985.

Matijasic, Thomas D. "The Reaction of the Ohio General Assembly to the Fugitive Slave Act of 1850." *Northwest Ohio Quarterly* 55, no. 2 (1983): 40–60.

Mattingly, Carol. *Well-Tempered Women: Nineteenth-Century Temperance Rhetoric*. Carbondale: Southern Illinois University Press, 1998.

Mayer, Henry. *All on Fire: William Lloyd Garrison and the Abolition of Slavery*. New York: St. Martin's Press, 1998.

Maynard, Christopher S. "Note: Nine-Headed Caesar: The Supreme Court's Thumbs-Up Approach to the Right to Travel." *Case Western Reserve Law Review* 51 (Winter 2000): 297–352.

Maynard, Douglas H. "The World's Anti-Slavery Convention of 1840." *Mississippi Valley Historical Review* 47, no. 3 (December 1960): 452–71.

McElroy, James L. "Social Reform in the Burned Over District: Rochester, New York as a Test Case, 1830–1851." Ph.D. diss., SUNY Binghamton, 1974.

McFadden, Margaret H. *Golden Cables of Sympathy: The Transatlantic Sources of Nineteenth-Century Feminism*. Lexington: University Press of Kentucky, 1999.

McFeely, William S. *Frederick Douglass*. New York: W. W. Norton, 1991.

McGill, Meredith L. *American Literature and the Culture of Reprinting, 1834–1853*. Philadelphia: University of Pennsylvania Press, 2002.

McHenry, Elizabeth. *Forgotten Readers: Recovering the Lost History of African American Literary Societies*. Durham, N.C.: Duke University Press, 2002.

McKivigan, John R., and Jason H. Silverman. "Monarchial Liberty and Republican Slavery: West Indies Emancipation Celebrations in Upstate New York and Canada West." *Afro-Americans in New York Life and History* 10 (January 1986): 7–18.

Melder, Keith E. *The Beginnings of Sisterhood: The American Women's Rights Movement, 1800–1840.* New York: Schocken Books, 1977.

Melish, Joanne P. *Disowning Slavery: Gradual Emancipation and "Race" in New England, 1780–1860.* Ithaca, N.Y.: Cornell University Press, 1998.

Miller, Edward A., Jr. *The Black Civil War Soldiers of Illinois: The Story of the Twenty-Ninth U.S. Colored Infantry.* Columbia: University of South Carolina Press, 1998.

Miller, Ericka M. *The Other Reconstruction: Where Violence and Womanhood Meet in the Writings of Ida B. Wells-Barnett, Angelina Weld Grimké, and Nella Larsen.* New York: Routledge, 1999.

Mitchell, Michele. " 'The Black Man's Burden': African Americans, Imperialism, and Notions of Racial Manhood, 1890–1910." *International Review of Social History* 44 (1999): 77–99.

——. *Righteous Propagation: African Americans and the Politics of Racial Destiny after Reconstruction.* Chapel Hill: University of North Carolina Press, 2004.

——. "Silences Broken, Silences Kept: Gender and Sexuality in African American History." *Gender and History* 11 (November 1999): 433–44.

Moody, Joycelyn. *Sentimental Confessions: Spiritual Narratives of Nineteenth-Century African American Women.* Athens: University of Georgia Press, 2001.

Morgan, Jennifer L. *Laboring Women: Reproduction and Gender in New World Slavery.* Philadelphia: University of Pennsylvania Press, 2004.

——. " 'Some Could Suckle Over Their Shoulder': Male Travelers, Female Bodies, and the Gendering of Racial Ideology, 1500–1770." *William and Mary Quarterly* 54, no. 1 (January 1997): 167–92.

Morris, Robert C. *Reading, 'Riting, and Reconstruction: The Education of Freedmen in the South, 1861–1870.* Chicago: University of Chicago Press, 1981.

Moss, Hilary J. "Education's Inequality: Opposition to Black Higher Education in Antebellum Connecticut." *History of Education Quarterly* 46 (2006): 16–35.

Muraskin, William A. *Middle-Class Blacks in a White Society: Prince Hall Freemasonry in America.* Berkeley: University of California Press, 1975.

Nadelhaft, Jerome. "Subjects and/or Objects: Abolitionists and 'Utopian' Women." *Reviews in American History* 21, no. 3 (1993): 407–14.

Neuman, Gerald L. "The Lost Century of American Immigration Law (1776–1875)." *Columbia Law Review* 93 (December 1993): 1833–1901.

Neverdon-Morton, Cynthia. *Afro-American Women of the South and the Advancement of the Race, 1895–1925.* Knoxville: University of Tennessee Press, 1989.

Newman, Louise M. *White Women's Rights: The Racial Origins of Feminism in the United States.* New York: Oxford University Press, 1999.

Nieman, Donald G., ed. *African Americans and Education in the South, 1865–1900.* New York: Garland Publishing, 1994.

——. *Black Freedom / White Violence, 1865–1900.* New York: Garland Publishing, 1994.

——. *The Day of Jubilee: The Civil War Experience of Black Southerners.* New York: Garland Publishing, 1994.

Norgren, Jill. "Before It Was Merely Difficult: Belva Lockwood's Life in Law and Politics." *Journal of Supreme Court History* 23, no. 1 (1999): 16–42.

Norlin, Dennis. "The Term 'the Woman Question' in Late-Nineteenth-Century Social Discourse." *Bulletin of Bibliography* 49, no. 3 (September 1992): 179–93.

Ogunleye, Tolagbe. "Dr. Martin Robinson Delany, 19th-Century Africanist Womanist: Reflections on His Avant-Garde Politics Concerning Gender, Colorism, and National Building." *Journal of Black Studies* 28, no. 5 (1998): 628–49.

Painter, Nell Irvin. Introduction to *Incidents in the Life of a Slave Girl, Written by Herself,* by Harriet Jacobs (1861), edited by Nell Irvin Painter. New York: Penguin Books, 2000.

———. *Sojourner Truth: A Life, a Symbol.* New York: W. W. Norton, 1996.

Pease, Jane H., and William H. Pease. "Confrontation and Abolition in the 1850s." *Journal of American History* 58, no. 4 (March 1972): 923–37.

Peck, Catherine L. "Your Daughters Shall Prophesy: Women in the Afro-American Preaching Tradition." In *Diversities of Gifts: Field Studies in Southern Religion,* edited by Ruel W. Tyson, James L. Peacock, and Daniel W. Patterson, 143–56. Urbana: University of Illinois Press, 1988.

Perkins, Linda Marie. *Fanny Jackson Coppin and the Institute for Colored Youth, 1865–1902.* New York: Garland Publishing, 1987.

———. "Heed Life's Demands: The Educational Philosophy of Fanny Jackson Coppin." *Journal of Negro Education* 51, no. 3 (Summer 1982): 181–90.

Perlmann, Joel, and Robert A. Margo. *Women's Work? American Schoolteachers, 1650–1920.* Chicago: University of Chicago Press, 2001.

Phillips, Christopher. *Freedom's Port: The African American Community of Baltimore, 1790–1860.* Urbana: University of Illinois Press, 1997.

Phinney, William R. *Maggie Newton Van Cott: First Woman Licensed to Preach in the Methodist Episcopal Church.* Rye, N.Y.: Commission on Archives and History, New York Annual Conference, United Methodist Church, 1969.

Piersen, William D. *Black Yankees: The Development of an Afro-American Subculture in Eighteenth-Century New England.* Amherst: University of Massachusetts Press, 1993.

Porter, Andrew C. "Comment: Toward a Constitutional Analysis of the Right to Intrastate Travel." *Northwestern University Law Review* 86 (Spring 1992): 820–57.

Porter, Dorothy B. "The Organized Educational Activities of Negro Literary Societies, 1828–1846." *Journal of Negro Education* 5, no. 4 (October 1936): 555–76.

———. "The Remonds of Salem, Massachusetts: A Nineteenth-Century Family Revisited." *Proceedings of the American Antiquarian Society* 95, no. 2 (1985): 259–95.

Portnoy, Alisse. " 'Female Petitioners Can Lawfully Be Heard': Negotiating Female Decorum, United States Politics, and Political Agency, 1829–1831." *Journal of the Early Republic* 23, no. 4 (Winter 2003): 573–611.

Priebe, Paula J. "Central and Western New York and the Fugitive Slave Law of 1850." *Afro-Americans in New York Life and History* 15, no. 1 (1992): 19–29.

Pritchard, Linda K. "The Burned Over District Reconsidered: A Portent of Evolving Religious Pluralism in the United States." *Social Science History* 8, no. 3 (1984): 243–66.

Quarles, Benjamin. *Black Abolitionists*. New York: Oxford University Press, 1969.

——. *Frederick Douglass*. 1949. New York: Da Capo Press, 1997.

——. "Frederick Douglass and the Woman's Rights Movement." *Journal of Negro History* 25, no. 1 (January 1940): 35–44.

Rael, Patrick. *Black Identity and Black Protest in the Antebellum North*. Chapel Hill: University of North Carolina Press, 2002.

Rhodes, Jane. *Mary Ann Shadd Cary: The Black Press and Protest in the Nineteenth Century*. Indianapolis: Indiana University Press, 1999.

Rice, Alan, and Martin Crawford, eds. *Liberating Sojourn: Frederick Douglass and Transatlantic Reform*. Athens: University of Georgia Press, 1999.

Richardson, Joe M. *Christian Reconstruction: The American Missionary Association and Southern Blacks, 1861–1890*. Athens: University of Georgia Press, 1986.

Richardson, Marilyn, ed. *Maria W. Stewart, America's First Black Woman Political Writer: Essays and Speeches*. Bloomington: Indiana University Press, 1987.

Riegel, Robert E. "Women's Clothes and Women's Rights." *American Quarterly* 15, no. 3 (Autumn 1963): 390–401.

Robertson, Stacey M. *Parker Pillsbury: Radical Abolitionist, Male Feminist*. Ithaca, N.Y.: Cornell University Press, 2000.

Rose, Willie Lee N. *Rehearsal for Reconstruction: The Port Royal Experiment*. Indianapolis: Bobbs-Merrill, 1964.

Ryan, Mary. *Women in Public: Between Banners and Ballots, 1825–1880*. Baltimore: Johns Hopkins University Press, 1990.

Salvaggio, Ruth. "Octavia Butler and the Black Science Fiction Heroine." *Black American Literature Forum* 18, no. 2, Science Fiction Issue (Summer 1984): 78–81.

Santamarina, Xiomara. *Belabored Professions: Narratives of African American Working Womanhood*. Chapel Hill: University of North Carolina Press, 2005.

Satterwhite, John H. "An Interpretation of History: Henry Evans, James Walker Hood, and Bishop James Wesley Wactor." *A.M.E. Zion Quarterly Review* 96, no. 3 (1984): 28–31.

Schechter, Patricia A. *Ida B. Wells-Barnett and American Reform, 1880–1930*. Chapel Hill: University of North Carolina Press, 2001.

Schwalm, Leslie A. *A Hard Fight for We: Women's Transition from Slavery to Freedom in South Carolina*. Urbana: University of Illinois Press, 1997.

Seraile, William. *New York's Black Regiments during the Civil War*. New York: Routledge, 2001.

Sernett, Milton C. "On Freedom's Threshold: The African American Presence in Central New York, 1760–1940." *Afro-Americans in New York Life and History* 19, no. 1 (January 1995): 43–91.

Shaffer, Donald R. " 'I Do Not Suppose That Uncle Sam Looks at the Skin': African Americans and the Civil War." *Civil War History* 46 (June 2000): 132–47.

Shaw, Stephanie J. "Black Club Women and the Creation of the National Association of Colored Women." *Journal of Women's History* 3, no. 2 (1991): 10–25.

———. *What a Woman Ought to Be and to Do: Black Professional Women Workers during the Jim Crow Era.* Chicago: University of Chicago Press, 1996.

Sheridan, Richard B. "Charles Henry Langston and the African American Struggle in Kansas." *Kansas History* 22, no. 4 (1999–2000): 268–83.

Sherman, Joan R. "James Monroe Whitfield, Poet and Emigrationist: Voice of Protest and Despair." *Journal of Negro History* 57, no. 2 (Spring 1972): 169–76.

Shippee, Lester Burrell. "Jane Grey Swisshelm: Agitator." *Mississippi Valley Historical Review* 7, no. 3 (December 1920): 206–27.

Siegel, Reva B. "She the People: The Nineteenth Amendment, Sex Equality, Federalism, and the Family." *Harvard Law Review* 115, no. 4 (February 2002): 948–1046.

Silcox, Harry C. "Philadelphia Negro Educator: Jacob C. White, Jr., 1837–1902." *Pennsylvania Magazine of History and Biography* 97, no. 1 (1973): 75–98.

Silverman, Jason H. *Unwelcome Guests: Canada West's Response to American Fugitive Slaves, 1800–1865.* Millwood, N.Y.: Associated Faculty Press, 1985.

Sizer, Lyde C. *The Political Work of Northern Women Writers and the Civil War, 1850–1872.* Chapel Hill: University of North Carolina Press, 2000.

Sklar, Kathryn Kish. *Women's Rights Emerges Within the Antislavery Movement, 1830–1870: A Brief History with Documents.* New York: St. Martin's Press, 2000.

———. "'Women Who Speak for an Entire Nation': American and British Women Compared at the World Anti-Slavery Convention, London, 1840." *Pacific Historical Review* 59, no. 4 (1990): 454–99.

Skocpol, Theda, and Jennifer Lynn Oser. "Organization Despite Adversity: The Origins and Development of African American Fraternal Associations." *Social Science History* 28, no. 3 (Fall 2004): 367–438.

Small, Sandra E. "The Yankee Schoolmarm in Freedmen's Schools: An Analysis of Attitudes." *Journal of Southern History* 45 (August 1979): 381–402.

Smith, Earl. "William Cooper Nell on the Fugitive Slave Act of 1850." *Journal of Negro History* 66, no. 1 (Spring 1981): 37–40.

Smith, J. Clay, Jr. "Black Women Lawyers: 125 Years at the Bar; 100 Years in the Legal Academy." *Howard Law Journal* 40 (Winter 1997): 365–97.

———. "Charlotte E. Ray Pleads Before Court." *Howard Law Journal* 43 (Winter 2000): 121–39.

———. *Emancipation: The Making of the Black Lawyer, 1844–1944.* Philadelphia: University of Pennsylvania Press, 1999.

Smith, Robert P. "William Cooper Nell: Crusading Black Abolitionist." *Journal of Negro History* 55, no. 3 (July 1970): 182–99.

Smith-Rosenberg, Carroll. *Disorderly Conduct: Visions of Gender in Victorian America.* New York: Oxford University Press, 1985.

Snorgrass, J. William. "The Black Press in the San Francisco Bay Area, 1856–1900." *California History* 60, no. 4 (1981–82): 306–17.

Soderlund, Jean R. "Priorities and Power: The Philadelphia Female Anti-Slavery Society." In *The Abolitionist Sisterhood: Women's Political Culture in Antebellum America*, edited by Jean F. Yellin and John C. Van Horne, 67–90. Ithaca, N.Y.: Cornell University Press, 1994.

Sokolow, Jayme A. "The Jerry McHenry Rescue and the Growth of Northern Antislavery Sentiment during the 1850s." *Journal of American Studies* 16, no. 3 (December 1982): 427–45.

Stauffer, John. *The Black Hearts of Men: Radical Abolitionists and the Transformation of Race*. Cambridge: Harvard University Press, 2001.

Steinhagen, Carol. "The Two Lives of Frances Dana Gage." *Ohio History* 107 (Winter–Spring 1998): 22–38.

Sterling, Dorothy. *Ahead of Her Time: Abby Kelley and the Politics of Anti-Slavery*. New York: W. W. Norton, 1991.

———, ed. *We Are Your Sisters: Black Women in the Nineteenth Century*. New York: W. W. Norton, 1984.

Stevenson, Brenda. Introduction to *The Journals of Charlotte Forten Grimké*, edited by Brenda Stevenson. New York: Oxford University Press, 1988.

Stewart, Maria W. "Lecture Delivered at the Franklin Hall (21 September 1832) [Reprinted in *The Liberator*, 17 November 1832]." In *Maria W. Stewart, America's First Black Woman Political Writer: Essays and Speeches*, edited by Marilyn Richardson, 45–49. Bloomington: Indiana University Press, 1987.

———. "Religion and the Pure Principles of Morality, The Sure Foundation on Which We Must Build. Productions from the Pen of Mrs. Maria W. Steward [*sic*], Widow of the Late James W. Steward, of Boston." In *Maria W. Stewart, America's First Black Woman Political Writer: Essays and Speeches*, edited by Marilyn Richardson, 28–42. Bloomington: Indiana University Press, 1987.

Strane, Susan. *A Whole-Souled Woman: Prudence Crandall and the Education of Black Women*. New York: W. W. Norton, 1990.

Sumler-Lewis, Janice. "The Forten-Purvis Women of Philadelphia and the American Anti Slavery Crusade." *Journal of Negro History* 66, no. 4 (Winter 1981–82): 281–88.

Sweet, Leonard I. "The Fourth of July and Black Americans in the Nineteenth Century: Northern Leadership Opinion Within the Context of the Black Experience." *Journal of Negro History* 61, no. 3 (July 1976): 256–75.

Swift, David E. *Black Prophets of Justice: Activist Clergy Before the Civil War*. Baton Rouge: Louisiana State University Press, 1989.

Tate, Gayle T. "The Black Nationalist-Christian Nexus: The Political Thought of Lewis Woodson." *Western Journal of Black Studies* 19, no. 1 (1995): 9–18.

———. "Prophesy and Transformation: The Contours of Lewis Woodson's Nationalism." *Journal of Black Studies* 29, no. 2 (1998): 209–23.

Taylor, A. A. "The Negro in South Carolina during the Reconstruction." *Journal of Negro History* 9, no. 4 (October 1924): 381.

Taylor, Henry Lewis, Jr. "On Slavery's Fringe: City-Building and Black Community Development in Cincinnati, 1800–1850." *Ohio History* 95 (Winter–Spring 1986): 5–33.

Terborg-Penn, Rosalyn. *African American Women in the Struggle for the Vote, 1850–1920.* Indianapolis: University of Indiana Press, 1998.

——. "Afro-Americans in the Struggle for Woman Suffrage." Ph.D. diss., Howard University, 1977.

Thornell, Paul. "The Absent Ones and the Providers: A Biography of the Vashons." *Journal of Negro History* 83, no. 4 (Fall 1998): 284–301.

Thorpe, Jessie. *An Introductory History of African Americans in Rome, New York.* Rome, N.Y.: Afro-American Heritage Association, 1994.

Trotter, Joe William, Jr. *River Jordan: African American Urban Life in the Ohio Valley.* Lexington: University Press of Kentucky, 1998.

Trudeau, Noah A. *Like Men of War: Black Troops in the Civil War, 1862–1865.* Boston: Little, Brown, 1998.

Tyrell, Ian R. *Sobering Up: From Temperance to Prohibition in Antebellum America, 1800–1860.* Westport, Conn.: Greenwood Press, 1979.

Ulman, Victor. *Martin R. Delany: The Beginnings of Black Nationalism.* Boston: Beacon Press, 1971.

Usrey, Miriam L. "Charles Lenox Remond, Garrison's Ebony Echo at the World Anti-Slavery Convention, 1840." *Essex Institute Historical Collections* 106, no. 2 (1970): 112–25.

Van Broekhoven, Deborah B. *The Devotion of These Women: Rhode Island in the Antislavery Network.* Amherst: University of Massachusetts Press, 2002.

VanderVelde, Lea, and Sandhya Subramanian. "Mrs. Dred Scott." *Yale Law Journal* 106 (January 1997): 1033–1120.

Venet, Wendy H. *Neither Ballots nor Bullets: Woman Abolitionists and the Civil War.* Charlottesville: University Press of Virginia, 1991.

Vickers, Gregory. "Modes of Womanhood in the Early Woman's Missionary Union." *Baptist History and Heritage* 24 (1989): 41–53.

Wade, Richard C. *The Urban Frontier: Pioneer Life in Early Pittsburgh, Cincinnati, Lexington, Louisville, and St. Louis.* New York: Negro Universities Press, 1959.

Walker, Peter. *Moral Choices: Memory, Desire, and Imagination in Nineteenth-Century American Abolition.* Baton Rouge: Louisiana State University Press, 1978.

Wallace, Maurice. " 'Are We Men?' Prince Hall, Martin Delany, and the Masculine Ideal in Black Freemasonry, 1775–1865." *American Literary History* 9, no. 3 (1997): 396–424.

Walls, William J. *The African Methodist Episcopal Zion Church: Reality of the Black Church.* Charlotte, N.C.: A.M.E. Zion Publishing House, 1974.

Wang, Xi. *The Trial of Democracy: Black Suffrage and Northern Republicans, 1860–1910.* Athens: University of Georgia Press, 1997.

Warner, Michael. *Publics and Counterpublics*. New York: Zone Books; Cambridge, Mass.: Distributed by MIT Press, 2002.

Warner, Robert A. "Amos Gerry Beman, 1812–1874: A Memoir on a Forgotten Leader." *Journal of Negro History* 22, no. 2 (April 1937): 200–221.

Weisenfeld, Judith. " 'Who Is Sufficient for These Things': Sara G. Stanley and the American Missionary Association, 1864–1868." In *This Far by Faith: Readings in African-American Women's Religious Biography*, edited by Judith Weisenfeld and Richard Newman, 203–19. New York: Routledge, 1996.

Weisenfeld, Judith, and Richard Newman, eds. *This Far by Faith: Readings in African American Women's Religious Biography*. New York: Routledge, 1996.

Wellman, Judith. "Crossing Over Cross: Whitney Cross's *Burned-Over District* as Social History." *Reviews in American History* 17, no. 1 (March 1989): 159–74.

———. *The Road to Seneca Falls: Elizabeth Cady Stanton and the First Woman's Rights Convention*. Urbana: University of Illinois Press, 2004.

———. "The Seneca Falls Women's Rights Convention: A Study of Social Networks." *Journal of Women's History* 3, no. 1 (1991): 9–37.

———. "This Side of the Border: Fugitives from Slavery in Three Central New York Communities." *New York History* 79, no. 4 (October 1998): 359–92.

———. "Women and Radical Reform in Antebellum Upstate New York. A Profile of Grassroots Female Abolitionists." In *Clio Was a Woman: Studies in the History of American Women*, edited by Mebel E. Deutrich and Virginia C. Purdy, 113–27. Washington, D.C.: Howard University Press, 1980.

Welter, Barbara. "The Cult of True Womanhood: 1820–1860." *American Quarterly* 18, no. 2, pt. 1 (Summer 1966): 151–74.

White, Deborah Gray. *Ar'n't I a Woman? Female Slaves in the Plantation South*. Rev. ed. New York: W. W. Norton, 1999.

———. *Too Heavy a Load: Black Women in Defense of Themselves, 1894–1994*. Rev. ed. New York: W. W. Norton, 1999.

White, Shane. " 'It Was a Proud Day': African Americans, Festivals, and Parades in the North, 1741–1834." *Journal of American History* 81, no. 1 (June 1994): 13–50.

Wilder, Craig S. *A Covenant with Color: Race and Social Power in Brooklyn, 1636–1990*. New York: Columbia University Press, 2000.

Williams, Jeanne B. "Loose the Woman and Let Her Go! Pennsylvania's African American Women Preachers." *Pennsylvania Heritage* 22, no. 1 (1996): 4–9.

Williams, Loretta J. *Black Freemasonry and Middle-Class Realities*. Columbia: University of Missouri Press, 1980.

Williamson, Joel. *A Rage for Order: Black/White Relations in the American South Since Emancipation*. New York: Oxford University Press, 1986.

Wills, David W. "Womanhood and Domesticity in the AME Tradition: The Influence of Daniel Alexander Payne." In *Black Apostles at Home and Abroad:*

Afro-Americans and the Christian Mission from Revolution to Reconstruction, edited by David W. Wills and Richard Newman, 133–46. Boston: G. K. Hall, 1982.

Winch, Julie. *A Gentleman of Color: The Life of James Forten*. New York: Oxford University Press, 2002.

———. *Philadelphia's Black Elite: Activism, Accommodation, and the Struggle for Autonomy, 1787–1848*. Philadelphia: Temple University Press, 1988.

———. "'You Have Talents—Only Cultivate Them': Philadelphia's Black Female Literary Societies and the Abolitionist Crusade." In *The Abolitionist Sisterhood: Women's Political Culture in Antebellum America*, edited by Jean F. Yellin and John C. Van Horne, 101–18. Ithaca, N.Y.: Cornell University Press, 1994.

Winks, Robin W. *The Blacks in Canada: A History*. Montreal; Kingston: McGill-Queen's University Press, 1997.

Woods, Randall B. "C. H. J. Taylor and the Movement for Black Political Independence, 1882–1896." *Journal of Negro History* 67, no. 2 (Summer 1982): 122–35.

Work, M. N. "The Life of Charles B. Ray." *Journal of Negro History* 4, no. 4 (October 1919): 361–71.

Yacavone, Donald. "The Transformation of the Black Temperance Movement, 1827–1854: An Interpretation." *Journal of the Early Republic* 8 (Fall 1988): 281–97.

Yarbrough, Slayden. "The Southern Baptist Spirit, 1845–1995." *Baptist History and Heritage* 30, no. 3 (1995): 25–34.

Yee, Shirley J. *Black Women Abolitionists: A Study in Activism, 1828–1860*. Knoxville: University of Tennessee Press, 1992.

———. "Gender Ideology and Black Women as Community-Builders in Ontario, 1850–70." *Canadian Historical Review* 75, no. 1 (March 1994): 53–73.

Yellin, Jean F. *Harriet Jacobs: A Life*. New York: Basic, Civitas Books, 2004.

———. *Women and Sisters: The Antislavery Feminists in American Culture*. New Haven, Conn.: Yale University Press, 1989.

Yellin, Jean F., and John C. Van Horne, eds. *The Abolitionist Sisterhood: Women's Political Culture in Antebellum America*. Ithaca, N.Y.: Cornell University Press, 1994.

Zaeske, Susan. *Signatures of Citizenship: Petitioning, Antislavery, and Women's Political Identity*. Chapel Hill: University of North Carolina Press, 2003.

Zipf, Karin L. "Reconstructing 'Free Woman': African American Women, Apprenticeship, and Custody Rights during Reconstruction." *Journal of Women's History* 12, no. 1 (Spring 2000): 8–31.

Acknowledgments

The research and writing of *All Bound Up Together* was made possible by generous financial support from the Charles H. Revson Foundation through the Revson Fellows Program; the Columbia University History Department through a Richard Hofstadter fellowship; the Columbia University Graduate School of Arts and Sciences through an Edmund G. Haynes fellowship and a Merit fellowship, and the Leadership Alliance through an Irene Diamond Foundation fellowship. At the University of Michigan support was provided through a Michigan Faculty fellowship at the Institute for the Humanities, a Ludolph Fund Junior Faculty Development award, and a grant from the Office of the Vice President for Research. Additional support was provided through research fellowships with The Library Company of Philadelphia and the Historical Society of Pennsylvania and the Gilder Lehrman Institute of American History.

The assistance of librarians, archivists, and curators has been indispensable. I have been the fortunate beneficiary of support by the staffs of the Bancroft Library at the University of California, Berkeley; the Boston University, Mugar Memorial Library; the Newberry Library; the Drew University United Methodist Church General Commission on Archives and History; the State Historical Society of Wisconsin; the AME Church Office of the Historiographer; the Fisk University Archives; the Beinecke Library at Yale University; the Oberlin College Archives; the Historical Society of Pennsylvania; the Library Company of Philadelphia; the Livingstone College, AME Zion Church Archives; the Howard University, Moorland-Spingarn Research Center; the Library of Congress; the New York Public Library, Schomburg Center for Research on Black Culture; and the William H. Clements Library at the University of Michigan. Special thanks go to Phillip Lapsansky at the Library Company of Philadelphia and Clayton Lewis at the William H. Clements Library for their attention and generosity as I was completing this manuscript.

My professional life has been full of generous, engaged, and encouraging colleagues. My thanks go to Eli Evans, the late Eli Ginzberg, and Karen Vrotsos at the Revson Fellows program. At Columbia University my work was possible through the advice and support of many, including Erica Armstrong, Betsy Blackmar, Marcellus Blount, Richard Bushman, Sharon Gamble, Farah Griffin, Alice Kessler-Harris, Manning Marable, Deborah McCoy, Daryl Scott, and Judith Weisenfeld. My Columbia writing group of Chris Capozzola, Mike Fuquay, and Ellen Stroud, the Donner Party, were generous, untiring, and humor-filled allies. My special thanks go to my mentor and adviser, Eric Foner. Back when I was just a lawyer "taking a break," Eric took my ambitions and ideas seriously. Since then he has shown me the way, while giving me plenty of room to make my own path. He has encouraged me to hold tight to my passions and to those unspoken streams that run through so many of us, moving us to devote our life's work to the stories that we believe matter.

At Barnard College, Chris Baswell, Vivian Taylor, and the students in the Mellon Minority Undergraduate Fellowship program saw me through a critical year of writing. At the University of Michigan I have been assisted by a fine group of research assistants, including Tracy Chichester, Nathan Connelly, David McNamara, Tiffany Riley, Brandis Taylor, and Kalyn Wilson. I have benefited from the support of an incomparable intellectual community that includes Paul Anderson, Susanna Blumenthal, John Carson, Rita Chin, Jay Cook, Kevin Gaines, Robert Genter, David Hancock, James Jackson, Philip Pachoda, Sonya Rose, Kelly Quinn, Hannah Rosen, Rebecca Scott, Victoria von Arx, and Penny VonEschen. A special thanks to my extraordinary writing group—Dena Goodman, Mary Kelley, and Carroll Smith-Rosenberg—from whom I have learned so much about history and more.

This manuscript was completed while I was a visiting professor at Paris's École des Hautes Études. There, colleagues including François Weil, Jean Hébrard, and Myriam Cottias provided me with a quiet workspace and warm collegiality as I worked through final revisions. Thanks also to the Women and Religion in the African Diaspora Project at Princeton University and the members of its working group, including co-directors Marie Griffith and Barbara Savage, Elsa Barkley Brown, Anne Boylan, Estelle Freedman, Glenda Gilmore, Leslie Harris, Nancy Hewitt, Mignon Moore, Judith Weisenfeld, Albert Raboteau, and Deborah Gray White, all of whom supported this project at critical junctures. The same should be said of Gray Osterud, whose insightful reading helped the manuscript become a book.

My appreciation for the University of North Carolina Press runs deep. Chuck Grench endured my early musings and has since then given his steadfast encouragement and keen criticism to the project. Katy O'Brien has helped by ably walking me through the many stages of the publication process with patience and persistence. Mary Caviness helped me see the delights of wonderfully detailed copyediting. I am proud to have *All Bound Up Together* included in the Press's John Hope Franklin Series in African American History and Culture, and I thank Waldo Martin and Pat Sullivan for making this honor possible.

For my friends there is not enough thanks to go around. Without their good humor, generosity, and deep faith in me this book would not have been possible. Erica Armstrong; Mia Bay; Christine Cain; Alvia Golden; Farah Griffin; Leslie Harris; Kelli Jareaux; Arlene Keizer; Miriam Martinez and her daughter, Alejandra; Mignon Moore; my cousin Carol Bonner Saulny; Barbara Savage; Meryl Schwartz and David Weinraub and their children, Elias and Lily; and Michelle Schreiber and Raun Rasmussen and their daughter, Nadia, have walked nearly every mile of this journey with me. Jean Hébrard came into my life just as this book was coming to an end. Jean read, edited, and generally spurred me onward with the writing. But, more importantly, he helped me see this book as just one part of my life's project. I can finish this book, in part, because we have so much else to do.

My family has sustained me in countless ways, and, of course, our collective story is very much bound up with the story of this book. My father, who did not live to see this book completed, my stepmother, Ronnie, and my sister Lori, her husband, Gregg, and their children, Emma and Aaron, have kept me grounded in life's simple joys. My brother Paul has been my greatest student, and my sister Laura has always stood ready to celebrate triumphs and weather moments of doubt. No one has supported me more than my mother, Suzanne Yager Jones, who has given me her infinite love and encouragement. As a woman of ideas and of deeds, a lover of social justice and of her garden, of public work and the privacy of solitude, my mother encourages me to live a life that is complex and dynamic. She inspires me to embrace life—to grasp for the things that matter to me and love them, nurture them, mold them, battle with them, and through that give of myself to others.

This book is dedicated to my paternal grandmother, the late Susie Williams Jones. My grandmother, by her example and by her deep love for me, has always been the yardstick by which I have measured my life. She was a woman of ideas and action, of graciousness and fortitude. Her life, as well as the lives of her mother and grandmother, inspired the questions that this book asks. They were women who made their lives in the many realms of African American public culture that this study visits, all the while negotiating the challenges that confronted them as public women. But my deepest gratitude is for my grandmother who was at home with family. In her Greensboro, North Carolina, home, during summer afternoons spent in the shade of the front porch, curled up in white wicker chairs and taking in the scent of magnolia blossoms and freshly cut grass, she taught me about the intimate relationships that quietly sustain our public work.

Index

Abdy, Edward, 55

Abolitionism. *See* Antislavery movements

Activism, 9; generational development of, 2, 88–90, 115–17; "cross-fertilization" of ideas and, 16–17, 166–67, 205–6; churches and, 39–40, 66, 105–6, 150, 152–55, 166–69, 193, 198–99, 202; as cross-gender activity, 69–70; women's associational life and, 82–85, 142; Fugitive Slave Act and, 95–96; cross-racial contact and, 164–65, 205; entrance into public life and, 174. *See also* Antislavery movements; Women's rights movement

Adams, J. J., 191

Adams, John Quincy, 50

Advocate of Moral Reform, 45–46

Afric-American Female Intelligence Society, 39

African Dorcas Association, 39–40, 57

African Methodist Episcopal (AME) Church: history of, 15, 66, 94, 154, 155, 170, 180; preaching by women in, 40–44, 67, 108, 148–49, 155–56, 183–84; Daniel Payne and opposition to women's authority in, 41, 75–76, 108–9, 113, 183–84, 196; women's traditional roles in, 66–67, 155, 180; women's leadership roles in, 75, 167; gender-neutrality of church law, 156–57; office of the stewardess in, 158–59; women's missionary societies, 159–61; church organization and hierarchy, 164, 183

African Methodist Episcopal Zion (AME Zion) Church, 154, 155, 189–90, 202, 205; ordination of women in, 11, 185–86; women's traditional roles in, 39, 148, 155; preaching by women in, 42–44, 75–76, 155–56, 173–74, 182–83; women's leadership roles in, 66–67, 173–74, 182–83, 186–87; history of, 94; voting rights for women

Jeffrey, Mary, 103, 208
Jeffrey, R. Jerome, 206, 208
Johnson, Harriet C., 146–47
Johnson, William, 46
Jones, Mary Jane Talbert, 161
Jones, Singleton, 161

Kachun, Mitch, 89
Kansas-Nebraska Act (1854), 93
Keckley, Elizabeth, 133
Kelley, Abby, 55, 63, 69
King, Alice, 153
King, Martha, 148–49

Lane, Hester, 54–57
Langston, Charles, 59–60, 80, 95
Langston, John Mercer, 102, 124, 135, 138, 147, 157
Lawrence, Thomas, 109
Laws and legal cases: Fugitive Slave Act, 7, 10, 85, 87–88, 93–98; Fifteenth Amendment, 10, 140–41, 146–47, 156; Fourteenth Amendment, 10, 140–41, 156; exclusion of African Americans and, 13; "black laws" and institutionalized racism, 13, 79, 167–68, 175, 202; church law, 42, 66, 76, 155–62, 182, 186, 191–92, 195–96; women's rights as legal issue, 80; *Dred Scott v. Sanford*, 85, 88, 97–98; Fugitive Slave Law, 94–95; *Passenger Cases*, 96–97; women as practitioners of law, 157; Civil Rights Act, 175; *Plessy v. Ferguson*, 175
Lee, Anne, 74–75
Lee, Jarena, 7, 40–41, 44, 66, 67, 88, 107, 185
Levine, Robert, 64
Levison, William H., 99–100
Lewis, Amelia, 48–49
Liberator, 16, 24, 33, 34, 38, 52, 55, 63, 72, 119

The Life and Religious Experience of Jarena Lee, A Coloured Lady (Lee), 40
Life in Philadelphia, 18, 84–85
Literacy. *See* Education; Literary societies; Print culture
Literary societies, 4, 26–27, 31–34, 39–40, 84, 88, 108–11, 111, 153
Litwack, Leon, 12
Livingstone College, 189, 202, 205
Loguen, Caroline Storum, 84
Loguen, Jermain, 71, 84, 95, 103, 104, 138
Lott, Eric, 98–99
Love and Theft (Lott), 98–99
Lovinggood, Lillie, 182
Low, Martha, 185
Lyceums, 117, 136–37, 154

Majors, Monroe, 181
Manly, Alexander, 188
Manly, J. N., 201
Marginalization, 2–5, 13, 23–24, 38–39, 92–93, 175
Market revolution, 12, 22
Martin, J. Sella, 133, 135, 138, 146, 197
Martin, Sarah, 133
Martin, Waldo, 64
Masonic order, 16, 73, 111–13, 169, 170–71
Matthews, Victoria Earle, 174, 184
McCrummill, James, 109
McCurdy, Mrs. M. A., 181
McHenry, Elizabeth, 31
McMullen, J. H., 195
Men: disfranchisement of, 14, 49, 175, 187–90; literary societies established by, 40; voting rights for black men, 51, 102, 141; as fugitives from slavery, 98; military service and manhood, 120, 121, 122, 124–25, 131, 133; church authority and manhood, 174–75, 192–95; as feminized by women's

rights, 177–78, 193; women as
defenders of manhood equality, 184–
85; competition for power and
authority among, 194; as missionaries, 199–200
—as allies, 10–11; in print culture, 24,
113; in political organizations, 50–51,
53–54, 57, 59–60, 80–81, 103–4, 143,
146–48; participation in women's
rights conventions, 70–71, 79, 104; in
church politics, 75–76, 161, 164, 185,
196–97; public speaking encouraged
by, 135; in legal issues, 157
Mercier, Charles, 143
Merritt, Jane P., 81, 88
Methodist churches, 155, 165, 182. *See
also* African Methodist Episcopal
(AME) Church; African Methodist
Episcopal Zion (AME Zion) Church;
Colored Methodist Episcopal (CME)
Church; Methodist Episcopal
Church (North); Methodist Episcopal
Church, South
Methodist Episcopal Church (North),
155, 165, 182
Methodist Episcopal Church, South,
165
Minstrelsy, 98–101, 126–30, 177–78
Missionary societies, 4, 66, 148; educa-
tion and, 138–39; women's roles in,
159–62, 174, 200, 202, 203–4; men as
missionaries, 199–201
Moore, Esther, 49
Moore, Rev. Mrs. W. L., 195
Morality: attacks on women activists on
basis of, 17, 40; female influence as
moral force, 25, 28, 63; American
Moral Reform Society, 33, 47–50, 75–
76, 103, 106; activism and, 39; of public women, 39; Female Moral Reform
Society, 45–46; women's rights as
moral issue, 45–46, 69–70, 155, 162,

182–83; of enslaved women, 126. *See
also* Respectability
Morel, Junius, 52, 103–4
Morrisey, R. A., 192
Mossell, Gertrude, 181
Mott, Lucretia, 35, 49, 56, 71–72, 77,
98
Mutual aid societies, 31, 37, 39–40, 57,
83–85, 137, 154, 170

National Afro-American Council, 188,
199, 202–3, 206
National Association for the Advancement of Colored People (NAACP),
199, 203
National Association of Colored
Women (NACW), 171, 184, 203
National Federation of Afro-American
Women, 184
National League of Colored Women,
153
National Woman Suffrage Association
(NWSA), 142, 158, 165–66, 201
Nell, William C., 25, 54, 62–63, 70, 71–
72, 116
Newspapers: African American public
culture and, 16, 26, 51; political
engagement of women encouraged
in, 50; audience for, 64–65; funding
for, 83–84. *See also* Print culture; *spe-
cific papers by title*
Nickson, Rosina, 200
Norris v. City of Boston (1849), 96–97
North Star, 63–65, 73, 74, 75, 76, 83, 89,
91, 197

Oberlin College, 60, 67–69, 80, 116,
131–32, 139–40
*One Hundred Years of the African Methodist
Episcopal Zion Church* (Hood), 182–83
Oser, Jennifer, 169

specific institutions); in Boston, 23; respectability as parameter for women's
public lives, 48, 63, 75, 168–69, 174,
182; sacred/secular divide, 66, 153–
54; celebrations as public events, 89–
90; freed people and, 120–21, 125–26,
130; slavery as barrier to creation of,
122–23. *See also* Churches; Print culture; Public speaking
Public speaking: woman question introduced as issue through, 7, 23–24;
political activism and, 48; antislavery
activism and, 64; popularity of
women speakers, 69, 135–38; fund-
raising for lectures, 83–84; minstrelsy
and mockery of, 100–101; accept-
ability of women speakers, 107–9, 117,
120, 134–35; as educational, 110, 135;
during Civil War and Reconstruction, 120–21, 125, 133; men as patrons
or allies of women, 135. *See also*
Preaching by women
Purnell, Hannah, 49
Purvis, Harriet, 77
Purvis, Robert, 77, 95, 98, 146

Quakers, 37–39
Quarles, Benjamin, 65
Quinn, William Paul, 105, 108

Racism: slavery and racial ideology, 17;
stereotyping and, 17–22, 32; sexism as
analogous to, 60, 63–64, 69–70, 79,
87–88, 185, 197; minstrelsy and, 98–
101, 126–30, 177–78; sexuality and,
167–68, 188–89; woman's era as
resistance or remedy to, 171, 176,
184–85; segregation as legal man-
date, 175; white supremacy movement and, 187–89
Ray, Charles B., 28, 32, 34, 46–47, 51,
52, 56–57, 157

Ray, Charlotte, 157
Ray, H. Cordelia, 56
Ray, Henrietta Regulus, 39–40, 56
Reckless, Mrs. A. [Hetty], 77
Reconstruction, 120–21, 140–47, 174–
75
Re-enslavement, 94, 131
Regulus, Henrietta. *See* Ray, Henrietta
Regulus
Reid, Susan, 116
Religion: enslaved people and women's
religious authority, 123; female chap-
lains, 173–74. *See also specific churches*
Religion and the Pure Principles of Morality
(Stewart), 23–24, 40
Remond, Amy, 119
Remond, Charles Lenox, 53–54, 69, 70,
77, 89, 95–96, 98, 116, 119, 135
Remond, Sarah Parker, 119, 135
Respectability: freedom and, 24; educa-
tion and, 32–33; domesticity linked
to, 32–33, 61, 114, 168–69; as param-
eter for public life, 40, 48, 63, 75,
168–69, 174, 182; political use of rhet-
oric of, 46; authority in public culture
and, 90, 179; caricatures and, 99–100;
sexuality and, 100, 126, 136, 193;
employment and, 106; public speak-
ing and, 107–9; women's rights and,
114; freedwomen and, 136; stereo-
types and mockery of, 177
Rhodes, Jane, 113
Rich, William, 103
Richards, Mary J. R., 138
Riching, G. F., 181
Riddick, Nannie, 160
Riddle, Alfred, 157
Riley, Elizabeth, 39
Rollin, Louisa, 147
Ruffin, Josephine St. Pierre, 133, 174
Ruggles, David, 50–51, 55
Ryan, Mary, 8

Women's rights conventions: Seneca
Falls, 10, 60, 70–71, 72, 75, 76, 79, 80,
85; Rochester, 60, 71–72, 79, 80;
Worcester, 91–93; Akron, 107
Women's rights movement: antislavery activism and, 7, 45–46, 63–64,
69–70, 76–77; African American
public culture and, 10; and "cross-
fertilization" of ideas, 16–17, 166–67,
205–6; as moral issue, 45–46, 69–70,
155, 162, 182–83; relative nature of
women's rights, 54, 72–73, 165–66;
race and participation in, 60, 70–71,
92–93, 141–42, 205; black men as
active participants in, 70–71, 79;
ultraism and, 71, 78–79; as marginalized, 87–88; generational shifts in,
88–89, 115–17; antislavery cause
severed from, 91–93, 101–3, 142; race
subordinated to gender as issue in,
92–93; minstrelsy and, 100, 126–30,
177–79; civil rights activism and, 101–
4; church standing and, 198–99. *See
also* Woman question debate;
Women's rights conventions
Woodson, Lewis, 32–33, 34, 170
Woodson, Sarah J. *See* Early, Sarah J.
Woodson
World's Anti-Slavery Convention (1840),
53–54
Wright, Theodore, 36, 53, 74

Yates, Josephine Silone, 203
Yellin, Jean, 18